Spaces of Consumption

Consumption is well established as a key theme in the study of the long eighteenth century. *Spaces of Consumption* brings a new dimension to this subject by looking at it spatially. Taking English towns as its scene, this inspiring new study focuses on moments of consumption – selecting and purchasing goods, attending plays, promenading – and explores the ways in which these were related through the spaces of the town: the shop, the theatre, the street.

Drawing on both traditional interpretations of urban space and new spatial analysis, this survey assesses lived spaces of everyday social action and perceived spaces of representation and explores how, from the level of the region to the individual, spaces of consumption were produced by and, in turn, moulded leisure and shopping practices. *Spaces of Consumption* argues that both spaces and practices were linked to broader social structures of sociability, politeness and respectability by providing a complex set of socio-spatial contexts that offered both choices and constraints to individual consumers.

This original study is essential reading for all those interested in consumption studies.

Jon Stobart is Professor of History at the University of Northampton. His current research focuses on the history of shopping, leisure and consumption, in both urban and rural contexts. He has also published widely on urban space, urban and regional identity and the Industrial Revolution.

Andrew Hann is a Research Fellow at the University of Greenwich and County Editor of the Victoria County History of Kent. His research interests include the history of retailing and consumption, urban and industrial change and the writing of community histories.

Victoria Morgan gained her doctorate at the University of Coventry where she was a Researcher in Historical Geography. She now works as a barrister in London and maintains a strong interest in eighteenth-century urban development and local history.

Spaces of Consumption

Leisure and shopping in the English town, *c.*1680–1830

Jon Stobart, Andrew Hann and Victoria Morgan

LONDON AND NEW YORK

First published 2007
by Routledge
2 Park Square, Milton Park, Abingdon, Oxon OX14 4RN

Simultaneously published in the USA and Canada
by Routledge
270 Madison Ave, New York, NY 10016

Routledge is an imprint of the Taylor & Francis Group, an informa business

© 2007 Jon Stobart, Andrew Hann and Victoria Morgan

Typeset in Baskerville by
HWA Text and Data Management, Tunbridge Wells
Printed and bound in Great Britain by
The Cromwell Press, Trowbridge, Wiltshire

All rights reserved. No part of this book may be reprinted or reproduced or utilised in any form or by any electronic, mechanical, or other means, now known or hereafter invented, including photocopying and recording, or in any information storage or retrieval system, without permission in writing from the publishers.

British Library Cataloguing in Publication Data
A catalogue record for this book is available from the British Library

Library of Congress Cataloging-in-Publication Data
Stobart, Jon, 1966–
Spaces of consumption : leisure and shopping in the English town, 1680–1830 / Jon Stobart, Andrew Hann, and Victoria Morgan.
    p. cm.
Includes bibliographical references.
1. Consumption (Economics)–England–History. 2. Consumers–England–History. 3. Cities and towns–England–History. I. Hann, Andrew. II. Morgan, Victoria, 1978– III. Title.
HC260.C6S76 2007
339.4′7094209033–dc22
                                                            2006039514

ISBN10: 0–415–42455–0 (hbk)
ISBN10: 0–415–42456–9 (pbk)

ISBN13: 978–0–415–42455–4 (hbk)
ISBN13: 978–0–415–42456–1 (pbk)

Contents

List of figures	vi
List of tables	vii
Acknowledgements	viii
1 Leisure, consumption and shopping	1
2 The region: hierarchies and spatial ordering	26
3 The town: politeness and place	57
4 The street: stage-set and performance	86
5 The building: representation and display	111
6 The individual: social practices and identity	140
7 Advertisements: re-producing spaces of polite consumption	171
8 Conclusions	189
Notes	196
Select bibliography	228
Index	243

Figures

2.1	The consumption hierarchies of north-west England and the west Midlands	43
3.1	Building land in the New Town of Leamington Spa, *c.*1810	61
3.2	Peter Robinson's plan for the area to the north of The Parade, Leamington Spa, *c.*1822	62
3.3	Plan of the proposed development of Green Ayre, Lancaster, 1784	63
3.4	Plan of the proposed development of Dalton Square, Lancaster by Edward Batty, 1783	64
5.1	The Guildhall, Worcester, 1721–3	114
5.2	Liverpool Athenaeum: first and second floor plan	120
5.3	Liverpool Athenaeum: ground floor plan	120
5.4	Trade Card of Henry Lilwall of London	127
7.1	Advertisement of William Cart, Coventry, 1767	173
7.2	Trade card of Hill and Turley of Worcester	177
7.3	Advertisement of John Grimes, Coventry, 1767	181
7.4	Trade card of Samuel Daniell of Stourbridge	183
7.5	Trade card of Henry Waterfall of Coventry	184
7.6	Media space: a matrix of advertisements	187

Tables

1.1	Corrigan's 'Changes in shopping brought about by department stores'	14
2.1	Leisure facilities and urban improvement in the towns of north-west England and the west Midlands in the long eighteenth century	29
2.2	Selected retailers and services in north-west England and the west Midlands, 1700–1830	34
2.3	Population and taxable wealth in north-west England and the west Midlands, c.1700–1830	37
2.4	The leisure hierarchy: exemplar towns	39
2.5	The retail hierarchy: retail scores and threshold activities	41
6.1	Status of customers at three Staffordshire shops	147
6.2	Groceries purchased from Thomas Dickenson of Worcester, grocer: January 1741–April 1742	153
6.3	Pattern of proxy purchasing by customers of Thomas Dickenson, 1741–2	154

Acknowledgements

Many people have helped in the research and production of this book. First, we acknowledge, with thanks, a research grant from The Leverhulme Trust (F/00732/A) which made possible much of the archival work for this project. We would also like to thank the staff at the record offices in Birmingham, Chester, Coventry, Lichfield, Preston, Stafford, Stratford, Warwick and Worcester for their assistance in locating the numerous documents upon which this work is based. Thanks also to the following for permission to reproduce images: the Bodleian Library, University of Oxford, John Johnson Collection; Lancaster Central Library; Lancaster City Museum, part of Lancashire Museums; The University of Leicester Library; and Warwickshire County Record Office. Finally, there are numerous colleagues who have helped to refine our thinking on the spaces and practices of eighteenth-century shopping and leisure, and who have provided useful feedback on earlier versions of the manuscript. In particular, we must thank Peter Borsay, Nancy Cox and Matthew McCormack.

1 Leisure, consumption and shopping

The rise of consumption

Twenty-five years ago, McKendrick, Brewer and Plumb wrote of the birth of a consumer society in the eighteenth century. They noted a shift in consumption patterns and practices, and traced their origins in and impacts on the social and economic transformation of the country. In the period since then, consumption has emerged as an important historical meta-narrative, especially in studies of the eighteenth century where it has displaced the former grand narrative of the industrial revolution.[1] This surge of interest has coincided with a contemporary spending boom which has placed the consumer at the heart of modern society, economy and culture. Yet it draws on a long tradition of academic interest in the transformative role of consumption, particularly its relationship with modernity. For modernists such as Sombart and Veblen, writing at the turn of the twentieth century, it was the 'decisive force behind modern capitalism, its dynamism and social structure'. More recently, post-modernists like Baudrillard have seen consumption as 'the semiotic code constituting post-modernity itself'.[2] This burgeoning interest in consumption, and its flexibility both as a concept and a set of practices, has resulted in a plethora of empirical studies and a profusion of theoretical viewpoints. Analyses have focused on, *inter alia*, consumer categorisation and consumer tactics, the visual and the spectacular, subject–object relationships, consumption and citizenship, consumption as experience, and more recently, the social agency and subjectivity of consumption.[3] What has emerged is a picture of consumption and the consumer as complex, relational and reflexive, with different modes and practices of consumption combining in time and space to produce new and shifting (sometimes temporary) identities, spatialities and social relations. This is most evident in studies of shopping malls, which Shields, Miller and others characterise as places of leisure as well as material acquisition, and as sites of social engagement and identity formation. Similar arguments have been made for other consumption sites: from late twentieth-century car-boot sales to nineteenth-century department stores. These are portrayed as places to spend time as well as money; where identities as knowing consumers can be (re)created, and where the agency of consumers is expressed.[4] Surprisingly, this approach is rare in historical analyses, especially of the eighteenth century, where the relationships between leisure practices and consumption remain largely unexplored. These activities drew on related social and cultural imperatives and, as we shall see, were enmeshed in the daily lives of consumers, not least through the routines and pleasures of shopping. But each remains marginal to historical analyses of the other.[5] Furthermore, there has been little attempt to explore the inter-relationship between consumption practices and the social and material spaces in which they took place. Whilst department stores and malls loom large in analyses of nineteenth and twentieth century consumption, the shops of earlier periods have remained largely the preserve of retail historians.[6]

This emphasis on space and spatial practices is not to deny the importance of gender and class, for example, in structuring consumption. Indeed, their significance is amply demonstrated by the considerable attention that they have received elsewhere.[7] Rather, it is to shift attention onto the neglected socio-spatial dialectics of 'polite' consumption and material culture; to address Soja's call for a critical spatialisation of (urban) history – one that recognises the divergent and fractured but interconnected nature of space.[8] The main aim of this book is to explore the spatiality of the interplay between consumption, leisure and shopping in the provincial towns of eighteenth-century England. We argue that spaces of consumption were socially produced – that is, they were created and given meaning by the social practices of consumers – and that these spaces acted back on consumers, shaping their practices and behaviour.[9] Moreover, we explicitly explore the ways in which space and practice were related at a variety of scales, from the region to the individual, and the different imperatives which surfaced at each geographical scale. The *region* offered a broad framework within which middling and upper rank consumers made choices; the *town* was a more or less polite place which formed the venue for individual consumer practices; these took place in the public *street* or in more private *buildings* – the setting for a variety of consumer performances and representations. At the heart of these spaces and practices lay the *individual* consumer, whose actions served to produce space and construct personal identity. Linking all these physical spaces was the *virtual* consumer space produced by advertisements and forming an imagined matrix of spaces, practices, values and attitudes. Moving down through a series of geographical scales in this way allows us to deconstruct the spatiality of urban consumption, whilst retaining the notion that consumer spaces were at once layered and discrete. We begin, though, by drawing a number of overlapping historiographical and theoretical contexts into which our analysis is placed.

Consumption, modernity and the town

Britain stood out from much of the rest of Europe in terms of its experience of urban development. Whilst many towns in the established urban societies of Italy and the Low Countries were experiencing demographic decline by the later seventeenth century, those in Britain grew rapidly.[10] Birmingham, Manchester and Liverpool, for example, quadrupled their populations in the second half of the eighteenth century, their growth underpinned and reflected in the equally rapid expansion of smaller centres such as Wolverhampton, Stockport and Warrington. Much of this urban growth was based on industry and commerce, but towns such as Chester, Warwick, Bath and Cheltenham prospered and grew as leisure towns, boasting extensive facilities, healthy living conditions and a relative absence of the labouring classes. Below these were a multitude of small towns – another peculiar feature of British urbanisation in the period. At the start of the eighteenth century, these housed over half of England's urban population; by the 1790s, the *Universal British Directory* listed 325 small towns 'over half of which, especially in the west Midlands and north-west, had a spectrum of consumer activities'.[11] Moreover, all towns were characterised by significant professional, service, administrative, building and retail sectors. They also had their own elites – often of merchants, industrialists or professionals – and housed a growing number of the middling sorts. As centres of supply and demand, therefore, towns were central to processes of consumption. Their role as central places marks them out as points of supply for their own populations, but also those of their hinterlands. As Braudel argues, 'every town … is first and foremost a market' and 'needs to be rooted in and nourished by the people and land surrounding it'.[12] It was in towns that consumers were concentrated, that most goods and services were acquired, and that information and ideas were exchanged. Indeed, towns were central to both the learning of new consumption practices and to their pursuit: the active arenas in which leisure and consumption took place.[13]

Conversely, leisure and consumption were central to eighteenth-century urban development. They were linked through the construction of a new material culture: one that incorporated consumer goods, together with the physical infrastructure of shops and leisure facilities, and an improved physical environment – what Estabrook terms 'artificial surroundings'.[14] Such developments lie at the heart of Borsay's notion of a post-restoration urban renaissance. He highlighted the role of sociability, social competition and commercialised leisure in shaping a physical and cultural renewal of many towns. This linked to the more general expansion of the arts and fashionable culture which were central to eighteenth-century modernity. It involved the introduction or proliferation of leisure infrastructure as well as a general but deliberate improvement in the urban environment. This culture of improvement permeated the fabric of urban life and individual aspirations.[15] It formed part of the wider programme of the English Enlightenment, the underlying mission of which was to rescue the nation from barbarity and ignorance: in essence to civilise it. Enlightenment promoted the primacy of the rational mind, which Ogborn refers to as the 'hallmark of modernity'.[16] Central to this was development of a milieu of civility and sociability, and a so-called public sphere. Although this was partly dependent on an 'imagined public space', it was also connected to tangible changes in the urban environment.[17] Ogborn draws on a particular and situated understanding of modernity which revolves around the politics of the public sphere and their spatial expression in the town. He demonstrates these links in terms of the projects of urban improvement which made public places and promoted sociability. Building on this, Breen links the urban consumer experience to political ideology, and suggests that this broader 'public' came to believe it had a claim on the goods and spaces of the market place.[18]

At a number of levels, it is possible to see the Enlightenment as being intimately linked with the urban. Towns were its engine rooms: perceived as innovative, supporting a public sphere and producing a civilised culture. They played an important part in disseminating education, literacy, and more cosmopolitan ideas; a role epitomised by their association with an emerging scientific culture in the second half of the eighteenth century.[19] In turn, the values of the Enlightenment supported the town: defining and designing it as cultivated, public, rational and secular, and engendering rationalist tenets of proportion and symmetry.[20] As such, towns were overtly contrasted with countryside; their modernity and sophistication being set against rural backwardness and vulgarity (see Chapter 3). But we must be wary of such rhetoric. First, there were tensions between the town as the symbol and vehicle of Enlightenment, and its role as the engine of modern consumerism. While the framework of Enlightenment suggests an increasingly rational and 'public' society, the world of consumerism that emerged out of the town appealed to the senses, was constructed around desires as well as needs, and heightened the notion of a private consuming self more than participation in a public arena which was open to all.[21] Second, the ideological, cultural and social divide between town and country is easily overplayed. Links between town and country remained strong, especially for shire towns, which acted as socio-political foci for the county gentry and as economic centres for increasingly commercialised agricultural and sometimes industrialising hinterlands.[22] Yet Weatherill, Estabrook and Overton all underline the distinctive nature of urban material culture.[23] Estabrook goes further, highlighting the importance of 'topographical setting' or localism in the construction of the material culture and identity of a community. There is a danger here, though, of obscuring the important inter-linkages which existed between town and country, and in collapsing the variety of towns (in terms of size, function, location and legal status) into a homogeneous 'urban'.

What is significant here is the need to recognise the variety of urban experience: the emergence of specialist towns, the increasingly different experiences of and in large and small towns, and the ways in which towns interacted with other towns and with the surrounding countryside. In this light, 'topographical setting' becomes a much more powerful concept. It invites us to explore the link between people and place, but also society and space; to imagine the urban space as spreading beyond the boundaries of the town to incorporate links with other towns and the surrounding countryside.

Politeness, leisure and the built environment

What set the eighteenth-century town apart was its role in promoting the values of and providing a venue for politeness (see Chapter 3). As Sweet argues, 'politeness was a quintessentially urban concept; the formation of a code of polite behaviour was a response to the pressures of urban living and the cultivation and display of polite manners took place in the social spaces of the urban locale'.[24] Politeness was a complex, multi-faceted and contested concept. Shaftesbury and others viewed it as a model of behaviour which distinguished and justified the position of a gentlemanly elite. In this gendered reading, sociability served to refine and civilise. Indeed, Hutton argued that 'man is evidently formed for society: the intercourse of one with another, like two blocks of marble in friction, reduces the rough prominences of behaviour, and gives a polish to the manners'.[25] Within such constructions, polite status was marked by a set of material and mental attributes – what Bourdieu, in a modern context, has termed cultural capital. This marked social distinction, signalling the taste and discernment of the individual and identifying them as a member of the social elite.[26] Courtesy writers suggested that gentlemen should maintain their rank through manners – dignity, easy assurance, repression of emotional display and distinguished speech all being lauded. Gentlewomen, meanwhile, should have 'dignified ease and graceful control', good table manners and diverting conversation. For both men and women, consumption and the construction of an appropriate material culture – of the body and the home – were essential in distinguishing their status as polite.[27] Other commentators, including Addison and Steele, emphasised politeness as a means of oiling the wheels of commercial and social interaction in liberal urban society. The manners of tradesmen and merchants would be refined as they sold their wares, whilst the language of commerce in part 'developed out of the patrician manners of the landed elites'. Again, politeness was linked to consumption, but this time the emphasis was on inclusiveness and complaisance. As Berg argues, 'merchants and tradesmen sold to each other through distinctive conversational style, expectations of hospitality, and the appropriate position, type, and decoration of their houses'.[28]

Politeness in both of these guises lay at the heart of Borsay's urban renaissance: the spaces and practices of polite society served to redefine urban culture and restructure the urban built environment. Leisure played a large part in these processes and, for much of the eighteenth century, the emphasis was on inclusive and public activities designed, in part, to embrace the middling sorts within an expanded urban elite.[29] This translated into a wide-ranging renewal of urban infrastructure and leisure facilities which together served to re-imagine the town as polite and modern. Improvements encompassed the building and rebuilding, refronting and ornamentation of the physical environment. Indeed, it was in this period that a distinctive architectural aesthetic, first seen in the public buildings and country houses of Jacobean England, spread across provincial towns. Consciously borrowing from both ancient Rome and Renaissance Italy, a style of classical architecture was adopted to link newly prosperous and dynamic English towns to their older-established counterparts in Europe, and to create uniformity, coherence and integration in the urban environment.[30] This helped to reinforce the town as a distinct entity, separate from a rural 'other'.

The application of these ideas took place in different spaces and for different purposes. In the public domain, order and improvement were a matter of 'political authority, polite sociability, self-control and commodity exchange': order was required in the way streets looked, and in the purposes for which they were used.[31] Newly beautified streets – the beneficiaries of revised programmes of paving, cleansing and lighting (see Chapter 4) – were improvements of practical and commercial significance: they eased movement through and regulation of the town. They also served as a tribute to the town and testament to the new discourses of civility.[32] Much the same could be said of squares. Based on the ideas of the classical civilisation, community and citizenship, their place in the town was central geographically and culturally. Most importantly, the square provided a visual image of the public sphere, a physical space upon which ideas of a collective public could hinge. Squares also provided venues for semi-public sociability.

Other spaces were more explicitly geared to polite sociability, amongst them walks, promenades and pleasure gardens, theatres and assembly rooms, coffee houses and libraries (see Chapter 2). These were sometimes provided by civic authorities (most notably in resort and county towns), but were often funded by subscription, part of what Plumb has called the 'commercialization of leisure', allowing easier access by the middling sorts and even plebeian society (see Chapter 3).[33] Such facilities served the practical needs of the leisured classes, and formed icons in the urban landscape, shaping the attitudes of residents and visitors. Together with new civic buildings, they transformed the built environment and the public image of towns across the country.[34] At the same time, the fundamental values underpinning the culture of improvement were invested in the landscape and became a measure of the success of the town, its gentility and civility, demonstrating its suitability as a place of residence for the gentry. Ideas were transmitted through the urban arena, imprinted on the landscape, and consequently given a spatial expression. Changes to the town, with at least hints of architectural grandeur, satisfied criteria of rational order whilst also providing new spaces of display. Through its streets and squares, promenades and gardens, combined with its educational and cultural institutions, the town offered a kind of public politeness. This spirit of improvement did not stop in communal spaces. Private individuals took these ideas into their shops and homes, extending the spaces for new forms of social behaviour and material culture. The heart of the town had been transformed into a consumer landscape.

This kind of axiomatic linking of urban renewal, cultural renaissance and politeness is not without its problems, as Borsay himself is quick to recognise. Tensions and contradictions were inherent within politeness and sociability, and these grew as the eighteenth century progressed. First, there was always a friction between inclusivity and exclusivity. Polite sociability was useful in absorbing and diffusing political, religious and ethnic tensions, and in accommodating the growing social ambitions of the middling sorts. It provided a mechanism for drawing together an elite divided by party strife and a means for (new) money and (established) title to unite in a mutually productive manner, not least through marriage. Yet, politeness was a status which had to be earned, demonstrated and defended. There were limits to the inclusiveness of sociability for, as Borsay puts it, 'the hand of friendship stretched only so far down the social ladder' – reach too far and politeness would lose its meaning and cachet.[35]

Second, placing emphasis on fashionable culture and the leisure pursuits of polite urban society obscures the persistence of traditional values, customs and activities. Markets and fairs remained important events in the weekly and annual rhythms of the economic and social life of towns. Similarly, bull-baiting, cock-fighting and public bonfires were important foci of urban leisure well into the eighteenth century, often providing a unifying focus for fashionable and plebeian society (see Chapter 4).[36] The rural gentry and the urban labourer came together at the cock-pit, epitomising an older order based on rank, patronage and manliness, rather than the affections of polite urban living.[37] This, of course, further encouraged the caricaturing of the rural squire as boorish and uncivilised, but complicates any easy equation of 'politeness', social rank and the urban.

Third, politeness – as a concept and an organising principle – changed through the course of the eighteenth century. The dichotomy of urban civility and rural vulgarity declined as a motif, to be replaced by finer distinctions between the vulgar and truly polite within the urban sphere. As the infrastructure of and participation in polite leisure spread across space and through different social orders, so the currency of politeness became debased. By the end of the century, Sweet argues, 'the term polite had lost some of its exclusivity and rhetorical power'. The self-evident link between politeness and good company, defined largely in terms of the presence of gentry, was gradually eroded. In its place emerged the notion of politeness as 'a generic quality of urban living'.[38] In short, politeness gradually transmuted from a concept of the gentry to one of an urban bourgeoisie. At the same time, the social exclusivity of a whole range of leisure facilities was in decline. Across the country, tradesmen were setting up their own assemblies governed by rules and rituals mimicking those of the gentry, whilst pleasure gardens were being invaded by the lower orders: an indication of the rise of new wealth and the difficulties of maintaining the exclusivity of facilities provided through the market. The response of the gentry was to refine the language of gentility and re-orientate their leisure space and practices. The term polite was increasingly replaced by notions of 'good taste' and respectability, the last of these carrying complex overtones of birth, morality and virtue.[39] Meanwhile, the gentry were deserting their local county towns in favour of the brighter lights of resorts or the metropolis, and were retreating into private entertainments, often centred on the home.[40] These ranged from tea parties to invitation balls, but all involved a removal from public to private spaces, and a concomitant and conscious emphasis on exclusivity.

Fourth, and compounding the temporal variability of politeness, was the understanding that not all towns were equally polite. Urban renewal was felt earliest and most profoundly in so-called leisure towns. These same places were labelled by town historians and travel writers as polite because they were the places where gentry congregated and where appropriate leisure institutions were most numerous and prestigious.[41] According to Defoe, Lincoln had 'a great deal of very good company', Lewes and the surrounding countryside were 'full of gentlemen of good families and fortunes', and Lichfield was deemed the best place in Staffordshire for 'good conversation and good company'. Moreover, such places *looked* the part, with their improved streets, modern architecture and grand civic buildings: Defoe thought Warwick 'a handsome, well built town', whilst Fiennes commented that the 'streetes are very handsome and the buildings regular and fine'.[42] The contrast was drawn between these places and two other types of town. First were those places, like Hereford and Coventry, with dark and narrow streets lined by medieval buildings, the former being described by Defoe as 'truly an old, mean built, and very dirty city'.[43] Second were the manufacturing and commercial towns which were growing increasingly numerous and populous in the later decades of the eighteenth century. Places such as Liverpool, Manchester and especially Bristol were viewed as centres of vulgar new money with only a thin veneer of politeness: the population was too engrossed with trade to consider higher things. It was a source of surprise when, as at Exeter for example, a town was found to be 'full of gentry, and good company, and yet full of trade and manufacture also'.[44] As industry spread, the environment of manufacturing towns deteriorated and polite infrastructure was swallowed up by commercial development.[45] Yet the supposed incompatibility of commerce and politeness was as much rhetorical as real. The polite nature of commercial towns was never seriously addressed: they and their inhabitants were characterised as impolite in order to 'validate the arguments that to be truly polite one needed the leisure and education of a gentleman'.[46] Moreover, as the eighteenth century progressed, the range and quality of facilities in towns traditionally viewed as 'polite', and in those thought of as vulgar, backward and unimproved, grew increasingly similar (see Chapter 2), making established stereotypes increasingly hard to sustain.

Overall, then, there is a clear need to explore more thoroughly the variety of experience seen in different sizes and types of town as the eighteenth century progressed. This enables a more precise mapping of the spread of urban renaissance, and also allows us to judge the extent to which the institutions and values of politeness penetrated the urban hierarchy (see Chapters 2 and 3). At the same time, it must be remembered that leisure and the built environment were only part of the new material culture which characterised the long eighteenth century. The changing acquisition, ownership and meaning of personal belongings were equally important in defining the status and identity of individuals and towns, and in making lives more comfortable or pleasant. These aspects of consumption have been extensively analysed across a wide range of times and places, the majority of studies falling, according to Trentmann, into one of two types: those which attempt to trace the birth of modern consumer society, and those which focus on shopping – or more correctly retailing.[47] We consider each of these in turn.

Urban consumption: status, meanings and identity

From a traditional focus on the late eighteenth and late nineteenth centuries – respectively seen as the birth of a consumer society and the advent of mass consumption – many recent historical analyses have sought to push back the bounds of modernity. In the British context, Peck argues for widespread luxury consumption in the early seventeenth century, whilst McCracken suggests a narrower but intensive consumer boom led by Elizabethan courtiers. Elsewhere in Europe, vibrant consumer societies have been identified in Renaissance Italy, and even in ancient Greece and Rome, where streets were lined with sellers of luxury goods. Further afield, China during the Ming dynasty and the Murghal empire are being redrawn as consumer societies, at least for elite groups.[48] Wherever we look, it seems, we find consumer societies or consumer revolutions. For Brewer, this effectively, and unhelpfully, inverts Latour's famous claim that 'we have never been modern': a criticism which is, at best, only tempered by moves to link early-modern and modern consumer society through stage models, such as that of Stearns.[49] The problem, as Stearns himself recognised, is that, within any over-arching understanding of the development of modern consumer society, there needs to be greater awareness of geographical diversity and temporal unevenness, and of the particular character of consumption in specific times and places.

What, then, do we 'know' about consumption in eighteenth-century England? Much recent work has focused on three related areas. First is the social and geographical variation in ownership of key goods. Contrasts have been drawn by Weatherill, Estabrook, Overton and others between consumption regimes in town and country: the former being seen as dynamic and modern, and the latter as torpid and traditional.[50] This is based, in part, on the role of the town as a nexus in the supply as well as the consumption of goods. Luxuries and semi-luxuries were imported in increasing quantities in the eighteenth century. Many came from the Orient or the New World, but Europe remained an important source of supply; and domestic manufacturers were quick to imitate these imported luxury goods, effectively spreading luxury amongst the middling sorts.[51] Significantly, imports, workshops and factories, and the middlemen and shopkeepers who brought goods to the consumer, were concentrated into towns. So too were the middling sorts – the most innovative and acquisitive group of consumers in the eighteenth century. Goods and people combined in a distinctive consumption milieu.[52]

The second area of interest lies in uncovering the motivations to consume more, new or particular types of goods. Here, Veblen's notion of conspicuous consumption and Simmel's 'trickle down' theory have been highly influential.[53] According to Veblen, the consumption of material goods and leisure is used to communicate wealth and status. Both quantity and quality were significant, as was behaviour, so that: 'closely related to the requirement that the gentleman must consume freely and of the right kind of goods, there is the requirement that he know how to consume them in a seemly manner'.[54] This imperative to consume spread down through the social hierarchy because, within an increasingly fluid post-feudal society, the 'leisure' classes set standards of consumption and lifestyle to which the rest of society aspired. It was upon this model of emulative consumption that McKendrick drew for his seminal work on eighteenth-century consumer society. He argued that:

> In imitation of the rich the middle ranks spent more frenziedly than ever before, and in imitation of them the rest of society joined in as best they might … Spurred on by social emulation and class competition men and

women surrendered eagerly to the pursuit of novelty, the hypnotic effects of fashion and the enticements of commercial propaganda.[55]

The driving force behind this emulative spending was social competition, which, aided by the close stratification of English society, penetrated even its lower reaches. Linked to the practices of Wedgwood, Boulton and others of producing cheaper versions of luxury consumer goods, this created an unprecedented upsurge in spending which, McKendrick argued, helped to stimulate the mechanised mass-production of goods which characterised British industrialisation. Although persuasive, many others have seen this emulation thesis as narrow and deterministic.[56] Emphasis is placed instead on the wide range of often mundane goods which appeared in increasing numbers in people's homes on both sides of the Atlantic.[57] In this way, 'modern' consumption was linked not to industrial-urbanism as McKendrick argued, but rather to de Vries' industrious revolution, Borsay's post-Restoration urban renaissance, and Berg's argument for the import-inspired production of semi-luxuries. Thus, the emergence of a consumer society involved heightened dependence on the market, growth in the number and wealth of the middling sorts, and the consumption of ever-larger quantities of cheaper goods – not least the semi-luxury manufactures pouring out of factories and workshops in the Midlands and north of England.[58] Growing consumption was also based on changes to the structure of and practices in the home emphasising the importance of utility as a stimulus to consume. As Berg argues, 'new consumer goods were frequently ascribed with values of usefulness, civility and ingenuity'.[59]

From a broader perspective, the growing heterogeneity of urban society and culture placed additional emphasis on the key role of consumption as a cultural marker, and created 'greater scope than hitherto for self-manipulation of status by choice of consumption practice'.[60] This places emphasis on the nature and quality of goods being consumed: their semiotic meanings rather than their intrinsic materiality. For Corrigan, this takes consumption beyond the individual and into a system of objects and signs wherein the individual consumes 'not so much specific objects to accomplish specific concrete ends, but signs in general for general social ends. Social differentiation becomes the name of the game'.[61] According to Bourdieu, this differentiation turns on the bundling of certain goods and attributes into particular combinations of social practices. Elites are thus distinguished not merely in terms of their wealth or their ownership of key goods, but in how these formed part of their broader lifestyle. Of particular significance here are goods and activities which mark out taste and judgement, either in terms of their aesthetic qualities or their rarity. Bourdieu, writing about France in the 1960s and 1970s, highlighted items such as luxury cars, crystal glasses and antique furniture, and a liking for 'difficult' composers such as Stravinsky or Boulez, as marking out the discernment of those with high levels of cultural capital. In eighteenth-century England, we might emphasise liveried carriages, imported porcelain, mahogany furniture, and lacquered tea-urns, but also conversance with architectural and scientific principles, and the classics. In both contexts, ostentatious display is not enough. Rather it is tempered or indeed challenged by 'a more subtle, detached and inconspicuous form [of consumption] to be appreciated only by those sufficiently cultivated or civilised'.[62]

In this respect, exotic and/or novel goods were especially significant. With the former, the spatial separation of production and consumption added extra interpretive scope to the consumer: the meaning of goods could be moulded around social aspirations or what Smith refers to as 'cultural contexts'. He argues that the consumption of coffee and the construction of coffee houses, for example, were important constituents of a 'rational masculinity' which underpinned the public sphere. Coffee was linked to sobriety and order, whilst the coffee house created an atmosphere of rational and businesslike sociability.[63] With new types of goods, their intrinsic novelty made them attractive, especially to newly wealthy professionals, merchants and the like, who marked their social (and economic) arrival through a new and distinctive material culture.[64] In Britain, and across Europe, we see a switch to lower cost, less durable goods with high cultural capital: pewter is replaced by earthenware and china, tapestries by wall-paper, and heavy oak and leather by lighter rush-bottomed chairs.[65] The rise of novelty over patina, and of cultural over economic capital, was important to the social mobility of the middling sorts, since lower costs meant that greater quantities of goods could be consumed and more emphasis could be placed on choosing items which carried the right meanings.[66] Moreover, their novelty and diversity made the consumption of these goods more open to interpretation – a tendency which was further heightened by the introduction of new designs or motifs on familiar goods. It was this constant reinvention of the familiar that lay at the heart of Wedgwood's business practices and the annual changes in design by the silk manufacturers of Lyon. It also drove the speculation in new types of tulip in seventeenth-century Holland.[67] Fashion, according to Simmel, served as a coding of objects in order to assert membership and allegiance. It was, moreover, a value system linked by eighteenth-century commentators such as Allan Ramsay to social status, since only those of rank could successfully attract imitators and thus establish fashion.[68] In combination, then, exoticism and novelty not only made goods highly desirable, but also provided scope for new rituals of consumption and new expressions of individual or group identity.

This links to the final aspect foregrounded by recent studies of consumption: the link between goods, rituals and identity. In this regard, consumption forms part of a broader view of culture as a 'conduit through which values and affinities are expressed', and identities created and projected: what is owned and what it means being an expression of and a key element in defining identity. As Campbell puts it: 'the self is built through consumption [and] consumption expresses the self'.[69] Consumption-based expressions of identity are often seen in terms of gender, with a special role being accorded to the relationship between women, consumption and the home. In contrast to the public nature of rational masculinity, Smith highlights domestic femininity as the context for consumption rituals centred on tea-drinking.[70] This can be seen, in some ways, as a prelude to the notion of separate spheres which supposedly characterised Victorian Britain, and shares with it the problem of ignoring women's role in public life and leisure.[71] Whilst it is true that women were often responsible for decisions about household consumption, they also took considerable time and trouble to acquire 'personal and expressive goods, conveying identity, personality and fashion', often to be displayed in public arenas such as assembly rooms, pleasure gardens and the street.[72] Consumption was central both to the social and economic roles of women in eighteenth-century England, and to their class and gender identities. Yet, as Finn observes, men were also actively engaged in acquiring and consuming goods. They were delegated to buy for the household and were enthusiastic shoppers on their own behalf, seeking out personal accoutrements, books and decorative items for the home.[73] Furthermore, Nenadic notes how Glasgow's 'arriviste colonial merchants' engaged in a 'spectacular form of self invention' through their 'conspicuous consumption and acquisition of elaborate and symbol-laden possessions'.[74] This underlines the importance of cultural capital and material culture to the middling sorts. They were defined, not simply in terms of their economic function or social status and aspirations, but also by their relationship with money and goods. On the one hand, it was the growing diversity of goods that 'met desires for individuality, self-differentiation and luxury by means of visual diversity'.[75] On the other, dependence on earned income made their social standing precarious and gave a special significance to material possessions: there was a heightened need to consume the necessary markers of their genteel status.[76] As Copeland observes: 'spending, like the hallmark on silver, marks Jane Austen's ambitious class as nothing else does'.[77] Thus, the middling sorts played a central role in shaping the world of goods through their constructions of genteel or polite consumption practices.

If politeness helped to structure consumption, then the reverse was also true. Indeed, the acquisition and consumption of material goods were central to Addison and Steele's commercially-orientated definition of the term. We have already discussed how politeness was often viewed as a model of behaviour, but it also 'lent itself as a descriptor to institutions, publications and patterns of consumption'.[78] Whilst it would be wrong to equate politeness unproblematically with the pursuit of fashionable goods and leisure activities or to see it as an expression of consumer consciousness, such practices were an important constituent of polite identity. As Vickery notes, gentility found its richest expression in material objects, so that consumption and lifestyle marked out a particular kind of genteel, polite, honourable and even virtuous citizen.[79] Consumption was not only necessary to demonstrate status; it also provided the means to engage in sociability through which 'private individuals' came together as a 'public', taking part in collective activities in the town. Goods both signalled and legitimised claims to genteel status, whilst the ideals of refinement and Enlightenment could be displayed through association with the new commodity culture, and through the practices of genteel leisure and shopping – a process which closely parallels the formation of 'life style tribes' in the late twentieth century.[80] Thus, new patterns and processes of consumption were not simple consequences of increased availability of goods, but rather the mark of a new cultural production. Polite identities were produced and reproduced through consumption and lifestyle, quality and refinement being the hallmarks of the elite.

The emphasis on the materiality and semiotics of goods links historical analyses with studies of consumption in the social sciences, but it produces what Pennell has referred to as an 'over-indulgence in the … world of goods'.[81] This has two drawbacks. First, it encourages neglect of those forms of consumption which do not involve material goods. Trentmann argues that late twentieth-century consumption has become as much about services and experiences as it is about goods.[82] But this is nothing new: eighteenth-century consumption involved leisure activities and professional services as well as a new material culture of personal possessions. As we argued earlier, there is a need to reconnect these various modes of consumption. Second, a focus on goods and their meanings obscures the processes of production and supply that linked commodities to consumers. These are important because, as Gregson and Crewe argue, social distinction could also be marked by the context and process of acquisition. More broadly, for Shields, the acts and spaces of shopping were central to the construction of particular, if mutable, lifestyles. What people do when they visit shops and malls is just as important in producing and reproducing their identity as the goods which they might (or might not) buy. Miller goes further, arguing that shopping is a reflective and relational activity and that the 'study of consumption should … be increasingly articulated with, and not become an opposition to, the study of the mechanisms by which goods are produced and distributed'.[83] Such a longitudinal perspective is exactly what Fine and Leopold attempted through their detailed exemplification of 'systems of provision', but has been attempted by few others, Styles and Berg being notable exceptions.[84] That said, recent years have seen a growing interest in the processes and practices which structured the end stages of supply: that is retailing and shopping.

Shops, shopkeepers and shoppers

It is a long-standing myth that retailing remained under-developed and primitive before the advent of department stores and multiple retailers in the second half of the nineteenth century. Conveniently analogous with the industrial developments at that time, these urban, innovative and 'large-scale' changes were promptly described in terms of a 'retailing revolution' in Britain and across Europe.[85] Any changes occurring before this monumental leap had to be minor and situated in some dark, atavistic and backward retail environment. The supposed contrast between these two modes of retailing is neatly summarised by Corrigan who creates a series of dichotomies covering retail organisation, consumer behaviour and cultural identity (see Table 1.1). Yet each of these is based on a serious misreading of retailing and shopping 'before the department store' and a misguiding assumption that, 'after the department store', every shop and all shopping took this apparently new form. In many ways, Corrigan's assessment – published in 1997 – is anachronistic.[86] The myth of under-development had already been exploded by the work of Willan, Mui and Mui, Shammas, and

14 *Leisure, consumption and shopping*

Table 1.1 Corrigan's 'Changes in shopping brought about by department stores'

Before the department store	After the department store
Purchase obligatory: 'just looking' impossible	Purchase optional: 'just looking' becomes possible
Ultra-specialisation: each shop sells only one type of good	Ultra-generalisation: each department store sells a vast range of goods
Retailing governed by guild system; restricted to goods available in artisanal system	Retailing in the department store a response to the availability of mass quantities of goods produced by the factory
No competition between guild members	Competition between department stores
No fixed prices: bargaining obligatory	Fixed prices: bargaining impossible
Need-centred: goods neither displayed nor advertised	Desire-centred: display and advertising of goods becomes vital to successful retailing
'Shopping around' impossible	'Shopping around' possible
Shopping restricted to one's local area	Department stores attracted shoppers from all over the city and beyond
Personal characteristics of seller relatively unimportant	Personal characteristics of the sales clerk must match 'cultivated' image of store
Public space generally male	Creation of new female public space for both shoppers and workers
Could not provide identity for new middle class	Cultural identity for new middle class can be bought off the shelf

Source: Based on Corrigan, *The Sociology of Consumption*, Table 4.1.

Glennie and Thrift, amongst others.[87] They demonstrated the growing number and range of shops in the eighteenth century, their organisation into complex retail systems, and the growing sophistication of retail practices. More recent work by Walsh, Cox, Berry, Stobart and Hann, and Peck has revealed seventeenth- and eighteenth-century shops as complex social as well as economic environments.[88] Yet even astute commentators such as Trentmann fail to acknowledge the depth and implications of this research for our understanding of consumption. The department store continues to hold many in thrall.

The eighteenth century was marked by rapid growth in the number of shops in England and Wales. In 1688 King thought that there were about 50,000 shopkeepers and tradesmen; Postlethwayt in 1757 estimated 100,000 and Massie two years later suggested a figure of 162,500.[89] These numbers are educated guesses, of course, but the reality of growth is clear enough: a response to population expansion, increased trade, urbanisation and a growing commercialisation of the household.[90] As well as being more numerous, eighteenth-century shops were increasingly specialised, particularly in larger towns, and offered an expanding variety of commodities, including novelties, imported wares and semi-luxuries. They were windows onto a world of goods. The impact of this on the 'mental horizons of town dwellers and countrymen alike must have been profound – literally and metaphorically a real eye-opener'.[91]

It is all too easy to take a Whiggish view of the shop as modern and progressive, developing to inevitably eclipse traditional forms of retailing such as markets, fairs and pedlars. Yet Europe's great fairs continued to be important international events through the eighteenth century, attracting huge numbers of people from across the continent. Berg argues that they operated in much the same manner as international exhibitions, or clothes, home or car shows do today. Thus, for example, Meissen porcelain was first displayed at the Leipzig fair; books from Holland, Germany and Geneva were sold at the Frankfurt fair; and both Boulton and Wedgwood exhibited their wares at the fairs at Brunswick, Leipzig, Frankfurt and Nuremberg.[92] Fairs also offered spectacle: people might go, not to buy, but 'out of curiosity only, to partake of the usual diversions of these public places'.[93] English fairs, in contrast, were far more modest and specialised events, increasingly associated with agricultural goods and wool, although some remained more significant in the supply of consumer goods. The fair at Stourbridge, for example, carried on an extensive trade in Nottingham glass, Sheffield cutlery and hardware from the west Midlands.[94] Pedlars persisted longer, and were far more widespread as a source of goods for English consumers. They were active in towns and the countryside: selling in the street, door to door and from inns, and offering their customers a personal service and often credit. Their impact in towns is apparent from the growing chorus of complaints from shopkeepers who sought to restrict this 'unfair' competition. Even though much of this was rhetoric aimed at easing their own tax burden, the antipathy shown towards pedlars suggests that they formed important competitors in the retail system of English towns.[95] In contrast, a more symbiotic relationship developed between markets and shops – the latter were often clustered around the market place and did much of their trade on market days when the town was filled with visitors from the surrounding countryside (see Chapter 3).

Despite the continuing importance of 'traditional' forms of retailing, it is clear that the role of the shop in establishing shopping as an everyday (not just market day) activity was achieved at the eventual expense of markets, fairs and pedlars.[96] Already in sixteenth-century Venice, shopkeepers were unwilling to sell on the market place, even though they were prohibited from selling from their shops during the period of the fair. The relative decline of Antwerp's opulent markets and fairs seems to start from a similar period, and for similar reasons.[97] One underlying cause, Walsh argues, is that shops were replacing street markets as the mental focus for consumers. It was in shops that the newest, most fashionable items were to be found and, by extension, where consumer desires were created and indulged.[98] Another is that shops were fixed premises which could be consciously moulded around the display of goods, and the social and economic practices of buying and selling. Certainly, the fabric of many shops gradually improved. Glazed and bow windows, and gas lighting brought the Georgian ideals of light and space into the shop.[99] Inside, fittings and furnishings became very important in creating an appropriate atmosphere and in displaying the goods to best effect (see Chapter 5). Walsh has revealed a high level of spending and concern for shop design in London, and the fittings which were central to the shop became more elaborate and numerous over the century.[100] More pliable glass encouraged the use of display cabinets to show off new goods to maximum effect. However, it is the front window upon which much attention has focused. Displays set up there were designed to encourage people to enter the shop, with shopkeepers going to considerable trouble and expense to produce a pleasing spectacle. Thus, the shop was transformed into a place for display and marketing: it was a site of commodities, information and persuasion.[101]

In addition to changes to the fabric of the shop, new practices were employed by the shopkeepers to encourage sales. At the heart of these were attempts to make the goods look as attractive as possible, in part dependent on the environment in which they were presented. The more prestigious retailers cultivated the shop as a leisure environment, encouraging browsing, looking and trying.[102] This heightened promotion of goods, along with new sales techniques, formed a key part of the shopkeeper's role, not least as a mediator of fashion and taste. In other shops, the process of buying was made as efficient as possible. In the second half of the century fixed prices and ready cash became more widely used, which brought the advantages of speed, avoiding the need to haggle with the shopkeeper.[103] Linked to this was the development of the showroom as a specialist space designed for displaying goods to their best advantage, and to facilitate different types of selling according to the status of the customer. Entry into private backrooms was reserved for privileged customers to whom credit might be offered, a practice which generated opportunities for 'the home as showcase'.[104] Economic aspects of shopkeeping were also enhanced. The eighteenth century saw a burgeoning literature on account keeping, along with other commercial guides, which indicated the increasing professionalisation of the trade. The shopkeeper was required to manage complicated credit networks, and the rise of the account ledger, day-book and billheads indicated the formalisation of the everyday exchange process.

The enhancement of the physical structure and appearance of shops, together with the introduction of more 'modern' marketing and selling strategies, made them an integral part of the wider urban renaissance.[105] Shops were, in effect, made more appropriate for selling the new goods which tapped into discourses of modernity and Enlightenment. This is of no surprise, as the shopkeepers who were redesigning and promoting their shops were also, as Beckett and Smith demonstrate for Nottingham, champions of and subscribers to a wide range of urban renewal projects.[106] Yet, the importance of shopping to the social and cultural development of a town stretched beyond investment in the physical infrastructure of the town. In addition to the acquisition of goods, consumerism embraced social practices that surrounded the moment of purchase.

Shopping involves going to places and engaging with people – the shopkeepers, fellow shoppers and friends whom one might meet whilst visiting shops, but also the 'significant others' on whose behalf, Miller argues, much shopping is undertaken. Shoppers develop all these social relations through viewing and selecting goods

– processes which link people to people as well as people to goods. Consumption, then, cements identity in relation not only to commodities (as we discussed earlier), but also to other people and other practices.[107] On the one hand, this underscores the ambivalence and mutability of lifestyle as a concept and as social practice. On the other, it links shopping as a process of acquiring material goods, to shopping as a social and leisure activity.[108] In the context of the eighteenth-century town, we need to view shopping in the wider framework of social practices and cultural mores which characterised the urban renaissance and polite society. Thus, the beautified spaces of the town provided a setting for promenading, shopping and engagement with the discourses of polite sociability. There is no doubt contemporaries were conscious of the importance of this blending of activities and intentions. On the Pantiles in Tunbridge Wells, for example, there was an enclosed gallery erected from which music was played while consumers moved from shop to shop along the street – entertainment, sociability and shopping coming together in time and space. Celia Fiennes visited the town to take the waters, but also commented favourably on the genteel society found there, the coffee houses and card rooms, and the 'shops full of all sorts of toys, silver, china, milliners, and all sorts of curious wooden ware'. Clearly, the fusion of various forms of flânerie and leisure with the practices of shopping was far from being the exclusive domain of late twentieth-century malls.[109]

It is possible to view shopping as a 'cultural context' through which goods and social practices were given meaning (see Chapter 6). Berry goes some way towards this by highlighting the emergence of a polite shopping culture as part of public sociability, especially for women.[110] Building on this, we can see shopping as an important leisure activity and a significant force in moulding the urban environment, and shaping class and gender identities. Shopping was part of the social round. More than a means of acquiring goods or knowledge about goods, it developed as a polite and respectable way of passing time: of seeing and being seen. Glennie and Thrift rightly argue that it is unlikely that eighteenth-century consumers had a 'complete intellectual framework through which they articulated their motives and which they deployed when encountering commodities, other consumers, and consumption sites' (be they shops or more overtly leisure facilities).[111] However, they undoubtedly made active choices to engage in leisure and shopping, and to visit particular places for particular purposes, even if those motives were complex and bundled together a number of related and sometimes subconscious objectives. In this way, shopping offered the consumer sociability and agency. It was a reflective process which drew on specific sets of social and economic skills that were important enough to be taught, and yet were learned and honed through repeated performance.[112] Shopping as leisure often involved visiting a number of different shops to inspect a variety of goods. The concentration of fashionable shops into definable and widely recognised shopping streets facilitated polite shopping and generated a distinctive urban shopping landscape (see Chapter 3).[113] The New Exchange in London (1609) encouraged sociability and impulse buying, the covered walk which linked the shops being 'an appointed place of meeting, for men to walk and stay on for another and, in that staying, a man sees one thing or other that he will buy'. They performed a similar function fifty years later when Samuel Pepys wrote of planned or casual encounters there, and of his browsing in shops to pass the time of day.[114] A century later, the shopkeepers on Cheapside and the Strand were well accustomed to having their wares inspected by well-to-do Londoners and visitors.[115] Such practices may have been most highly developed in London, but provincial shopkeepers were clearly attuned to them by the early eighteenth century (see Chapters 5 and 6). Shops thus formed an increasingly important part of the polite public sphere of the eighteenth-century town – as central to the new notions of politeness as were the assemblies, promenades and circulating libraries.

Many different elements came together to create what may be termed a consumer culture or lifestyle. Centring on the material goods, these produced new social practices – shopping, looking, learning, displaying – which were absorbed into everyday life and ritualised. As Miller and others note, these activities were 'in process': people engaged in performances which were acted out in the town and in specific spaces within the town, so that social practices were also spatial practices.[116] In order to understand more fully the related nature of leisure and shopping in the eighteenth century town, it is therefore necessary to shift attention onto the largely neglected social-spatial dialectics of polite consumption and material culture, and to explore the spatiality of the interplay between retailing/shopping and leisure development in the eighteenth-century town.

The spatiality of consumption

There is a wealth of research on the nature, spaces and practices of provincial culture – much of it inspired by Borsay's seminal study – and on the role of social structures, most notably gender, in shaping consumer practices.[117] However, the topographies and social processes of consumerism, and especially shopping, have not been fully spatialised.[118] Consumer behaviour has been located in particular spaces, but has not been seen as contributing to those spaces, or being shaped by those spaces. Not only is it a surprisingly 'people-less' account of consumer behaviour that has been recovered, it is also one that relies on orthodox understandings of how the eighteenth-century town was made. On the one hand, Berry notes that: 'material goods transport themselves from shops into people's homes and are mysteriously described as part of the process of the "flow of goods" … with little attention paid to the social interactions which were required to procure them'. And on the other, Ogborn argues for 'more accounts to be constructed of the experience of modernity and modernism in the streets, built environments and representations of a wider range of cities than has yet been considered'.[119] However, this is not only about a recovery of people's actions in space, but also understandings of the complexity of spaces which engendered socio-cultural processes.

In focusing on space as well as practice, studies of twentieth-century consumerism by Miller, Shields, Jackson, Gregson and Crewe, and others have shown that space and place matter. They highlight the need to focus more closely on the ways in which consumer spaces (both leisure and shopping) can be at once material sites for commodity exchange and symbolic and metaphoric territories.[120] The rejection of modernity's geography as simply a planned, rational and panoptic space, focuses attention onto the varied, multiform, and hybrid spaces of consumption. It also helps us to recognise that the socio-spatial manifestation of different discourses was found in layered spaces in which different consumer meanings coexisted. Acknowledging that spaces and meanings were continually in flux, we come upon the need to fix meanings in actions and draw together the relationships between material reality and perception, and embrace the contradictory nature of such intersections. This implies a relationship between doing (or spatial practice) and the environment (or the material). However, it is essential to recognise that this was a two-way relationship. The processes and practices of leisure and shopping served to produce and reproduce urban space, from squares to shops, promenades to coffee houses. Conversely, they were themselves shaped by those spaces. As Miller and others have argued, space was not merely a passive backdrop to the unfolding performances of consumption. It was both the 'geographical site of action' and the 'social possibility for engagement in action'.[121] Thus, just as the socio-spatial requirements of politeness and respectability moulded the urban environment, so the pleasure garden and assembly room structured the behaviour of those attending concerts and balls, whilst shops and shopping streets informed the routines and actions of shoppers (see Chapter 5).[122] This links closely to Goffman's differentiation of front-regions and back-regions, the former – which equates with these public spaces – being characterised by the self-conscious acting out of particular 'public' identities. More recent analyses have placed greater emphasis on the repetitive and intuitive nature of consumer behaviour, and the flexibility of its attendant social relations. But the link between behaviour, identity and space remains at the foreground of contemporary research.[123] There is, therefore, a need to spatialise more completely the relationship between consumption practices, material culture and urban space in historical analyses, both through empirical evidence of consumer behaviour, and in terms of a deeper theoretical understanding of the socio-spatial dialectic.[124]

Traditional thinking has recognised two long-established schools of thought which define urbanity first according to density and proximity (the built form or morphology), and second as a way of life.[125] Whilst very different in their conceptualisation of the town, both definitions depend on intrinsically spatial understandings of urban. The notion of the urban as a distinct form underpins ecological models which represent the city as stable and homogeneous (although subject to repetitive 'waves' of change), allowing the production of typologies and ideal types. This, in effect, presents the city as an 'end-product', created by a single perspective on the urban phenomenon and by narrative and progressive conceptions of history. Benjamin rejected the vision and the approach, arguing that they totalised and homogenised the historical geography of the city. Instead, he sought to create a deeper understanding by disrupting both the progressive narrative of history and the Euclidian geometry of geography. To do this, he focused on the particular – the 'debris of history' – abstracting these fragments from their 'all-too-familiar, taken-for-granted' context, and placing them in a heterogeneous montage of objects, images and texts.[126] For Benjamin, these better represented the complexities, discontinuities and serendipities which characterised the modern city. An equally powerful and more widely shared critique of morphological analysis argues that it ignores the active place of people in making the town.[127] One way in which people produced urban space was through planning: of the orderly use of streets and squares, extensions to the town, or complete new towns. Such calculated interventions into urban space draw on modernist perspectives of the town as a unit comprising elements that can be rearranged to produce a different spatial and social order (see Chapter 3). The process is thus portrayed as rational and progressive, with the planners themselves seen as technocratic spatial engineers – part of the existing urban elite – or occasionally inspired visionaries.[128]

The second definition of urbanity – as a way of life – gives centre-stage to the role of people in making the town. In many ways, the people were the town. This perspective turns on the pioneering work of Lewis Worth, who forged a crucial link between place and way of life. His ideas gave expression to a set of practices which are embedded within broader urban culture. It is on this key tenet that current understandings of the spatial form depend, emphasising the role of human agency in spatial constructions, but also recognising that those spatial constructions denote a particular set of practices.[129] This is highly significant because it draws a fundamental link between practice (or behaviour) and space (or place): the mutual constitution of society and space. These ideas have been central to the spatial turn, and the recognition of the social production of space. The essence lies in a move away from the Kantian conception of space – that is, as an empty and primordially-given container of things – to space as process and in process.[130] Thus, the town can be viewed as specialised space with particular meanings.

Understanding of the close relationship between space, society and culture rests on the twin notions of urbanity as built form and way of life. As Soja argues: 'spatiality is socially produced and, like society itself, exists in both substantial forms (concrete spatialities) and as a set of relations between individuals and groups, an "embodiment" and medium of social life itself'.[131] This assertion reflects the earlier work of Simmel, who highlighted the importance of space as an active context for human interaction, and echoes Frisby's argument that 'space is not a reflection of society, it is society'.[132] Its implication is that any consideration of urbanism should be a consideration of behaviour, practices and spaces. Consumer behaviour 'takes place': it has a spatiality of *where* it happens and *how* it happens – a point made clear in Hägerstrand's time-geography, paraphrased by Pred as the 'choreography of existence'.[133] Within this approach, emphasis is placed on the importance of everyday lives – of the mundane and the ordinary – and on the ways in which the movement of people through time and space intersected to shape both individual experiences and the spatiality of the city. Hägerstrand pictorialised movement in space through diagrams showing paths, nodes and bundles, a device adopted by Pred as a means of tracing individual lifeworlds and linking them to wider socio-economic worlds.¹³⁴ Processes of leisure and shopping can also be viewed in this way: incorporating the flow of shoppers and pleasure seekers, the nexus of the shop, and the bundling of social, economic and cultural activities in the polite social round.

Such activities took place within the built environment of the town. Even everyday consumption practices, which Glennie and Thrift characterise as repetitive, intuitive and non-reflexive, involved people making choices about what they did and where they went: between different goods, shops, plays, assemblies, routeways and destinations. Yet, as de Certeau argues, spatial practice is about action in and the transformation of space. For him, the city is created by people's movement through and appropriation of space: 'their intertwined paths give their shape to spaces. They weave places together'. In this respect, pedestrian movements form 'one of those real systems whose existence in fact makes up the city. They are not localized; it is rather they that spatialize'.¹³⁵ The actions of individuals are thus central to the production of urban space: humans, as free and active agents, make choices which make, re-make and reform spatial and social structures. But these structures are also seen as exerting an influence on the individual and on society. Indeed, for Giddens, structure was the 'medium and the outcome' of social practices, and was also 'implicated in every moment of action … at once constraining and enabling'.¹³⁶ Consequently, consumer behaviour is framed by and produces distinctive urban environments: assembly rooms and shops; world exhibitions and department stores; multiplex cinemas and shopping malls. It also depends upon place or location, sign and symbol to give significance from which meaning can be constructed.¹³⁷ Consumers perceive the city and then reformulate their reading into a conceptualisation. These cognitive or mental spaces cannot be separated out from other types of space – social or physical – because, as Soja argues, 'semiotic imagery and cognitive mappings, as ideas and ideologies, play a powerful role in shaping the spatiality of social life'.¹³⁸ At one level, this imagery can be seen in Benjamin's portrayal of the cultural landscape of nineteenth-century Paris as a dream-world or phantasmagoria: a succession of intensely visual yet not quite 'real' images and experiences.¹³⁹ Perhaps more practically, individuals' perceptions are central to Rendell's depiction of rambling as a mode of consumption in the early nineteenth-century West End. Here, we see the significance of the conceptual map of urban space in negotiating the city. Similarly, the eighteenth-century consumer was actively engaged in mentally putting together a consumer landscape, which was determined by personal choice (as a free agent) and possibility (itself shaped by provision). Thus, 'conscious decisions can be made on the basis of perceptions of the world, but actions are played out in the real world'.¹⁴⁰

At the heart of the new spatial theory has been the work of Lefebvre.¹⁴¹ His project directs a new framework for theorising space, encapsulated in the concept of 'the production of space', and brings together many of the preceding ideas. Whilst his immediate political framework and project are temporally and spatially removed, Lefebvre's core ideas lend themselves well to analysis of urban spatiality in Georgian England because he uses the city and urbanism as 'touchstones' throughout his work, and shows a particular sensitivity to the emergence of modernity and its associated spaces.[142] Lefebvre's central tenet was that space was socially produced and embraced a multitude of intersections. The conceptual triad that he developed, and which Soja has subsequently refined, reflects his attempt to overcome the traditional duality of society and space, material and mental, real and abstract.[143] Within the so-called 'trialectics of spatiality', *spatial practices* – what Soja terms 'Firstspace' – link the geographies of individuals to the production of space through routine and routinised activities: Pred's daily pathways. It is through such routine spatial practices (visiting shops or walking the streets) that space is subconsciously (re)constructed and transformed. In its emphasis of the everyday and its spaces, and in placing a value on knowledge derived from everyday practice, this overcomes the separation of concept and reality.[144] It also reminds us that people living at the time experienced a coherence of space and practice which can be lost in retrospective analysis. In contrast, *representations of space* or 'Secondspace' are codified, and subsume ideology and knowledge within practice; that is to say, space itself becomes 'represented'. Effectively, this is the space of capital. Representations of space, as they are 'conceived' spaces, controlled by professionals or elites (such as the town corporation and the gentry), reflect the operation of power structures in society around which individuals move. These spaces are imaged, fashioned and shaped. It is these spaces which urban planning dominates or, in the context of the eighteenth century, which supported emerging forms of urban design and renewal. Finally, *spaces of representation* are spaces of everyday experience, in which the individual (rather than society) may be 'represented'.[145] Typically, these are associated with counterspaces or 'Thirdspaces', which challenge or subvert dominant spatial practices and spatialities. De Certeau, for example, highlights the tactics of consumers which allowed them to reappropriate space for uses other than those for which it was intended. 'Felt more than thought', it is through these lived spaces that people construct meaning for themselves, through the use and interpretation of signs, symbols and icons.[146]

Themes and scales of analysis

A consciously spatial perspective has much to offer the study of consumption, and yet these ideas have been drawn on only tangentially in the analyses of the eighteenth- and nineteenth-century town.[147] The aim in this study is to introduce a critical spatiality to our understanding of the inter-relationships between eighteenth-century leisure and shopping, material culture and built environments. An appreciation of the socio-spatial dialectic underpins our approach by insisting that there must be relationships drawn between space and society, and that space must be interpreted at a number of levels, both material and mental. In arguing this, we do not seek to discard traditional empirical analysis – indeed, a wealth of empirical evidence is deployed to underpin our argument throughout the book. Rather, we draw on our reading of Lefebvre, Soja and others to offer new perspectives and ask fresh questions about seemingly familiar topics and processes.

This theorisation structures our approach in three ways. First, we seek to identify a range of consumer spaces and elucidate their production before considering each as encompassing different types of space in addition to the physical materiality. Second, we focus on the actions of individuals as consumers within these spaces, and thus link space with practice. In this regard, we are interested not simply in where consumer and leisure sites were located, but how they were made, perceived and lived. Third, we take a contextualised approach to the socio-spatial dialectic, recognising the importance of place as well as space, but also the (spatial) relationship between places. Buildings, streets and towns were not produced, and nor did they operate, in isolation from one another. We therefore place each into their spatial as well as their socio-cultural context. This requires analysis that is sensitive to a variety of different scales of activity, the two-way relationships between space and social practice that occurred at every scale, and the different imperatives surfacing at each scale.

These ideas are not explored through the milieu of a wealthy elite of aristocrats and landed gentry, or through the lens of metropolitan experience – both of which give a clear, but very particular view of eighteenth-century consumption. Rather, attention centres on shopping and leisure as they were experienced by a broadly defined middling sort who inhabited the market, manufacturing and county towns of two broadly defined regions: north-west England (taken as Lancashire and Cheshire) and the west Midlands (Staffordshire, Worcestershire and Warwickshire).[148] We do not pretend that these were necessarily conscious and self-aware socio-spatial units, although there is good evidence of broad coherence.[149] Instead, we would argue that they offer three important aspects to the analysis. First, at a pragmatic level, they give us boundaries within which to work: a finite number of towns for which to collect data on consumption spaces and practices. Second, by focusing our attention in this way, they allow us to undertake comprehensive analysis: we are able to say something of the spaces of consumption in every town within the study areas, rather than 'cherry-picking' examples from across the country. This is vital in allowing us to assess the extent to which consumption spread through the urban network, and relate towns to one another as spaces of consumption or as points of supply from which consumers could choose. Third, without claiming that these regions or their constituent counties were representative of the country as whole, they offer a wide variety of different *types* of town. There were large industrial or commercial centres, such as Birmingham and Liverpool; substantial county towns, notably Chester and Worcester; smaller administrative centres, like Warwick, Lancaster and Stafford; old established and newly emerging manufacturing towns, including Wolverhampton and Bolton, and Burslem and West Bromwich, respectively; prosperous market towns, like Stratford and Knutsford; and places right at the margins of urban status, from Malpas to Dunchurch. This variety is important in gauging the extent to which consumption spread through different levels of the urban hierarchy and was related to local socio-economic conditions.

Each chapter focuses on a different theme within the overall exploration of the spatiality of leisure and shopping. Chapter 2 centres on *hierarchies* as a means of conceptualising the relationships between towns and as a socio-spatial structure conditioning individuals' experience of and access to goods and leisure activities. We begin by detailing the distribution of leisure and retailing functions across the two regions, highlighting differences between towns in terms of size, location and socio-economic character. We then attempt to (re)construct hierarchies of consumption: exploring how these were spatially ordered and temporally variable, and assessing how any urban renaissance spread across space and time. Finally, we explore the ways in which regional spaces of consumption were integrated through retail and transport networks, and the spatial practices and perceptions of individual consumers. This chapter provides contextual bedding for the discussions of consumption spaces in Chapter 3 which focuses on attempts to construct the town as a spatial focus of *politeness* and civilisation. This was affected in part through the accretion of a critical mass of appropriate activities and spaces, and in part through the cultivation and projection of a polite image. Central to the discussion here is an examination of the identity and motivations of those engaged in constructing a new, civilised material culture which embodied urbane politeness. Looking beyond such rhetoric, we also explore the intra-urban geographies of polite consumption, in terms of the spatial distribution of shops and leisure facilities, and argue that the 'critical mass' of politeness was given extra weight by the functional and spatial inter-linking of practices and infrastructure.

In Chapter 4, attention focuses down onto the street as a *stage-set* for polite, commercialised *performances* of consumption. We begin by assessing environmental improvement as a practical process for creating an appropriate venue for public life and social intercourse, and then consider the socio-spatial imperatives which shaped the layout and architecture of the street. In this, we highlight the privileging of visual readings of the urban environment and other people. Turning to the performances themselves, we examine how these produced the street as social space, and how different kinds of performance could bring conflicting meanings to the street. Moving further down the spatial scale, Chapter 5 considers the nature of individual buildings and relates their material structure – particularly the distinction between public and private space – to the ways in which they were experienced, utilised and imbued with meaning. Attention initially centres on the façade as symbolic capital, a *representation* of space and of social practices, but we argue that this masks a more complex layering of spaces: differential access reflecting and (re)conferring status accordingly. Building on this, we examine how these different layers of space were used to direct consumption practices through the *display* of goods, the body, and ultimately status; but also how they were contested and transgressed, producing counterspaces and alternative identities.

Issues of *identity* are considered more fully in Chapter 6, which begins by exploring the patterns and rhythms of leisure and shopping, and emphasises that these activities engendered social mixing as they brought together (different types of) people in space and time. We then examine the customs, norms and *social practices* which characterised shopping and leisure, arguing that these were central to the construction of leisure facilities and especially shops as lived spaces. From this basis, we explore some of the motivations of consumers and the identities created and recreated through acts and spaces of consumption. In Chapter 7, we broaden our perspective once more and explore the ways in which advertisements conveyed images of modern consumer spaces in the town and how this involved the construction of *virtual* consumer spaces, projecting consumerism into the public realm in new ways. This brings together the themes of the spatiality of consumer processes and the production of consumer space; the inter-locking of material culture and the town and provincial and metropolitan identity. Through this series of spatial scales, we seek to further understanding of the mutually constituted practices and spaces of consumption in the provincial towns of eighteenth-century England. Specifically, we aim to show how new forms of urban space were both produced through the practices of consumption (from dancing at assemblies to browsing in shops) and served to shape the possibility for social action.

2 The region

Hierarchies and spatial ordering

Introduction

Regional space can usefully be viewed in Lefebvrian terms. Patterns of spatial interaction were socially produced – they were the result of personal mobility, trading networks and so on – but they also shaped both the socio-economic characteristics of particular places and their external relationships with other localities. Thus the region was not merely the container in which economic and social change might occur, but an active agent in structuring these changes.[1] To understand how the region might structure as well as arise from the individual's experience of and choices in leisure and shopping, we need to recognise both the differences between places and the spatial and functional links that bound them together. We must address Soja's call for a critical spatialisation of (urban) history – one that recognises the divergent and fractured, but inter-connected nature of space – and make our analysis spatially as well as topographically sensitive.[2] The difficulty here is identifying ways in which this might be achieved, not least because systematic theorisations of the spatial arrangement of socio-economic activities are remarkably rare. One profitable, but surprisingly under-explored, approach is to marry older paradigms with this critical spatiality. Too often dismissed as meaningless spatial science, Christaller's central place theory offers us a useful way of conceptualising the spatial and hierarchical relationships that bound together locations within regional space.[3] In essence, it draws the spatial practices of people's everyday lives – as they shopped, visited friends or attended social events – into a structured hierarchical representation of space. Importantly, we can use this approach to explore the relationship between individual action (social practice) and the wider spatial patterns of supply and (collective) demand, in part because the model explicitly acknowledges the region as a network space. Indeed, the central place system is essentially a hierarchical network of towns and their interlocking hinterlands – a network that allowed both individuals and settlements to 'transcend their localism' and adopt aspects of regional and metropolitan culture.[4]

Of course, there are many problems with the Christallerian model: not least its inflexibility which fails to accommodate the variable importance of towns through time and across different functions. A slavish application of central place theory would be as tedious as it is unproductive. However, adopting a broad spatial-hierarchical mode of analysis to explore the practice of and relationship between shopping and leisure in the towns of the west Midlands and north-west England can provide a more spatially sensitive reading of the processes underlying urban renaissance and the emergence of polite consumption. It focuses attention on the diversity of leisure and retail provision found in Georgian towns, whilst recognising the common threads that ran through the urban experience in small and large towns alike. Moreover, it allows us to consider the region and the urban hierarchy as structure and agent – shaping individual shopping and leisure habits – and as the product of the myriad decisions and activities of shoppers and pleasure seekers.

In this chapter, we explore the spatiality of shopping and leisure development during the long eighteenth century at a regional level. A systematic approach is essential here if we are to present a comprehensive region-wide analysis of leisure and retailing – one that allows us to explore the spatial and hierarchical distribution of goods and services. Thus we present analysis of the leisure and retail infrastructure of *all* towns in the west Midlands and north-west England: over 100 towns, varying in size and structure from large commercial towns like Liverpool, Birmingham and Manchester, through established county capitals including Chester, Worcester and Stafford, to lesser manufacturing centres such as Burslem, Dudley and Blackburn, and small market towns, some at the very margins of urban status, like Penkridge, Abbots Bromley and Malpas.[5] We begin by tracking the spread of facilities and shops across space and time, highlighting differences between towns in terms of size, location and socio-economic character. This allows us to assess the spatial and hierarchical spread of urban renaissance. Building on this basic survey, we attempt to (re)construct hierarchies of consumption, exploring how these were temporally variable and spatially ordered. From this, we can identify the key centres in the emergence of regional and local consumption milieus. Finally, we explore the ways in which regional spaces of consumption were integrated through retail and transport networks, and the spatial practices of individual consumers.

Geographies of urban renaissance: leisure and retailing

Notions of sociability and civility lay at the heart of eighteenth-century leisure development. They involved the construction of space and of carefully conceived images of that space; both being shaped by the needs of increasingly commercialised fashionable culture that provided a polite public arena where men and women could meet and interact.[6] This incorporated all three aspects of Lefebvre's analytical matrix. The spatial practices of polite society (promenading, theatre-going and so on) combined with representations of space (conceived by corporations and architects) and the lived space through which individuals perceived their urban surroundings. Together, these produced leisure space in the eighteenth-century town: spaces for clubs, assemblies, horse races and plays. As the century progressed, these polite pleasures were overlain with an infrastructure of improvement of the urban environment, society and the individual. Thus we see the spread of infirmaries and charitable bodies, libraries and philosophical societies, and new forms of urban design. In Borsay's original iteration of his urban renaissance thesis, the chronology of this set of transformations ran from the Restoration through to the 1760s, with bursts of activity in the 1690s and again in the 1730s. More recently, Sweet has offered a revised, and two-tier, chronology of development. She argues that, whilst county or leisure towns had experienced profound change by the early decades of the eighteenth century, most places did not feel the full impact of improvement until the 1760s.[7] Thereafter, development was rapid and widespread: by 1800 few towns or even large villages were without a range of new leisure institutions, public spaces or civic infrastructure. To what extent do our data from the west Midlands and north-west England support this revisionist perspective?

Before 1770, leisure facilities were restricted in their distribution across the two regions: over half of the towns had no recorded activities and a further third had only one or two.[8] The most widespread forms of commercialised leisure were horse races, assemblies, music societies and theatres, which were each present in around one-fifth of towns (see Table 2.1). Race meetings could be hugely important social events, mixing sociability and display with the frisson of gambling and the excitement of crowds. They were found in a wide variety of places, including small towns such as Malpas, Neston and Tenbury. Those in county towns were major regional events. Lichfield, for example, hosted an important county meeting, attracting large numbers of the Staffordshire gentry. In 1748 the *Worcester Journal* reported that the races there were so well attended that the company had to dine in a garden as no house could accommodate them, and many gentlemen were forced to retire to Tamworth for board and lodgings.[9] In contrast, racing in small towns was more sporadic and became less widespread than had been the case in the early decades of the eighteenth century. This was partly a consequence of the 1740 Act 'to restrain and prevent the excessive increase of horse-races', which stipulated that all prizes should be at least £50 in value, resulting in the closure of 91 out of 138 courses across the country by the end of the decade.[10] Some surviving meetings struggled to attract audiences and competitors. Sir Roger Newdigate counted just fifteen couples dining on the first day of Rugby races in 1752, and one day of the 1772 meeting at Stratford-upon-Avon was abandoned 'for want of horses'.[11] Assemblies were similarly widespread, appearing in county towns, large commercial centres and a range of smaller manufacturing and market towns: places such as Bewdley, Congleton and Ormskirk. Like racing, many drew on and strengthened links with gentry families across their hinterlands. Those in Chester, Worcester, Preston, Warwick and later Leamington Spa attracted local nobility as well as the rural and urban gentry, but smaller towns were also linked to the surrounding countryside: Congleton had a regular hunt ball by the 1750s, attended by the gentry of south-east Cheshire, and Knutsford's races and assemblies were said to be 'honoured with a more brilliant assembly of nobility and gentry than any other in the county, not excepting Chester'.[12] Larger commercial towns – including Warrington and

Table 2.1 Leisure facilities and urban improvement in the towns of north-west England and the west Midlands in the long eighteenth century

	1770		1790		1830	
	No.	%	No.	%	No.	%
Horse racing	24	23.1	26	25.0	42	40.4
Assembly	18	17.3	38	36.5	49	47.1
Theatre	17	16.3	29	27.9	37	35.6
Music	18	17.3	27	26.0	34	32.7
Town Hall	15	14.4	23	22.1	48	46.2
Circulating library	14	13.5	21	20.2	59	56.7
Walk/pleasure garden	11	10.6	14	13.5	26	25.0
Baths/spa	11	10.6	17	16.3	25	24.0
Newspaper	10	9.6	9	8.7	22	21.2
Subscription library	9	8.7	18	17.3	48	46.2
Improvement	7	6.7	9	8.7	36	34.6
Square	6	5.8	10	9.6	17	16.3
Infirmary	5	4.8	6	5.8	9	8.7
Lit. and Phil. Society	3	2.9	3	2.9	16	15.4
Painter/artist	2	1.9	7	6.7	28	26.9
Market hall	1	1.0	6	5.8	28	26.9
Dancing master	1	1.0	9	8.7	12	11.5
Dispensary	0	0.0	4	3.8	27	26.0

Source: various

Wolverhampton as well as Liverpool, Manchester and Birmingham – possessed assemblies from the early eighteenth century. However, like those that appeared in lesser manufacturing towns during the 1780s and 1790s, these were oriented more towards urban professionals, merchants and tradesmen. The presence of large numbers of such consumers in these towns also helps to explain the early appearance of purpose-built theatres and the support given to charity concerts and music societies.[13] In part due to complex licensing procedures, theatres were largely restricted to larger centres – even when they were housed in multi-function buildings like St Mary's Hall in Coventry or in converted commercial premises, such as the refurbished wool hall in Chester. Musical performances, in contrast, also took place in smaller centres, if on a rather sporadic basis. A 'grand concert of vocal and instrumental music' was held in Stockport's assembly rooms in 1757 and again in 1764; Blackburn had a Handel Society by 1754; and oratorios were performed in the parish church during Stratford-upon-Avon's Shakespeare jubilee festival in 1769. In the majority of small towns music was restricted to occasional recitals or choral concerts at the local church or chapel, although Leigh's music society (established in 1768) was clearly not exceptional: a performance of Handel's *Messiah* in Manchester in 1765 drew on choral and music societies from across the industrial parishes of eastern Lancashire.[14]

Other leisure activities had a still narrower distribution. Libraries, walks and gardens, and newspapers were recorded in around 10 per cent of towns by 1770, whilst just 3–7 per cent had Literary and Philosophical Societies, infirmaries or schemes to improve the broader urban environment. Again, whilst such developments were most numerous in the largest centres, their distribution was often not simply a reflection of hierarchical diffusion. The spread of subscription libraries was at least partly a spatial phenomenon, since they appeared notably earlier in north-west England than the west Midlands. Established first in Manchester (1757) and Liverpool (1758), subscription libraries had spread to six other towns in the region by 1770, including Rochdale, Blackburn and Macclesfield.[15] It was another decade before the first west Midlands library was established, in Birmingham (1779).[16] The distribution of walks is difficult to accurately assess, since they need not have been purposely laid out. Promenading could take place informally in streets or churchyards, as on Foregate Street, Worcester, the Rows in Chester, The Parade in Leamington Spa and St Philip's churchyard in Birmingham.[17] Moreover, private parks and gardens were often opened up to the public, as with the so-called 'Ladies Walk' leading from Chorley to Gillibrand Hall.[18] However, formal facilities were most common in corporate towns, which accounted for about two-thirds of the places recorded as possessing walks or gardens by 1770. This reflected the importance of town corporations in their construction and maintenance (see Chapter 3). Moreover, facilities in such towns were often developed on a more elaborate scale than those seen elsewhere. Chester possessed two extensive sets of walks (the Walls and the Groves), plus the Cherry Gardens at Boughton, whilst Liverpool had three formal walks and its own Ranelagh Gardens. The people of Manchester, in contrast, had to make do with an informal riverside promenade.[19] Attempts to extensively remodel the urban environment, in the form of squares and crescents, were initially restricted to the larger commercial centres and, to a lesser extent, county towns. Before 1770, only 6 per cent of towns contained such features and, even within this group, the scale of development varied hugely. Liverpool had six named squares; Manchester and Stockport had two apiece; and Chester and Warwick just one each, both very small if grandly conceived developments. The pace of population growth and the need for housing fit for the new urban elite of professionals, merchants and industrialists appears to have been critical in marking the divide between these sets of towns. In county towns much of the elite continued to live in grand houses along the main streets or in villas on the outskirts of what were still relatively small and unpolluted towns.[20]

A generation later, in 1790, leisure facilities were distributed more widely: two-fifths of towns were still without any recorded facilities, but around one-third now had three or more. The best served were, of course, the county towns and large commercial centres, but several smaller towns, including Nantwich, Ormskirk and Walsall now had a good range of facilities. The most widespread forms of leisure remained assemblies, theatre- and concert-going, and horse racing (see Table 2.1) – a set of activities which increasingly defined a town's pretensions to respectability. Assemblies were found in twice as many towns as they had been in 1770: growth which meant that certain areas were particularly well served. In central Cheshire, for example, there were periodic assemblies in Nantwich, Northwich, Knutsford and Middlewich, as well as the grander gatherings in Chester. Yet the quantitative and qualitative distinction between these smaller centres and their larger neighbours remained strong. In Chester, subscribers to the assemblies at the Talbot Inn in the 1780s could enjoy dancing every Monday and card games every Thursday from early November to mid-May. By the turn of the century, there were also assemblies in the Albion Hotel and the Blossoms Hotel. In contrast, Northwich had just one event a month throughout the year, whilst Elizabeth Shackleton's diary records only five assemblies in Colne during the decade 1770–80, the most lavish of which celebrated the opening of the town's Piece Hall in August 1776. By the early 1800s, balls and concerts were held more regularly at the Piece Hall, but still only three or four times a year.[21] Theatres also became much more widespread. A burst of activity in the 1780s led to the opening of playhouses in a range of manufacturing centres such as Macclesfield, Blackburn and Bury, where the theatre collapsed in 1787, trapping 300 people under the ruins.[22] To an extent this growth – and the relative scarcity of theatres in even reasonable sized market towns like Knutsford, Uttoxeter and Evesham – reflected the commercial nature of these facilities, driven forward by entrepreneurs, and thus requiring a certain threshold audience to justify construction, although such economic arguments are not easy to sustain given the presence of theatres from an early date in centres as small as Leigh.[23] Race meetings were struggling in smaller market towns, but were established in Birmingham and Manchester by the 1730s – a reflection of the growing wealth and social pretensions of local industrial elites. Much the same was true of subscription libraries, which were increasingly important cultural institutions within industrial towns. In both large and small towns, they helped to define polite and later bourgeois masculinity, drawing subscriptions from and re-emphasising the status of the male urban elite (see Chapter 6). In Liverpool, the Athenaeum limited membership to 500, with subscriptions rising to 30 guineas by 1800, which effectively debarred many of the middling sort.[24] Such people patronised the plethora of circulating libraries established by booksellers and printers during the closing decades of the eighteenth century. In contrast to the weighty religious and historical volumes held by subscription libraries, they offered the middling consumer access to more popular literature.[25]

Whilst such facilities were growing in number and stature in industrial towns, others were coming under increasing pressure as ever greater amounts of land were given over to industry and housing for the labouring classes. Indeed, there was a growing distinction between county and industrial towns, with walks and gardens in the latter struggling to maintain their integrity. In Liverpool, Duke Street Walk, along with the Ladies Walk and the Ranelagh Gardens had all been swallowed up by industrial and residential development by the 1790s; Birmingham's two pleasure gardens had both closed by the 1760s; and in Wolverhampton, Jenning's Gardens, Grea Pea Walk, Green Hill Walk and New Walk, visible on Isaac Taylor's map of 1750, had all gone by the end of the century.[26] Similarly, although new squares were being built in smaller towns during the 1780s, many of those in larger commercial towns were being overtaken by industrial growth – a process seen in Liverpool and Birmingham, and later in Wolverhampton, Bury and elsewhere.[27]

The forty years to 1830 witnessed a huge growth in the number and spread of leisure facilities in north-west England and the west Midlands. Less than one town in five had no recorded facilities, well over half had three or more, and about one-quarter had at least ten. The best served towns were evenly spread across the two regions and included county towns (such as Chester and Worcester); established commercial centres (Liverpool, Manchester and Birmingham); middle-ranking industrial towns (Stockport, Rochdale and Wolverhampton); and a number of more specialist centres (most notably Stratford-upon-Avon). The 'basic' provision of assemblies and libraries was found in nearly half the towns; racing had revived and was found in about two-fifths of towns; and theatres and music societies or concert rooms in around one-third (see Table 2.1). Certain of these leisure activities had changed in character, even from the later decades of the eighteenth century. Most notable here are assemblies, whose subscribers and purpose were rather different from those which characterised their heyday.[28] They were increasingly seen as gatherings for the lower middle classes: the elite withdrawing to parties in private houses. However, links to the nobility remained strong in certain places. In 1829, a fancy-dress subscription ball at the Royal Hotel in Chester, held in aid of Spanish and Italian refugees, was attended by over 500 of the local elite, headed by Robert Grosvenor, whose costume was said to be valued at £2,000.[29] The provincial theatre was also increasingly colonised by the lower orders, elites often preferring to patronise concert halls instead. Horse racing too had lost some of its cachet. Meetings associated with industrial towns in particular drew few if any members of the gentry and nobility, depending instead on their appeal to the masses (but see Chapter 5). Subscription libraries, in contrast, retained an air of exclusivity, even as they spread to a larger range of centres, including Walsall (1801), Stratford-on-Avon (1810), Oldham (1817), Evesham (1819), and Hanley (1824).[30] This was helped, in part, by the even more rapid diffusion of circulating libraries which gave a wider section of the urban populace access to print culture, and helped to disseminate the values of politeness, and later personal improvement, down the urban and social hierarchy.

As such facilities became ever more widespread, what increasingly differentiated towns was the presence of certain higher order activities. These were epitomised by Literary and Philosophical Societies. Dating back to the 1770s, only a handful were successfully established by 1800, mainly in the larger commercial centres of Liverpool (1779), Manchester (1781) and Birmingham (1799). Similar institutions were spreading to other, smaller towns in the early nineteenth century, but even by 1830 only sixteen towns across the west Midlands and north-west England could boast a Literary or Philosophical society of some form.[31] These were augmented in larger towns by a growing range of other societies. Manchester, for example, boasted an Agricultural Society, Natural History Society, Horticultural Society, Philological Society and the Royal Manchester Institution, which was devoted to the arts.[32] Combined with philanthropic institutions such as infirmaries, which remained confined to larger towns because of their cost and nature (many were conceived as facilities for the county as well as the town),[33] such learned societies marked an important distinction between the leading provincial towns and lesser centres.

The presence and importance of leisure activities was reinforced by the provision of goods and services. As Estabrook argues, this formed the other aspect of urban material culture, helping to define respectable living for both men and women. Adoption of a polite lifestyle required the acquisition of material possessions, such as household furnishings, fashionable clothing, and consumables such as tea and coffee, as well as the practice of civilised behaviour, including speech, deportment and artistic accomplishments. This created a surge in business for upholsterers, mercers and drapers, grocers, hairdressers, language teachers, dancing and drawing masters, and so on.[34] The construction of towns as spaces of leisure was thus overlain by one of towns as spaces of commerce, and the practices of leisure and shopping combined to produce new spaces of consumption. In this way, what we might call the 'leisurisation of commerce' combined with Plumb's commercialisation of leisure to make many towns centres of consumption in a newly polite manner. Given this, it is significant that the shops and professional services central to eighteenth-century consumerism were not the preserve of large towns but were found throughout the urban network. By the 1790s a typical small town such as Alcester in Warwickshire could boast a druggist, clock and watchmaker, hatter, hosier, milliner, confectioner, three perukemakers and a toyman as well as the usual assortment of mercers, grocers and general shopkeepers.[35] Estimates from Mui and Mui suggest that the ratio of population to shops declined in the mid-eighteenth century to levels far below those seen before or since. Although partly due to the spread of small retail outlets into rural areas, many of the new shops were in towns, their distribution determined by population, accessibility and local demand.[36] These, however, are broad impressions: how did the detailed distribution of shops change during the course of the eighteenth century? And how did the regional geographies of consumption relate to patterns of leisure and improvement?

Probate evidence reveals the presence of mercers and drapers, apothecaries and surgeons in nearly all towns in the west Midlands and north-west England in the early eighteenth century (see Table 2.2). These tradesmen, along with tailors, shoemakers and grocers, formed the bedrock of service provision.[37] In both regions, they served to distinguish towns from the expanding industrial villages found particularly in southern Lancashire and the Black Country. Indeed, their absence from a settlement raises a question mark over its urban status. For example, Abbots Bromley had just a single grocer recorded in probate records for the 1700–50 period and was described by Blome in 1673 as 'a very poor town'

34   *The region*

Table 2.2 Selected retailers and services in north-west England and the west Midlands, *c.*1700–1830

Occupational category	c.1700–40		c.1795		c.1830	
	No.	%	No.	%	No.	%
Mercer or draper	71	78.0	82	89.1	96	90.6
Surgeon/Doctor of medicine	40	44.0	83	90.2	103	97.2
Grocer and tea dealer	37	40.7	87	94.6	98	92.5
Tallow chandler/chandler	37	40.7	66	71.7	70	66.0
Hairdresser and perfumer	34	37.4	76	82.6	90	84.9
Apothecary/druggist	32	35.2	48	52.2	89	84.0
Gardener/seedsman	32	35.2	66	71.7	75	70.8
Clock/watchmaker	26	28.6	66	71.7	93	87.7
Bookseller, stationer, binder and printer	21	23.1	57	62.0	88	83.0
Tobacconist	20	22.0	11	12.0	14	13.2
Attorney	18	19.8	76	82.6	96	90.6
Wine and spirit merchant	18	19.8	50	54.3	73	68.9
Cabinet maker/upholsterer	11	12.1	54	58.7	74	69.8
Painter/artist/musician	10	11.0	18	19.6	28	26.4
Silversmith, jeweller and toyman	10	11.0	26	28.3	16	15.1
Confectioner and specialist baker	9	9.9	38	41.3	69	65.1
Teacher – dancing/languages	6	6.6	18	19.6	0	37.7
China, glass and earthenware dealer	3	3.3	40	43.5	71	67.0
Architect/builder	1	1.1	10	10.9	22	20.8
Coach builder	1	1.1	12	13.0	33	31.1
Banker	0	0.0	26	28.3	59	55.7
Music and musical instrument dealer	0	0.0	5	5.4	15	14.2

Source: Probate records, *UBD*, Pigot's *Directory*.

Note: Attorneys were frequently listed as gentlemen in probate records.

whose market was 'very mean'.[38] At the opposite end of the scale, the best served towns were the county capitals and large commercial centres: probate records for Manchester, for instance, record 15 different categories of retailer, including 52 mercers and drapers, 11 cabinet makers and upholsterers, 8 perukemakers, 7 booksellers or printers, and 1 glass and china dealer. The status of tradesmen and professionals, of course, varied with location, as did the quality of goods and services they offered. For example, William Jordan, a mercer in Malpas (with a population around 500 in 1700), left just £20 1s 4d in shop goods, whereas his contemporaries in the larger centres of Nantwich, Stockport and Congleton had between £450 and £700 of stock.[39] Both Jordan as a tradesman and Malpas as a central place had a limited hinterland. Such small town shops relied on market days for much of their custom, many of their customers coming not from the town itself, but the surrounding countryside. Both John England (a Northwich apothecary) and Edward Twambrooks (a Warrington mercer) had many rural customers: their inventories list book-debts from people in fourteen and twenty-two villages respectively.[40] Towns clearly acted as central places for the surrounding countryside, providing rural dwellers with access to leisure facilities and a new polite material culture of consumer goods.

More specialised and high status shops and services had a narrower distribution, and were most numerous in county and large commercial towns, although they still penetrated all parts of the two regions. At least one luxury tradesman – a bookseller, gold and silversmith, or hairdresser – could be found in around 60 per cent of towns across the five counties. These outlets were only absent from the very smallest places such as Malpas, Kenilworth and Abbots Bromley and some emerging industrial centres like Bilston, Oldham and Dudley. Indeed, we find clockmakers in Frodsham, Middlewich and Brewood; booksellers in Knutsford and Kidderminster; vintners in Clitheroe and Coleshill; and a goldsmith in Altrincham. Fewer towns could boast a musician or artist, but even these occupations were not limited to the largest centres: there was, for instance, a musician in both Stockport and Leek. Significantly, the hierarchical distribution of shops and services in the north-west was broadly similar to that in the west Midlands, suggesting the patterns revealed were the norm for provincial England.

By the end of the eighteenth century the provision of goods and services had improved substantially in both the west Midlands and north-west England, as is clear from the increase in the range of tradesmen (see Table 2.2). The core of shops and services found in most towns at the beginning of the century had now expanded to include other retailers and professionals such as clock and watchmakers, booksellers and attorneys. To some extent this simply reflected the prodigious growth of town populations. However, for most towns there was a genuine fall in the ratio of people per shop, so that by the 1790s over half the towns in both regions had fewer than 100 inhabitants for each shopkeeper. As for the early eighteenth century, these core activities appear to have constituted the minimum threshold of service provision and helped to define places as urban. Thus, whilst settlements such as Malpas were arguably sliding off the urban scale, many growing industrial centres had gained a reasonable range of shops and services and were cementing their status as towns. Amongst the latter were several of the Potteries and Black Country towns. In Dudley, for instance, there were three attorneys, two grocers, twelve mercers and drapers, five perukemakers and two clockmakers by the 1790s. More specialised outlets were also emerging, increasing the diversity of retail and service provision at all levels of the urban hierarchy. Most notable amongst these were the glass and china sellers, who could be found in almost half of the study towns by the 1790s, including Burnley, Ulverston and Uttoxeter. Such shops gave consumers across the two regions improved access to fashionable new tableware, and with it access to rituals of polite sociability such as tea drinking. Other specialist activities could be found in relatively small towns: there was a silversmith in Alcester, a musical instrument seller in Stockport, and two drawing masters in Macclesfield. However, these trades remained largely the preserve of the major county and commercial towns, though here there was a growing gap between the two. The *Universal British Directory* (*UBD*) lists eight artists, musicians and silversmiths in Chester, but forty in Liverpool, a disparity largely due to rapid population growth in the latter.

Further expansion had taken place by 1830 (see Table 2.2). Almost all towns now had a more diverse retail and service base: even somewhere as small as Penkridge could boast an attorney, two surgeons, a clockmaker, three grocers, a wine and spirits dealer, three general shopkeepers, a hairdresser and a seedsman. Particularly notable was the increased presence of specialist shops and services in industrial towns. In the north-west only six towns had a newspaper in the 1790s, whereas this had risen to nine by 1835. Booksellers, confectioners and china dealers were also present in 83 per cent, 65 per cent and 67 per cent of towns respectively, including manufacturing centres such as Bury, Burslem and Wednesbury. The hinterland ties of such towns were often relatively weak,[41] so this expansion of provision must have stemmed largely from the growing demands of middle class urban consumers. Only trades dealing with goods at the extreme luxury end of the market continued to have a restricted distribution: silversmiths and jewellers, for instance, were found in just 15 per cent of towns, and music and musical instrument sellers in 14 per cent. Greater demand, of course, allowed greater specialisation in larger towns, so that in Manchester it was possible to find an animal painter, two artificial flower makers and five artists' colourmen, as well as a thriving market in art – both paintings and prints.[42] Increasingly, the distinction between large and small centres was marked by the number and quality of the shops and services available rather than the range of outlets. Shoppers in Manchester, for example, could choose from forty booksellers and eight dentists; those in Blackburn had the choice of only seven and one respectively; and in Ashton under Lyne there were just three booksellers and not a single dentist. County towns like Chester, meanwhile, were developing reputations as high-class shopping centres with fashionable retailers like the drapers and furnishers Browns who served the elite of both city and county.[43]

The leisure infrastructure, environmental improvement and consumerism that characterised the urban renaissance became increasingly widespread during the long eighteenth century, filtering down from county towns and other major urban centres to smaller places. Whilst Borsay has argued that such innovations took hold earliest in southern counties, there is little evidence here to suggest a spatial diffusion of new forms of leisure and retail activity from London or the south. In general, the trends in the two regions appear very similar: if anything, the spirit of social and individual improvement appears to have taken root in the north-west a little earlier than in the west Midlands, but differences were slight. Retail and service provision, especially in terms of the luxury and semi-luxury trades, developed rapidly in both regions, so that novel items and high class services were readily available even in relatively small towns.[44] This is not to say that London was insignificant (see Chapters 3 and 7), but developments in provincial England also fed off and into local growth in population and wealth. Between the late seventeenth and early nineteenth centuries, the population of the five counties surveyed grew by an average of around 300 per cent and their rankings in terms of taxable wealth rose by an average of sixteen places (see Table 2.3). Yet this flowering of urban culture and economy reflected real changes in the leisure and consumption demands of the elites and middling sorts. Change was both widespread and deep-seated. Indeed, by the 1760s, one commentator could claim that there was 'scarce a town of any magnitude but has its Theatre Royal, its concerts, its balls and card parties'.[45] Such rhetoric reflects the diffusion of the spatial practices of polite society, but also the ways in which they were conceived and represented as a set of activities and institutions that defined respectability for the town and its inhabitants. Yet our survey makes clear the limits of this respectability and the urban renaissance of which it formed a central part: many of the smaller towns were largely or entirely excluded, having few, if any, leisure facilities, even by the early nineteenth century.

These findings support the notion of a two-stage urban renaissance in the north-west and west Midlands.[46] However, we find less evidence of the divide between the two stages that Sweet and others identify in terms of the location and character of that renaissance. There is something attractive in a simple dichotomy

Table 2.3 Population and taxable wealth in north-west England and the west Midlands, c.1700–1830

County	Population					Wealth rank		
	1701	1781	1801	1831	% growth 1701–1831	1693	1843	Change
Cheshire	100,221	154,279	197,871	338,116	237.3	28	9	19
Lancashire	238,735	422,328	694,202	1,351,745	466.2	35	3	32
Staffordshire	124,151	188,977	246,786	415,085	234.3	30	16	14
Warwickshire	97,387	171,816	214,835	340,359	249.5	12	5	7
Worcestershire	102,721	121,165	143,780	213,719	108.1	14	7	7

Sources: Deane, P. and Cole, W., *British Economic Growth 1688–1959: Trends and Structures*, Cambridge: Cambridge University Press, 1967; Buckatzch, E., 'The geographical distribution of wealth in England 1086–1843', *Economic History Review*, 3, 1950–1, pp. 180–202.

of, on the one hand, established county and market towns and, on the other, industrial and commercial centres. Urban renaissance in the former is seen as being elite-led and leisure-oriented, drawing on metropolitan notions of politeness in servicing the leisure needs of the gentry. The latter was the product of middling, consumerist cultures and built a rival provincial culture on the bases of hard work, and physical, intellectual and moral improvement. Whilst this contrast works in principle, it is more difficult to sustain in the face of the diverse experiences of large and small, county and commercial, established and newly growing towns. Development was, in general, earliest in county towns and they did, indeed, enjoy the closest links with the rural gentry; but in Liverpool and Birmingham, amongst others, facilities were provided by and for the gentry as well as industrialists and merchants (see Chapter 3). Conversely, a culture of improvement might have been most characteristic of commercial towns, but county towns were prominent as centres of intellectual development and scientific culture. And everywhere there was a spirit of consumerism and the influence of a middling sort of professionals, tradesmen and their like.[47] Certainly, there is little to distinguish county and the larger commercial towns in terms of their cultural and leisure infrastructure, and their shops, especially up to the mid-eighteenth century. Arguably, distinctions broadened towards the end of the century as commercial development in the latter overshadowed and swallowed up some earlier cultural infrastructure: what was left, and what subsequently developed, was perhaps inspired by 'improvement' as much as leisure.[48]

The regional space: hierarchies of consumption

As the new infrastructure of respectable leisure and retailing spread ever wider, the material culture linking consumption and leisure diffused through space. Patterns of provision nevertheless remained uneven: some centres had a wide range of facilities, whereas elsewhere these were more basic. The range and mix of high and low order leisure functions in each town can be used to determine its position within a leisure hierarchy (see Table 2.4). Liverpool, Manchester and Chester took the top positions in the north-west, each with a much wider range and depth of leisure functions than the next tier of towns. Within the west Midlands, Birmingham, Worcester, perhaps Coventry,[49] and later Leamington Spa held equivalent positions with a similar range of leisure facilities. Significantly, most of these places do not easily fall into the category of 'resort' towns, suggesting more dispersed provision and a different hierarchical ordering of leisure outside southern England. Nor were they necessarily the location of important religious and political institutions. Chester, for example, was a cathedral city, garrison town and parliamentary borough, making it an important focus of activity for ambitious local families such as the Grosvenors;[50] but Manchester, Birmingham and Leamington held few of these advantages.

To this upper tier we could add Preston, Warwick and Lancaster. The first two were respectively described by Defoe as 'a fine town [with] a great deal of good company', and a 'really fine town ... now rebuilt in so noble and so beautiful a

Table 2.4 The leisure hierarchy: exemplar towns

Liverpool	Warrington	Knutsford	Altrincham	Malpas
Many good inns	Several good inns	Several good inns	Two good inns	Good inn
Horse racing	Horse racing	Horse racing	Horse racing	
Frequent assemblies	Regular assemblies	Monthly assemblies	Occasional assemblies	
New/rebuilt town hall	New/rebuilt town hall	New/rebuilt town hall	Town hall improved	
Subscription libraries	Subscription library	Subscription library		
Circulating libraries	Circulating library	Circulating library		
Theatre	Theatre	Basic theatre		
Concert hall/ series	Concert/music society	Occasional concerts		
Square	Square	Terrace		
Walk/pleasure garden	Walk/pleasure garden			
Spa or baths	Spa or baths			
Improved marketplace	Improved marketplace			
Dancing masters	Dancing master			
Newspaper				
Town history				
Improvement Act				
Infirmary/ dispensary				
Lit. and Phil. Society				
Coffee house				
Artist/painter				

Source: Various

Note: Facilities are those present in 1790.

manner'. He dismissed Lancaster as having 'little to recommend it … little or no trade, and few people', but it developed strongly as a fashionable leisure town through the eighteenth century. Its growth was limited, however, by the split of county functions with Preston; the lack of development in its hinterland; and ultimately by the collapse in its maritime trade around the turn of the nineteenth century.[51] More realistically, though, these bridged the divide between the major centres and a larger group of secondary towns such as Lancaster, Warrington, Nantwich, Wolverhampton, Lichfield, and, by the end of the eighteenth century, Macclesfield, Bolton and perhaps Walsall. It was the range of leisure facilities in such towns (around six to eight categories each by the 1800s) which marked them out from smaller centres such as Knutsford, Kidderminster and Tamworth (with only three or four). Yet even these smaller places had pretensions to respectability, either through links with the local gentry or an expanding resident bourgeoisie. They were certainly better provided with leisure infrastructure than places like Newton-le-Willows, Altrincham, Nuneaton or Penkridge; whilst at the very bottom of the hierarchy small towns like Malpas, Frodsham, Abbots Bromley and Southam had few, if any, dedicated leisure facilities. These quantitative distinctions were, moreover, reinforced by qualitative differences, with facilities and activities in the larger centres being more refined and attracting 'superior' company. Although the tentacles of commercialised leisure had extended to all corners of the west Midlands and north-west England by the late eighteenth century, a vast social gulf remained between large county and commercial towns, and those at the bottom of the hierarchy. If anything, it increased through time.

Retail provision was also structured within a hierarchical framework. In this case, a more precisely differentiated hierarchy can be developed, based on the relative number and variety of shops. The position of each town is determined by its 'retail score', measured by multiplying the number of shops or services by the range of different types of outlet.[52] As with leisure, the data suggest a five-level hierarchy in both study regions (see Table 2.5), although the relative position of individual towns changed during the course of the eighteenth and early nineteenth centuries. In north-west England the retail hierarchy was again based around Liverpool, Manchester and Chester. These had a greater range and number of retail outlets than those at the next level down, which included social centres such as Preston and Nantwich as well as industrial towns like Warrington, Stockport and later Bolton and Blackburn. There was a rather smaller gap in provision between these second-tier towns and those at the next level down – places such as Ormskirk, Prescot and Knutsford – and below them others including Colne and Middlewich. At the base of the hierarchy were small market towns like Frodsham, Clitheroe, Malpas and Newton, which had very few shops in the early eighteenth century, and remained poorly provided into the early nineteenth century. In the west Midlands, a mix of commercial and county towns again predominated: Birmingham and Worcester stood at the top of the hierarchy, followed by a group of social and industrial centres including Coventry, Warwick, Wolverhampton and Stourbridge. The third order comprised large market towns such as Evesham and Stratford-upon-Avon, and a growing number of industrial centres, including Walsall, Dudley, and later Hanley and Burslem. Below them came smaller towns like Cheadle, Pershore and Rugeley. As in the north-west, at the bottom of the hierarchy were places like Tutbury, Abbots Bromley and Solihull, which barely merited urban status. These occupation-based hierarchies correspond closely with those identified from the shop tax returns of 1785.[53] The returns show Liverpool,

Table 2.5 The retail hierarchy: retail scores and threshold activities

	Rank				
	1	2	3	4	5
Retail score:					
1700–60	4,600–5,500	250–700	50–250	10–50	0–10
1790s	5,000–23,000	1,500–4,000	600–1500	100–600	0–100
1830s	10,000–83,000	4,000–10,000	1,500–4,000	150–1,500	0–150
Threshold activities for inclusion in given rank					
1700–60	silversmith and jeweller	bookseller and stationer	apothecary and druggist	mercer and draper	petty shopkeeper
	confectioner and specialist baker	clock and watchmaker	ironmonger	grocer	
1790s	tobacconist	silversmith and jeweller	bookseller and stationer	clock and watchmaker	mercer and draper
(as above, plus)	musical instrument dealer	china and glass dealer	ironmonger	hair dresser and perfumer	grocer
c.1830	carpet warehouse	silversmith and jeweller	china and glass dealer	ironmonger	mercer and draper
(as above, plus)	artists' repository	musical instrument dealer	cabinet maker and upholsterer	bookseller and stationer	grocer

Source: Probate records, UBD, Pigot's Directory.

Note: Retail score is calculated by multiplying the number of shops or services by the range of different types of outlet. The gap between the top of level 2 (1790) and the bottom of level 1 (1700–60) reflects the real 'space' between the two levels.

Manchester and Chester as the leading centres in the north-west, paying at least three times more than towns in the next group. In the west Midlands Birmingham, Worcester and Coventry were similarly dominant. Both regions then had a group of towns with shop tax receipts of between £25 and £60, including Preston, Warrington, Stockport, Wolverhampton, Warwick and Bewdley. Below them a group of towns such as Macclesfield, Ormskirk and Walsall had tax receipts of between £10–£20, and a far larger number collected sums of between £2–£10. Places like Clitheroe and Abbots Bromley, which were on the margins of urbanity, paid very little shop tax at all.

The structure and composition of these two hierarchies was remarkably similar, reflecting the mutuality of leisure and shopping as social practices. Bringing them together allows us to create a consumption hierarchy for each region *c*.1790, with five broad orders of town (see Figure 2.1). Significantly, this hierarchy matches quite closely the depictions of towns by earlier commentators. Blome, for instance, writing in the 1670s, uses a variety of different terms to describe a town's condition. These can be employed to group towns into five distinct categories similar to those used to define the consumption hierarchy. Places noted as 'much frequented by gentry' (Chester, Preston, Lichfield and Wolverhampton, for instance) were invariably in the top two levels of our consumption hierarchy, whilst phrases such as 'fair' or 'well built' are often used to describe towns of somewhat lesser importance, like Warrington and Nantwich. Further down the scale, in orders three and four, most small towns are noted simply for their 'good market', and those at the very bottom of the hierarchy, such as Abbots Bromley and Sutton Coldfield, are simply described as 'mean' or 'indifferent'.

The precise configuration of this consumption hierarchy was, of course, continually changing. The relative fortunes of towns rose and fell: a process that was etched on the urban consciousness and recorded in town histories, diaries and travel guides. Some towns, including Nantwich and Evesham, noted as important social and commercial centres by authors such as Blome and Defoe, have fairly low retail and leisure rankings in the 1790s and paid relatively little shop tax. Others, such as Stockport and Stourbridge, regarded by these authors as not particularly distinguished, have higher rankings and were taxed more heavily. As we saw earlier, the spread of shops and facilities during the long eighteenth century was both uneven and spasmodic. Towns acquired new leisure and civic infrastructure in piecemeal fashion; streets were improved when political will allowed; new shops emerged where openings were perceived. Towns could rise up or drop down the hierarchy when circumstances changed. For instance, at Nantwich the loss of Quarter Session meetings in 1759 was both a reflection and a contributory factor in the relative decline of the town's social status and leisure facilities from their height in the early eighteenth century. Similarly, the fashionability of a town could rise and fall: Lichfield was regarded by Blome as 'much frequented by the gentry', and during most of the eighteenth century retained its reputation as a regional centre of fashion. Its races, for instance, were an important event in the social calendar, with as many as 233 gentlemen attending the race dinner during the 1750s. Yet by the 1830s the town was in relative decline, having lost its role

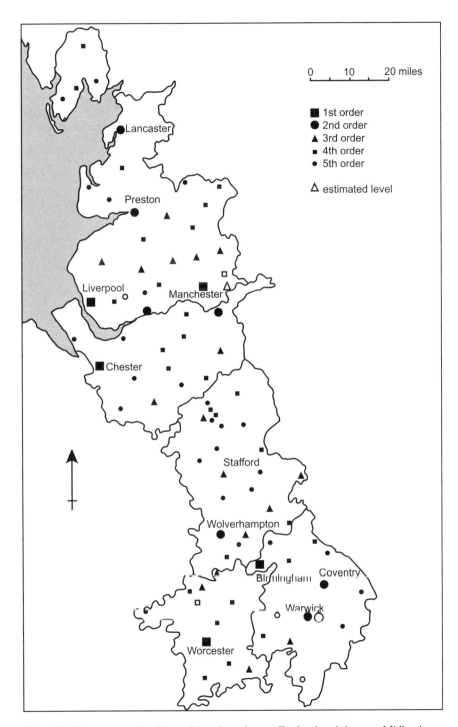

Figure 2.1 The consumption hierarchies of north-west England and the west Midlands

as a transport hub and any pretensions as a leisure centre beyond its immediate locality.[54] In other cases the founding of an important institution could raise the profile of a town, attracting other retail and leisure facilities. Warrington forms the best example here, the famous Dissenting Academy being associated with the town's library, printing press, and literary society. Its closure in 1786 can be linked to decay in other facilities, the demand for which ebbed as the tutors and pupils, and the atmosphere of intellectual enquiry that they engendered, moved elsewhere.[55]

The re-sorting of towns within the hierarchy was far from being arbitrary, however, and some clear trends can be observed, particularly between the early eighteenth century and the 1790s. Most notable is the rise of commercial and industrial towns at the expense of market and county centres. In both regions commercial hubs, most notably Birmingham, Liverpool and Manchester, pulled away from traditional county towns such as Chester and Worcester, which had almost been their equal in the earlier period. Amongst other towns, medium ranking industrial centres, such as Walsall, Blackburn and Bolton, and some smaller manufacturing towns, including Burslem, Hanley and Burnley, appear most dynamic. They rose up the hierarchy as they gained a greater range and volume of shops, services and facilities. Defoe might have seen 'nothing remarkable' in Bolton, and dismissed Bury as 'a small market town' in the early 1700s, but by the close of the century they were both thriving industrial centres with well-developed retail sectors and a growing range of leisure facilities.[56] Of course, we should be wary of overplaying the pretensions of such places, not least because, as facilities improved, so too did the expectations of consumers. Despite its theatre, library, booksellers, glass and china dealers, perfumers, music teachers, miniature painter and so on, a wealthy resident could still complain in 1816 that 'Bolton is proverbially dull just now'.[57] However, the material culture of many industrial towns was considerably improved during the eighteenth century, making them significant local centres for respectable consumption. This development was notably stronger and occurred earlier in the north-west than the west Midlands, reflecting in part the different economic structure and industrial organisation of the two regions. The factories of north-west England produced a class of wealthy industrialists with social pretensions for themselves and their towns. The workshop and artisan production seen in much of the west Midlands often left the region's towns without this substantial body of *nouveaux riches*: the industrial luminaries of the Lunar Society (men like Boulton, Wedgwood and Keir) were the exceptions rather than the norm.[58] The different pace of development was also linked to the fact that, unlike those of the Black Country or Potteries, few of the Lancashire textile towns were genuinely new: most had long histories as market centres and an established tradition of supplying goods and services to both the town and its hinterland. Moreover, they were far less densely concentrated. Even in south-east Lancashire, the towns were at least five miles apart, allowing hinterlands to develop in a way that was impossible in the Black Country or the Potteries, where five towns were growing within six miles of one another. Importantly, though, manufacturing towns across both regions experienced retail and leisure development, suggesting that there was no axiomatic repulsion of culture and commerce, despite the rhetoric of certain contemporary commentators.[59]

Along with these long-term changes, Borsay argues that fashionable leisure was organised within both a spatial and temporal framework.[60] Thus the position of a town within the hierarchy could vary over the course of the year, and indeed be raised temporarily by a particular event. For instance, Tamworth temporarily became the social centre of the west Midlands for two days in late September of 1809 when it played host to a large-scale music festival to raise funds for the rebuilding of the parish church.[61] In simple terms, three social cycles can be identified. The first was a long-term cycle and involved large-scale events that occurred only infrequently. The most striking example of this was the Preston Guild. Held every twenty years ostensibly for the registration of burgesses, this was in reality a two-week festival of pleasure attended by town residents, the county elite and gentry families from across the north of England. In 1742 a visitor reported that the

> entertainment was quite handsome and Genteel, everything that the season cou'd afford, there was approx two setts of players, an assembly besides Private balls and two masquerades ... I never saw so great a Crowd of good Company as there was at the assembly, the room is but small, and there was four Hundred and forty five Tickets taken out.[62]

The second was an annual cycle, punctuated by a series of events and generally organised into distinct 'seasons'. As in London, many large provincial towns, particularly county centres, packed the bulk of their cultural activities into a winter season. In Worcester this lasted from early October to mid March by the 1770s. There were fortnightly assemblies at the Guildhall, two sets of weekly card assemblies at the Long Room and Tom's Coffee House, regular concerts at the Hop Pole Inn, and a series of theatrical performances at the King's Head theatre in the High Street every Tuesday, Thursday and Saturday from early December.[63] In commercial centres such as Liverpool, however, seasonality was generally less pronounced. Social events catered mainly for the resident bourgeoisie, augmented by visiting local gentry, so it made more sense to spread activities more evenly over the year. In some cases the precise timing of events was dictated by the availability of performers: the theatre in Liverpool hosted a company of comedians from the Theatre Royal in London who could only tour the provinces during the summer months, just as the Three Choirs Festival, held in early September, was able to attract famous London musicians and singers because it took place before the start of the winter season in the capital. That said, an essentially winter season was predominant. In Bolton assemblies were held from late December to early April in the early nineteenth century. Similarly, during the winter months of 1793/4, Blackburn's residents and visitors were entertained by a production of 'New Brooms' at Mr Stahan's Large Room and by the 'Original Stone-Eater' from Germany, who performed for three nights in a room at the White Swan. They could also attend regular card assemblies and a ball at the new assembly rooms hosted by the dancing master, Mr Winder.[64] Through the spring and summer, members of fashionable society retired to their country estates or visited spa resorts, reducing the demand for fashionable urban leisure. Thus Leamington Spa received most of its visitors during the summer months, although it developed a distinctive winter season based on fox hunting.[65] In a similar fashion, many county towns, including Chester, Worcester and Warwick, managed to construct a short summer season, often centred on the Assize meetings and involving horse races, public breakfasts and musical concerts. At Worcester visitors to the August Assizes in 1772 were entertained by concerts and assemblies in the Guildhall, and the festivities continued the following week with the city's annual race meeting, which, the *Worcester Journal* noted, had never been

> honoured with a greater number of nobility and gentry, who were present every day on the course, at the Balls in the evening, and at the Public Breakfasts both mornings – Upwards of 680 persons assembled the first morning, and near 600 the second.[66]

At Liverpool too there was a summer season, which, during 1770, was centred on a series of concerts in early August to mark the opening of a new organ at St Thomas's church. The theatre, as we have seen, also opened during the summer months, with performances every Monday, Wednesday and Friday from June till September.[67]

Set within this annual cycle was a weekly round of events. Even in the larger towns, certain nights offered more entertainment than others: in Liverpool and Worcester Monday and Tuesday nights were the busiest, with regular concerts and card assemblies over the winter months. In the latter, Wednesday was usually reserved for grander occasions such as the fortnightly subscription assemblies held in the Guildhall. In smaller places, the night of the monthly assembly had to be carefully chosen to match in with events in neighbouring towns. For instance, during the 1750s the Northwich Assembly was held on the second Wednesday of each month, judiciously avoiding Chester's Monday and Thursday gatherings.[68] Only this way could sufficient company be assembled in any one place for the event to be successful in financial and social terms. Yet, for that night, the host town took on extra importance: it was *the* central place within that area. Moreover, during such periodic events, levels of demand within a town were temporarily raised, making viable other facilities which would not have been at other times during the year or week, and temporarily distorting the consumer landscape of the region.

Cutting through these temporal variations was a strong spatial ordering of retail and leisure provision (see Figure 2.1), the features of which help us to understand the regional spatiality of material culture. First, there was a fairly even distribution of high-ranking towns interspersed with smaller centres. Nowhere in either region was further than twelve miles from at least a middle-ranking town, so that most people could make a return journey to one of several such places within a single day. This meant that leisure facilities and specialist shops were accessible to almost everyone, and many could make choices about where to acquire their goods, services and entertainment. This was a reflection of the second feature of the spatial hierarchy: that higher order centres had larger spheres of influence and prompted longer journeys than did smaller towns. Jack Dickenson, the son of a country squire living at Taxal in north-east Cheshire, went five miles to the races at Mottram, but was prepared to travel eighteen miles to attend the Music Meeting in Manchester.[69] At a similar time, Elizabeth Shackleton's diaries also reveal that, whilst luxury items were acquired via friends and relatives in London, or during occasional shopping expeditions to fashionable centres such as Preston, Chester, Wrexham or York, everyday purchases were made locally in Colne, Barrowford, Burnley or Bradford.[70] The distance people were willing to travel varied depending on their personal resources and on the range of the goods or services. This was, in turn, determined in part by their value and scarcity, but also by the prestige and cachet of the outlet or institution. For instance, visitors flocked to Worcester from across the country to tour Flight and Barr's porcelain factory after a much publicised Royal visit in 1788.[71] In stark contrast, almost all of William Wood's thirty or so account customers during the period 1767–91 lived within four miles of his shop in Didsbury.[72] This tended to produce a nesting of spheres for particular retail and leisure functions in different places – the third key feature of this hierarchy. Thus, the races at Chester drew people from as far afield as the Midlands, north Wales and Lancashire, whilst those at Malpas were frequented only by local residents and the gentry of the neighbourhood. The hinterlands for these two facilities were quite different in scale, the former subsuming the latter. They did not compete with each other for the attention of the public, but were complementary: timed so as not to clash and drawing on a different, if overlapping clientele.

A fourth notable feature is the relationship between population size and retail/leisure provision, reflecting the fact that demand came from the town's resident population and from that of its hinterland, including smaller central places. There was a close correlation between town population and overall service provision, suggesting that internal markets were important in determining the level of provision in a town.[73] Certainly, the resident urban population formed a significant body of consumers, even in relatively small towns. By the mid-eighteenth century, a prosperous middling sort eager to acquire the latest fashions in order to demonstrate their polite credentials, could be found in most places, including many manufacturing towns. There were clear exceptions to this relationship, however. In rapidly expanding manufacturing towns such as Bury, Oldham and Dudley, provision appears to have fallen some way below what might be expected. In contrast, slower growing, established towns such as Nantwich, Lichfield and Stratford-upon-Avon were arguably over-provided. These differences are best understood in terms of the contrasting socio-political structure of these various towns, their different wealth levels, and variations in the size and character of their hinterlands.

County towns were prominent amongst those which had higher levels of leisure and retail provision than one would anticipate given the size of their populations. The array of functions which often characterised such towns gave them more varied occupational structures than other places, whilst their status as parliamentary boroughs made them the focus of attention for politically ambitious gentry families. More specifically, the high proportion of professionals, clergymen and administrative or military personnel underpinned the blossoming of leisure, cultural and retail facilities. As Elliott puts it, their 'juridico-political and ecclesiastical status allowed them to ... "punch above their weight" in cultural terms'.[74] In contrast, commercial towns were characterised by a much higher proportion of labouring sorts who would have been unable to engage in such leisure and consumption. Compounding this, many smaller manufacturing towns often lacked or were slow to develop an indigenous middling sort, although this was far from being true of larger centres like Manchester, Birmingham and Wolverhampton. Such distinctions can be approximated in terms of the wealth of the consumer base of the town, measured using the 1785 Window Tax assessment. This tax applied only to the houses of people paying church and poor rates, there being an additional graduated levy for houses with more than seven windows. Thus it effectively measures the distribution of wealthier townspeople who generally formed the key consumers in the eighteenth century.[75] Towns ranked highly on the basis of tax collected also generally had large populations and well developed leisure and retail infrastructure. Indeed, there was a close correlation between window tax receipts and both retail and leisure rankings in the two study regions.[76] Significantly, the higher levels of leisure and retail provision in county towns such as Worcester and Warwick are reflected by the relative wealth of their inhabitants; whilst towns with surprisingly poor provision often scored relatively badly in terms of wealth levels too: for example, Blackburn, Oldham and Dudley.

The socio-economic character of the town was thus important in shaping the distribution of facilities, services and shops, and hence in determining the status of a town. Such explanations, however, overlook the importance of demand from the surrounding countryside. Whilst larger centres tended to have more extensive hinterlands, there was no straightforward relationship between town and hinterland size. Whereas market and service centres like Nantwich and Stratford-upon-Avon could draw on more established and wider hinterlands, the lack of a clear sphere of influence limited retail development in eighteenth- and early nineteenth-century Burslem.[77] Again, the social profile of the hinterland population was important. The presence of a wealthy aristocrat in the neighbourhood was important in some cases: the Leghs at Dunham Massey had considerable influence in nearby Altrincham, helping to explain the presence there in the early eighteenth century of numerous gardeners, a lawyer and a goldsmith. Despite clearly giving a boost to the local economy, however, these grandees acquired many of their luxury goods from London or larger provincial centres. More often it was the abundance of local gentry families that provided the stimulus. For example, contemporaries argued that the proprietors of ten nearby 'elegant villas very materially contribute to the prosperity of Knutsford by the patronage which they afford'.[78] Similarly, Bentley noted that visitors to Evesham would find 'excellent society' there 'as the town and neighbourhood abound with respectable families, whose mansions are seen in various directions enlivening and adorning the landscape'.[79] It was not merely that these wealthy consumers were numerous in these areas: they were intimately tied to the town.

Overall, the hierarchical status of a town was determined by a complex mix of factors: its size and wealth, and that of its hinterland, plus its relative location within and integration into the urban network, its economic character, and its reputation. That said, it is important to recognise both the temporality and spatiality of this hierarchy. None of these characteristics was determined or judged in isolation. Towns were often in tacit competition with one another for the custom of wealthy consumers: they operated within a spatially integrated economy. It is to the issue of integration that we turn next.

Integrating regional spaces of consumption

Towns were intimately tied to their hinterlands and to neighbouring centres, their relationship with each being mutually informed by the other. As Lepetit argues, the integration of the regional space was thus a product of bipolar (town–country) and multi-polar (inter-urban) linkages.[80] At the local scale, polite consumption brought together rural gentry and an urban elite of tradesmen and professionals, both socially and spatially, within the arenas of commercialised leisure. Whilst not producing cultural convergence, this did introduce the rural population to a more urbane lifestyle, and rural–urban links certainly contributed to the cultural and economic vitality of many small towns.[81] Conversely, without the patronage of hinterland consumers, most towns at the foot of the urban hierarchy would have lacked sufficient demand to support even the most basic leisure facilities. Influential in bringing rural consumers into towns were a range of periodic events, including fairs and courts of law, which served to renew hinterland and network connections and helped to spread the values of a polite and commercial society more widely through provincial England. This underlined the traditional role of county and, to a lesser extent, market towns in integrating urban and rural socio-economies during the early modern period.[82] The contrast between the socio-cultural links of such places and those of the burgeoning commercial towns is clear from the distribution of subscribers to novel urban institutions such as infirmaries. Of the founding subscribers of the Liverpool Infirmary (1749), 88 per cent came from the town itself. Worcester Infirmary was established largely through the efforts of the town's elite, but external subscribers accounted for 54 per cent of the total and came from all parts of the county, as well as further afield. Many of these distant subscribers were recruited through the extensive social and family networks of the Bishop of Worcester and local aristocratic families such as the Earls of Coventry.[83]

This contrast accepted, the size of a town's socio-cultural sphere of influence generally reflected its size. As noted above, larger and more established towns had bigger market areas because they contained more, higher order and superior quality functions. For instance, during the 1770s Birmingham offered a choice of two theatres, including the edifice in New Street, described by Hutton as 'one of the first theatres in Europe'. In contrast, the small playhouse in Stafford was 'a mean looking building in St. Martin's Lane'.[84] In terms of retailing, the market areas of small town retailers are exemplified by the Northwich apothecary John England. Most of the 149 book-debts listed in his probate inventory were for small amounts (only twelve were for more than £1) and the majority were from local people: 116 were owed by people of an unspecified location – most were probably from Northwich itself where England spent most of his active life – and a further eight were from Knutsford where he had latterly moved. Of the other twenty-five, only five were from places further than six miles from Northwich. One step up the hierarchy were men such as the Warrington mercer, Edward Twambrooks. His market area was somewhat larger, reflecting a more expansive business network and Warrington's greater sphere of influence. Twambrooks was owed a total of £147 16s 0½d by sixty-six individuals. The greatest number were from Warrington or the immediate area, but there were fourteen from places more than six miles distant.[85] If cloth could be sold over longer distances than apothecary's remedies, then high quality furniture appears to have had an even larger range, and Chester certainly commanded a much bigger market area than did either Northwich or Warrington.[86] The business activities of Abner Scholes, a Chester upholsterer, covered a large area and involved considerable amounts of money. His probate inventory lists book debts of £1,134 19s 6d owed by 151 individuals, including sums of £89 14s 10d, £18 0s 1d, £80, £54 7s 6d and £44 4s owing from particularly wealthy customers.[87] Clearly he had a substantial business which could meet large orders from customers which spread over a wide part of west Cheshire and north Wales, and included two baronets, five ladies and thirteen esquires. Such people, and many others, were obviously willing to overlook the service available at smaller towns to acquire furniture from what was clearly a high status craftsman.

The integration of such widespread hinterlands was dependent upon effective communication. Information about cultural events and consumer goods was carried by word of mouth, via trade cards and through advertisements in the provincial newspapers (see Chapter 7). Both the distribution network of these newspapers and the places mentioned in advertisements give a good impression of a town's hinterland for higher-order goods and services. On this basis, Chester's sphere of influence stretched from Beaumaris to Buxton and from Preston to Shrewsbury, whilst that of Worcester covered a large swathe of the west Midlands from Shrewsbury to Lechlade and Hereford to Warwick. Both encompassed the hinterlands of many smaller towns and also overlapped with those of other major centres. From the 1740s, Stephen Bryan's Worcester newspaper was in competition with *Aris's Birmingham Gazette* and *Jopson's Coventry Mercury*, whilst *Gore's Liverpool Advertiser*, *Williamson's Liverpool Advertiser* and the *Manchester Mercury* all offered alternatives to the Chester newspaper, *Adams Weekly Courant*. By the 1800s there were also newspapers being published in towns such as Blackburn, Macclesfield, Wolverhampton, Stafford and Warwick, and more sporadically in a number of smaller towns. Indeed, there is evidence of retrenchment in the circulation area of the *Worcester Journal* between the 1740s and 1770s, suggesting that the town's sphere of influence was being challenged by emerging industrial centres to the west. In the earlier period, advertisements regularly refer to Warwickshire towns such as Alcester, Warwick and Stratford-upon-Avon, but rarely do so after 1770. A reflection, perhaps, of their more complete absorption into the hinterlands of Birmingham and Coventry.

Wider integration of the region took place through a variety of media, including transport networks and services, customer and supply networks, urban institutions and personal contacts. Transport shaped the region as a space of production through facilitating spatial divisions of labour and linking local production to distant markets. It also helped to create regional spaces of consumption: first by easing the distribution of consumer goods and encouraging the dissemination of new cultures of consumption based on novel and desirable goods; and second by facilitating the flow of capital, ideas and information, allowing the expansion of credit networks and helping to spread market information, new ideas of fashion and so on. In short, effective transport services were essential to the operation of a regional economy and specifically to the distribution of consumer goods and services. Indeed, Elliott convincingly argues that turnpikes were particularly significant in facilitating the appearance of travelling players or itinerant lecturers.[88] It is significant, then, that the nature and intensity of transport varied considerably from place to place, often in response to the structure and geography of the local economy. Thus, for example, the specialist industrial towns of the Black Country had relatively few but intensively used routes linking them to neighbouring centres, especially Birmingham. In contrast, the textile towns of eastern Lancashire, and market towns across both regions, were served by a denser network of roads and had more dispersed service patterns.[89] The obvious corollary of this is that some towns were more effectively integrated into the regional urban system than were others, and that this would affect both the urban hierarchy and regional integration. Whilst this holds good in principle, in reality transport services were largely 'fashioned to the contours of the existing urban hierarchy' and therefore served to reinforce the essentially hierarchical structure of regional urban systems.[90] Communication lines fed into larger centres from smaller towns and were focused on the pre-eminent towns in each region: Chester, Manchester and Liverpool in the north-west, and Birmingham and Worcester in the west Midlands. These towns dominated both intra- and extra-regional linkages and were therefore pivotal in the integration of the regional space. They were central to the dissemination of new goods and ideas – the latter often via the pages of their newspapers, themselves distributed via mail coaches and carriers – and formed the key social and cultural centres, drawing in people from across their respective regions.

This reminds us that transport services were part of a much larger range of activities through which the regional space was produced and drawn together. Customer and subscriber networks were centred on retailers and institutions in particular towns, but could encompass other urban centres as well as the town's immediate hinterland. This was evident in the extensive area served by Abner Scholes from his Chester shop and is echoed in the broad geographical distribution of customers holding accounts with the Worcester grocer Thomas Dickenson. Whilst 83 per cent of his customers lived within ten miles of the shop (58 per cent in Worcester itself), others lived much further afield in places such as Bridgnorth, Birmingham, Hereford and Stafford.[91] Such links again reflect the hierarchical structure of the urban system: Chester and Worcester shopkeepers effectively having greater reach than their counterparts in smaller towns. A similar argument might be made for the Birmingham Library, which drew its subscribers from across the west Midlands, including Lichfield, Solihull, Pershore and West Bromwich.[92] Similarly, as noted above, an important minority of subscribers to the infirmaries in Liverpool and Worcester were widely dispersed. Indeed, the Liverpool infirmary established a string of agents, often clergymen, based in towns across north-west England, whose job it was to canvass for and collect subscriptions. The intention – only partly successful – was to make the infirmary a facility for the whole region, drawing on and underlining Liverpool's status as an entrepôt and arguably the leading town in the north-west. The scaling back of these ambitions following the establishment of competing infirmaries in Manchester and Chester reflects the way in which spatial integration increasingly took place through the urban system rather than the enlarged reach of a single town.[93]

Integration was also affected through business connections. Attorneys were especially significant in this regard, not least through their role in integrating local and regional money markets. This involved contact with a large web of people making deposits and seeking loans. From his business base in Liverpool, John Plumbe developed an extensive money-lending business which incorporated individuals across south-west Lancashire; he had dealings with other attorneys in Liverpool, Prescot and Warrington. From Daniel Lawton, his contact in Prescot, the network stretched further to encompass attorneys in Wigan, Manchester and Ormskirk.[94] This professional networking drew together the regional space and created lines of communication and flows of information. In a similar fashion, traders in the leading towns formed connections across and down the urban hierarchy through means of multiple branches and partnerships. For example, Sara Bazeley, a Coventry ironmonger, had a branch shop in Southam, and the printer Merridew had shops in both Coventry and Warwick. James Keating owned a printing office and bookshop in Stratford-upon-Avon, and also shops in nearby Alcester and Shipston-on-Stour, whilst Roger Lowe was set up in Ashton-in-Makerfield by a shopkeeper from nearby Leigh.[95] Inter-urban partnerships were less common; yet they indicate both a willingness to combine the business acumen and capital of two traders, and an awareness of the wider consumer space of the region. An interesting example is that of two Warwickshire drapers, Richard Blick of Warwick and John Fulford of Coventry, who agreed to form a 'co-partnership' in 1784 with the intention of establishing a shop in Newcastle-under-Lyme, some 70 miles to the north.[96] That these men were willing to invest in a new business venture so far from home reflects the intense interchange which often took place between traders and towns. Indeed, another south Warwickshire tradesman, Thomas Burbidge of Dunchurch, near Rugby, also had trading links with Newcastle-under-Lyme, purchasing £22 9s 7¾d worth of stock from the drapers, Fletcher and Fenton in 1769.[97]

Such networks and relationships underline the fact that the consumption hierarchies outlined earlier are not abstract constructions: they were the product of decisions by individual traders and customers about where to locate and where to go in order to acquire certain goods and services. In Lefebvrian terms, the regional consumption hierarchy was lived space, produced through everyday social practices. Yet the hierarchy also structured the behaviour of both traders and customers: some places were better connected, offered a greater range of goods or formed a more profitable business environment. Of course, spatial networks and retail hierarchies were not how consumers perceived their consumption milieu. It was the shops and coffee houses, local newspapers and circulating libraries, assemblies and race meetings which formed the real nodes of consumer space and established preferences in people's minds. This consciousness of availability and choice shaped the shopping and leisure trips of the middling sorts and the rural gentry. Their decisions were based on relative levels of retail and leisure provision, and on the reputation of towns and individual events and traders, all of which were judged in the light of personal experience and shared information, from newspapers, correspondence and conversations.[98] In many ways, Blome's classification of towns, or the pen-pictures of travel writers like Defoe, Macky and Fiennes, were formal iterations of these perceptions. Yet, in turn, they fed into the wider 'knowledge' about the goods and services available in and worth of the various towns in a region, often reinforcing existing readings of the consumer landscape.

The consumption space of the region was therefore produced not only by retailing hierarchies, but also through the actions, preferences and perceptions of individual consumers. It was a perceived hierarchy: a space of representation. Consumers' images and imaginings of leisure and shopping space, through records of behaviour and the way in which they wrote about towns, constitute vital information on how places were constructed in their minds and featured in their lives. Often particular towns loomed large in the mental landscape of consumer opportunities. For Nicholas Blundell in west Lancashire, Liverpool appears as the preferred central place.[99] He shopped in Ormskirk and Preston, and at fairs in nearby Prescot and Weeton, bought from itinerants who called at his door, and ordered luxury goods from London. Yet, it was to Liverpool that he travelled most regularly to buy goods, see plays or visit friends, and his relationship with certain Liverpool shopkeepers clearly went beyond the purely economic as he often took meals with his preferred suppliers.[100] Despite the closeness of these relationships, Blundell also shopped at places that were far less convenient and seemingly offered little extra by way of choice. He bought goods at Chester, Ashbourne and Holywell in north Wales, often when he was in these places for social reasons. Clearly, his decisions about where to visit and which shops to patronise were, to an extent, opportunistic, but they were also based on his perceptions of the retail hierarchy of the region. A century later, similar practices can be seen in the shopping and leisure habits of an anonymous female diarist from Lutterworth on the Warwickshire–Leicestershire border. In this case it is Coventry that forms the key focus of her consumption milieu, with regular trips to the city's fair and shops, and to visit friends being recorded in her diary.[101] In contrast, Warwick and Birmingham do not feature on the pages of her diary nor, presumably, in her perception of the retail hierarchy of the area. Of course, these towns were more distant and less convenient than was Coventry, yet Leicester, just fifteen miles to the north, accessible via carrier and coach services, and offering a similar range of goods and services to Coventry, is mentioned only three times in the two years covered by the diary. Coventry also seems to have dominated the local shopping habits of the Leighs at Stoneleigh. Although Warwick lies a similar distance to the south, the receipts and vouchers of purchases made by the family during the eighteenth century show Coventry traders being used around five times more often than those in Warwick.[102]

For some consumers, it is possible to discern a hierarchy of preferred centres, apparently chosen on the basis of the quality and range of goods and services on offer, and the particular products being purchased. The Leighs in the Midlands, and Blundell and Shackleton in the north-west appear to have operated in this way, using local towns for mundane purchases and sending to London for higher order goods. For costly items, the distance and expense involved seems to have offered little barrier to metropolitan supplies reaching even quite distant provincial consumers, no doubt reflecting the cachet of London goods as much as the difficulty in acquiring them more locally. Certainly the silver plate sent from London to the Ardernes in eastern Cheshire or the metropolitan wine and books dispatched to the neighbouring Leghs could have been bought in Manchester, if not in the local centre of Stockport. However, these places were used instead to supply everyday items: corn, groceries, ironmongery, shoes, paper, cloth and the like.[103] The attraction of London goods is clear: they were seen as fashionable and gave kudos to the consumer (see Chapters 6 and 7). Even in her relatively remote rural home on the Lancashire–Yorkshire border, the fashion-conscious Elizabeth Shackleton insisted on tableware and textiles coming from London. Indeed, she wrote frequently to her friends in London to gain information about the latest fashions – or at least those which she and her correspondents thought suitable for a woman of her age, status and geographical situation – and commissioned them to make purchases on her behalf. Similarly, the wealthy industrialist Michael Hughes furnished his new house near St Helens (Kinmel Park, 1805–6) from Gillows in London.[104] Yet the desire to obtain high order and fashionable goods from the metropolis was not consistent. In late eighteenth-century Burslem, John Wood sent to London for tea and linen drapery, yet he purchased more and higher quality cloth (including silk and buckram) from drapers in Burslem and had all of his tailoring carried out in the town or in neighbouring Newcastle-under-Lyme.[105]

Choices of venue made by eighteenth-century leisure consumers could appear equally peculiar. Notwithstanding his Liverpool-centred professional and business networks, the attorney John Plumbe regularly attended Preston races rather than the meetings at Manchester, Liverpool or Newton-le-Willows, possibly because he combined his visits with duties at the Assizes held in Preston. Jack Dickenson visited Matlock baths and Parkgate on the Wirral, but overlooked the delights of nearby Buxton.[106] Other leisure consumers, such as Ann Sneyd, appear to have been almost constantly on the move, attending social events in the different towns that she visited. Diary entries reveal that between 1766 and 1782 she often spent the summer season in Bath, attending card assemblies, concerts, plays and the Winter Gardens, before travelling to Shrewsbury in the autumn for the races and a winter season of concerts and assemblies. Over the winter and spring, journeys to other places such as Lichfield, Oswestry and Oxford provided opportunities to attend further events: for instance, in September 1772 she paid £1 5s for five ball tickets at Lichfield Races.[107] Even if their strategies may not make apparent sense to us today, eighteenth-century consumers were clearly making conscious choices about where to shop and where to visit. They were not simply going to the nearest centre where a good or service might be available. Instead they reveal their preferences for certain towns – and, by extension, the structure of their perceived consumption hierarchy – through the pattern of their purchases. Moreover, their decisions about where to shop and socialise served to integrate the regional consumption space in ways that were informed by, but also cut across, the consumption hierarchy outlined above.

Conclusions

Consumption and leisure were important in shaping economic, social and cultural life in virtually all towns in eighteenth-century England. Whilst clear concentrations were apparent, the infrastructure of sociability and improvement, display and conspicuous consumption were far from being the preserve of a select few towns. Moreover, the tangible possessions of fashionable material culture were readily available from a growing number of specialist retailers across the country. This widespread distribution reflected growing demand from the rural gentry and the burgeoning urban middling sorts. As Borsay argues, provision responded to (local) economic prosperity; but this could mean industrial as well as propertied wealth, so that manufacturing as well as county and market towns developed a wide range of facilities, even if they did not always win approval as polite towns (see Chapter 3). In this way, regional as well as urban spaces of consumption were produced by diverse social processes and interactions. Yet, as Soja argues, society was also shaped by space, not least as hierarchical and spatial relationships between central places focused leisure facilities and material goods into certain locations. In general terms this meant towns; more specifically, it meant so-called leisure towns like Chester, Worcester and Warwick (and perhaps Knutsford and Stafford), and larger commercial centres such as Birmingham, Liverpool and Manchester, and later Wolverhampton and Stockport.

Three broad points arise from this regional analysis. First, the plethora of influences which drove consumer practice, shaped fashionable leisure and moulded the urban built environment were brought together through the spatial matrix of the urban network, and, within this, through the social practices of the polite men and women who consumed material goods and leisure experiences.

In other words, the places and practices of consumption were formed by the intermeshing of personal identities, and local interactions of space and society, economy and culture.[108] But they were also structured by broader relationships between the constituents of the urban network. Regional spatial–economic relationships were therefore just as important as local socio-cultural forces in shaping consumption and material culture in eighteenth-century England. Second, there was a remarkable similarity of experience across the two regions in terms of the nature, and often the timing and subsequent fortunes, of the new urban material culture which developed through the eighteenth century. Indeed, the growing ranks of professionals, shopkeepers, merchants and industrialists in the manufacturing towns appear to have encouraged the development of the same type of facilities as did the rural gentry. As Vickery argues, these different groups increasingly shared a common polite culture expressed through their cultural activities and their material possessions (see Chapter 3).[109] These values appear to have spread across 'the genteel' in town and country, although this is far from saying that they formed a homogeneous socio-cultural group. Third, and following from this, a leisure-consumption economy developed in parallel with industrial growth: through much of the eighteenth century there seems to have been no ideological or large-scale spatial separation of the two. As comparisons of Liverpool and Chester, or Bristol and Bath suggest, leisure towns might appear as such because of their relative lack of other economic activities rather than their extraordinary concentration of leisure facilities.[110] The quality of facilities was also a distinguishing factor, but the significant difference was probably in terms of the status of subscribers and customers. This was itself a product of the carefully constructed and often self-fulfilling image of these places as exclusive, fashionable and polite. The construction of this image, in space, on the pages of town histories and in the minds of visitors and residents, requires further investigation.

3 The town

Politeness and place

Introduction

From the late seventeenth century, towns were increasingly conceived and perceived as integral spatial units, both in terms of their material culture – comprising the built environment and ways of life – and their body politic.[1] This emphasis on the collective was manifest in many different ways, but is perhaps best encapsulated in two closely related sets of processes: the re-organisation and representation of the town, and the construction of a 'polite' urban society. The first, centring on the built environment, encouraged the proliferation of maps and prospects of the town, uniting it through an encompassing visual representation, and the associated 'will and capacity to arrange or reorganise large blocks of the landscape' through planning.[2] These developments were linked in both conceptual and practical terms: maps showed how the various elements of the urban space fitted together, providing a model of the town and suggesting how it might be reordered. For Lefebvre, maps were archetypal representations of space, replete with symbolism and loaded with power, whilst planners were central to the processes of producing this conceptualised space.[3] And, of course, remodelling of urban space also involved – indeed, it was frequently intended to produce – a remodelling of society. Planners and architects from John Wood and John Nash, to Ebenezer Howard and Le Corbusier saw social reform as the end goal of their spatial engineering.

This takes us to the second set of processes: the constitution of a civilised and 'polite' urban society, and conversely the production of the town as a site of polite consumption and its representation as the individual and collective embodiment of politeness. As highlighted earlier, politeness was a mutable and slippery concept. Its links with leisure and consumption can be traced back to Shaftsbury, but are most explicit in the arguments of Addison and Steele, and the Scottish Enlightenment.[4] The former offered a distinctly commercial view of politeness, wherein the rules and regulations of polite conduct helped to open up consumption and leisure to a wider urban population by smoothing over traditional distinctions of status and origin.[5] David Hume and Adam Smith drew on this rhetoric of politeness and presented it as a distinctively urban phenomenon – part of the equation of civilisation with urbanisation which characterised Enlightenment thinking across

Europe. Hume's political philosophy emphasised the notion of the civilised city that was created and understood through the events that unfolded within the cultural and commercial spaces of the public sphere. New forms of social organisation thus informed the ways in which private individuals interacted with and through modernity in the public spaces of the town.[6] As Habermas argues, however, the construction of a public sphere was also an environmental and political project. On the one hand, urban improvement comprised the reconceptualisation, formalisation and regulation of urban space. On the other, it was an important instrument in attempts to extend and reconfigure local governance, to make towns locales for political association and citizenship, and to reconcile public and private interests.[7] In this way, the production of a public sphere was gendered: the body politic and the citizen being defined as male. In socio-spatial terms, Smith links it to the coffee house, which was also central to the construction of rational masculinity. Yet, as Vickery argues, we should be wary of an unthinking dichotomy of male-public and female-private. Whilst these associations had 'considerable hold on the eighteenth-century imagination', polite public life, defined more broadly as those practices and spaces open to 'the public', was populated by men and women.[8]

Sweet notes that contemporaries saw towns as the 'the prime location of polite society, and the connection between a "polite and commercial people"'.[9] Yet, whilst the relationship between towns and politeness was seen as axiomatic, it was not automatic, and could only be achieved with time, effort and money. It was dependent upon a series of constructions and representations, both in terms of the built environment and the rhetoric of urban institutions and town histories which subtly infiltrated the urban consciousness. Towns were rebuilt and improved – part of Borsay's urban renaissance – and were reconceived and re-presented as polite places – often in opposition to a traditional and unpolished countryside, but also in contrast to neighbouring urban centres portrayed as less civilised and genteel.[10] Unpicking the relationship between politeness and the town thus involves exploring the physical infrastructure and spatial practices of politeness, and the rhetoric of town histories and travel guides.

To this end, our analysis focuses on three closely related themes. The first two explore the town as a representation of space, planned, paid for and produced by elite groups. Initially, attention centres on attempts to present the town as a polite place. As Sweet reminds us, whilst all towns might harbour ambitions of politeness, only some justified and could effectively lay claim to this status.[11] Success was dependent upon a variety of factors encompassing the projected image of the town and the 'reality' on the ground, as moulded by regulation and planning of the built environment. In some places, politeness and polite spaces were compromised by conflicting activities and land uses; everywhere, there was the need to establish a critical mass of polite activities and spaces. Building on this, we next examine the identity and motivations of those engaged in constructing a new, civilised material culture. The provision of commercialised leisure and retail facilities of the kind noted in Chapter 2 was sponsored by a variety of urban and non-urban actors, each with their own motivations and ambitions. These individuals and groups were producing urban space in both a physical and conceptual sense. They paid for buildings to be erected, but also constructed the town as a representation of space: writing ideology and power-relations onto the townscape. Finally, we attempt to look beyond the rhetoric, plans and growing regulation to discover something of the geographies of polite space. In Lefebvrian terms, we might view these as the lived spaces of politeness, created through the spatial practices of consumers and mapped onto the urban environment through their multiple identities as shoppers, promenaders, theatre-goers and so on. At one level, we explore the geographies of politeness expressed through urban renewal and polite consumption. Here we argue that the 'critical mass' of politeness was given extra weight by the functional and spatial inter-linking of practices and infrastructure. This meant that the same spaces might be used for shopping and promenading, for business and pleasure, or for display, access and performance.[12] At a second level, we sketch out the spatial practices of politeness, arguing that leisure space was produced through social processes – the everyday activities of those engaged in polite sociability.

Making places polite: conceptions, order and identity

Eighteenth-century towns can be seen as spaces of capital, authority and order, conceived and controlled by elites. The planned town formed the ideal opportunity to produce an ordered, regular and civilised urban environment: the physical manifestation of the vision of architect and patron. Yet, in contrast with developments elsewhere in Europe, England lacked a coherent tradition of town planning.[13] There were some initiatives: the early Stuart monarchs had ambitions to stamp their authority on their capital and subjects through an ambitious redesign of Whitehall; the Fire of London (1666) prompted a number of proposals for redevelopment, including ambitious plans from Wren, Hooke and others; and in the 1680s Charles II began a grandiose scheme to turn Winchester into his own Versailles. Little came of the first project – beyond Inigo Jones' magnificent Banqueting House – because of the lack of money and sufficient monarchical power. The second foundered on vested property interests and the need to rebuild quickly, although it did lead to the introduction of a new regime of building regulation which was very influential in shaping urban environments across the country. The third ended abruptly with the king's death.[14] As Borsay argues, however, there were other more general problems that restricted the scope for planning. These included fragmented landholding, the diffuse nature of the building process and resistance from established interests. Enfield, writing at the end of the eighteenth century, summarised the situation rather neatly, arguing that:

> Leverpool, in common with most other large towns, labours under the inconveniences which arise from the want of a regular plan of building, when it first began to flourish. At that time every one, probably, built in whatever place and form best suited his own purposes, without consulting the appearance of the town, or so much as imagining that it would afterwards be of any consequence to the public, what situation he chose, or what style of architecture he adopted.[15]

Despite these difficulties, planning became increasingly important in shaping the eighteenth-century town and urban society. Scope was greatest in new towns, where a blank canvas gave free reign. Such opportunities were rare in England, with its dense network of market and industrial towns, and the best example is probably Sir John Lowther's development of Whitehaven.[16] *Ab initio* industrial and resort towns in the west Midlands and north-west England were also subject to careful planning. In Ashton-under-Lyne, nine-tenths of the town were 'laid out with great regularity by the Earl of Stamford and Warrington's Surveyors' in the late eighteenth and early nineteenth centuries.[17] Similarly, Leamington Spa developed rapidly as a fashionable resort in the early nineteenth century. Here speculative development was set within an overall framework determined by the principal landowner, Bertie Greatheed, who laid out his land for building: constructing and gravelling roads, digging culverts, and staking out and levelling sites. The plan was a simple grid of streets centred on Union Street (later The Parade) leading up from the old town, with Warwick Street marking the northern limit of the initial development (see Figure 3.1). An 1822 survey, prepared for Greatheed, shows that the plots along The Parade were the smallest, reflecting the intensity of demand there, whereas land on the back streets was sold off in larger units.[18] Although simple, the layout shows that the development was conceived as a whole, and contrasts sharply with the more cramped web of streets making up the old town. It thus reveals a conception of the new town not merely as a speculative development, but as an attempt to create an orderly urban environment. This vision, and indeed the grid plan, informed subsequent expansion of the new town. There were plans from Samuel Beazley and Peter Robinson which incorporated grand circuses lined with large detached villas, and others from John Nash for roads laid out in romantic sweeping curves with areas of parkland interspersed. But these came to nothing.[19] Instead, there was a continuation and agrandisement of the grid. Robinson's final (1822) plan for the area to the north of The Parade was formal and imposing: it incorporated two grand squares and a circus at its western end.[20] The local press lauded the development, reporting that 'a Square [Beauchamp] has been formed and ornamentally planted, of the same size with Grosvenor Square in London, around which, houses of the first class are now building' (see Figure 3.2).[21] The plan was holistic, with Beauchamp Terrace – described in Robinson's plan as '400 yards long & 100 feet wide, planted as a … Promenade with a double row of Lime Trees' – being echoed in Binswood Terrace, a block to the north. Moreover, the designs suggested by Robinson for elevations of the principal crescents, terraces and villas were to be 'enriched with columns of the Corinthian order, with proper entablatures; and as all those will be covered with Roman cement in imitation of stone, the effect of the whole, when completed, will be imposing …'.[22]

Away from new towns, fire presented the best opportunity for extensive urban planning, although here the canvas was far from blank. Following the fire of 1694, which destroyed much of the centre of Warwick, the town was extensively remodelled, but within the framework of the original street plan and plot holdings.[23] The rebuilding involved straightening and widening streets, and closely

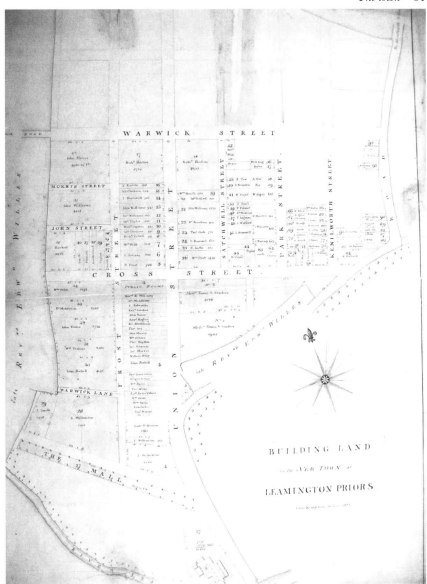

Figure 3.1 Building land in the New Town of Leamington Spa, c.1810
Source: Warwickshire County Record Office, CR 1563/299.

regulating building materials, heights and design. It also established a hierarchy of spaces within the town. There were three principal foci: the castle, the church of St Mary, and the intersection of Church and Castle streets (which linked these two buildings) and Jury and High streets (the major thoroughfare through town). This crossroads was marked by particularly ornate decoration of the buildings

62 *The town*

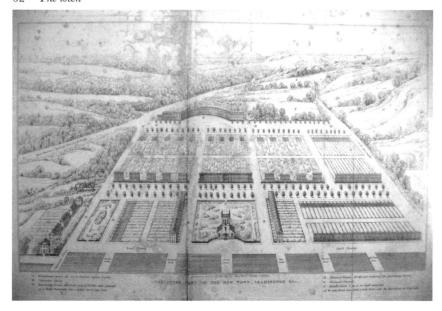

Figure 3.2 Peter Robinson's plan for the area to the north of The Parade, Leamington Spa, c.1822

Source: Warwickshire County Record Office, CR 351/220.

and its prestige was heightened by the erection of a new court house there in the late 1720s – part of its envisioning as a 'fine avenue ... closed at either end by the awesome masses of the St Mary's and Guy's towers'.[24] St Mary's itself, and the area immediately around, received similar treatment: the church was rebuilt and a new square laid out at its western end. This was a plan which conceived the town as a unit and sought to reaffirm its social standing through careful urban design.

The burgeoning of the middling sorts prompted large planned extensions to many provincial towns. Development was more common in rapidly expanding commercial centres than the more overtly 'polite' county towns and was often characterised by the addition of entire blocks of roads and squares. In the early eighteenth century, the focus was on large centres, but as growth accelerated elsewhere so did the impetus for planned expansion. In Liverpool, the estates of Sir Edward Moore and Lord Molyneux were systematically developed in the late seventeenth century and, if later commentators such as Enfield were less than impressed, contemporaries were struck with the quality of development. Defoe declared that 'there is no town in England, London excepted, that can equal Liverpool for the fineness of the streets, and the beauty of the buildings ... as handsomely built as London it self'.[25] The developers sought to produce ordered spaces which would ornament their town and augment its claims to be civilised and polite. Not only were commercial centres thus aligned with the architectural qualities of elegant spas and fashionable developments in west London, they also echoed, if only faintly on occasions, the great cities of Renaissance and baroque

Italy. William Roscoe went further: in portraying Florence and its ruler, Lorenzo de Medici, as the 'apotheosis of the union between culture and commerce', he drew an implicit parallel with Liverpool and its merchant elite.[26] Much the same agenda can be seen in late eighteenth-century Lancaster, where two extensions were planned for a town enjoying considerable prosperity as a port and a social centre for north Lancashire and beyond.[27] The first, drawn up by the Corporation in 1783–4, was for the area between the old town and the planned new bridge across the river Lune (see Figure 3.3). The plan included twenty-three plots along Cable Street (most measuring 26 or 27 feet by 185 feet) and a further forty either side of Parliament Street (ranging in size from 32 by 180 feet down to 20 by 76 feet). The design was punctuated by several new streets, named Barbados, Jamaica and Antigua to reflect the trading links of the town, and a series of public buildings, including the new toll house which faced the bridge across a large open square. The Corporation imposed strict building controls, specifying a uniformity and quality of development which included provision for a gravel footpath. The second scheme was even more ambitious, involving a grid of new streets laid out around the grand Dalton Square, some 206 by 354 feet (see Figure 3.4). As at Warwick, there was a clear spatial hierarchy in the planned development. The plots on either side of the square, intended for the finest houses, were between 51 and 60 feet wide and ran back at least 173 feet. Those further removed were considerably smaller (as little as 19 by 42 feet) and sometimes irregular in shape.[28]

Of course, as representations of space, the plans of architects, city fathers and others were, at best partial. Neither of the plans for Lancaster was executed according to the original design and several schemes for the development of north Leamington Spa were only slowly or partially completed. In both cases,

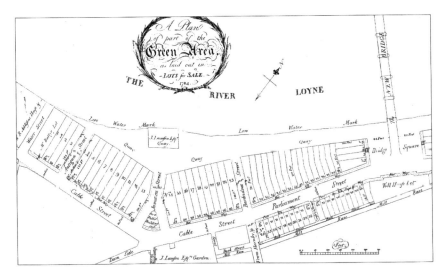

Figure 3.3 Plan of the proposed development of Green Ayre, Lancaster, 1784

Source: Reproduced by permission of Lancaster Central Library.

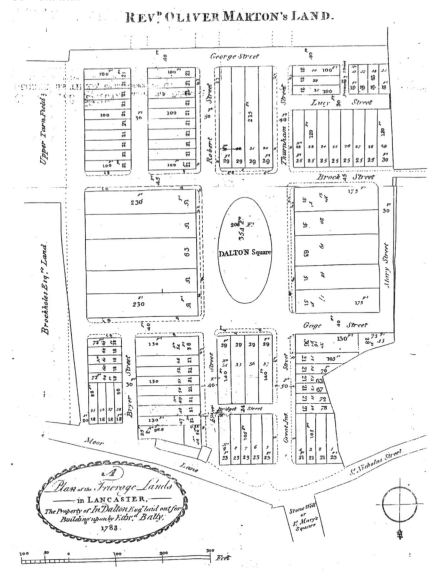

Figure 3.4 Plan of the proposed development of Dalton Square, Lancaster by Edward Batty, 1783

Source: Reproduced by permission of Lancaster City Museum.

the demand for additional housing was slow to materialise, the consequence of a downturn in trade and post-war recession respectively. Historic elements of the town – old buildings, the sinuous network of streets and alleys, even the entrenched localism of corporations and land owners – continually resisted the agenda of modernisation and improvement. Even in 'polite' towns like Chester, the back lanes often remained 'narrow, filthy and inconvenient' lined by houses 'generally of the meanest description'.[29] The Rows, meanwhile – almost universally condemned by visitors as 'old and ugly' – were fiercely defended by the Corporation as a vital part of the town's commercial real estate (see Chapter 4).[30] But this is to miss much of the importance of these schemes: their significance lay as much in their conception of the town as in the difference that they made on the ground. They reveal a re-imagining of the town as something which could be shaped to the will of the architect. The planning of streets, squares or even entire districts according to preconceived principles of design was thus a key element of attempts to modernise and regularise urban space and urban society. That many of these designs were based on classical models added to their symbolic power and their distanciation from the situation on the ground. They could be used to impose order on the perceived chaos of organic urban growth.

Improvement both as an ideal and a practical exercise spread down the urban hierarchy through the course of the eighteenth century (see Table 2.1). From the outset, but increasingly explicitly with the spread of Improvement Commissions, these efforts to improve the town had two related objectives which ran through the more overt rhetoric of bringing order to the urban environment. The first was to produce urban space conducive to polite and civilised behaviour. The second was to bring together public and private ambition, and to help to coalesce disparate groups into a polite urban society. The detailed provisions of corporation-led initiatives and Improvement Acts are dealt with in Chapter 4. What concerns us here is how improvement was used as a tool for constructing the town as a polite place. An important part of this was the upgrading of the physical environment through the appointment of scavengers and pavers, the installation of lamps, and the removal of obstructions such as shop boards, steps and palisades. Lighting held particularly strong symbolism, rendering the remodelled and improved town visible for all to see: a testament to the new discourses of civility. Indeed, Falkus argues that the development of artificial lighting provides one of the major divisions between modern and pre-modern towns.[31] This transformation was especially dramatic in Wolverhampton, where a large gas lantern mounted on a 40 foot cast-iron pillar illuminated the marketplace and surrounding streets.[32] This impressive structure not only served a practical purpose, it also stood as a beacon of modernity, emphasising the forward-thinking attitudes of the local elite.

Just as significant were attempts to regulate and civilise the use of space, most obviously through the removal of markets from central streets and their policing to discourage undesirable activities, from vagrancy and prostitution to blood sports. Once an important part of civic ceremony in many towns, corporations gradually withdrew support from activities such as bull-baiting in the late seventeenth and early eighteenth centuries. In part, this was linked with a wider shift in public values that increasingly saw the slaughtering of cattle in the market place as distasteful.[33] But it was also to do with public order. Preston Corporation explained its decision to end its sponsorship of bull-baiting by stating that: 'the power and authority of the magistrates or other civil superiors hath not been sufficient upon these occasions to restrain the turbulent and unruly passions of the common people'.³⁴ In Birmingham too, the Street Commissioners made bull-baiting a fineable offence. In 1798, when a bull was baited in a field behind the Salutation Inn on Snow Hill,

> in conformity with the wishes of the respectable inhabitants (who desired to put down the nuisance) the Birmingham Association – a body of militia voluntary, formed by the trading classes – undertook the formidable task of capturing the bull and dispersing his tormentors.³⁵

Civilised taste and the production of ordered and regulated space thus came together in opposition to such sports. Whilst they continued well into the nineteenth century, they were increasingly marginalised as plebeian. In these ways, the improved urban environment was linked to the lived spaces of the town, both being redrawn through the provisions of Acts which defined the remit and powers of a new form of local governance. Typical was Coventry's Act of 1763 entitled, 'An Act for paving, lighting and cleansing the City of Coventry and its suburbs for preventing Annoyances therein and for better ordering the public wells and pumps there'.³⁶ The 1790 amendment ordered that no swine were to be kept or slaughtered within the city; spouts and gutters of buildings were not to project; and posts, steps and palisades were to be removed.³⁷ The 1777 Act for Wolverhampton also included provision for the allocation of street names and house numbers, indicating a new emphasis on the ability to navigate through the town and on a modern ordering of urban space.³⁸

We should be wary of taking the rhetoric of Improvement Acts at face value. Appointing scavengers did not necessarily mean that the streets were effectively cleaned, and introducing lamps did not always mean they were lit (see Chapter 4). Modernisation was a fragmented process, one that divided space as well as unifying it. It was, as Ogborn argues, a process that could have a differing, uneven and often contradictory impact on particular spaces and social groups. Nonetheless, both the intention and outcome of improvement was to render the town more civilised and polite. This was a process which necessitated changing spaces and changing attitudes to space. It also required the enforcement of collective responsibility over private interest: a key element of Hume's notion of politeness and civility. He argued that municipal regulation played an essential role in the formation of a civilised society 'by restraining the natural liberty of men', but had also to be accompanied by self-control on the part of the citizen.³⁹ The making of a public sphere thus involved the construction of both public authorities and private individuals, and the formalising of relationships between the two through the political structures of improvement legislation. Improvement commissions effectively played a co-ordinating role, acting on behalf of individual ratepayers in the 'public' interest: they had the powers to address issues of improvement systematically and thus give these developments public direction. A two-way relationship existed wherein the changing urban environment came to represent the emergence of a public sphere and, in turn, the public sphere was constructed through the image of the urban as controlled and civil. Moreover, the process of regulation and improvement was instrumental in creating public space and the public sphere: it was about extending and enforcing elite values of politeness and respectability in both social and spatial terms.

It was also concerned with inclusivity: the bringing together of different social groups in a newly defined urban elite. This was achieved in part by the means of funding these improvements. Levying rates on house occupants and public buildings enforced a collective responsibility for urban improvement. More importantly, gentry, professionals and tradesmen came together in the formal organisations or informal alliances that attempted to improve the urban environment. For example, in the midst of the rebuilding of Warwick, the fire accounts show the keen involvement of Lord Brooke and the county gentry along with those townspeople who had lost their livelihoods.[40] The composition of Improvement Commissions could be similarly diverse. In county towns such as Worcester, Stafford and Chester the gentry had a substantial presence, whilst elsewhere the lord of the manor, local members of Parliament or Justices of the Peace often played an important role. However, in Leamington Spa, Bertie Greatheed was unwilling to join the subscribers to the Upper Assembly Rooms. His concerns were partly financial – the project was by no means a certain success – but also appear to have been linked to the lower social status of other shareholders who included a grocer, a printer, an undertaker and a publican.[41] Such reluctance was both cause and effect of the growing domination of subscription lists, improvement commissions and so on by the urban bourgeoisie. Indeed, Langford has argued that Improvement Commissions were instrumental in widening participation in urban governance, especially amongst the middling orders.[42] In Manchester improvement legislation enabled the commercial elite to wrest some control of town governance from the lords of the manor, although the Mosley family maintained their hold over the markets and their valuable toll income. Similarly, in Wolverhampton authority had long been exercised by the High Steward acting on behalf of the county Justices of the Peace, but 51 of the 125 commissioners appointed in 1777 were shopkeepers or professionals, and a further 33 manufacturers or craftsmen, whilst only 18 were clearly identifiable as gentlemen.[43] By the end of the century, even some established 'gentry' towns, such as Preston, were firmly 'middle class'; though, where industrialisation was less pronounced, there remained a strong desire within corporations and commissions to unite the interests of town and country.[44]

These improvements enhanced the status of towns as orderly and polite: the improved built environment formed a physical representation of its good manners and good government. Such representations of the urban space were projected outwards through town histories, guides and prospects. Many of the larger centres were the subject of numerous publications, especially in the early nineteenth century when their tone became increasingly celebratory. Chester, for instance, had at least seventeen histories and guides between 1781 and 1851. Each devoted attention to the most important structures, institutions and social facilities of the town, outlining their polite credentials and applauding the beneficence of those responsible for their establishment. Hemingway, for instance, whilst critical at times, offered the following endorsement of Chester's cultural attractions:

There are few cities in Europe that have a stronger claim to particular notice than Chester: the curious stranger will here find an ample field for admiration; the man of taste will not leave its precincts ungratified; nor will the research of the antiquary pass unrewarded, in exploring the rich and valuable treasures contained within its walls.[45]

Worcester received similar treatment from a number of writers, most notably Valentine Green. He described the northern entrance into the town along Foregate Street as:

exceeding grand, being a series of spacious modern-built houses of a long extent, and the street equally spacious end to end; well paved and clean; and the view, which is finely terminated by the elegant spire of St Nicholas church, at a due distance, has a most delightful effect. This, with an uninterrupted length of spacious street, continues to the College grates, of which, out of London, is not to be found its equal.[46]

The author of the 1799 Worcester Guide was equally impressed, commenting that 'the general appearance of the whole city does credit to its inhabitants, and indicates at the same time both taste and opulence'.[47] Such positive images were not limited to established county towns. Aikin, writing in 1795, noted that Manchester had nearly doubled in size in recent years, and that the new streets were mostly 'wide and spacious, with excellent and large houses, principally of bricks'. Similarly the principal streets of Birmingham were 'mostly of good widths, and contain the better description of houses and retail shops', whilst Liverpool was reckoned by Baines to have improved immeasurably in appearance in the half century before 1825.[48] Even smaller towns were frequently presented as well-built, commodious and forward-looking. In Macclesfield, 'the general appearance of the town … was greatly improved, by a number of handsome modern mansions, built and furnished in a very elegant style, by opulent manufacturers'. Similarly, Rugby consisted of 'various clean and cheerful streets', and Tamworth had 'a very clean and respectable appearance', whilst Bewdley enjoyed 'eminent qualifications, both as a place of business and for genteel residence'.[49]

The character of towns was also praised in many urban histories. Moss argued that charity was the hallmark of a civilised society and praised Liverpool for its many publicly-funded charitable institutions: the Poor House, Infirmary, Dispensary, Seaman's Hospital, Blind Asylum, and so on. Similarly, histories of Lancaster celebrated the town's long list of charities, including Gillison's Hospital, the Samaritan Society, the Marine Society and the Dispensary. By the early nineteenth century, the demise of blood sports was seen as a mark of the growing civilisation of a town.[50] Such rhetoric suggests that Barker's argument for the construction of an alternative model of politeness – based around economy, morality and respectability – spread beyond northern industrial towns to include more overtly 'polite' places.[51]

Just as much as the physical structures of the town, then, this literature formed part of its cultural capital. Indeed, it was through published histories and guides that towns could broadcast their credentials as polite places.[52] That these were polemic and partial is undeniable, and a point which was recognised by contemporaries. In the introduction to his history of Liverpool, Wallace noted that many town histories 'which hath hitherto appeared, are evidently written with a view to please the inhabitants, and are therefore replete with eulogy and partial panegyric'.[53] And yet, whilst his complaint was perhaps well-founded, it missed an important point of what these histories were about. The inhabitants of the town formed one element of the audience, but another arguably more important constituency was the visitor and armchair tourist.[54] For the latter especially, colourful descriptions, inventories of good works and comparisons with familiar places, especially London, were essential in creating a positive image of the town as polite and cultured. Using London as a point of reference did not necessarily mean that places aspired to be like the capital, but it did provide a model of modernity against which places might be graded. It was adopted not only by metropolitan visitors such as Defoe and Fiennes, but also by the authors of local histories.[55]

As Sweet so persuasively argues, however, these histories could cut both ways: they could also form damning critiques of the facilities, physical environment, accomplishments or polite pretensions of the town.[56] This highlights a third audience for these histories: the urban authorities who had the power to make the improvements seen by these authors as necessary to produce a material culture of politeness and respectability. For Wallace, Liverpool in 1775 'presented to the eye little or nothing calculated to excite admiration or interest': its streets, particularly those around the Exchange, were 'narrow, irregular, and ill built', it could support only two weekly newspapers, and had 'not a single erection or endowment for the advancement of science, the cultivation of the arts, or the promotion of useful knowledge'.[57] Wallace was writing to debunk earlier descriptions of the town, but even those with a more sympathetic view of their subjects could be critical. Enfield complained that, from a lack of planning and 'from that spirit of frugality which always prevails among a people who are beginning the career of commerce, it has happened, that in a far greater part of the streets of Leverpool, there is little appearance of elegance, much less of magnificence'.[58] Aikin focused on more practical considerations in his description of Manchester, complaining about the common practice of building flights of steps 'projecting nearly the breadth of the pavement, which make it very inconvenient for foot passengers'. He also criticised the lack of flag paving, the inadequacy of street lighting, and the crowding of the poor into 'offensive, dark, damp, and incommodious habitations, a too fertile source of disease'.[59] Failure to keep up with changing standards also brought opprobrium to established towns. Defoe likened early eighteenth-century Coventry to 'Cheapside before the Great Fire', whilst other writers commented on the age and poor condition of the buildings, and the dirtiness and narrowness of the streets within the town.[60] Complaints were, of course, not restricted to the larger towns. Butterworth noted of Oldham, for example, that 'some of the back streets and lanes are extremely loathsome and unpleasant', whilst the narrowness of the High Street is 'disgraceful to the town itself'.[61]

In their combination of eulogy and critique, town histories were both conceptions and perceptions of the urban space. They were part of the attempt by elites to construct a representation of urban space, and thus formed an ideal to which the town approximated and aspired, and an advertisement for the town and its elite. Conversely, they were spaces of representation which challenged the imposed identity of politeness, either by debunking cultural pretensions (as Wallace sought to) or by presenting an alternative reading of culture (which Moss had sought to establish for Liverpool on the basis of easy sociability, harmony and philanthropic works).[62] Town histories thus shaped external and internal perceptions of the town as polite and fashionable, or commercial and vulgar. In this way, they helped to shape its identity and influenced consumer choices. For many towns, politeness was both an aspirational image and a social nirvana: a representation produced through plans and regulation, new social groupings and the rhetoric of histories and guides. Yet it was built into the material culture of the town through the bricks and mortar, stone and plaster, tiles and slates of its buildings and streets. It is to this materiality that we turn next.

Producing polite places: actors and ambitions

In each town, there was a variety of individuals, groups and institutions, each with their own ambitions and motivations, and each with their own image of what the town should be, how it should look and who it should be for. In considering the production of space, it is possible to identify four main sets of agents active in constructing the material culture of polite leisure and consumption: corporations, the gentry, subscribers and private entrepreneurs. The importance of each group varied from place to place, and changed through time, whilst hybrids of these ideal types were quite common. Here, we outline these different agents, their motivations and the ways in which they impacted on the built environment and identity of different towns.

In many towns, corporations were central to the provision of leisure infrastructure and thus the promotion of the town as a place of polite sociability. Typical of this was the provision of assembly rooms within town or guildhalls. Such an arrangement is most often associated with established county towns, but was a feature of most corporate towns. In Chester the brick-built Exchange (1695–8) included a richly ornamented assembly room measuring 39 feet by 26.5 feet on the south side of its upper floor; whilst the grand Council Chamber on the upper floor of Worcester's new Guildhall (1723) doubled as a concert and assembly room.[63] Much the same expenditure and prioritisation of polite society were apparent in Liverpool, where the Exchange (1748–55) contained a large assembly room adjoining the council chamber, in which the Corporation entertained guests at regular banquets, concerts and assemblies. When this building was destroyed by fire in 1792 its replacement, erected in 1803–9 at a cost of £110,848, offered even more extensive leisure facilities. On the south side was a well-furnished saloon with drawing rooms to either side. A 'lofty ball room' occupied the whole of the north front, and there was also a smaller ballroom and a banqueting room available for the magistrates to entertain invited guests.[64] Even in smaller towns, the civic authorities were engaged in constructing facilities for assemblies and balls: in Knutsford, the sessions house contained assembly rooms, as did the guildhall in Newcastle-under-Lyme, rebuilt in 1818.[65]

Promenades too were frequently funded in this way. In Chester, the walls, long obsolete as a means of defence, were repaired in 1707 and subsequently maintained by the Corporation at considerable expense to provide an attractive circular walk.[66] The development of Avenham Walk in Preston was also initiated by the town fathers, eager to enhance local recreational infrastructure. In 1698 a corporation committee was appointed to negotiate 'for the ground upon Avenham now and heretofore used as a walk', which was to be 'planted with trees and made into a gravel walk'. Once established, the Corporation devoted considerable efforts to maintaining and improving the facilities: in 1710 and 1736 seats were repaired and in the late 1730s they raised funds along with private subscribers for 'enlarging, repairing, and beautifying' the walk. A little later, the Corporation in Lancaster laid out the extensive Ladies Walk, and another at the foot of the castle walls, and planted trees on Castle Hill.[67] The importance of corporations in this regard is apparent from the fact that non-corporate towns rarely enjoyed formal promenades, relying instead on other open spaces to serve this purpose (see Chapter 2).

Corporate bodies were also keen to encourage horse racing. Town or common land was often set aside for race-courses as at Chester, Warwick, Worcester and Lancaster, amongst others, and in some cases corporations helped to finance the laying out of the course and provision of infrastructure such as grandstands. This is most famously seen at York, but was also apparent in Lancaster and Worcester.[68] More important, however, was the provision of prize money. Most meetings included a race for the Town Plate, which was usually funded at least partially by the Corporation itself. In the 1770s, the £50 purse for the third day's racing at Worcester came from 'County and City Subscription', and at Lancaster the Town's Plate was also worth £50 to the winner. A generation later, the highlight of the revived Lancaster races was the Corporation Gold Cup, valued at 100 guineas. On a lesser scale the authorities in Walsall gave an annual contribution of £5 for the encouragement of the races there.[69] Additionally, town authorities often laid on evening entertainment, particularly at the more important meetings: at Lichfield in 1748, for instance, there were balls at the Guildhall every night during the races which attracted 169 gentleman and 120 lady subscribers.[70]

The motivations which lay behind such investment are not difficult to discern, but were not necessarily as simple as might be assumed. The close association between cultural facilities and urban authorities added prestige to the Corporation and the town, allowing it to keep up with changing standards and to match (or outdo) developments in rival centres. Corporations were also able to draw the rural and urban gentry into the political process by effectively acting as hosts at social gatherings which gained their prestige in part from those attending and in part from the opulence of the surroundings. Thus, investment in costly fitments and furnishings helped the civic leaders to make the right socio-political connections and thus enhance their social capital. At the same time, ensuring that the buildings and decoration were tasteful and fashionable enabled them to build up their cultural capital: it communicated their discernment and good taste, bolstering their position as the legitimate authority within the town.[71] Moreover, this investment reinforced the status of the town hall as an iconic building: a social and cultural as well as political symbol for the town. In this way, investment in civic and cultural infrastructure formed an important constituent of urban identity, but built a specific identity for each particular town, since, as Jacobs argues, identity is constituted not only by looking inwards, but also through awareness of self and other.[72] Awareness of and rivalry with developments in other towns can be seen in the rhetoric of eighteenth-century town histories, but was also built into the fabric of the town through corporations' investments in their civic infrastructure.[73] More pragmatically, such investment was also commercially motivated: better facilities helped to attract families of rank to visit or settle in the town, increasing spending on goods and services and adding to the prosperity of tradesmen and the town as a whole.[74]

The gentry and aristocracy, at which much of this investment was directed, form the second set of agents in urban improvement. They loom large in Borsay's discussion of the urban renaissance, as consumers of goods, space and leisure, and as important players in the production of leisure infrastructure and polite urban space more generally. In parliamentary boroughs, there was a political incentive to invest in civic and cultural facilities. As Sweet argues, MPs (and prospective MPs) had to court their electorate, *inter alia*, through subsidising urban improvement.[75] In Wigan, for example, the town hall was erected in 1720 at the expense of the then representatives, Lord Barrymore and Sir Roger Bradshaigh; and in Chester the Grosvenors aggrandised the Royal Hotel (formerly the Talbot Hotel and the centre of polite leisure in the town) and commissioned performances at the theatre.[76] However, investment by the gentry clearly spread well beyond such political agendas since non-borough towns also attracted patronage. Thus, Lord Paget was responsible for replacing the old Market House in Burton-upon-Trent with a more modern structure in 1772; the Earl of Derby provided £1,338 11s 7d in 1780 for the rebuilding of the Town Hall at Ormskirk; and the 1802 town hall in Chorley was erected 'at the sole expense of the late John Hollinshead Esq.'.[77] Even at the margins of urban status, gentry investment could be considerable, as in Tarporley in Cheshire, where the county gentry, meeting as the Cheshire Hunt, commissioned the construction of banqueting rooms at the Swan Hotel.[78]

The impact of the gentry spread well beyond the construction of individual buildings. In post-fire Warwick, Lord Brooke used various architectural devices to enhance the status of the town's main cultural and leisure spaces, drawing inspiration from the rebuilding of London after the Great Fire and from Versailles. As previously discussed, this involved a remodelling of the townscape and close attention to the detail of the reconstructed buildings along the principal thoroughfares. The overall effect, Borsay argues, was to make 'the reconstructed landscape ... a material articulation of Brooke's authority'.[79] Such all-encompassing vision and impact were rare, and the social and political attraction that towns held for the gentry was diminishing by the late eighteenth century. As they refocused their attention onto London and the fashionable resorts, the gentry became less interested and less influential in most provincial towns. By the early nineteenth century, the wealthy landowners in Leamington Spa, for instance, were reluctant participants in the construction of infrastructure: they preferred to sell off the land and leave its development to an urban middle class.[80]

In the absence of a wealthy and willing local aristocrat to act as financier, the usual mechanism by which moneys were raised was subscription – a central element of Plumb's notion of the 'commercialisation of leisure' and one which theoretically democratised elite culture.[81] All manner of facilities were funded in this way, as were the town histories that celebrated or critiqued these developments. Indeed, without this device, many towns would have been largely devoid of leisure infrastructure. In Hanley, for example, subscribers funded the library (1794) and newsroom (1834) in the marketplace, the grandstand at the racecourse (1825), the North Staffordshire Infirmary (1815), and even the general market, erected in 1776.[82] Elsewhere, subscription reflected the need for dedicated facilities or more prestigious settings. Chester already had assembly rooms in the Exchange and in Booth's Mansion, but this did nothing to discourage enthusiasm and plentiful subscriptions for the grand assembly rooms built in the renovated Talbot Hotel (1777).[83]

Subscriptions for the construction of such facilities were limited to those who could afford shares, the minimum investment in which was generally £25 – beyond many middling-sort incomes. In county and smaller market towns, as well as some larger commercial centres, subscribers were drawn from across the urban elite and local gentry families. Berry notes that 42 per cent of subscribers to the new assembly rooms in Newcastle-upon-Tyne were drawn from the nobility and gentry, with 35 per cent being merchants, bankers, professionals and tradesmen from the town itself.[84] Whilst these were not necessarily the same people who made use of the facilities, those attending balls at subscription assembly rooms across the country were drawn from similar backgrounds. Chester's assemblies were graced by the presence of the Grosvenors, and a plethora of county families, as well as worthies from the town; whilst in neighbouring Derbyshire, the assemblies accompanying the annual races were presided over by the Duke of Devonshire. Similarly, the opening of Lancaster's subscription theatre in June 1782 was marked by the presence of the Earl of Surrey (MP for Carlisle) and 'consequently, every person of distinction and taste visited it'. At a more general level, Knutsford was said to benefit greatly from the 'public spirit and liberality of the opulent gentry who reside in its neighbourhood'.[85]

In the commercial centres, the constituency was more closely defined by the town itself. In Burslem, those sponsoring the construction of the first 'town hall' (1761) included the two Lords of the Manor (Sir Nigel Gresley and Ralph Sneyd, esquire), but principally comprised local pottery manufacturers, notably the Wedgwoods, Daniels, Taylors and Warburtons. Similarly, at least half of the members of Liverpool's subscription library (1758) and two-thirds of subscriber-shareholders of the new theatre (1772) were merchants. In Birmingham, all of the original subscribers to the New Street theatre in 1773 came from amongst the leading merchants, industrialists and professionals of the town.[86] For them this was partly a commercial venture, but also an opportunity to boost the prestige of the town. Writing in support of a licence for the theatre in 1777, the industrialist Matthew Boulton, noted that:

> Of late years, Birmingham hath been visited much in the summer season by persons of fashion, and it is some inducement to prolong their stay when their evenings can be spent at a commodious, airy theatre. This is a fact I mention from experience, and it is certainly our interest to bring company to Birmingham, as it contributes much to the public good, not only from the money they leave behind them, but from their explaining their wants to the manufacturers themselves, and from their correcting the taste and giving hints for various improvements, which nothing promotes so much as an intercourse with persons from different parts of the world.[87]

The message is clear: by encouraging genteel visitors to spend time in Birmingham and converse with its people, the town might be civilised and educated in the intricacies of polite living, which the manufacturers could then turn to their advantage. And, to do this, there had to be appropriate spaces. Here the social and economic benefits of polite leisure activities are explicitly interrelated, something that was recognised by those subscribing to leisure facilities in towns throughout the west Midlands and north-west England. Indeed, it is striking that not just the facilities, but also the funding mechanism and the motivations behind their provision were common to a wide range of different towns; to urban middling sorts as well as the rural gentry.

Self-interest came not just in terms of the pleasures to be had in attending assemblies or visiting the theatre, but also in the prestige that reflected back onto the subscribers. As with the activities of corporations, association with prestigious and fashionable buildings enhanced the cultural capital of subscribers. Subscription was also a good way of imparting a sense of commitment and ownership which galvanised support for particular leisure facilities. More than this, it helped to construct a polite leisure community made up of people who shared a sense of civic pride and responsibility, and a liking for public sociability and for the prestige which membership of such a social circle conferred.[88] Certainly, Boulton and the other promoters of Birmingham's New Street theatre, such as the toymaker, John Taylor, and the publisher, Samuel Aris, recognised that, as subscribers, they constituted an exclusive body. Indeed, a code of conduct adopted by the proprietors in 1779 stipulated that no shares were to be sold, other than to an existing subscriber, without the prior agreement of the general body, in order to 'prevent improper persons from becoming proprietors in the Theatre'.[89] This links closely with Borsay's argument about the dual nature of polite sociability that lay at the heart of much leisure activity in the eighteenth century. Assembly rooms, theatres and so on were inclusive, bringing together people within the bounds of polite and genteel society. Yet they were also exclusive: marking out the extra worth of those – the subscribers – who lay behind their construction, forming them into a separate, coherent social grouping. This kind of argument is perhaps best illustrated in terms of libraries. Subscription libraries were often funded and built with the deliberate intention of being exclusionary. Thus, subscribers to the Liverpool Library were required to present a specially struck medal to the librarian in order to gain admittance and be able to borrow books. To police this system the library committee voted on 14 May 1771 that 'a bar or rail be fixed across the Library room … in order to keep out all persons without subscription from entering the room'.[90]

Infirmaries and dispensaries were also largely paid for by subscription, although here the motives of subscribers were rather different. Whilst altruism and paternalism played a part, it is clear that they were overlain with notions of boosterism and the wider cultural identity of the town. By the last quarter of the eighteenth century, an infirmary was a necessary ornament for any civilised place. Both Worcester and Chester had one by 1760, as did Liverpool and Manchester, with Stafford following in 1766. Birmingham had to wait a little longer, but by 1780 all of the study counties could boast at least one infirmary, each sponsored largely by subscribers from within that county.[91] In Liverpool, as we have already seen, there were initially attempts to project the town's infirmary as a facility for the region as a whole. This enterprise is worth exploring in more depth as it reveals much about the significance of these institutions and the motivations lying behind their funding and construction. The auditors' report for the year 1749 noted that the inhabitants of Liverpool had expressed an 'earnest desire' that an infirmary should be established 'not with any partial view of serving the town only, for which a very small building would have been sufficient, but to make provision for the many objects that appeared in distress from all parts of this nation and Ireland'. The inhabitants, it was argued, had a duty to support all those in need, regardless of their place of origin, since Liverpool was first and foremost a centre of trade. 'It is well known', one of the trustees reasoned

> that this town to carry on her great commerce employs hands not only from the circumjacent but the more distant places: hereby is occasioned a great concourse of people from all parts of which many must perish with their crying distresses, and many become burdensome to the community for want of the assistance'.

Subscriptions were thus solicited from across the north-west and beyond, drawing on the commercial networks centred on the town, but subtly spreading its influence and broadcasting its importance beyond the immediate hinterland. Indeed, the annual reports outline a network of correspondents to receive subscriptions which stretched across the region from Lancaster and Preston to Nantwich and Macclesfield, along with a representative in London. Ultimately, though, this bid for regional predominance was unsuccessful. Subscription lists for 1759 and 1769 show that fewer than 10 per cent of contributors came from outside Liverpool and its immediate hinterland. If anything, the importance of 'Country and Foreign' subscribers tended to decline over time. In 1749 they provided 19 per cent of the money for building the infirmary, and 14 per cent of the first annual contributions, followed by 31 per cent in 1750. By 1759, however, income from outsiders had dropped to just 6 per cent, in part reflecting the opening of competing infirmaries in Manchester (1752) and Chester (1755), and underlining the fact that, above all, people's ambitions and loyalties were closely tied to space and to place identity.[92]

Subscription was not a panacea, however: sometimes, ambitions were unrealised. In early nineteenth-century Chester, for example, a campaign was briefly run by the local newspaper to galvanise support for the construction of a replacement for the old wool hall which had long housed the town's theatre. The editor wrote that, 'we wish a few of our wealthy citizens would put down their £500 each and erect a new Theatre. We are confident the speculation would be well repaid'.[93] Here, we have the essence of subscription: drawing on local elites to act in their own interest (pecuniary and cultural) as well as that of a more general public and, of course, the town. Yet, Chester's elite did not respond, showing that the links between improvement and the elite were neither stable nor guaranteed. Perhaps the cost was too great or the investment uncertain, or perhaps the theatre was not seen as an appropriate vehicle through which to enhance their standing. Whatever the cause, such instances emphasise the importance of the final route by which spaces for leisure and consumption were constructed: that is, as private commercial ventures. In some instances, this approach overlapped with subscription, with one individual collecting contributions to help fund an essentially private initiative. Many theatres appear to have been developed in this way: an impresario attracting subscribers through the provision of special season tickets. In late eighteenth-century Lancaster, subscription was organised by Joseph Austin and Charles Whitlock, managers of a circuit of theatres in Newcastle, Whitehaven, Sheffield, Manchester and Chester. In Walsall, individuals holding £50 shares in the theatre, erected in 1803, received interest on their money and a silver ticket which was 'transferable at pleasure'. Over twenty years earlier the twenty subscribers to the new Worcester theatre in Angel Street benefited from a similar arrangement: essentially they were engaged in a commercial venture whereby money was advanced 'on the security of the building' in return for preferential access to the facilities.[94] Similarly, assembly rooms funded through subscription were sometimes included in private developments, as was the case at the Talbot Hotel, Chester (see above), but the model of owner-developer was more common. Premises might be purpose-built, as at the assembly rooms on Back Lane in Lancaster (1759) or the Parthenon Assembly Rooms in Leamington Spa (1821), the latter being sponsored by Robert Ellison, lessee of the Drury Lane Theatre in London.[95] More often, assemblies were held in private rooms within inns. Perhaps the most famous example of these was at the Lion Hotel in Shrewsbury, but it was a model repeated – albeit at a less grand scale – in small towns across the west Midlands and north-west.[96] In each case, the owner of the inn or hotel benefited financially from the subscriptions to the assemblies and the food and drink consumed, and socially from the kudos of hosting such fashionable gatherings.

Pleasure gardens were almost invariably private ventures. These were sometimes developed by innkeepers as part of a more general provision for polite sociability. In late eighteenth-century Chester, for example, gardens with 'lawns, extensive flower gardens and a bowling green' were laid out behind the Albion Inn on Lower Bridge Street. In Coventry, Spires' Spring Gardens, behind the Mermaid Inn on Broadgate, offered similar facilities. Evening concerts were often held here during the summer in the mid-eighteenth century, sometimes accompanied by a firework display.[97] Elsewhere, pleasure gardens operated as stand-alone facilities, many of them fashioned on the London model. There were Vauxhall Gardens in Birmingham, and Ranelagh Gardens in Liverpool and later Leamington Spa. In some towns, there were competing attractions: in Worcester there were gardens attached to Diglis bowling green and the assembly rooms to the south of the city, and pleasure grounds around Sansome Lodge in the north, and Birmingham had both Vauxhall Gardens at Dudleston Hall and the Apollo gardens.[98] More ephemeral facilities, such as the 'Israel's tent ... made of poles covered with sail cloth, about 15 yards long by 6 broad' erected for a *ridotto al fresco* on Liverpool's Maiden Green in 1736, were also commercial ventures.[99] All such facilities were designed to make money for those who built and operated them. They were designed to attract the public and to extract payment from them, sometimes through subscription and sometimes through an entry fee.

This commercialisation of leisure was an important part of making polite society inclusive: facilities were open to all those who could pay and, because rates were generally fairly low, this included the middling sorts and many artisans too. Ogborn has argued that the Vauxhall Gardens in London were far from exclusive, and the same appears to have been true in the provinces. Admission to concerts at Ranelagh Gardens in Liverpool typically cost one shilling, well within the budget of an artisan or petty tradesman; even the *ridotto al fresco* staged at Maiden Green cost only 2s 6d.[100] By the same token, the cheapest seats at the theatre usually cost no more than one shilling, and well-to-do consumers often paid for their servants to attend the theatre or races. Ann Sneyd, for instance, noted that she had 'treated the servants to a play' on three occasions in 1767 at an accumulated cost of £1 9s.[101] Moreover, complaints against the theatre often focused on its reputation for encouraging dissolute behaviour amongst the lower orders. Writing to oppose the granting of a Royal patent to the New Street theatre in Birmingham, the Revd J. Parsons argued that it was 'a thing which must be productive of idleness and dissipation'. Indeed, he suggested, the practice of 'forcing playhouse tickets upon dependent workmen as part of their wages' was a common abuse.[102] That said, the cost of participating in commercialised leisure clearly did exclude large sections of society (and deliberately so), whilst spatial and temporal divisions in the use of theatres, assembly rooms and promenades (see Chapter 5) reinforced social divides. As Borsay argues, the point of polite society was to include some whilst excluding others.[103]

78   *The town*

In sum, the material culture of leisure and consumption produced by these different groups of investors served to transform both the physical appearance and social character of the town, rendering it a civilised and polite place. Yet, as we have already seen, these developments were far from uniform in time or space – some towns were seen as polite whilst others were not, and some parts of towns were planned and improved whereas others were left largely untouched. Towns thus developed particular geographies of polite consumption. It is to these spatial patterns and relationships that we turn next.

Geographies and spatial practices of polite consumption

Looking beyond the attempts of planners, urban authorities and elites to construct and represent urban space allows us to explore the lived spaces of leisure and shopping and the spatial practices through which they were experienced, produced and reproduced. The changing geographies of polite leisure, civic infrastructure, high status shopping and elite residential areas indicate a 'modern' ordering of space, marked by the emergence of specialist areas in all but the smallest towns by the end of the eighteenth century. However, it would be wrong to see these spaces as separate or as being produced by distinct processes, an impression which can emerge from Ogborn's treatment of different sites of modernity within eighteenth-century London. The specialist spaces found in many provincial towns were often geographically proximate (in part, a result of the modest size of many towns) and were closely bound together, blurring the spatial and experiential boundaries between them and encouraging 'mixed' use. This might be conceived of as a layering of space but it might be more usefully envisaged as a complex matrix within which polite consumers operated.[104]

Whilst the range of leisure infrastructure built up in towns across the west Midlands and north-west was common to centres of different size and function (see Chapter 2), the distribution of these activities within the town could vary considerably. In established county and cathedral towns, such as Chester, Worcester and Coventry, facilities were often concentrated along the main thoroughfares or adjacent streets reflecting the relatively slow pace of urbanisation and long history of commercial leisure development. In many cases activities took place in existing buildings, sometimes renovated or modified for the purpose. For instance, Chester's theatre was contained within the wool hall, which was itself built on the base of the chapel of St Nicholas.[105] Even the infirmary at Worcester initially occupied a large house in Silver Street, close to the heart of the town, before moving to purpose-built premises on a larger peripheral site overlooking the Pitchcroft in 1770. Where leisure facilities were newly built in these towns they frequently stood on the site of earlier structures often serving a similar purpose. For instance, the Draper's Hall on Bailey Lane in Coventry, used regularly for assemblies and concerts, was rebuilt in 1775 and again in 1830, replacing the original 'dark and gloomy' hall with a fashionable ballroom.[106]

In contrast to this central clustering, leisure facilities in fast growing commercial centres were often more marginal to the urban space or were located on back streets – a reflection, in part, of the availability of suitable venues or land, but also of the move to locate such facilities amongst newly built residential areas for the expanding middling sorts. This was an explicit part of John Wood's vision of Bath, and is echoed in the distribution of facilities elsewhere. James Guest's 1834 map of Birmingham shows social facilities concentrated in the fashionable area around St Philip's churchyard and at the western end of New Street, some distance from the old town core centred on the Bull Ring and St Martin's Church. In Manchester buildings such as the Assembly Rooms (1792), Portico Library (1806), Theatre Royal (1807) and Royal Institution (1825) were grouped along Mosley Street – a fashionable area lined with wealthy homes and fine churches, but some distance from the centre of town.[107] The pattern in Liverpool was more complex, with development often being shaped and reshaped by the very rapid growth of the town. The Ranelagh Gardens were established to the north of the old town around 1722. By 1743 they were complemented by two Ladies Walks, and in the 1760s by St James' Walk, also in peripheral locations. On the south side of the town, the first purpose-built theatre was erected on a side street, Drury Lane, in 1759, before moving further north to more lavish premises in Williamson Square (1772). Later developments also tended to be situated away from the main thoroughfares of the town: the Athenaeum (1799) was on the south side of Church Street, the Royal Institution (1817) on Colquit Street, and the Botanic Gardens (1802) at the top of Mount Pleasant.[108] Similar patterns were apparent in Wolverhampton, where leisure facilities were generally located on back streets or at the margins of the built-up area: Isaac Taylor's plan of 1750 shows two bowling greens, one to the north of the Deanery Hall, the other in Cock Close on the western side of the town. Tree-lined walks were also laid out to the west and south across land later used for the racecourse and St John's square respectively. Later in the century leisure facilities continued to be sited away from the main thoroughfares: the theatre in a yard behind the Swan Hotel, and the library and assembly rooms in Queen Street.[109] Perhaps surprisingly, such marginality could also be an issue in smaller towns, although here it was often seen as a disadvantage. In Nantwich, for example, the theatre was described as lying in 'an obscure and ineligible situation',[110] despite it being only 200 metres from the High Street and the market. Similarly, the grandly named 'Imperial Sulphureous Medicinal Font and Ladies Marble Baths' off Clemen Street in Leamington Spa was short-lived, being too far from the increasingly fashionable new town.[111]

Concentrations of shops, particularly high status outlets, became ever more apparent in eighteenth-century towns of all sizes. Urban retail space had long been organised around the marketplace, a location which had advantages clearly recognised by those selling or letting shop premises. The situation of one 'good-accustomed shop' was described as 'inferior to none ... being in the Heart of the Market', whilst another 'very desirable shop ... fronted to two different Aspects of the ... Market' was thus in 'a good Situation, if not the best of any in Town for a Retail Business'.[112] The close association of shops and market stalls clearly made shopping more convenient, particularly for those who were passing through the town on business. Moreover, with goods displayed outside under canopies, shops could appear an extension of the market itself, presenting shoppers with a reassuringly familiar retail environment.[113]

By the second half of the eighteenth century, the market was being pushed to the economic and physical margins of the town, whilst progressive intra-urban specialisation meant that shops were concentrated in the town centre, principally along the main thoroughfares. This was most pronounced in large commercial towns, where the size and complexity of the retail sector and the physical extent of the town encouraged a distinct geography of retailing to emerge. In the 1760s, trade directories reveal that Liverpool's fixed shops were predominantly located along the principal streets, Dale Street and Water Street running down to George's Dock, and High Street, Castle Street, Derby Square and Pool Lane, which ran on a perpendicular axis to the Old Dock. These streets contained more than half of Liverpool's high status retailers, one-quarter being concentrated into the stretch between St George's Church in Derby Square and the Exchange on the corner of High Street and Water Street.[114] Perhaps because of their spatial constancy, these institutions of sacred and secular authority were more influential in shaping the geography of retailing than were other more overtly leisure facilities such as the theatre or pleasure gardens. The port itself, though, formed the key spatial axis of Liverpool's changing commercial and retail geography. The movement of merchants and others between the docks and the exchange undoubtedly helped to concentrate retailing along these key routes in the mid-eighteenth century. Two generations later, the commercial infrastructure of commodity exchanges, specialist office blocks and merchants' clubs dominated these same streets. Higher quality shops were then drawn out along some of the principal routes between this commercial core and the better residential areas to the south-east of the town. For this reason, Bold Street became known as 'the Bond Street of the North'.[115] Patterns of retailing were thus far from static, but the underlying logic that determined the location of shops remained the flows of people to and from the port. Similar anchors can be found for the retail geographies of smaller towns. In Walsall, for instance, shops were arranged along the High Street from the market house to the Guildhall, and then on to the George Hotel in Digbeth, site of the town's largest assembly rooms. In Burslem the new town hall not only housed the market, but also became the focus for subsequent shop development.[116]

In many county towns, concentrations of shops were even more pronounced.[117] This often involved a strengthening of traditional retail patterns as they coincided with the emerging geographies of leisure. In Coventry 52 per cent of shop tax payments in 1785 were for Cross Cheaping ward, which included the marketplace, shambles and principal shopping streets such as Cross Cheaping and West Orchard. From here, shops spread out along Broadgate, Smithford Street and the High Street. This part of the town was also close to the main concentration of leisure facilities along Bayley Lane overlooking St Michael's Church, whilst the gentry and wealthy townsmen had houses in Much and Little Park Streets immediately to the south.[118] Similarly, in Worcester high status retailers tended to cluster together in a few centrally located streets. A wide selection of specialist shops and most of the town's banks were found around the Cross, whilst booksellers, cabinet makers, milliners and drapers were particularly prominent in the High Street, and Broad Street was home to many apothecaries and grocers, plus numerous attorneys and several of the main coaching inns.[119] The extent of this fashionable shopping area was clearly recognised by contemporary commentators: Valentine Green noting that 'the many elegant and well-furnished shops that fill the Cross, the Broad street, and the High street, give them a near likeness to Cheapside, London'.[120] These streets were also home to some of the main leisure facilities in the town, such as the Guildhall and King's Head theatre on the High Street, and the Bell Inn and Crown Inn on Broad Street, both of which had large assembly rooms. In Chester, the four main streets (Eastgate Street, Bridge Street, Watergate Street and Northgate Street) contained well over three-quarters of the city's high status retailers.[121] Rather than being evenly spaced along the streets, however, Batenham's early nineteenth-century etchings suggest that shops were more numerous around the Cross, where the four main streets met, thinning out as distance from this central focus increased.[122] Moreover, there was a strong concentration of drapers, mercers, grocers, goldsmiths and other high status retailers along the east side of Bridge Street and the south side of Eastgate Street – areas which had a 'decided preference … shops let here at high rents and are in never-failing request'.[123] This clustering went still further with the Row level shops (those raised on open galleries on the first floor of the buildings) being considered the best.[124] Thus, on the south side of Eastgate Street, the Rows were dominated by mercers, linen and woollen drapers, goldsmiths and toy shops, whereas the street level shops contained a large number of victuallers and especially butchers.[125] The town's leisure facilities were mostly located within or at the fringes of this retail core: the theatre and exchange on Northgate Street, Booth's Mansions on Watergate Street, and the Talbot Assembly Rooms further along Eastgate Street. This spatial proximity encouraged those attending the theatre, public gardens, card parties and so on to walk along the city's shopping streets, an activity that was further encouraged by the changing nature of retailing and shopping in the eighteenth century.

These burgeoning shopping districts were also shaped by patterns of high status residence. This is evident at the city-wide scale from Mui and Mui's study of York, which shows 94 per cent of shops concentrated in the fifteen parishes with the highest socio-economic ranking. But it also emerges in terms of the residential status of individual streets: the development of Foregate Street and the Tything as a gentry suburb on the north side of Worcester, for instance, encouraged the northwards expansion of the shopping area in the mid-eighteenth century, colonising premises in the lower reaches of Foregate Street itself.[126] Only occasionally did newly created 'polite' suburbs fundamentally alter the established retail patterns of a town in the manner seen in London. In Birmingham, the development of a wealthy quarter on the high ground around St Philip's churchyard from the mid-eighteenth century led to a reorientation of the town's polite shopping area away from the crowded narrow streets of the old medieval town by the Bull Ring towards New Street, Bull Street and the upper reaches of the High Street.[127] More typical was Liverpool, where the new and fashionable squares to the south and east drew few high status shops in their wake. Indeed, Cleveland Square quite literally went down-market, becoming filled with shambles used for the twice-weekly produce markets.[128]

Specialist shopping areas are more difficult to discern in smaller towns, not least because such places had fewer streets through which shops could disperse. Even so, the same broad processes of clustering can be recognised. In early eighteenth-century Warwick, retailers were spread across the central streets of the town, but the principal focus was the crossroads of High, Jury, Church and Castle streets, around which were clustered at least two woollen drapers, four apothecaries, three barbers and two gunsmiths, as well as a mercer, a watchmaker, a milliner, a bookseller, a cutler, a saddler and the town's premier inn.[129] This concentration of high status retailers reflected the number of wealthy customers attracted to or resident in even a relatively small county town – a point illustrated by the list of debtors attached to the 1733 inventory of a Warwick mercer, John Fairfax. Those owing him money included Dr Heath, Lady Hubam and William Knight, esquire, with residences on the High Street, and Dr Greenwood, Mrs Prescott and Mrs Howitt on Jury Street.[130] Other concentrations of professionals and gentry were to be found in Sheep Street and the southern end of Smith Street, whilst the market place was characterised by a mix of butchers, shoemakers, hatters and tailors. Even in fairly modest market towns like Nantwich, the fixed shop increasingly over-shadowed the market: by the 1780s, higher status retail tradesmen were mainly found along Hospital Street and especially the High Street, both some distance removed from the town's market.[131] Indeed, only mercers and grocers were found in any number away from these principal streets.

What appears to have been critical in structuring these geographies of retailing was the visibility of the shop, governed principally by the role of the street as a thoroughfare. In London, Francis Place noted that, when setting up in business, his wife had:

> found two or three shops in streets which ran into Holborn, from the window of any one of which she thought I could scarcely fail to sell as much as would pay the rent and perhaps to something more, but my ambition had risen considerably and I no longer contemplated a shop in a bye street. I now looked for a shop in a principal thorough fare or in a street of good name where a large quantity of business might be done.[132]

Changes in the flow of people along the street could have profound effects on its attraction as a retail location and hence on the retail geography of the town as a whole. So too could changes to the type of person passing along the street. Thus, we see the development of Bold Street in Liverpool as it became an important thoroughfare into and out of town, and the rise of Mosley Street in Manchester as it was developed as a fashionable residential area. Once established, though, there was a remarkable degree of continuity in the geographical locus of polite society within most towns in the study regions. In part, this reflected heavy investment in real estate, so that moves were often forced – as was the case in Liverpool – or relatively localised, as in Birmingham. But it also reflected the fact that concentrations of shops and leisure facilities quickly became self-reinforcing – a sort of spatial lock-in.

Important in this process was the growth of shopping as a leisure activity in its own right (see Chapter 6). By the early eighteenth century, shopping had become part of the social round: shops were visited to see what was new and what was fashionable. Walsh argues that the early shopping galleries of London were 'places for an outing, and spaces to meet friends', and much the same was true of fashionable shops in provincial England.[133] Moreover, these social practices spilled out onto the streets. In many towns, the principal shopping streets also became fashionable promenades (see Chapter 4). This meant that both shops and shopping streets were leisure spaces. Streets were rendered fashionable and polite promenades by the spatial practices of shoppers as they moved from shop to shop, inspecting goods, but also their fellow customers. Further, the quality, status and fashionability of streets, shops, goods and customers were intimately tied to one another. Politeness was, almost by definition, a quality that could be gained through association and interaction as well as through the innate qualities of the person or place. Thus, a polite clientele might define a shop as fashionable, but their own polite status could be developed through being seen in the right places, including fashionable shops. Wedgwood certainly recognised this, and indeed sought to maximise the aura of exclusivity surrounding his retail business by not issuing trade cards and choosing a prime location for his showrooms, noting that the wealthy shoppers whom he sought to attract 'will not mix with the rest of the World any further than their amusements or conveniencys make it necessary'.[134] Similarly, Messrs Flight, Barr and Barr, proprietors of the Worcester porcelain manufactory, sought to exploit royal patronage by establishing a warehouse on Haymarket 'at the court end of the metropolis', taking note of the advice proffered by the king himself during his visit to the works in 1788.[135] An air of exclusivity was, however, also apparent in many of the leading shops in provincial towns such as those which lined New Street in Birmingham, or Eastgate in Chester.

As consumer spaces, shops and shopping districts were defined by the type, range and quality of the goods they contained; they were produced through the behaviour of, and interaction between, shopkeeper and shopper. A shop became a shop because of the social practices of buying and selling which took place therein. Much the same was true of other leisure activities, since many took place in non-dedicated spaces. The appropriation of the quayside of St George's Dock, Liverpool, the churchyard of St Philip's in Birmingham or the sea wall at Parkgate by polite promenaders defined these spaces as promenades. They were not created as formal walks, but were characterised as such through their use. Equally, social practice could transform buildings such as St Mary's Hall, Coventry. It could be a theatre, 'whenever a company of sufficient merit and character required it for that purpose'; but was also a concert room, as in September 1760, when the oratorios 'Samson' and the 'Messiah' were performed before 'a numerous and brilliant audience of nobility and gentry', and even a formal dining hall, as in 1761 when it

84 *The town*

formed the venue for a lavish civic banquet to celebrate the coronation of George III.[136] In such circumstances, leisure spaces were defined by their use, and that definition lasted only as long as the use itself. Outside these periodic activities, St Mary's reverted to being a council room or an empty shell. Yet the significance of these practices went far beyond the moment of the event itself. Contemporary perceptions of the town were shaped by activity as well as space. Indeed, the spatial practices of polite leisure and shopping were central to the sociability and easy interaction which characterised Addisonian conceptualisations of politeness as quintessentially urban. They combined to make the town the prime location of polite society, linking, as they did, politeness and commerce.

Conclusion

Consumer spaces were socially produced; in turn, they served to shape attitudes and behaviour. This social-spatial dialectic lay at the heart of the economic and cultural renaissance of the eighteenth-century town. It also fed into the identity and image of towns: making (some of) them polite places as well as containers of polite spaces. In part, this politeness was constructed through, and judged in terms of, the assemblage of 'polite' infrastructure and fashionable shops. As such, it can be seen as a representation of space: conceived and codified by elite groups who shaped the town through selective investment in key infrastructure, through planning and regulations, and through the projection of carefully constructed images. These issues formed the focus of the first half of this chapter, and it is clear that contemporaries often viewed urban politeness in such terms. Indeed, Sweet argues that eighteenth-century travellers often had a clear set of criteria by which to judge the politeness of a town, usually based on comparison with London or Bath. They weighed each town according to the number of visitors it could attract, its physical appearance, the range of shops and social facilities (particularly coffee houses, libraries and schools), and the number of gentry or nobility residing nearby, although it was generally assumed that politeness would be steadily dissipated as one moved further from the capital.[137] On this basis Worcester could be deemed polite: its streets were 'broad, handsome, well built, and very well paved', with 'flag pavements for foot-passengers'; there was an absence of projecting signs, and a 'great concourse of polite strangers that come here to reside from every quarter'. By the same criteria, Liverpool was not: it 'presented to the eye little or nothing calculated to excite admiration or interest; nearly every house and [nearly] all the public buildings of a secular nature, were built of dingy brick'. Moreover, there was a lack of the scientific or cultural institutions that spoke of taste.[138]

However, politeness was also a product of the social practices of urban elites and middling sorts – they and their town were rendered polite through their behaviour, their mode of living. To an extent, this can be read from physical infrastructure, but two things complicate this simple equation. The first is that there was, as we have already argued, a range of interpretations of what comprised politeness. Shaftesbury argued that, to be truly polite, one needed the leisure and education of a gentleman; thus commerce and manufacturing, with their emphasis on hard work and the pursuit of wealth, could be dismissed as incompatible with a polite lifestyle. From this perspective the elites of towns such as Manchester, Liverpool and Birmingham appeared vulgar money-makers, devoting all their energies to profit and leaving little time for patronage of the arts, public conviviality or the pursuit of leisure. An alternative thesis of politeness – emerging in part from these commercial towns themselves, but drawing strongly on notions of civilisation as conceived by Hume and Smith – centred on civic pride and a developing infrastructure for individual improvement, built with the profits of commerce and industry. This provincial and commercial view of politeness celebrated the growing economic power of such towns, and the general civility and sociability of their leading citizens, which were both its underpinning and its consequence.[139] As Hutton argued, 'The prosperity of a town depends upon its commerce; as that increases knowledge, freedom, taste, luxury, power and civilization increase'.[140] The second complication is that, as with the town as a whole, urban space was rendered polite through social practices. This places great emphasis not just on how the town looked, or even how behaviour might be characterised (as polite or not), but the way in which individuals and groups produced space through their daily routines, and, conversely, how those spaces served to influence that behaviour. To understand more fully these complex relationships, we must explore the streets and buildings of eighteenth-century consumption in closer detail.

4 The street

Stage-set and performance

Introduction

Many towns contained areas where it was unwise for respectable people to go, but streets were effectively open to all.[1] They were spaces of commerce – the setting for markets, fairs and shops, as well as a growing range of commercial leisure infrastructure – and important arenas of public consumption, where people could access goods, knowledge and information. For Benjamin, the street – or more specifically the arcade – brought together all forms of commodity in a bewildering juxtapositioning of images and promises, from the uplifting to the sordid. To walk through these arcades was to pass through a series of real and imaginary encounters, prompted by goods stacked in shop windows and notices pasted to walls.[2] But streets were also social spaces, full of people and characterised by considerable social mixing between the polite and the plebeian, shopkeepers, customers and flâneurs: a place of encounters and relationships. They were, as Benjamin puts it, 'the dwelling place of the collective': they formed the principal arena for urban politics, where identities and power relationships could be negotiated, whether this was through mob violence, customary ritual or elite spectacle.[3]

As intensely public spaces, streets were 'front regions' where people acted out particular social roles.[4] They were carefully constructed stage-sets: representations of space wherein the symbolism of design and architecture were significant because of the meanings they could add to the self-conscious performances which they framed. Yet the street was also the setting for many other performances and practices, many of which were unknowing, repetitive and habitual.[5] Seen in this light, streets were lived spaces, the physical character and meaning of which were produced by the routines of individuals and groups of actors, but also by the social and cultural structures which framed and informed their daily routines. They were part of the 'sites and circuits … through which social life [was] produced and reproduced'.[6] For the polite consumer in the eighteenth century, walking the streets brought a wide range of social encounters with other 'respectable' citizens, but also with the 'vulgar' pastimes of the common people, with street crime and disorder, and with the traditional fairs and festivals which punctuated the urban calendar.[7] The street was a liminal space: a site of social mixing but also of contest, between commerce and leisure, conscious performance and intuitive action, polite and plebeian activities.

The production of the street as public space – a stage-set for polite, commercialised rituals and performances of consumption – had many different dimensions. In this chapter, we focus on three. We begin by referring back to notions of a redefined public sphere and consider environmental improvement, less as a vehicle for political reform, and more as a practical process of constructing a stage for public life and polite social intercourse. Building on this, we next explore the social and design imperatives which informed the construction of a setting appropriate for these performances. This focuses attention on the layout and architecture of the street and their semiotic meanings. Here, we emphasise the growing vision of the street as a unit, and the increasing importance of the façade, but also of perspective, and thus the privileging of visual readings of the built environment and other people. Finally, we turn to the performances themselves. We explore how, both conscious and subconscious, these helped to produce and reproduce the street as social space, and the ways in which different performances gave different, sometimes conflicting, meanings to the street.

Setting the stage: improvement and public space

Both Shaftesbury's and Hume's notions of politeness placed emphasis on the street as public space. For Shaftesbury, the 'noisy streets overrun with carriages' that characterised eighteenth-century London needed to be reorganised along classical lines in order to provide places for civilising public discourse. Less utopian in his outlook, Hume argued that the street had a central role in reconciling public and private interests, providing the stage for enlightened conversation.[8] Each of these conceptions emphasises the importance of the street as a setting for polite and especially male sociability. Whilst the street had always been a social space, Sennett argues that the eighteenth-century town was the subject of an explicitly 'modern' project: 'the first attempts at making streets fit for the special purpose of pedestrian strolling as a form of relaxation'.[9] The emphasis on seeing and being seen, which this implies, underlines the importance of visibility in making effective 'politeness' as a means of regulating and policing commercial conduct. Thus, the orderliness of the street became a matter of 'political authority, polite sociability [and] self-control'.[10] Order was required in the way streets looked, and in what they were used for.

Initially in larger towns, but increasingly in smaller places as well, there was growing regulation and improvement of urban space, in terms of both the area and aspects of urban infrastructure covered (see Chapter 2). Whilst pavers and scavengers were a feature of medieval and early modern urbanism, the eighteenth century saw a proliferation of activity. In Chester, for example, a paver was first appointed by the Corporation in 1584 and three scavengers in 1670, the latter being ordered to remove all 'dirt and ashes' at least twice a week. To judge from the city's Assembly Books, all were kept busy as their duties and areas of responsibility were expanded during the eighteenth century – a trend common to many substantial provincial towns.[11] However, the impact of such appointments and activity should not be over-emphasised. One late eighteenth-century observer noted that the piles of refuse in Liverpool often remained for eight to ten days so that 'passengers in a dark night, and often in the day, tread in them to the midleg, and children are sometimes nearly suffocated by falling into them'.[12] Moreover, the town's pavements were 'laid with small sharp pebbles that render walking in the town very disagreeable, particularly to ladies' – a complaint echoed in Birmingham and elsewhere.[13] Over time, standards improved and the process of environmental upgrading diffused down the urban hierarchy. In Warwick, for instance, subscribers raised £4,600 during 1811, allowing the main streets to be 'handsomely paved with Yorkshire flag stones'.[14] Yet it was well into the nineteenth century before most small towns felt any real benefit.

Lighting was also made an issue of improvement and of expanded urban governance in the early eighteenth century.[15] In Chester street lighting had traditionally been the responsibility of individual householders, but the Corporation petitioned Parliament in 1725 for powers to install lamps along the principal streets, rows and other public places of the town. Householders in Coventry were also required to hang a lantern outside their property until 1725, when the constables started purchasing and setting up lamps with money levied for the purpose.[16] The level of investment varied considerably: in Preston, the Corporation agreed to install just four lamps at strategic points in 1699, whilst Liverpool Corporation erected forty-five in 1718, and in 1738 offered to set up lamps outside the houses of any inhabitants who offered to light and maintain them.[17] By mid century, most respectable towns had some form of public oil lighting in the streets, although the results were sometimes limited. In Birmingham, for example, the commissioners had only erected a few lamps by the 1790s, a feeble effort that drew criticism from various commentators including William Hutton.[18] Notwithstanding such complaints, street lighting had a transformative effect, blurring boundaries between day- and night-time activities even in relatively small towns. Provision of such amenities facilitated the growing use of city streets after dark, for shopping, socialising and frequenting leisure facilities. In many larger towns, the effect of public street lighting was enhanced by the night-time illumination of shops. Describing an evening walk through the streets of London, William Hutton remarked that the 'innumerable multitude of lamps affords only a small quantity of light, compared to the shops. By these the whole city enjoys nocturnal illumination; the prospects are preserved, and mischiefs prevented'.[19] Lighting could also be a source of novelty and amusement in its own right. For Johannes Neiner, the streets of Vienna in 1721 offered a wondrous night-time spectacle: 'these beautiful night lights are laid out so prettily that if one looks down a straight lane … it is like seeing a splendid theatre or a most gracefully illuminated stage'. Indeed, the contrast between the lights of the town and the darkness of the countryside became itself a defining feature of urban life.[20]

Improvement of streets was not a one-off event: it required continued financial investment from civic authorities and formed a key point of contact in the dialogue between public and private interests. Throughout the eighteenth century, the re-occurring themes of Coventry's Constables Presentments were the removal of muck from the streets; the repairing of pavements in front of individuals' houses; and the hanging of lanterns outside them. As early as 1683 an alderman, upholsterer, mercer and others were presented for failing to hang out lanterns, and in the same year a clothier was brought before the court for 'his house built too far into the street being an encroachment'.[21] Later, newspapers were often enlisted to spread the message of improvement to the reading public. In December 1778 a notice was placed in *Piercy's Coventry Gazette* entitled 'Coventry Streets'. This stated that, following 'complaints to the commissioners, they have resolved … to enforce the late Act of Parliament'. It highlighted the problem of dumping ashes, rubbish and timber in the streets, and concluded that the commissioners would 'prosecute and punish in the most exemplary manner all lampbreakers, as enemies to all good order'.[22] This link between light and order is significant, suggesting that the importance of lamps was symbolic as well as practical. The growing concern with order was re-echoed across provincial England, although the precise focus of attention varied. In 1793 the *Blackburn Mail* thought it necessary to remind its readers 'not to throw pea and bean shells, or other offals of greens upon the foot pavements'. In a similar vein, a notice in *Gore's Liverpool Advertiser* in November 1770 called for an end to the practice of 'laying, setting or putting empty casks, timber, lumber, dunghills, heaps of rubbish, wagons, carts, carriages and other annoyances, in the public streets, highways and other places'.[23] Complaints such as these might reflect a deteriorating urban environment. Given the growth in population, trade and traffic in many towns, 'improvement' would be necessary merely to preserve the *status quo*. But complaints were also a product of the rising expectations of both town authorities and the public: by the late eighteenth century most were agreed that the streets should be kept accessible, clean, ordered and safe. They were to be rendered appropriate settings for polite sociability and consumption.

Improvement in the early eighteenth century was piecemeal and, almost of necessity, restricted to corporate towns. Others generally lacked the civic authority or finances to implement such changes. From the 1740s, however, the establishment of Improvement Commissions both formalised and diffused the process of environmental improvement, offering an effective mechanism for raising money and implementing improvement schemes. The 1777 Act for Wolverhampton allowed the imposition of penalties for those depositing rubbish or washing brass in the street. It also gave the Commissioners powers to improve the marketplace by clearing away the old market hall and shambles, and to widen 'several streets, lanes, alleyways and other public passages'.[24] This spirit of rationalising improvement could be found even in relatively small towns. Burton-on-Trent, Dudley and Stourbridge all acquired Improvement Acts well before 1800, and during the first two decades of the nineteenth century commissions were also established in places such as Blackburn, Burnley and Kidderminster. The commissioners addressed familiar concerns. Those in Dudley appointed a scavenger and prohibited the use of footways for such diverse activities as wheeling barrows, rolling casks, slaughtering animals, hewing stones or repairing wagons. Shopkeepers were also required to remove bulk windows that obstructed free passage along the footways.[25] This concern for the free flow of traffic had long exercised urban authorities. It was heightened by the growing volume of vehicles and pedestrians that accompanied commercial and demographic growth. Yet it also linked in with the desire on the part of corporations, landowners and many citizens to reconceptualise the street and the town as ordered and civilised spaces. Attempts had long been made to improve streets in this way, but they were often frustrated by the necessity for piecemeal improvement due to different land ownership and the ossified pattern of medieval streets and lanes. In late seventeenth-century Liverpool, Sir Edward Moore was hindered in his plans for Fenwick Street. He wrote that: 'if it had not been for this piece of land, I had made Fenwick Street as straight as any street in town. But this being none of my land, I was forced to wind the street in that place'.[26]

Fires sometimes allowed a fresh start, and in Warwick, the rebuilding Act made provision for road widening. Two of the main routes through the town, Church Street and Sheep Street (later Northgate Street), were to be widened in the vicinity of the churchyard, as were several lanes leading from the marketplace. All this, the Act suggested, would contribute towards 'the common Convenience and Safety of the said Borough'.[27] Equally, a determined corporation could force through improvements, as in Preston, where Fishergate Lane was widened in 1713 with the help of an Act of Parliament.[28] More commonly, however, such schemes required the wider and revenue-raising powers of an Improvement Commission whose impact could be considerable. In Liverpool, Commissioners oversaw the widening of Castle Street and Dale Street, and thus created a broad and straight route between the town hall and the customs house by the old dock.[29] This transformed the appearance of the main business conduits of the town, replacing streets that were 'confined and ill built', and 'so narrow in some parts that it was with difficulty that two carriages could pass at the same time', with broad thoroughfares providing clear passage and unimpeded views of the two key sites of Liverpool's commercial success.[30] That these were also the principal shopping streets of the town (see Chapter 3) served to underline the importance and impact of this scheme. Such streets were the public face of Liverpool and the image of rational modernity projected by their conspicuous improvement epitomised the forward-looking commercial ethos of the town. Similarly, in Coventry, repeated attempts were made to widen the thoroughfares and bring order to the medieval street plan. At the beginning of the nineteenth century, a town guide noted the impact on the town's shopping streets, observing that:

> Coventry has not been wanting in efforts to remove the most prominent inconveniences of its streets, and much has been done to that purpose, by the Commissioners under the Street Act, by individual public spirit, and lastly, by the aid of a toll, granted in 1812; which has already been the means of producing a new street [Hertford Street] forming a commodious entry to the City from Warwick; a widening and enlargement of the entrance of Much Park Street, in the London Road; and an entire removal of the houses forming the Western side of Broadgate; at once enlarging the marketplace and avoiding a much frequented, narrow and dangerous passage.[31]

Improvement Commissions strove to assert control over urban space, aligning the street with the norms and aspirations of polite society and rendering it a suitable stage for refined activities. This reconceptualisation of the street also involved sharpening the distinction between different uses of street space and, ultimately, defining those parts of the street network which were suitable for different uses. Some spaces were residential; others were for polite sociability and consumption; others were for commerce. Whilst this separation was never complete, the eighteenth-century town was increasingly marked by a rationalisation of the use of space. The process is perhaps most clearly seen, and was certainly vigorously pursued, in the reorganisation of markets within, and often their removal from, the street.[32] In Chester, there were markets for fish, meat, vegetables and corn on Northgate Street; fowl, butter and cheese on Eastgate Street; coal on Bridge Street; and livestock on Further Northgate Street. During the fairs, stalls spread out along all these streets and the rows above them. From the 1770s there were attempts to move elements of the fairs off the principal streets and into trading halls.[33] Similarly, after at least one unsuccessful petition, the residents of Further Northgate Street managed to get the livestock market moved to Gorse Stacks, outside the city walls, whilst the 'frequent complaints of public-spirited and respectable citizens' convinced the Corporation to build a market hall on Northgate Street (1829) to house all the street traders.[34] The rhetoric here is as revealing as the process. Long established market customs and practices once deemed acceptable were now attacked as distasteful, vulgar or contrary to the public interest, reflecting the growing culture of politeness amongst the middling ranks of urban society. Just as bull-baiting was condemned as barbaric and football discouraged as an 'annoyance and personal danger of the public', so the street market was attacked because

> the too often filthy and unsightly appearance of the stands themselves, and the idle, the rude, and the dissipated loungers that collect in a market street, all tend to produce an uncivilised state of society … [that is] repulsive to persons of taste and refinement.[35]

A similar attitude seems to have prevailed when it came to butchers who were increasingly seen as inappropriate tradesmen to be operating on the main fashionable shopping streets. Chester's Corporation was active from the mid-eighteenth century, corralling market tradesmen into shambles on Northgate Street, and squeezing shopkeeping butchers from their premises on Eastgate Street.[36]

Through such processes, the street was re-imagined and reoriented as polite as well as commercial: a suitable venue for promenading and browsing by the middling sorts. But the degree of 'success' was far from certain and some well-intended plans never came to fruition. In Coventry, for example, attempts were made from the early eighteenth century onwards to alleviate over-crowding in and conflicting uses of the street by moving the markets. In 1719 the 'women's marketplace' was moved from Great Butcher Row to Peacock Inn Yard off Cross

92 *The street*

Cheaping, where a market house was erected. However, a century later, the town's market committee was still confronted with disputes between shopkeepers and market traders, the remaining markets in Cross Cheaping and Broadgate being seen as detrimental to the image and use of these as polite shopping streets.[37] Thus, whilst unity, integration and order were the principles informing change to urban spaces, behind these conceptions, spatial practices presented a force for the making of spaces of representation – a point explored in more detail below.

The paving, cleansing and widening of streets created a stage on which the performances of urban life could unfold. Like the twentieth-century shopping malls discussed by Shields, Jackson, and Goss, the principal streets were divested of some of the traditional functions, associations and symbolism of shared public space. Attempts to clear vulgar and disorderly activities, from vagrancy to bull-baiting to street markets, aimed to make the street more civilised – a fitting space for polite commerce and consumption. Yet, as a conceived and constructed space of representation, the street still required an appropriate backdrop, befitting a modern urban place: one which would enhance and add meaning to the actions of polite consumers.

Building the set: architectural improvements

Central to many of the improvements made to the street was its reconceptualisation as a holistic architectural unit. The street was conceived less as a succession of plots and buildings, and more as a unitary space, drawn together by the design and layout of the thoroughfare and the buildings with which it was lined. Within this re-imagining and redesign of the streetscape, four features are of particular significance: the residential square, the terrace, the grouping of buildings (partly through the creation of new perspectives along the street), and classical architecture.[38]

Residential squares, along classical or continental lines, often formed the centrepiece of plans for extending eighteenth-century towns. Following the late seventeenth-century expansion of London's West End, squares became fashionable architectural and residential features. Indeed, Borsay traces a direct link between the construction of a square in Warwick and Lord Brooke's experiences of London's changing streetscape.[39] Warwick's square marked the social prestige of both the town and its patron. Yet it was modest in scale (just 14,000 square feet) and was compromised by the intrusion of the rebuilt St Mary's tower on the east side. Moreover, it lacked the coherent and unified building lines seen in London and in later provincial squares: a problem exacerbated by the fact that significant portions of three sides were taken up by access streets.[40] This was a problem to which John Wood was very much alive. He wrote that:

> I preferred an enclosed square to an open one, to make this as useful as possible: For the intention of a Square in a City is for People to assemble together; and the Spot wherein they meet, ought to be separated from the Ground common to Men and Beasts, and even to Mankind in General, if

Decency and good Order are necessary to be observed in such Places of Assembly.[41]

For Wood, then, the square was a microcosm of polite public space. It was designed to look like the courtyard of a palace, thus appealing to the status-seeking side of politeness, but was also intended to provide a forum in which polite society could come together, socialising with one another, yet removed from the common order. It was to be a stage-set for polite public performance.

This dual function was repeated in the squares that appeared across the west Midlands and north-west England from the early 1700s. In Liverpool, a series of new squares was built from the 1720s. These were conceived at an increasingly grand scale: the largest, Cleveland Square, had a tree-lined walk along each side and a fountain in its centre, supplied with piped water from a nearby spring.[42] All were occupied, at least initially, by the town's professional and mercantile elite: Cleveland Square counted eight merchants, nine sea captains and a schoolmaster amongst its residents in 1766, whilst Clayton Square remained a secluded and select residential quarter well into the nineteenth century. Following the London fashion it was centred on the house of the lessee and developer, Mrs Clayton. Through the use of regulatory clauses she ensured houses fronting the square adopted a uniform façade. Care was also taken to safeguard the quality of the interior space by prohibiting activities likely to cause a nuisance and obliging residents to keep the streets clean and properly lighted.[43] A similar approach was taken in Birmingham where restrictive leases on buildings around the Square stipulated that 'no building for a butcher, or a baker, or a smith should be erected'. Laid out with a lawned garden, trees and gravelled walks, it was largely inhabited by prosperous merchants – ironmongers taking nine of the sixteen houses.[44] Such exclusivity was sought in county towns as well as growing commercial centres. Abbey Square in Chester was developed in the 1750s to provide housing for the prebendaries and other members of the cathedral establishment, and by the early nineteenth century housed a range of clergy, professionals and annuitants. In Lichfield, the cathedral close operated in much the same way. It was dominated by the clergy and other members of the town's established elite: 'cultural arrivistes such as Michael Johnson, who still had to make a living, lived by the marketplace'.[45] The exclusive nature of these developments gave them extra kudos and meaning as social spaces. Just as John Wood argued they should, residential squares offered prestige and some degree of seclusion from the common order. They provided both the stage-set for polite performance and an audience appropriate to the unfolding scenes of sociability. Thus, the *de facto* square comprising the churchyard of St Philip's, Birmingham, was 'ornamented with walks in great perfection; shaded with trees in double and treble ranks; and surrounded with buildings in elegant taste'. The stage was set and the audience provided, *inter alia*, by the wealthy residents of Temple Row and Colmore Row.[46]

Squares also epitomised the tension between inclusivity and exclusivity inherent in polite sociability. The physical limits of the square often defined membership of the elite. Where those boundaries were breached, and social distancing was undermined, polite residents moved elsewhere and the square became the setting for very different social practices. This is most famously seen in London's Covent Garden, but is also apparent in Cleveland Square in Liverpool and St James's Square in Wolverhampton. The former was first crowded by the permanent erection of shambles for the twice-weekly markets and was slowly abandoned to shops and taverns. The latter was quickly engulfed by industrial and commercial development associated with the nearby canal basin. The failure of both squares to maintain their polite identity reflected the ongoing conflict between polite and commercial uses and conceptions of space.[47] Commerce provided the wealth that enabled a growing section of the urban population to aspire to a respectable lifestyle, yet the everyday activities of manufacturing and trade undermined the genteel environment that this group sought to create. Not that commercial interests always prevailed. As late as 1847, the wealthy residents of Stanley Place in Chester successfully resisted the construction of a locomotive works on corporation land immediately to the west of the walls and scarcely a stone's throw from their houses.[48]

Whilst the longer term fate of residential squares was variable, they were conceived as being spatially and socially homogeneous. These twin ambitions were realised through the employment of restrictive leases, which governed the use of buildings, the upkeep of the urban environment and building styles – the aim of the last of these being to impose a uniform façade on all houses lining the square.[49] The physical and aesthetic linking of buildings in this way was seen more widely in eighteenth-century towns through the construction of terraces of houses. These were not a new feature of urban design, but the fragmented nature of property ownership restricted their development before the renewed growth of towns in the eighteenth century.[50] They diffused rapidly through the urban hierarchy so that by the early nineteenth century, there were terraces of elegant houses in most provincial towns, offering the lustre of fashionable design to places such as Nantwich, Stratford-upon-Avon, Bolton and Walsall. The regularity of the terrace was often lauded in town histories, the virtues of a uniform street architecture being contrasted with scathing criticisms of any deviation from this model.[51] This classical vision of the street and the wider town emphasised the public, rather than private, significance of development. Whereas houses had previously been built to individual taste and convenience, such impulses were now to be subordinated to the aesthetic and practical requirements of the wider community. In 1769, Chester Corporation, concerned that the houses on Paradise Row should be of a uniform appearance, stipulated standards of design and materials. The result was such that they were still praised as being amongst the most pleasant houses in the town some sixty years later.[52] This quality was reflected in the status of the street's inhabitants. Despite its location close to the wharfs and riverside industries, Paradise Row housed a cross-section of the provincial middling sorts, including an architect, a merchant, an engineer and a gentleman. Other terraces were more homogeneous. Birmingham's Temple Row was 'inhabited by people of fortune, who are great wholesale dealers in the manufactures of this town'. On Nicholas Street in Chester, a terrace of three-storey houses, built in 1781, was rapidly adopted by the professional classes: its nickname of 'Pill-box Promenade' is revealing of both the occupation and habits of its residents.[53]

Terraces drew together the street socially, spatially and visually. They were part of the wider project for redesigning public space which sought to unite the streetscape through the re-alignment and re-building of streets, and, in so doing, create appropriate perspectives from which to view the townscape, its surroundings and its inhabitants. In some instances, this meant opening up vistas of the countryside beyond the town, as at Bridge Street, Worcester: 'an entire new street of forty feet width, letting in a beautiful view of the Malvern hills'. More often, it involved creating new lines of vision within the town itself. Such was the effect of the improvements made to Castle Street in Liverpool, which opened up perspectives to the town hall and St George's church. The new west side of Castle Street was lined by brick and stucco terraces, designed by William Turner, who also made designs for the ornamentation of the town hall. The street was thus recreated as a single unit. At a more modest scale, the lord of the manor at Henley-in-Arden gave a house and garden in the centre of the town to the high bailiff on the understanding that the site would be 'laid wast and open to the street, for the better ornament of the said town'.[54]

In many instances, public buildings formed the focus of the view and of urban design more generally. They rarely stood alone and often drew on neighbouring buildings to help transmit their splendour. Thus, the most fashionable assembly rooms in Birmingham, at the Royal Hotel, stood at the top of Colmore Row overlooking St Philip's churchyard.[55] Public buildings also offered a focus for development, with churches being placed either within or along one side of squares. From such foci radiated out the most prestigious streets of the town, often the fashionable shopping areas which drew on and contributed to the grandeur and spectacle of the urban stage (see Chapter 3). In this way, public buildings were the equivalent of anchor stores in modern malls: socio-spatial nodes, focusing pedestrian movement and shaping the identity of the street. They formed landmarks in mental landscapes, and were used as points by which to navigate the city, not just as signposts but also reference points that could carry status.[56] It is no surprise that shopkeepers frequently described their location through reference to these buildings, familiar to all town dwellers and easily found by newcomers. For instance, the Worcester stationer, Elias Andrews, noted that his 'Reading Library' was to be found 'opposite the Town Hall in the High Street'. Similarly, the Liverpool hatter, hosier and laceman, William Farrington, described his newly opened premises as being 'near the Exchange', whilst Susannah Phillips advertised that she had moved to better premises 'opposite the New Shambles'.[57] Some town descriptions also used the literary device of a tour round the city streets, with various circuits focused on a prominent public building (see below).[58] This type of imagery acted to reinforce the centrality of such buildings in the minds of the inhabitants and visitors alike.

The arrangement of buildings along the street was important in creating a setting appropriate for performances of polite sociability and consumption. So too was their individual and collective appearance.[59] This was achieved through the use of classical architectural styles, which conveyed meanings of civilisation and democracy, but also order, harmony and modernity. Such ideals were propagated through a growing number of printed manuals and treatises which placed emphasis on a flush façade; the rigorous pursuit of proportion and symmetry; the employment of classical ornamentation; and the use of new and standardised building materials such as brick, ashlar stone, tile and slate. It was further strengthened by the emphasis placed on the façade as a means of modernising, beautifying and unifying the street. The classical model was adopted across the country, albeit with local variations and interpretations, and a gradual evolution from baroque to palladian.[60] Developments in Chester were fairly typical. Initially, it was individual houses that were built in the classical style, one of the earliest being the stuccoed five-bay mansion built in *c.*1676 for Lady Mary Calveley on Lower Bridge Street. By the early 1700s, whole streets were lined with brick houses (often older properties that had been refronted), notably Castle Street and White Friars. Only in the 1750s, though, were terraces being erected, initially around Abbey Square, subsequently along King Street, along the north side of Pepper Street and on Newgate Street, and later on Nicholas Street, Abbey Green and elsewhere.[61]

The growing emphasis on classical uniformity can be seen in the post-fire reconstruction of Warwick.[62] The Act made provisions for the 'more regular and uniform rebuilding [of] the houses demolished by the fire', stipulating that they should be two storeys of ten feet each, with garrets and cellars. Projections from the façade, most especially jettied upper storeys which were anathema to the sought-after uniformity, were severely restricted. Stone, brick, slate, tile and lead were to be used instead of timber, wattle and daub, and thatch, and vernacular types of ornamentation were replaced by cornices, pilasters and capitals. A uniform roof line was introduced and a single row of small dormer windows prescribed. These standards were vigorously enforced: one citizen was forced to remove a double row of dormers and an order was issued that nobody should 'build contrary to the schem' and that they 'put up one row of luthern [*sic*] lights and noe more in the fore front of their houses'.[63] In a similar fashion, Sir Edward Moore tried to establish a common house design for each road laid out as he developed his estate in Liverpool. Without the statutory power of a parliamentary act, he was sometimes thwarted, complaining of one builder that he 'should have built two dormer windows as others did: but when he had got me fast and he was loose, he would build none, but made the house like a barn, much to the disparagement of the street'.[64] Significantly, it is both the loss of uniformity and the unfashionable and bucolic appearance of the building that aggrieved Moore. Despite these setbacks, he was, in general, successful in producing a fashionable urban landscape in Liverpool. Fiennes' comment, that 'the houses [are] of brick and stone built high and even … the streetes are faire and long, its London in miniature as much as ever I saw any thing', was echoed two decades later by Defoe.[65] Later in the century, the Corporation continued to strive for uniformity of appearance. In June 1770, a notice appeared in *Gore's Liverpool Advertiser* addressed to those laying out building plots in the town. It noted that no lease would be granted or renewed unless plans were first laid before the Corporation for scrutiny. Main streets were to be no less than fourteen yards in breadth, and cross streets at least twelve yards across; building materials were specified and projecting signs and bulks prohibited.[66]

It was not only in newly built streets that the ambition for fashionable and modern buildings was realised. The civic authorities, Improvement Commissions and citizens of many historic towns also sought to improve the appearance of their main streets. Shopkeepers were especially active in this context: many improved the façade of their premises, recognising its importance in projecting a positive image for the business.[67] This was fundamental to the development of retailing in this period and enhanced the benefits of street improvements. Thus, most of the timber-framed buildings of the High Street and Broad Street in Worcester were refaced in brick by the late eighteenth century, creating a streetscape that was felt worthy of comparison with Cheapside in London.[68] In Chester, the eighteenth century saw a process of almost continual reconstruction and refacing of the old half-timber buildings with more modern brick and plaster, along with fashionable sash or casement windows.[69] The Assembly Books are littered with petitions from traders wishing to extend the ground floor of their premises to produce a flat frontage. Many suggested that the desired extension was 'to align his shop with the row above'; others even suggested that it would 'contribute to the uniformity of the street'.[70] The rows themselves were also subject to improvement. As individual buildings were taken down and reconstructed, the ceilings were raised and floors were repaired or re-laid. The wooden pillars and banisters were either ornamented with carving (common on Watergate Street) or replaced with stone columns and iron railings (especially along Eastgate and Bridge Street).[71] Such improvements were not universal, of course: lanes and alleys were still lined by buildings 'generally of the meanest description' and even along main streets, the impact could be uneven. The north side of Eastgate Street remained largely unimproved, whilst Brown's shop on the fashionable south side of the same street was described as 'a splendid mansion, flanked by two mud-wall cow houses'.[72]

Despite such variability, architectural improvements undoubtedly enhanced the quality of the main shopping streets. The shop, theatre or assembly room were not autonomous islands, but were set within a street increasingly bound by regulation, designed to produce a unified setting appropriate to respectable and elegant lifestyles. William West acknowledged this in his description of Colmore Row in Birmingham, noting that 'the style of architecture, and the light and airy mode of fronting the houses, together with the elegance of the shops, has rendered this quarter of the town very attractive'.[73] Buildings and streets were thus harmonised. They increasingly presented a unified and coherent space, the whole being critical in creating attractive environments for polite social activities. Moreover, much as Benjamin notes of the nineteenth-century city, the street was an intensely visual space.[74] Those walking along the principal thoroughfares of even quite modest provincial towns were bombarded with visual messages: the symbolism of the neo-classical architecture, with its overtones of polite fashionability and progress;

the shop window, in which could be glimpsed the world of goods; the theatre playbill, telling of the latest dramatic offerings; and, of course, fellow pedestrians, fashionably dressed and exhibiting polite behaviour. It is these experiences of being in the street, engaging in the social practices of leisure and consumption, which form the focus of the next section. We consider how they were structured by and drew meaning from the street, and how they helped to produce the street as a space of consumption.

Performance: sociability and consumption

We have argued above that the improved urban street formed a preconceived stage-set on which polite performances were acted out. Panelli defines performance as the way in which everyday life, social differences, identity and power are enacted through practices which draw on both social meanings and the spaces in which they take place.[75] Building on this, we can see that an individual's status as polite or leisured or a consumer was produced through their activity as such: that is, their movement through and performance in (public) space. As Glennie and Thrift argue, performance was central in judging the politeness of others. It therefore has many possibilities and provides the means of understanding space as lived: as 'an order of concrete spatial and temporal ... relations that is not only imbued with cultural meanings but also serves to direct ... cultural activities'.[76] The coming together of technology and social organisation in the built form of the town creates sites that focus specified needs, desires, habits and practices in order to reproduce them. The consumer spaces of the town – the mall, department store, arcade or shopping street – exerted a gravitational pull of social necessity which brought audiences together and structured the performance. At the same time, the performers shaped these spaces, making them places where everyday practices of pleasure were legitimised, celebrated and intensified.[77]

Yet there is a tension within the idea of performance. Goffman saw the individual – the performer – as active and conscious. Indeed, for him, 'the self [is] a performed character'. Social interaction is thus an engagement between individuals and audiences, and performances are preconceived, scripted and carefully staged.[78] As Rappaport suggests, consumers were active agents in shaping their own identity, through their performances and the spaces which they occupied and drew upon. In contrast, Butler and others have argued that 'identities are in some sense constructed in and through social action'. Self is seen as being constituted through repeated behaviour and is conditional upon that behaviour, and consumer practices are viewed as habitual and intuitive, rather than strategic and knowing.[79] Applying these different readings to polite consumption, promenading and window-shopping might be seen, in part, as self-conscious and scripted performances, staged on a carefully designed set and undertaken for the mutual audience on the street. Nonetheless, leisure and shopping practices were also routinised: consumers followed a set of normative actions learned from repeated use. Whilst shoppers did not set out to produce spaces of polite consumption, the aggregation of their individual actions effectively produced them as lived space.

The spatial practice of shopping, then, had different manifestations as a leisure activity and a polite performance.

Given these different interpretive frameworks, we should be wary of simple readings of the practices of consumption as they took place in the street. We have already seen that the street served many different, often contradictory functions. It is unsurprising, then, that the performances that took place, and the identities and social relations that built on and into these, were themselves varied and contradictory. Indeed, there was conflict in and over the use of the street as public space. This was linked, in part, to the issue of who constituted the 'public', and what the 'public interest' might be. By designating separate spheres for different activities, the rationalising rhetoric of civility and politeness sought to exclude certain performers and performances from polite street space. As we have already seen, the level of success in achieving such goals was varied and continues to be debated: there was often some distance between rhetoric and reality.[80] Nonetheless, the ambition was apparent.

In this section, we explore these ideas through a series of performances which varied both in the level to which they were 'scripted' and conscious, and in the ways in which they produced and were produced by the streetscape. We begin with those most carefully constructed and encoded with symbolism and move through to others with more flexibility and spontaneity. In doing this, we recognise that the latter were also shaped by social convention and assumed roles, and that the former retained a strong element of individual freedom of action. Indeed, we explore these internal contradictions and the ways in which these various performances could be disrupted by other perceptions of and activities in the street. At the same time, the typology is useful in highlighting the varied relationship between stage and performance, space and society. We argue that the more closely scripted ceremonies drew on established conceptions of urban space: the street being consciously seen and used as an elaborate stage-set. Conversely, through processes like shopping, the street was produced as a space of consumption through the spatial practices of shoppers and shopkeepers.

Carefully orchestrated processions and spatial expressions of social status formed an essential element of civic ceremonies such as the Preston Guild Merchant. The procession that marked the opening of the Guild in 1682 began at the house of the Mayor. Accompanied by a small body of attendants, he walked to the Guild Hall, where the twelve aldermen, common councilmen, and gentlemen from the town and county were waiting in their robes and gowns. The Mayor and his retinue, ordered according to rank and office, then proceeded to the High Cross in the marketplace, where they were joined by all the Companies of Trade and the soldiers stationed in the town. The assembled body then processed to the parish church with the Companies in the lead. They too were arranged in order of seniority, headed by the Company of Smiths, then the Cutlers and Saddlers. After a short sermon the procession made its way to each of the gates of the town, where a speech was given and a toast of ale offered, before returning to the marketplace. Here all the Companies, soldiers and Mayor's escort stood 'in good order surrounding the High Crosse' and listened to a speech from the school master. Finally the Mayor, aldermen and their retinue of gentlemen and merchants processed to the Guildhall for a feast, whilst the Companies dispersed to their respective Halls for similar festivities.[81] In this heavily ritualised ceremony, the ordering of the procession and the route that it followed were both highly significant. Indeed, one of the most prominent corporate officials during the Guild procession was the 'Master of Ceremonies', whose job it was to ensure that Companies, gentry and aldermen lined up in the correct order for the procession, and later, during the feast, 'to attend, conduct and see placed, the Gentry according to their due procedency at Table'.[82] The precedence given to the Mayor and Corporation, and their movement through the town as a single body, emphasised their secular authority. So too did the wearing of civic regalia, which linked each man to his office and established the corporate hierarchy: aldermen in their brown fur robes, councilmen in gowns. The prominent position in the procession reserved for the local nobility and gentry, and their inclusion in both the church sermon and feast symbolised the close relationship between town and county elites.[83] Equally, the growing presence of merchants and manufacturers amongst this elite illustrated the importance of commerce and industry to the town; whilst the movement of the procession between civic and religious buildings, and to each of the town's gates, underlined topographically the bases of corporate power and defined its spatial limits.

Such rituals had all the characteristics of Goffmanesque performance: this was 'front-region' behaviour in a range of public arenas. The sequencing of people and events, the routes followed by the processions, and the spaces occupied by the key moments of the events were carefully chosen and managed to heighten their symbolic effect.[84] In this light, we can view the street as a space conceived and produced as a setting for elaborate social practices of consumption, but it also became a space that was consumed through the unfolding events. As Goffman argued, the performance affected all those involved, whatever their station, whether as performers or audience.[85] It would be easy to view these events as unproblematic public rituals through which the elite cemented their position in the urban social order and stamped their authority on the streets and public spaces of the town. Yet there was considerable conflict over the meanings that these processions held for their various participants, and for the other townspeople who stood and watched the spectacle. Borsay argues that, during the eighteenth century, a 'powerful undercurrent of cultural alienation' increasingly drew polite society away from participation in such traditional social rituals. Growing contempt for customary practices was, for instance, largely responsible for the end of the Midsummer Show at Chester in 1678, and the Rogation Week processions at Walsall around 1765. The withdrawal of upper social groups from some practices led to their evolution into a genuinely popular culture, whilst other events became more narrowly identified with the governing elite.[86] Festivities such as the Preston Guild found themselves increasingly divided into polite and plebeian activities as the cohesive powers of traditional civic ritual declined. For instance, at the 1782 Guild oratorios, masquerades, assemblies and races provided diversions for the polite consumer, whilst the traditional processions played a less prominent role and were aimed primarily at the plebeian spectator. Yet even here the distancing of mostly polite participants from plebeian spectators is clear to see. During the ladies' procession in 1762 'the companies of trade were drawn up in lines, on each side, to prevent the ladies from being interrupted, or incommoded by the numerous crowd of spectators'.[87] This polarisation of polite and popular culture represented a transformation of the spatial and temporal context of ritual and ceremony, which will be explored more fully in the sections that follow.

Other forms of public performance were less elaborately staged, but still formed conscious and carefully choreographed rituals of polite urban living. One of the most obvious examples of this was promenading. Here, both the act and the space within which it took place were prescribed with some care to project the polite identity assumed by the performer. Etiquette books outlined the purpose and meaning of promenading, and the behaviour which it demanded from the promenader. Writers such as Adam Petrie focused on the relationship between pedestrians, recommending that a gentleman should allow social superiors, women and the infirm either to walk on the right, or be given the safety of walking nearest to the wall away from the dirt of the street. It was also rude to stare too directly at other people or to peer closely through the windows of private houses, although shops generally welcomed such interest. The Oxford dancing-master Matthew Towle advised against 'walking on the heel or toe of the foot, taking too short or long steps, or swinging the arms'.[88] Departure from these social mores could provoke censure. It was in this vein that Elizabeth Montagu wrote that: 'the misses waddle and straddle and strut and swagger about the streets here, one arm akimbo, the other swinging'.[89]

There were, of course, specialist spaces for promenading: gardens, walks and parades were found in towns across the country (see Chapter 2). Yet many streets were also conceived of and used as informal promenades – a function that at once built on and fed into their environmental and architectural improvement. The paving, cleansing and ornamentation of these thoroughfares rendered them ideal as fashionable leisure spaces regardless of whether purpose-built promenades were available elsewhere in the town. Borsay noted that high-class residential streets acted as a 'series of pseudo-promenades in which the company could exercise themselves, without running the risk … of dirtying their clothes and shoes [or] offending their noses'.[90] Yet it was shopping streets that perhaps offered most to the polite promenader, not least because they provided a mutual audience, essential to Goffman's reading of performance as the projection of a particular 'public' self. In Birmingham, New Street – the best shopping street in town – afforded 'an agreeable promenade', as did Foregate Street in Worcester. The eponymous Parade in Leamington Spa, lined with 'fine buildings' and 'shops of every description', formed 'a favourite promenade for visitors' despite the presence of numerous other walks and rides in the vicinity. Similarly, in Chester, the rows were a 'quiet lounge to ladies and others engaged in shopping'.[91] They formed, in effect, the ultimate promenade: the well-to-do could parade along them, quite literally raised above the common order.

The street was rendered polite not just through its physical improvement, but also through the presence and spatial practices of promenaders and shoppers, residents and shopkeepers. The spatiality of street promenading was quite clear: some streets were appropriate; others were not. In Chester, it was the rows on the south side of Eastgate Street and the east side of Bridge Street, lined with high-class shops, which were the fashionable routes. Those on the opposite sides of these streets and on Watergate Street were much less frequented. The particular geography of such promenading was linked to its self-conscious nature. The object was to see and be seen, to engage in polite sociability, and perhaps to do a little window-shopping along the way (see Chapter 6). These intentions depended upon a clean and safe environment, a decent surface underfoot, some good shops to browse and an audience. Promenading was a conscious performance, played for spectators on a particular stage – polite identity was projected (and reinforced) through the activity and the spaces in which it took place. Yet both space and identity were fragile. The delicate balance of manners and mutual respect that characterised promenading on the streets or walks could easily be tipped by overly ostentatious behaviour or the (private) rebuke that it might provoke. The opportunities for both were perhaps greatest in London and the resorts. Thus, Mrs M. Sneyd wrote from Bath that:

> the Duchess of K- is come up again and exhibits herself on the Parade sometimes; has Chairs brought out, and sitts down to be view'd by the populace; and has her French Horns playing before her; a very pretty imitation of a Country Fair.[92]

The Duchess, it seems, had stepped over the bounds of politeness and, in the eyes of some, at least, was seen as faintly ridiculous. Moreover, the comparison with the country fair stripped her of the urbanity and civility of her station and setting. Promenaders, especially men, had also to avoid affectation, a show of external refinement devoid of inner civility, since this challenged the supposed morality of polite conduct.[93]

Alongside the ritualised and self-aware practices of promenading was a range of more loosely guided performances that characterised polite use of urban streets. Some of these were provided through guide books. The most famous of these, John Gay's *Trivia: or the Art of Walking the Streets of London*, formed a general introduction to the social mores of street life. As Corfield argues: 'there were constantly new sights to be seen, strangers to be evaluated, judgments to be made, routes to be navigated, addresses to be found, footsteps to be placed'.[94] Yet guides such as Gay's also aimed at providing readers with a handbook to the city that said where to go, what might be encountered, and even what should be made of the buildings, streets and city. Ramblers should always conduct themselves with decorum and assured bodily control, walking neither too fast or slow, too stiff or slovenly. Indeed, Gay censures the Frenchified fop for treading too daintily, and for avoiding the curb in order to protect his clothes from dirt and so contravening the polite practice of 'giving the wall' to women and male superiors.[95] This genre of writing was most common in London, where urban life was at its most confusing and fascinating, especially for newcomers. More widespread in provincial England were volumes offering detailed itineraries for walks through the town. Here, the aim was to showcase the attractions of a particular place, rather than instructing the rambler on the etiquette of walking its streets. The guides provided detailed routes which took the walker through the improved streets of the town, calling at the most important locations, including civic and ecclesiastical buildings, leisure facilities, charitable institutions and, significantly, shops.

Two examples serve to illustrate the main thrust of these guided performances. William West's *History of Warwickshire* takes the reader on a tour of Birmingham and its environs, tracing out six circuits of the town, each centred on the Royal Hotel at the top of Colmore Row. This iconic building, housing the main concert and assembly rooms, is described as lying on 'the meridian line of Birmingham'; at the social and cultural heart of the town.[96] From here, each circuit forms a carefully guided tour which reinforces West's central message of Birmingham as a town whose prosperity and status is built on the industry and commerce of its inhabitants. The tours steer the reader around the main streets. Along the way, he highlights all that is worth noting in a commercial town: public buildings, places of worship and leisure facilities, but also shops, banking houses and manufactories. Each description is framed by a rhetoric of modernisation which emphasises the dynamism and respectability of the town. Much of this is centred on a close inspection of the streetscape. West focuses on architectural detail and on the relative positioning of buildings, drawing attention to the aesthetic qualities of particular façades. The New Library in Temple Row, for instance, is described as 'somewhat obscured' and its exterior as 'neat, plain and unassuming'. Much attention is given to New Street, with its 'well stocked shops, in articles of taste, of luxury, and of general consumption'.[97] Whether taken as a virtual tour or a practical guide, West's description entices the reader along the main streets and into each shop to marvel at the richness of the setting and the goods on display. It therefore provides a framework both for the performance of walking the street and for the production of the street as a space of consumption.

Much the same is true of Bentley's *History and Guide to Dudley, Dudley Castle, and the Castle Hill*, although this appears to have been aimed at the more ardent rambler. The route, the action of walking and noteworthy features are all framed by Bentley's guidebook, making the perambulation of the streets a performance that is heavily structured. He begins by recommending that we carry a map in our pocket, and a stout staff 'to poke for firm footsteps in some of the caverns, and to assist in climbing or descending the steeper parts of our journey'. Starting in the marketplace, the route takes us down Castle Street and into the castle grounds. There follows a detailed account of how best to navigate the ruins in order to fully appreciate the massive extent of this 'once impregnable edifice'. Bentley leads the reader along a secluded terrace walk, through a Saxon archway and up the castle mound. From here, he notes, 'a most delightful panoramic view of Dudley is obtained, more than one half of the town lying like a map at the spectator's feet'. In stark contrast to West's account of Birmingham, the walker is not encouraged to linger within the town itself, but to strike out for the nearby castle ruins with their 'sylvan foliage', 'sequestered walks' and 'delightful ... subterranean caverns'. Only passing reference is made to the buildings that line the route to the castle gates. Indeed, elsewhere in his *History*, Bentley dismisses Dudley's public buildings and houses alike as 'not very remarkable as specimens of architecture', although he concedes that they are spacious and substantial in appearance, and surrounded by 'an air of comfort and neatness'.[98] Again the guide is partly an aid to navigation, and partly publicity material for the town, in this case focusing on Dudley's principal asset, its picturesque castle ruins. It structures movement through space and produces space through its pages and through the footsteps of the rambler.

These guidebooks formed important conceptualisations of the improved town and street, as much a part of the constructed representations of modern urban space as Improvement Acts or architects' plans. They imagined and fashioned the street as polite and ordered space, offering a set of guidelines as to how the space should look and be perceived. In this way, they linked the mental and the material. The tours also helped to produce urban space through spatial practices: they structured behaviour and shaped the experience of the street and the town. There was no script for performances of mutual display and sociability. Rather, the polite visitor was allowed to deviate from the proposed route and to interpret their surroundings and their fellow walkers according to their own criteria. And yet these guides helped to orchestrate the performances of walkers, shoppers and tourists. The performances of the tourist moving along the streets, whether virtually or in person, shaped both the identity of the individual and the town. This links to de Certeau's argument that the city and the street were the product of multitudinous footsteps whose 'intertwined paths give their shape to spaces'. Given his assertion that 'there is a rhetoric of walking', we can view the guidebook as a primer which shaped the language and messages carried in the walkers' footsteps.[99] Both West's and Bentley's tours drew on the space of the street, but produced and reproduced that space through the actions of individual peregrinations. As such, they brought together the street as conceived, perceived and lived space.

Woven around these orchestrated performances – and in many instances binding them together into the fabric of street life – were the unscripted and routine performances which lie at the heart of Soja's conception of firstspace.[100] Here, the identity of individuals as polite and respectable, walker and shopper, browser and buyer was shaped in part by the architecture and layout of the improved street, but also by their actions in and movement through that space. This draws on Butler's notion of performativity, of identity contingent upon social action, but also Gregson and Rose's argument that the performance of everyday activities shaped not just individual identity, but also the spaces in which those activities took place.[101] This focuses our attention firmly on the street as a lived space: the product of performance. We can see action, space and identity coming together in the practices and processes of shopping. These were structured by the customs and conventions of polite consumption: what was desirable to own, how to conduct oneself and how, in turn, one expected to be treated by others, including the shopkeeper. These same customs and conventions came into play before the shop was entered and the processes of choosing and buying engaged in, so that shopping was overwritten with a whole series of encounters and interactions.[102]

Polite shopping, as we argued earlier, was closely equated with promenading in the shopping street. Before even getting to the shop, there were friends and neighbours to greet, windows to be looked through, traffic and crowds to be negotiated, steps to be trodden. In 1804, Christian Goede, a German visitor to London, found the pavements of Bond Street 'so perfectly covered with elegantly dressed people as to make it difficult to move'.[103] At a similar time, Anne Lister noted how her trips to shops in York were often part of broader perambulations of the streets, involving planned or chance encounters. On 21 April 1823, 'Miss Yorke called at 2¼ for me to walk. We went to Rigg's garden, bought geraniums, then sauntered to the white house at the bar'. Four days earlier, she had gone out walking and 'passed Mr Christopher Rawson & Mrs Empson near the bridge'. She then 'went to Breary, the coachmaker, to inquire about a pony-carriage' and again saw 'Mr Christopher Rawson, Mrs Empson and Eliza Belcombe on the other side of the street'.[104] This mixing of shopping and leisurely social interaction was also evident amongst male consumers. Henry Prescott, for example, noted that 'After a Turn, to Mr Minshalls where Mr Murrey buys a Bible for 1li. 2s. 6d. Wee go, Mr Denton with us, to the Fountain where wee carry on the discourse in singular pints'.[105] The transition appears seamless: Prescott moved from promenading, to shopping and to socialising, gathering friends along the way. Importantly, such spatial practices were part of the everyday lives of consumers, and it was through their regular repetition that identity – as browser and pleasure seeker, shopper and consumer, polite and respectable – was constructed and reaffirmed.

For the privileged, shopping formed part of the social round: morning trips to bookshops or drapers were mixed with visits to pump rooms or gardens, walks along promenades, or tea with friends. Lady Luxborough wrote that, in Bath, starting 'from the bookseller's shop we take a tour through the milliners and toymen; and commonly shop at Mr Gill's, the pastry-cook, to take a jelly, a tart, or a small basin of vermicelli'. This routine was already established by 1725, when visitors from Cambridge noted that 'the streets though narrow have many handsome and well-appointed shops which are well accustomed by the great resort of nobility and gentry to this place'.[106] Such routines of leisurely promenading and shopping were also a feature of ordinary towns. In the 1770s, the ladies and gentlemen of Colne would walk the streets and gather at Betty Hartley's general store for tea.[107] This ritual, it seems, was not pre-arranged, but became part of the everyday lives of polite society in this small Lancashire town – their status as respectable at once legitimised and re-confirmed by their presence in the tea rooms.

Activity might focus on particular locations, but it was in moving through the street that it gained meaning and importance. The street was a place in which to display one's fashionability and respectability, and to inspect these qualities in others. As Jane Austen said of Bath, visiting the shopping streets provided opportunities for 'learning what was mostly worn, and buying clothes of the latest fashion'.[108] Fashionable shopping streets were thus produced and reproduced by the spatial practices of (polite) shoppers as they moved from shop to shop, inspecting goods and their fellow customers. This involved browsing within and visiting several different shops. Henry Prescott went to several different booksellers and auctions looking for books to add to his considerable library, whilst Anne Lister's search for a gift for her riding instructor took her to a number of silversmiths in York.[109] It also involved window-shopping: taking in the visual spectacle of the street, whilst absorbing something of the world of goods presented in the shops. The impact of such images could clearly be significant, one visitor to London commenting in 1725 that on seeing the attractive shops of the Strand, Fleet Street, Cheapside and Cornhill, 'a stranger might spend whole days, without ever feeling bored, examining the wonderful goods'.[110] Whilst we might see London as exceptional, the difference was one of degree and possibly timing rather than fundamental character: similar environments and practices characterised provincial towns. In the 1790s, Johanna Schopenhauer commented on Buxton's 'elegant shops', libraries and coffee houses, noting that the 'covered columned walk protects strollers from the rain'. Around the same time, Batenham's etchings of the main shopping streets in Chester show windows filled with goods and shoppers peering into them. A generation later, the streets and shops described in West's tours of Birmingham were still more spectacular, with their neo-classical architecture and dazzling array of goods.[111]

These varied shopping trips and perambulations had some real if vaguely conceived and expressed objectives. In walking the shopping streets, polite consumers from Samuel Pepys to Anne Lister may have been seeking particular items, either from need or desire; they may have been meeting friends; or simply passing a few leisurely moments. Almost certainly, they wanted to see and be seen. Yet their actions were far from being carefully scripted: their behaviour as shoppers, respectable citizens or cognoscenti were, in part at least, constantly made and remade through their behaviour in the street and in shops, theatres, assembly rooms and the like. As such, their identities – and that of the street – were negotiated through encounters and social interaction. Sometimes, these encounters were compatible with the practices of polite consumption, but on other occasions, they were not. Streets could be crowded and boisterous places and – like later department stores, arcades and shopping malls – they were used for many other purposes which served to disrupt these polite performances, not least as they were appropriated for traditional and plebeian activities. These different activities and priorities brought competition over the use of space, but also over the identity of the performers. People on the street might simultaneously be shoppers and pleasure seekers; participants and onlookers; polite and plebeian. These multiple practices and identities were complex and cannot be fully explored here. Instead, we consider three examples to illustrate their overlapping and sometimes contradictory nature.

Perhaps most significant was the tension between the polite performances discussed above and traditional leisure pursuits, many of which took place in and around the open marketplace – a space where social interactions were at their most visible and intense, and over which all sections of the community felt they had ownership. As Postles and Griffin both argue, this was a place of social negotiation and conflict where a multitude of spatial practices and symbolisms interacted and overlapped.[112] For some the marketplace and the streets leading from it were places for genteel strolling and refined conversation, but for many townspeople it provided a venue for more boisterous pastimes. As noted already, bull-baiting remained popular in many parts of north-west England and the west Midlands into the nineteenth century, drawing large disorderly crowds in both old-established towns and new industrial centres. Birmingham's bull-ring was used up until c.1773; Chester witnessed baiting through to 1803, and it was not until the 1830s that the sport was removed from the streets of Wolverhampton.[113] Moreover, these events took place in the marketplace or the principal shopping streets: baiting in Chester took place at the High Cross, in Preston it occurred in the marketplace; in Manchester at Hydes Cross, and in Stockport on Chestergate, the principal thoroughfare. In Liverpool, bears were processed through the main public and commercial spaces of the town – from the marketplace to the exchange and thence along Derby Street to the stock market – baiting taking place in each location.[114]

All this was in direct contrast with the milieu of leisure shopping. Derby Street was also a significant shopping thoroughfare and the exchange contained the town's assembly rooms. Diurnal segregation ameliorated conflict to an extent, but there was, to modern eyes, a fundamental contradiction in the behaviour and identity of the elites and respectable middling sorts who enjoyed both the spectacle of bull-baiting and the polite sociability of the assembly room. This tension became increasingly apparent through the eighteenth century, with a rising chorus of disapproval which portrayed baiting as uncivilised, incompatible with other uses of key public spaces and inappropriate as part of civic ceremonies designed to inspire awe and respect amongst the governed.[115] Hutton captured this modernising mood when he wrote that bull-baiting in Birmingham was finally ended by 'the commissioners of lamps [who], in the amendment of their act, wisely broke the chain, and procured a reprieve for the unfortunate animal'.[116] Cock-throwing was also viewed with growing opprobrium. Henry Prescott, Chester's deputy recorder, noted in 1718 that he had witnessed 'in the Eastgate street the barbarous divercion of throwing at a Cock notwithstanding my application to the Mayor to prevent it'.[117] Significantly, however, cock-fighting was not subjected to the same degree of censure, reflecting its continued popularity amongst the gentry. Indeed, a new cockpit was built in Chester in 1825, with tickets costing 5 shillings apiece during race week.[118]

Tensions were also apparent between shops and fairs, despite the economic and spatial inter-dependence of the two (see Chapter 1). Fairs were associated with unregulated social mixing and a breaking down of the traditional barriers policing polite space, practices and identities. Shopping streets were invaded by itinerant traders, and many shops given over to these same periodic visitors. The September hop fair in Worcester, for instance, attracted large numbers of dealers and speculators 'not only from the neighbourhood, but all parts of the kingdom'.[119] At this time, the street was full of shoppers, anxious to benefit from the better prices and greater range and availability of goods traditionally associated with the fair. This bustle of retail activity was underscored by the leisure and entertainment aspect of the fair: it was a traditional time of festival. However, concern was increasingly voiced over 'uncivilised' crowds. For respectable town dwellers, street trading and the crime, filth and disorder by which it was allegedly accompanied was not suited to the polite shopping spaces of the eighteenth-century town. In Manchester it was argued that street stalls were not only a hindrance to traffic but also brought together 'a class of persons of indifferent character and generally lowered the tone of the immediate neighbourhood'.[120] Linked to this were modernist critiques of the 'low-brow' nature of leisure associated with the fairs and the way in which this spilled over into the street, transgressing other, more respectable uses. Yet the very fact that many of these leisure attractions, including the 'amazing and stupendous elephant' displayed at the Cross in Worcester in 1772,[121] were advertised in newspapers suggests that they sought an audience from amongst the middling sorts. Taste and discernment were not, it seems, entirely incompatible with gazing at the bizarre or the exotic. Anne Lister, for all her affected high-brow nature, was not above going to the 'Talbot great room [in Halifax] to see the 2 Esquimaux Indians now exhibiting there'.[122] Less easily accommodated into notions of respectable curiosity were the Wakes processions which could bring chaos and disorder to the streets. Hutton thought them 'the lowest of all low amusements, and compleatly suited to the lowest of tempers'. The three Wakes in Birmingham, he concluded, were of relatively recent origin, having been 'hatched and fostered by the publicans, for the benefit of the spigot'.[123] Yet elites were often involved in such festivities. In Coventry the Mayor led a procession to announce the opening of the annual Show Fair, whilst in Wolverhampton the tradition of 'walking the fair' survived until 1783. Each year on the eve of the great July 9 fair twenty men in armour would process through the streets accompanied by musicians and a crowd of onlookers.[124] Again, this illustrates how apparently specialised modern and polite spaces could equally be places of popular appeal: the identities of their patrons being similarly fluid, depending on the performance in which they were engaged.

The most widely occurring activity which cut across the practices of polite shopping was the hawking of goods in the street.[125] Itinerant tradesmen and women were a familiar part of urban life and operated at a variety of scales. Some travelled to the Midlands and north-west from London, bringing huge stocks of used clothing, for example, and announcing their arrival and their sales through advertisements in local newspapers.[126] Such dealers generally took space in fixed shops (see Chapter 5). Most hawkers were of far more modest means, and sold their wares from door-to-door or in the street. The activities of both types of itinerant brought protests from fixed-shop retailers as they were seen as threatening their livelihoods: hawkers were not freemen and sold goods which were neither uniform nor subject to inspection.[127] In consequence of this, and the more general public nuisance they were seen as causing, there was a vilification of hawkers. The vitriol was particularly strong in the nineteenth century when their dealings were seen as 'vulgarising the shopping encounters of the decent workingman's wife'.[128] More pertinent to our present discussion, they were also seen as a disruption to the regularity and respectability of the shopping street. In accosting passers-by, their activities might be interpreted as upsetting the processes of leisurely browsing which characterised polite shopping. Yet it seems unlikely that many polite shoppers were personally troubled by street hawkers whose principal markets were the urban poor. Indeed, the series of illustrations of street traders which appeared from the late seventeenth to the early nineteenth century seems to suggest that they were viewed as picturesque elements of the street scene, at least during this period. That said, some towns did introduce local restrictions on itinerants during the eighteenth century, often in programmes linked with clearing markets from the streets. Birmingham, for example, acted in the 1750s and 1760s to limit stall-building, establish mandatory off-street facilities and issue 'hawking' licences.[129] Whilst the attitude of authorities and elites to hawkers moved between ambivalence and hostility, it is clear that the activities of street sellers added another layer of experience and hence meaning to the street as a commercial and social space. Not only were goods carried through the streets to be sold from door-to-door, hawkers also brought the moment of acquisition out into the public arena: as in the shop or at the market stall, goods were viewed, selections made and prices negotiated.

The street was increasingly a space of consumption: a stage which structured and, in turn, was shaped by polite and not so polite performances. Streets were increasingly conceived and designed with sociability in mind, and the activities carried on there encouraged their making as social space. Following Lefebvre, we argue that it was in the street that individuals and groups gave expression to themselves, carved out their identities and encountered contestation and prohibition. The social spaces produced by different practices interpenetrated one another.[130] Through the spatial practices of shoppers and others the space of the street was experienced, lived and produced. The street not only provided a sense of spectacle through its geographical function as a channel of movement, but also through the access it provided to sociability and consumerism.

Conclusion

The production of new urban streetscapes was announced in the provincial press and applauded by travellers. The improved street, far from simply being a means of connecting places and ordering spaces, had become part of a wider idealisation of the urban, conveying meaning to those who walked in it. For who could fail to feel a sense of progress in the streets of improving towns, with their pavements and lights, their elegant squares and terraces, and their fashionable buildings in brick and stone? In this way, the street was a key space of representation within the town, produced by urban elites through Improvement Acts and the implementation of the principles of classical architecture. It formed the physical manifestation of a particular view of the town and of public life. It was, or at least was conceived and engineered to be, orderly and rational: a reflection of the ideals of urban civility. Moreover, as Wood and others were well aware, producing space in this way allowed the architect to mould society. The street, as the principal spatial unit for urban public life, thus became a front-stage space, in which the performances of polite sociability and consumption took place. Remodelling the street as a stage-set for the dramas of urban life largely meshed with the agenda for urban improvement, with the clear emphasis being on order, regulation and respectability.

Yet we have also seen that, as a stage-set, the street provided not merely a backdrop, but rather an active context to social practices: it was a structure within and through which operated the agency of individuals and groups of actors.[131] At the same time, as Gregson and Rose argue, performances shaped both the identity of these individuals and groups, and the topography and meaning of the street. Whether conceived as conscious and scripted, or as routine and everyday, performance was critical in making and remaking polite society and polite space. This underscores the essential spatiality of consumption: that is, the mutually constitutive relationship between society and space. Empty shops, promenades, theatres, and above all, streets meant that these spaces ceased to be fashionable. In other words, a threshold of politeness was whether, in Blome's terms, these places were 'well frequented'.[132] Thus the fashionable, polite places were created by the presence and participation of middling and upper sorts in these places – visiting the races, promenading and shopping. People made the street and the town through their use of its spaces. This was recognised at the time, as towns required patronage in the form of financial support through consumption and subscription, but also through the socio-cultural activities of families of rank which brought money into the town and which gave places greater standing. An important part of the re-conceptualisation of space was not just about how it looked, but how it should be used. Disruptions to polite performances could thus (temporarily) compromise the street as respectable and civil space. As de Certeau insists, 'tactics' could be just as significant as strategies in shaping social space.[133] In Lefebvre's terms, representations of space were challenged and compromised by spaces of representation.

The street, though, was more than simply a space unto itself. It was permeated by other spaces of consumption: most obviously the buildings with which it was lined. As we have seen, these formed façades – backdrops which shaped the character of the street and the performances which took place therein. But they were also three-dimensional spaces, shaped by and, in turn, moulding the spatial practices of polite consumers.

5 The building

Representation and display

Introduction

Urban renaissance was based on a particular urban aesthetic and a new sorting of space. The growing emphasis on the façade as a means of unifying the street and modernising the urban landscape can also be seen as heightening the divide between public and private. On one side lay 'front space', open to the public gaze. On the other was 'back space', closed to all but the chosen few. Yet this simple dichotomy of public and private masks a far more complex layering of space – a reality to which Borsay was very much alive.[1] We have already seen that representations of the street as polite and modern were challenged by transgressive behaviour and the persistence of medieval street plans. It is also clear that the differentiation of space, social practice and relationships continued inside individual buildings. Indeed, it is at this scale that the spatiality of consumption was at its most intense. Placing a magnifying glass on the inter- and intra-building distinctions thus reveals further the complexity of consumer space in the eighteenth-century town. As Glennie and Thrift note, in the construction and use of individual buildings, the spatial and the social came together in a manner that was mutually constitutive.[2] Certainly, the significance of these small-scale consumer spaces was well understood by contemporary observers, as is apparent in these fictional words by the wife of an ironmonger to her husband:

> I have told you; you want more space. Besides, you do not make half enough show. You ought to go with the times. Why, at Cross's at Cambridge their upstairs windows are hung full of spades and hoes and such things, and you can see it is business up to the garret. I should turn the parlour into a counting-house. It isn't the proper thing for you to be standing always at that poky little desk at the end of the counter with a pen behind your ear. Turn the parlour, I say, into a counting house, and come out when Tom finds it necessary to call you. That makes a much better impression. The rooms above the drawing-room might be used for lighter goods, so as not to weight the floors too much.[3]

Here, the emphasis is on the need for space and display, and the 'proper' etiquette for the shopkeeper is bound up with the space that he produces and occupies. Attention is even paid to the movement between different spaces, as the wife suggests to her shopkeeper husband that he should emerge from a new counting-house into the shop when a customer calls.

Consumer spaces were clearly under the spotlight. They were an important part of the emergent consumer culture and being seen in particular places, just as much as displaying fashionable goods, could augment and advertise social status. Institutions such as theatres, pleasure gardens, assembly rooms and shops served to bind physical space to the leisure activities which were being consumed. This placed great emphasis on the design and layout of such buildings. Of course, they had to be fit for purpose, prompting concern for stages and balconies, gates and entrances, windows and counters; but they also had to properly reflect the status and tastes of the people who built and used them, and the ideologies which they supported. The use of fashionable architectural styles and the inclusion of specific decorative features thus enhanced the cultural and symbolic capital of these buildings. They were chosen because of the specific associations they had with exemplar cultures and societies, most notably ancient Greece and Rome, and the city-states of the Italian Renaissance and baroque periods. In this way, these buildings conveyed particular messages about those who owned them: they were conceived spaces, intended to make clear statements about judgement and taste, power and authority.[4] But these meanings also rubbed off onto the people who frequented them. It is a commonplace that visiting pleasure gardens, attending the assembly, and buying goods in fashionable shops could augment social status. Yet it is important to recognise that, whilst spatial practice was significant, so too was the space itself: what people did was given additional meaning by where it was done. As we have already argued, space was not simply the site of action, but also shaped engagement in action.[5]

In focusing on the individual components of the built environment of consumption, this chapter considers the ways in which space was produced, differentiated and given meaning on a micro-scale. The aim is to explore the nature of individual buildings and to relate their material structure to the meanings with which they were imbued, and the ways in which they were experienced and utilised. Here, distinctions between public and private were important in giving different meaning to spaces and the practices through which they were composed and defined. We begin by focusing on the façade as a representation of space and of social practices, and also as symbolic capital: a means of projecting onto the public street key messages about the 'private' space which lay behind. However, as we go on to argue in the second section, sub-divisions of space were more subtle than this allows: the internal structuring of buildings produced a layered hierarchy of spaces, with degrees of publicity and privacy, affording differential access and conferring social status accordingly. It was this division and re-division of space which created a spatiality that embodied the culture of consumerism; not just in the way these spaces were consumed by the people who occupied them, but also how they facilitated the consumption of other aspects of urban material culture. Specifically, in the third section, we explore how these different layers of space were used for the purposes of display: to promote wares, leisure activities and modes of living. In this, we bring together representations of space, as conceived by the shopkeeper, theatre-manager or assembly-room committee, and the lived spaces of daily routines: shopping trips, visits to the theatre, attendance at card-parties and balls. Finally, we turn to the politics of space, and consider the ways in which space was used to direct consumption practices and, conversely, how it was – as de Certeau suggests – subverted and transgressed by those intent on engaging in forms of consumption other than those intended by the shopkeeper/proprietor. This leads us to a consideration of representations of spaces or 'counterspaces', through which identities were contested and in which individuals created their own spaces of consumption.[6]

Public and private: representation and the façade

Conceptually, the idea of the 'private' was anathema to the ethos and conventions of polite society. Sociability was central to the redefinition of the urban elite, just as the spaces and practices of polite leisure and consumption were central to its cohesion and internal layering.[7] In reality, of course, this inclusivity had its limits – John Wood famously set the lower boundary of polite society at the gentleman and, as the eighteenth century progressed, public sociability increasingly fragmented into more private and exclusive gatherings. There was, Vickery argues, a growing distinction drawn 'between inclusive sociability, open to all, and discriminating assemblies accessible to the few' – generally by invitation.[8] Indeed, these public–private distinctions – in terms of space, access and behaviour – were an established part of the consumer landscape. Buildings which housed leisure and consumer facilities were discrete spaces with a particular form of internal organisation and external contextualisation that was characterised by: their position on the street; their status as privately-owned space, distinct from the public thoroughfare; and the particular functions for which they were produced.

As discussed earlier, the street was increasingly – if not straightforwardly – re-conceptualised as part of an ordered public sphere, subject to the norms and mores of polite society. This 'public' might be conceived as male. It was in public that men defined their status and gender identities, whilst a woman's place, according to much contemporary rhetoric, was in the home.[9] Yet, as we argued earlier, public space could also be seen as anywhere to which (paying) visitors could gain access. Theatres, assembly rooms, libraries, pleasure gardens and shops were central to this broader conceptualisation of 'public', the practices of sociability, and the polite consumption of goods and leisure. Yet, whilst they were open to the public, they were not themselves public spaces. Rather, they were built, owned and operated by private individuals or groups who were often interested in making a good return on their capital investment; in the very public statements made by the appearance these buildings, and the opportunities they afforded for more or less private activity. These matters of structure and design, and the intent which lay behind their manifestation, indicate that these were highly 'conceived' spaces. Indeed, Lefebvre suggests that representations of space often coincide with 'frontal' relations, which are a part of the dominant order of space, formalised

114 *The building*

and subject to signs and codes.[10] Bound up in the rhythms and routines of genteel and respectable living, these buildings conveyed important visual messages about their roles in the urban arena. They comprised no less of 'a rich iconography' than the urban industrial spaces which followed them: they were indeed 'message boards with many meanings'.[11]

One of the most important aspects of this iconography was the façade. From town halls to shops, this allowed architects and owners to send important signals to the public in the street: messages about the function of the building and about the taste and respectability of the owner, subscriber or customer. The Guild Hall in Worcester (1721–3) can be read in this way. Built on a grand scale for use by both the city and the county assizes, its elegant fifteen-bay brick frontage was ornamented with stone-moulded windows. Two large Corinthian pilasters flanked the central bays and the doorway was framed by columns, also of the Corinthian order. Viewed from the High Street, the building offered an unambiguous statement about the status and wealth of both city and shire. It also declared its judicial function and Worcester's royal associations, and thus communicated messages about the values of the governing society and about social order and control. Statues of Justice, Peace, Plenty, Chastisement and Labour were lined up along the parapet; monarchs surrounded the entrance, above which were the city arms and, in the main pediment supported by angels, the royal arms (see Figure 5.1).[12] This mixing of symbolism reflected the varied activities taking place in the Guild Hall, and was typical of the period. Later in the eighteenth century, there was a move to ornament town and shire halls in a simpler manner, more fitting to their legal and administrative functions. The Greek Revival incorporated

Figure 5.1 The Guildhall, Worcester, 1721–3

Source: Valentine Green, *Survey of the City of Worcester*, Worcester, 1764.

plainer Doric or Ionic orders and a more restrained ornamentation. At Chester, the castle was extensively remodelled by Thomas Harrison between 1788 and 1813. He produced a grand ensemble of buildings – a new shire hall, a grand jury room, an armoury and barracks for the garrison – around a large parade ground entered by a pillared 'propylaeum'. Ornamentation was minimal, with Doric used for the main buildings and Ionic elsewhere. This was a façade designed to impress with its monumental scale and grandeur.[13]

This refinement of architectural taste and symbolism was important in signalling the meaning of these official buildings. Those responsible for other public buildings generally appear to have been more concerned with the overall effect or with explicit symbolism than with the niceties of particular classical orders. Birmingham's New Street theatre, for instance, was praised by Hutton as a 'noble edifice' and 'one of the first theatres in Europe' after the addition of a 'superb portico' in 1780. This consisted of a massive piazza, supported by two pairs of Ionic columns, with wings at either end, on the front of which were positioned medallion busts of Shakespeare and Garrick.[14] No one could have failed to see the significance of the theatre in promoting and celebrating the cultural ambitions of the town. This kind of statement made it clear that gone were the days when the theatre occupied the margins of polite society. Similarly, the New Street furniture shop of Mr Hensman had an entrance adorned with 'an Ionic colonnade', whilst the nearby Pantecnetheca of Mr Charles Jones was fronted by a 'double tier of massive columns, the lower fluted doric, the upper ionic' between which were 'handsome balustrades'. Supported by the upper columns was 'a series of allegorical figures, illustrative of the fine arts'.[15] The trouble taken with this detailed level of description in contemporary guides is as telling as the elaborate façades themselves.

With their imposing frontages, such buildings could dominate the street, prompting Lefebvre to comment on the 'reign of the façade over space'.[16] But façades were about more than simply expressing power, symbolising purpose or communicating discernment on the part of the owners. They also served to advertise what lay beyond and to tempt consumers in off the street. In effect, they bridged the public–private divide. Indeed, most façades were pierced by windows and doors that gave insights and access into what lay beyond. In shops, windows were dressed with displays of the goods available within – a practice which effectively projected an image of the shop and shopkeeper to those passing in the street. The importance of this presence in the public realm was marked by the lamentations of a failing early nineteenth-century provincial shopkeeper in Rutherford's novel *The Revolution in Tanner's Lane*:

> Somehow the business fell off. Customers as used to come didn't come, and I got no new ones. I did my work pretty well; but still for all that, things went down by degrees. … The shop, too, ought to have been painted more often, and I ought to have had something in the window, but, as I say, I was always dull …[17]

Many shopkeepers did have something in the window. In London, Francis Place took the trouble to change items in his expensively glazed window on a regular basis, sometimes displaying fashionable garments such as waistcoats, but mostly smaller items like gloves, ribbon and handkerchiefs. He saw his displays as vital in attracting passers-by who might make one-off purchases.[18] Evidence from provincial towns is more impressionistic, but indicates the importance of windows and window displays.[19] The 'window grates' listed in the inventory of Henry Bolt, a mercer in Bromsgrove, or the 'wire lattice' in the shop of the Liverpool grocer Robert Rownson, suggest that there were goods in the window that needed some protection. More revealing is the inventory of the Birmingham watchmaker Isaac Stretch which includes a 'glass case that stands upon the window'.[20] However rudimentary, these window displays gave a taste of what lay inside the shop; they were a representation of the shop goods and the shop itself, and projected important messages to the passing public. Windows also helped to illuminate the shop interior, allowing the stock to be displayed more effectively. Indeed petitions from Chester tradesmen wishing to enlarge their windows repeatedly stressed the desire to 'lighten [the] shop and ornament it to public view'.[21] Thus the shop was opened up to the gaze of the passer-by: as with modern shopping malls, illumination and visibility transcended the divide between interior and exterior space. Similarly, the façades of many social facilities presented a semi-permeable barrier to what lay beyond, seemingly with the intention of advertising their attractions. The wrought iron gates and railings that often bordered walks and pleasure gardens, for example, provided little in the way of seclusion for those gathered within. Theatres bridged the divide in a different way, adorning the entrance with playbills advertising recent and current attractions.

This use of the façade as an advertisement did not make what lay within a mere extension of the public realm of the street. Access to many leisure facilities was limited to ticket holders or subscribers. Tickets were relatively easily and cheaply obtained for theatres and pleasure gardens, but libraries, in particular, were more exclusive. Privacy and exclusivity were made possible by the limits imposed on the number of subscribers (Liverpool's Athenaeum had 500 and Manchester's Portico Library 400); the issuing of membership tickets or tokens (strictly non-transferable); and the private nature of the library buildings – the entrance was often guarded by the keeper or manager.[22] The spaces of commercial leisure facilities and shops were, in this sense, duplicitous. Much like modern shopping malls, they were open to the public yet controlled as a private space.[23] In crossing the threshold, the consumer became subject to subtly different sets of mores and norms: that is, particular cultures of consumption (see Chapter 6). The specificities of these cultures varied, so that what was seen as appropriate in one place might be frowned on elsewhere. Equally varied were the ways in which norms were brought to bear on the consumer, but through each space and activity ran a common thread of politeness and civility, propriety and respectability. These values and norms were structured by the movement of the individual from the public realm of the street into the public–private realm of particular buildings, and by the sub-divisions of space within shops and leisure facilities.

Internal divisions of space: public or private?

Behind the façade, consumer space was no more neutral than that which was overtly public. Indeed, the creation of space designed for consumers and to promote consumption was dependent upon a physical division of space to maintain the required 'frontal relations'. The layering of public onto private was therefore integral to the ways in which the spaces of consumption were structured. Hierarchies of privacy characterised assembly rooms, theatres and libraries, and shaped the ways in which people moved through and used these spaces, drawing on and adding to their meanings through differentiated social practices.

These distinctions, and their blurring, are best illustrated with reference to the shop, and particularly its relationship with the home. In most instances, provincial shops were bound into the fabric of the domestic dwelling, as were store rooms and workshops. Indeed, it is possible to see internal space as increasingly specialised, each room having its own purpose and character: shops were for selling, workshops for production, warehouses for storage, bedrooms for sleeping, and parlours for family living. To an extent, this view is supported by evidence from probate inventories. The workshop of Joseph Bourn, a tallow chandler in Dudley, contained two furnaces, 'a chopping trough, two knives and a mould to make candles', tallow, scales and weights, and three tubs, with a combined value of £8 6s 5d. That of the Warwick gunsmith, Nicholas Paris, contained three vices, two anvils, twelve hammers, a pair of bellows and a trough, files and tongs, 22 cwt of iron and large quantities of brasswork for guns.[24] In Liverpool, the contents of Robert Rownson's warehouse included 200 lbs of rice, 1.5 cwt of starch, 70 lbs of tobacco, 40 lbs of caraway seeds, 12 lbs of coriander seeds, 24 lbs of raisins and 8 gross of tobacco pipes. Similarly, the Leek cheesemonger, John Finney, had £10 6s of hops, £13 of cider, £12 1s 6d of malt and £5 17s 4d of bacon as well as cheese in his cellar.[25] None of these rooms contained any shop fittings: they were places of manufacture or storage, not selling. However, these easy distinctions are too simplistic when the house as a whole is considered: the boundaries between commercial and domestic space were often fluid. At one level, this can be seen in the practice of storing 'shop goods' in rooms throughout the house. The grocer Robert Rownson, for example, had boxes of oranges, lemons and almonds, and a parcel of sweetmeats in a first floor parlour; John Finney had hops and yarn in a bed-chamber; Edward Clifton, a Liverpool mercer, had oils and yarn in his garret; and Simon Ames, an ironmonger from Burton-on-Trent, had twenty-five frying pans and two dozen candlesticks stored in his 'house place'.[26]

Shopkeepers also made use of private domestic space as well as quasi-public shop space to secure sales. Cox has amply demonstrated the ways in which private parlours were used to entertain the privileged consumer: a more personal mode of selling which also marked out the status or esteem of particular customers.[27] Nicholas Blundell, for instance, frequently dined with Liverpool shopkeepers such as the mercers Mr Cottom and Mr Hurst. In one diary entry he records that, after purchasing a livery suit, Cottom 'treated me at his Hous and gave me a dooble Snuff Box'; in another he notes, 'My Wife and I got a Snap of a dinner at

Mrs Lancasters, we bought some lofe Sugar there'.[28] For Blundell these tradesmen were not merely suppliers of goods, they were also his friends. Indeed, it is the ambiguity of their relationship which goes some way to explain the absence of a clear demarcation between shop space and private space. We need to be careful of such dichotomies: in many cases, it was not a question of the privileged customer passing through a door and moving from a quasi-public space (the shop) into a more private space (the house). Many shopkeepers had a range of spaces – often separate rooms – for the display and selling of goods, some more open and 'public' than others, but none essentially 'private'. The itemisation of rooms and goods in probate inventories reveals the ways in which shop space was produced and how it was perceived by appraisers. In the 1680s, the sales rooms of the Warwick grocer and mercer, Hatton Atkins, were designated as 'little shop', 'shop' and 'warehouse', suggesting a differentiation of function as well as space. Similarly, in 1703 the Coventry draper, Jonathon Daniel, had an 'upper shop', a 'lower shop' and 'shop', along with a kitchen, hall, stairhead, and numerous other chambers.[29] The shop formed a substantial part of this large property and the structure of the inventory suggests a suite of rooms which perhaps led off from one another, as the shop extended backwards and upwards. Sub-dividing space in this way hints at the employment of a variety of sales strategies tailored to the different types of stock, or different types of customer (see below and Chapter 6).

These complexities can be summarised through detailed analysis of a single property: that of the Coventry tallow chandler, Nicholas Blithe.[30] His house contained eleven rooms, including a street shop, workshop, warehouse, cellar and 'glass room', as well as domestic rooms. Production, retailing and family life spilled over into one another, shop goods being stored in various rooms including the middle chamber. Yet specialisation was more apparent, as was a clear hierarchy of retail space. The workshop contained: 'twenty eight dozen of candle rods; five dozen of candles and two load of wood; two coppers, a lading dish and old kettle; one candle mould and old tubs; three knives, an old trough, and rendering strips', whilst his warehouse contained 'eight hundred[weight] of tallow'. His street shop contained candles, brushes and baskets, plus small looking glasses, coarse and 'middle sort of earthenware', white ware, glassware and bottles. Although quantities are not specified, the ceramics and glassware were valued at just 21s 6d. The impression is of inexpensive items, sold quickly, perhaps through the window or over the counter to a range of customers. In addition, Blithe also had a 'glassroom', situated away from the street, which contained 'white earthenware and Nottingham ware', flint glass ware, vials and looking glasses. This, whilst not domestic space, was altogether more private; the emphasis here was probably on more service-oriented selling (see Chapter 6).

This layering of space to create a hierarchy of specialised but overlapping public–private realms was also evident in other elements of the built environment of polite consumption. Both assembly rooms and subscription libraries were comprised of a suite of interconnected and inter-related spaces, each with its own function. The basic requirements were for a ballroom, card room and tea room, thus accommodating each aspect of the assembly in its own dedicated space. The assembly rooms built in Manchester in 1792 fulfilled these criteria and added a billiard room; those in Liverpool town hall had two ballrooms, a card room, tea room and separate eating room, as well as a saloon and drawing room, covering a total area of over 10,000 square feet.[31] Each room needed to suit its purpose: ballrooms had to be heated, with good ventilation, equipped with adequate illumination and space for musicians, and large enough for dancing.[32] This checklist is closely echoed in the specification and description of the ballroom at Manchester. Measuring 87 by 34 feet, it was just wide enough for two parallel sets of country dances; there were fireplaces, and three pendant and twelve wall chandeliers, whilst the 'orchestra is on one side ... over the principal entrance'.[33] That the billiard and card rooms were under separate management added to the flexibility of the space: these smaller rooms would be opened (and heated) separately at card assemblies and during the day. This gradation of privacy was clearer still in the complex of 'public' rooms built by subscription at Chester's Talbot Inn, which included two ballrooms, a newsroom, a coffee room and two billiards rooms.[34] Whilst the assembly rooms themselves were very public arenas – places of display for the social elite of the city and county – the others formed more private spaces: access was probably more restricted and use was certainly more introspective. With a greater degree of intimacy, such spaces were about learning, conversation and conviviality.

This ensemble of rooms closely resembled provision within private clubs, newsrooms and subscription libraries.[35] Here purpose-built premises again allowed the designation of specific functions to different spaces. At the Liverpool Athenaeum, for example, there was a newsroom, library and committee room, as well as space 'fitted up for the reception of ... specimens in Natural History' (see Figures 5.2 and 5.3).[36] The first of these rooms, which originally opened directly onto the street, was the most public and convivial, being 'fitted up after the manner of a Coffee-room, where the newspapers, reviews, magazines and pamphlets may always be met with'. It was here also that refreshments would be served to members and where business would be transacted. Above this, in a galleried room lit by a central dome, was the library proper. This was conceived as an altogether more sober and private space, lined with bookshelves and intended primarily for reading. Significantly, the prospectus emphasised the spatial and practical separation of newsroom and library, stating that 'the two establishments will be kept perfectly distinct from one another'.[37] Leading from the library was the committee room: the most private and secluded space in the Athenaeum. Here the twenty-one elected members of the committee met to discuss the running of the institution: their status and function marked by their (private) location within the building.

This same hierarchy of internal space, differentiated in terms of function, accessibility and relative location within the building, was also seen in theatres, where social distinctions were clearly denoted by the seating arrangements. Polite customers were separated from the common order through their occupation of boxes, whilst ordinary men and women were generally restricted to the pit and gallery. This spatial arrangement was effected, in part, through differential

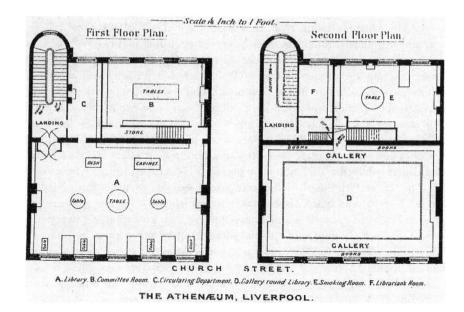

Figure 5.2 Liverpool Athenaeum: first and second floor plan

Source: G.T. Shaw, *History of the Athenaeum, Liverpool, 1798–1898*, Liverpool: Committee of the Athenaeum, 1898.

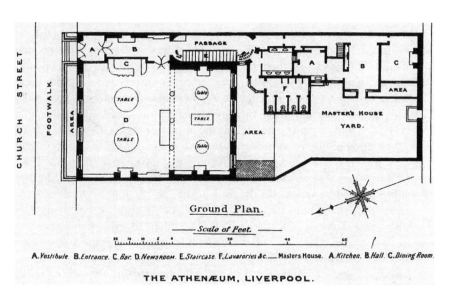

Figure 5.3 Liverpool Athenaeum: ground floor plan

Source: G.T. Shaw, *History of the Athenaeum, Liverpool, 1798–1898*, Liverpool: Committee of the Athenaeum, 1898.

pricing: typically, box seats cost 3s, those in the pit were 2s and in the gallery 1s. However, spatial segregation, and with it the meanings attached to specific spaces, was undermined in some cases by theatre proprietors offering half-price tickets for entry during the performance and in others by subscribers or other wealthy customers allowing servants access to their boxes – an indication that, even where boundaries existed, they could be transgressed.[38] It was further disrupted by the lack of a consensus regarding the relative respectability of different parts of the theatre. Most contemporaries drew 'sharp distinctions about status and sexual propriety based on a viewer's position in the auditorium', but their opinions varied considerably. Johanna Schopenhauer wrote of the London theatre that the pit was 'quite a respectable place'; yet, for many, this was far from being the case (see below). In Liverpool's Williamson Square theatre, the gallery was considered one of the better parts of the house for hearing and seeing the performance. As a consequence, it was frequented by many of the town's more respectable citizens.[39] Despite these complications, theatres were generally able to offer entertainment to a wide spectrum of society whilst keeping social distinctions clearly marked in spatial terms. The gallery of the theatre in Williamson Square may have accommodated a social mix, but, as Brooke noted, respectable theatre-goers were 'accustomed to sit on the left side ... when looking towards the stage, whilst the lower classes, by a kind of tacit arrangement, seldom interfered with them, but took their seats on the right of it, and in the wings'.[40] Boxes formed the most exclusive and, in some senses, the most private spaces in the auditorium. After its rebuilding in 1795, boxes at the New Street theatre in Birmingham were accessed through a separate entrance and occupants had exclusive use of a 'handsome Saloon' and large ballroom where refreshments were provided. In a similar manner, if rather lower key, one visitor to Liverpool's theatre in the 1760s noted that 'behind the boxes there is a table spread, in the manner of a coffee house, with tea, coffee, wines, cakes, fruit and punch'.[41] These arrangements – both the use of and access to these private spaces – reveal starkly the hierarchy of spaces within the theatre.

In this way, space asserted a social imperative: the divisions within buildings were an essential part of the consumption of space and the construction of society. Indeed, these spatial hierarchies can be seen as an essential part of the social differentiation occurring within polite society: the need to delineate and defend such spaces mirrored the importance of demarcating and defending social status. Spaces of consumption, from shops to theatres, therefore offered the opportunity to reinforce social distinctions through spatial practices. Accessing some of the internal spaces of shops or theatres, for example, both depended upon and bolstered social status. In as much as this depended upon the ability to pay, economic differences were also mapped onto spatial distinctions. Yet the possibility for the proprietor to play an active role as gatekeeper to these spaces meant that the process was far more subtle. When divisions and hierarchies of space, and of differential access to space, were less easily defined and defended, there was the possibility of heterogeneous mixing which brought with it both the frisson of excitement and the threat of social disorder. The lack of clear spatial and social boundaries was most evident in outdoor leisure spaces, where external barriers and internal sub-divisions were more difficult to effect and to police. This was, in part, a product of the large volume of space and people that they comprised; but it also reflected the nature of the leisure activities themselves.

In pleasure gardens, whilst a veneer of exclusivity was maintained through the charging of entry fees (themselves often set too low to exclude any but the poorest), there were few restrictions of movement once inside and little escape from the constant scrutiny of the public gaze.[42] At Vauxhall, private parties might occupy more secluded 'booths' for dining, but there was considerable freedom and a great inter-mingling of classes and genders. For some, this was liberating; for others it formed an unwelcome and unsettling challenge to the basis of social interaction. Smollett's young and wide-eyed Miss Liddy waxed lyrical. For her, Vauxhall was 'crowded with the gayest company … enlivened with mirth, freedom, and good-humour'. Conversely, the bucolic and acerbic Sir Matthew Bramble opined that 'when I see a number of well-dressed people, of both sexes, sitting on covered benches, exposed to the eyes of the mob … I can't help compassionating their temerity, while I despise their want of taste and decorum'.[43] Promenades offered similar possibilities for social mixing. In London, The Mall was possibly the most prestigious venue for perambulation, but it was also promiscuous. De Saussure reported in 1725 that

> the park is so crowded at times that you cannot help touching your neighbour. Some people come to see, some to be seen, and others to seek their fortunes; for many priestesses of Venus are abroad, some of them significantly attired, and all on the look-out for adventures.[44]

The same concerns also troubled those organising and attending events in provincial gardens. In addition to the moral censure reported by John Nicholson in Liverpool (see Chapter 6), he also noted that women attending the *ridotto al fresco* 'had good assurances given 'em not to be affronted by any' of the other participants.[45] The problem was the lack of spatial as much as social differentiation. There was little privacy or 'private' space in pleaure gardens and on promenades. They were, as Vickery notes, 'the most public of public places where women and men congregated'.[46]

Race meetings too attracted huge crowds, from the nobility to the artisan. One Midlands correspondent wrote enthusiastically of his visit to Lichfield races in 1733, 'where we met with the whole world, indeed, I never saw so much good company together in any place before'.[47] This 'good company' and the conspicuous consumption of food and drink which marked race meetings in many county towns, took place very much in the public domain. Following the races at Chester in 1705, for example, Henry Prescott noted that many gentlemen were treated to drinks in the Pentice.[48] As with other social and leisure activities, large race meetings formed important marriage markets, especially for the rural gentry: Nicholas Blundell, for instance, considered Ormskirk racecourse a suitable venue for an initial meeting between his daughter Mally and the wealthy Mr Strickland of Sizergh.[49] However, these practices, and with them the social meanings of race meetings, depended upon a mutual audience of the rural elite. At the start of the eighteenth century, Prescott was complaining of the 'mob' who attended the races, and the problem of maintaining exclusivity grew over time. By the 1800s, the races in Manchester were described as 'motley pleasures', populated by 'a body of men, women and children, of every description'. In this environment it was the private carriage and the grandstand which allowed some spatial and social distance to be maintained.[50] By the early nineteenth century the latter were often sophisticated structures offering many of the facilities of a private club. That at Wolverhampton, erected in 1827, was described as having 'all the appearance of the conservatories of our nobility, upon a grand scale; the refreshment and assembly rooms, and the orchestra, are all in a similar good taste'. In Walsall the lower room of the grandstand (erected in 1809) held a billiards table which was 'open by annual subscription'.[51] These semi-private spaces within the public arena of the racecourse provided a locus for elite sociability, but also a chance to be seen socialising in public. Raised up above the crowd, grandstands offered a better view of the racing, but for many race-goers it was the opportunity for display that appears to have been more important. Ann Sneyd, for instance, spent much of her time at Shrewsbury races in 1771 gossiping and playing cards, whilst Elizabeth Parker and Jane Pellett acquired new silks with the aim of aiding their 'conquest' of 'Southern beaus' at Wakefield races in 1749.[52]

Internal divisions of space – or the lack of them – were thus critical in determining access to and relative location within shops and leisure facilities. Differential access to a hierarchy of public–private spaces both reflected and constructed social status. Social distinctions were thus written into the micro-geographies of consumption. Moreover, the construction, meaning and use of these spaces shaped the social practices of consumption, not least in the ways in which they structured and promoted display.

Space, display and the consumer

Display was pivotal to the creation and representation of buildings for polite consumption. The external displays mounted by leisure facilities and shops through their fashionable façades represented both the functions of these buildings and the people that lay behind their construction. Yet, display was also central to the folding of public onto private space. It centred on the tangible commodities of urban material culture and on the consumers themselves. The intention of many leisure activities was, after all, to see and be seen. In this section, we direct attention onto the role of display in structuring the spaces of polite consumption, the messages which this was intended to convey, and the impacts it had on the use of these spaces. In focusing on visual image we emphasise both material objects and their arrangement in space as active agents in shaping human behaviour.[53]

Although the rhetoric of town councils and architects emphasised polite sociability and spatial order, a core function of public walks and gardens was personal display. Their structure, layout and setting both reflected and moulded processes of mutual exhibition. In essence, a walk had to provide a good surface which protected the feet of strollers from dirt and offer some shelter from the elements. It also helped if the walk was wide enough to let two parties pass by one another with ease. In Worcester, Charles Trubshaw Withers transformed the narrow path across Sansome Fields to the hamlet of Barbourne into a gravelled walk, shaded on each side by 'embowing' elms, with further footpaths radiating off it across the surrounding fields.[54] This formula was repeated across the country, and matched the materiality of the walk with the social practices of promenading in small groups.[55] Seats allowed for orchestrated displays of self and self-importance, as when the Duchess of K- sat on the Parade at Bath with her French horns playing before her (see Chapter 4). Display could be aural as well as visual and polite discourse formed an important part of the experience of promenading. Ornaments and follies were focal points around which groups might pause and discuss the good taste (or otherwise) of what lay before them. Henry Prescott, for example, recorded of his visit to a garden that 'wee walk about, admire the situacion of a gentile [sic] and convenient seat, in a Garden, the furniture suitable'.[56]

Assembly rooms too were arenas for personal display, and contemporaries always commented upon the quality and fashionability of the company. Eliza Parker remarked that, at the early nineteenth-century assemblies at Preston, there was 'a great deal of Genteel company … and tonight is expected a brilliant meeting. I never saw so much dress required at Preston before'.[57] The importance of displaying oneself and one's dress influenced the arrangement, decoration and use of space. The spatial and functional heart of the rooms was the ballroom, which needed to accommodate those being gazed upon and those who wished to gaze.[58] Given this, it is unsurprising that most descriptions of ballrooms emphasised their commodious nature. That at Worcester was a 'spacious handsome room'; whilst the ballroom at the George Inn in Walsall would 'admit fifty couples to dance without inconvenience'.[59] Yet size alone was not sufficient to make these effective spaces for display – a point made clear in Berry's account of the lavish interior of the new assembly rooms in Newcastle-upon-Tyne.[60] Those attending elegant and prestigious assemblies expected their surroundings to be decorated in a fashionable and tasteful manner; providing an arena in which to display their personal, social and material attributes. This meant stuccoed walls and ceilings, tall casement windows, ornamental fireplaces and above all lighting that would adequately illuminate fashionable clothing and expensive jewellery. Worcester's assembly room was wainscoted up to a height of seven feet, with plaster work above, and was illuminated by three large sconces hanging from the ceiling, plus twenty-two smaller ones attached to the walls; whilst in Manchester there were twelve wall and three pendant chandeliers, 'their united brilliance [having] heightened effect, from three very large mirrors'.[61] When all the rooms in these buildings were opened and illuminated for grand balls, they presented an impressive sight as the following description of the Exchange in Liverpool in April 1798 amply illustrates:

The Concert and assembly rooms were appropriated for dancing, and had a most brilliant and pleasing appearance when viewed from the saloon; the upper room … formed the grandest spectacle of the kind, perhaps, ever seen in this country. The Doric order of which this room is composed was correctly preserved, and lighted by a profusion of variegated lamps beautifully arranged; the interior columns being wreathed, and the lines of the pilasters on the side walls and the cornices hung with lamps. In the interior part of the room was a quadrangle of columns, supporting large semicircular arches, brilliantly illuminated. These columns were ornamented with wreaths of artificial flowers, and the ceiling of this interior quadrangle, was elegantly painted in compartments, of laurel and oak devices, from which were suspended five superb glass chandeliers. Over the doors at the entrance, on the east and west sides, were two large regal crowns, in crystal lamps; and in the recesses of the south part of the room, between the pilasters, were introduced nine large emblematic transparencies, executed in a masterly style, by artists of the first distinction.[62]

These buildings provided 'a labyrinth of spaces through which the company could circulate', flirting, gossiping and inspecting one another. However, the use of space was not a free-for-all. The gentry sometimes danced at separate assemblies, on different nights or in a separate area within the ballroom, raised on a platform or roped off from the common people. Often, there was an expectation that the young and single would dance and display themselves, whilst the older and married would remain more in the background. Nash enshrined this in one of his Rules: 'that the elder ladies and children be content with a second bench at the ball, as being past or not yet come to perfection'.[63] Such distinctions were perhaps not formalised at provincial assemblies, but they were certainly apparent. Indeed, they might even extend to the preferential use of different spaces within the assembly rooms, as one early nineteenth-century report makes clear:

The assemblies of Nottingham are, as in all other places, the resort of the young and the gay, who go to see and be seen; and also of those, who, having played their matrimonial cards well in early life, are now content to sit down to a game of sober whist or quadrille.[64]

There was an implicit understanding of which groups would attend assemblies, what they would be doing there, and where they would be found. The arrangement of assembly rooms thus effected a spatial segregation on the basis of status and age, but not gender.

Display was also an important subtext for those attending the theatre: performances in the auditorium offered an attraction as alluring as those on the stage. The process of mutual display and inspection was assisted in London theatres by the practice of lighting the audience as brightly as the actors. The extent to which this was also common in the provinces is more difficult to judge, although the regularity of theatre fires suggests that they were extensively illuminated.

Location within the auditorium was important. Box seats offered clearly defined personal space and helped to augment or confirm status, but they also made their occupants visible and well-placed to see who else was there to be seen. They were the most conspicuous as well as the most private part of the house.[65] A description of the newly rebuilt New Street theatre in Birmingham noted how the two tiers of sixteen boxes surrounding the house were individually illuminated by 'brilliant cut glass chandeliers' suspended from elegant brackets, providing those in the pit with a clear view of these richly decorated cubicles and their equally bedecked occupants.[66]

The scope for manipulating space was perhaps greatest in the shop. Here the display of goods and people came together, and again we can see how material systems structured behaviour and communicated important messages about those occupying the shop space. Display served three main purposes: as a means of marketing and selling wares; to communicate the status, professionalism and knowledge of the shopkeeper; and to serve new 'polite' modes of shopping, particularly browsing.[67]

An orderly arrangement of stock indicated the competence of the shopkeeper, whilst attractive or fashionable goods placed on shelves or pinned onto boards created an ambiance of elegance. Inventories and trade cards of London shopkeepers reveal opulent settings within which goods were often displayed in glass-fronted cases, or framed by plaster moulding and gilded cornices.[68] The fittings of provincial shops were more modest, but their purposes and the messages they conveyed were essentially the same. Simon Ames, a Burton-upon-Trent ironmonger, was fairly typical. His shop contained a counter, 'a little nest of drawers' and 'open boxes that the nails are in'. Similarly, if at a slightly larger scale, the apothecary John Chamberlain had two counters, several chests of drawers and extensive shelving in his Warwick shop; whilst the Rochdale grocer, Thomas Taylor, had at least seven sets of drawers, including one described as 'Alphabet drawers'.[69] Drawers and shelves were, in part, to do with storage, but they also facilitated display. Goods would be laid on the counter for inspection, whilst nests of drawers produced a visual impression of order and plenty, especially when combined with shelves piled high with goods open to public view. Moreover, drawers might be taken out and placed on the counter: a practice that appears to have been common amongst haberdashers when selling their lace and ribbons. The visual impact of the interior of such shops is difficult to gauge, but cannot have been so different from that of Henry Lilwall, a London grocer (see Figure 5.4). Certainly, the description of shop fittings offered for sale in mid eighteenth-century Worcester emphasises their visual impact as much as their practical use:

> To be SOLD at a very reasonable rate, A good FRAME of an Apothecary's Shop, with handsome Boxes and Bottles neatly painted and titled, and likewise Pots of all common Size for customary Use, with Mortars, Still, and other Utensils proper to an Apothecary's Business.[70]

Figure 5.4 Trade Card of Henry Lilwall of London

Source: Bodleian Library, University of Oxford, John Johnson Collection, Trade Cards 11 (30).

The growing complexity of eighteenth-century shop fittings was characterised by the Stafford grocer and ironmonger, Thomas Clarke. His inventory runs to eight sides and includes nearly £340 worth of shop goods.[71] It ends with an impressive array of fittings:

One new counter	1	0	0
One old counter	1	2	6
Three nests of drawers and frames	1	12	0
Nail boxes and shelves	0	12	0
One chair	0	8	0
2 rails and pegs	0	2	0
2 shelves	0	1	6
2 more shelves	0	10	0
One square table	0	2	6

Worth a total of £5 10s 6d, Clarke's shop fittings include novel items for displaying goods and an apparently more conscious and sophisticated manipulation of the retail space: perhaps a response to the growth of polite consumption and browsing within shops.[72] Smallwares could have been hung from the rails, or lengths of cloth draped over them, allowing shoppers to inspect the goods at their leisure. Significantly, such innovation was not the preserve of larger towns: Ralph Edge's shop in Tarporley (with a 1664 population of around 260) had '2 counters, shelves, ranges and boards pinned to the wall'. Likely, these boards were used to display some of the ribbons, lace and other haberdashery which made up much of his merchandise. A generation later in Prescot (itself with no more than 500 inhabitants by that date), the shop of the mercer and innkeeper Ambrose Pierpoint contained a glass case worth 16s as well as the usual counters, shelves and drawers.[73]

Elaborate fittings involved considerable capital expenditure, which only the more successful tradesman could justify in terms of their likely turnover and their sales strategies. However, the impact of such investment in the material fabric of the shop could be striking. Some of the most elaborate shop interiors were the showrooms used by specialist high status retailers such as china dealers and upholsterers. The layout of these rooms was tailored specifically to present the goods in a familiar setting and to encourage the customer to browse at their leisure, examine the goods on display and converse with the staff and fellow customers.[74] The glassrooms of Nicholas Blithe and his fellow Coventry tallow chandler, Richard Lindsey, were both fashionably furnished. Blithe's had an oval table and six leather chairs; that of Lindsey had three tables and four chairs; both included looking glasses. Neither was particularly wealthy – even including the debts owing to them, their estates were valued at just £202 9s and £156 19s 6d respectively – and yet both were taking significant time and trouble, and going to some expense, to display their superior wares to the best possible effect.[75] Such arrangements, even if executed at a modest scale, show the innovative and imaginative production of display space on the part of provincial shopkeepers. They were based on essentially the same principles as the grand West End showrooms of Wedgwood and the Worcester porcelain manufacturers, Flight and Barr. McKendrick has highlighted Wedgwood's use of such displays in his London showrooms where the aim was to dazzle the visitor and impress upon them the attractiveness and fashionability of the products.[76] These were conceived representations of space, consciously recreating the ambiance of the country house or assembly hall. To this end, the showrooms were lavishly decorated, dramatically lit with lamps, candlesticks and sconces, and filled with elaborate furnishings: tables were set with dinner services and cabinets filled with decorative items.

The Chester upholsterer, Abner Scholes, took this attention to the arrangement of his stock a stage further. From his 1736 inventory it appears that Scholes placed furniture in a series of co-ordinated assemblages in a large galleried showroom.[77] These groupings were apparently laid out to resemble rooms, often including a bed, chairs, screens and accessories such as looking glasses or prints. They also appear to have been grouped according to quality and price. For example, we see:

N3)	1 Green Harrateen folding bed at	3	15	0
	1 Green Easy Chair, black frame at	1	0	0

6 Brown Chairs matt seats	1	4	0
1 4-leaf map Skreen	1	10	0
4 messitintas in black frames with glasses	0	4	0

and, rather more up-market:

N7)	1 Yellow Camblet Bed lined with Sattin	15	0	0
	1 Scarlet Harrateen Bed at	9	0	0
	1 Scarlet Worsted Damask Bed Chair at	4	0	0
	1 Scarlet Damask Easy Chair	2	5	0
	1 Yellow Do	2	2	0
	1 Blue Do	1	18	0
	1 Chimney Glass and brass branches	1	10	0
	1 Mahogany Close Stool	0	10	6
	1 Large Landskip and small Dutch pieces	0	7	6
	4 Prints in black frames and Glasses	0	4	0

By arranging his stock in this way, Scholes perhaps hoped to introduce his customers to new fabrics or new styles of furniture: juxtaposing these items with other familiar goods such as the framed liliputians and hudibrass prints which were in vogue at the time. Wedgwood certainly adopted this technique in his London showrooms, using a model dining room laid out with a full dinner service to inform customers how new items should be properly incorporated into an accepted set of tableware. As Bianchi and Saumarez-Smith suggest, by placing novel items alongside the familiar, they could more easily be accepted by a conservative public.[78] Alternatively Scholes may have been trying to impress upon his wealthy clientele the quality of his furniture and his skills in designing and furnishing entire rooms in a fashionable manner – a central attribute for the successful upmarket eighteenth-century upholsterer, who often operated as a designer rather than simply an artisan. Or perhaps, as Benjamin might argue, his aim was simply to create a spectacle that was likely to have the maximum visual impact. In all likelihood Scholes had all three of these goals in mind. Certainly, surrounded by fashionable prints and displayed in a lavish setting, his furniture must have had bestowed upon it an aura of luxury and fashionability.

When laying out their premises, eighteenth century shopkeepers were concerned not only that their wares were displayed to the best possible effect, but also that the visual appearance of their shop fostered and projected an appropriate image for the business.[79] Thus, in the tour around Birmingham included by West in his *History of Warwickshire*, he noted that the interior of the cut-glass show room of Mrs Bedford and Co. excelled:

> in architectural taste, and is well stocked with superior cut glass, {manufactured by the proprietor,} china and earthenware: the shop and show rooms are well arranged, and the latter is ascended by a handsome geometrical staircase, the ballustrades of which are formed of exquisitely cut glass, producing an airy,

brilliant, and uncommonly beautiful effect. The show rooms and gallery of above 150 feet in length, are supported by chaste doric columns, from the best Grecian models; the whole evinces much taste and spirit in the proprietor.[80]

Here, Benjamin's emphasis of the visual image ties in with Lefebvre's notion of the conscious manipulation and projection of space. Through careful attention to the façade and interior décor, the astute tradesman could consciously construct a shopping environment designed to appeal to a discerning and polite clientele. The spaces produced were symbolic as well as practical: they linked ideology with everyday practices.[81] An elaborate window display and well-furnished interior conveyed an image of opulence and sophistication, and demonstrated the taste of the shopkeeper. By association, it also suggested that a business was successful and that a shopkeeper was able to access and supply a wide range of high quality goods, including others not present in the shop itself. Customers would therefore be able to order, with confidence, expensive or exotic items.[82] These front-spaces were therefore the focus of attention, whilst activities which did not actively enhance the image of the shop – storage and manufacturing – were tucked away elsewhere.

Cultivating such an image was particularly important for those involved in the luxury trades, who needed to attract polite consumers – a point made clear by the trouble to which Francis Place went when fitting-out his London shop, and equally apparent from the complex layout of Scholes' show rooms. Money was spent not only on shop fittings, but also on furnishings such as chairs, tables and looking glasses: all with the aim of creating a congenial setting for the goods on display and projecting messages of reliability and politeness. Comfortable seating encouraged customers to linger; whilst lamps, candlesticks and sconces illuminated both the interior and shop window to dramatic effect. Daniel Defoe commented disapprovingly on such developments in 1726, noting that 'never was [there] such painting and gilding, such sashing and looking-glasses among the shopkeepers as there is now'.[83] What dismayed Defoe was the growing tendency for the high-class shopkeeper to build his reputation on the basis of the luxuriant imagery of his shop rather than his retailing expertise. The shop had become a space of representation, a carrier of coded messages, projected by the tradesman and interpreted by the discerning customer.

Space within the shop was generally organised around the counter, which formed the interface between shopkeeper and customer. This spatial separation helped to maintain a certain distance, an 'otherness' which bolstered the authority of the tradesman. He was the guardian of specialist knowledge and gatekeeper – both literally and metaphorically – to a world of goods. The way in which goods were laid out in the shop also carried symbolic meanings. The methodical description of shopkeeper's wares in probate inventories owed much to the diligence of the appraisers, but it does suggest that different types of goods were stored separately within the shop. The distinction is especially clear in the case of the Coventry shopkeepers Julius Billers and Samuel Gibbard. Billers' inventory includes the entry '5 duble chests on the grocery side'. That of Gibbard contains a large stock of cloth and haberdashery listed as 'shop goods', whilst his groceries appear under a separate heading of 'grocery ware' further down the page.[84] Given that appraisers generally worked through rooms in a systematic fashion, this is suggestive of spatial distinctions within the shop. This, of course, makes eminent practical sense, since the display requirements of these goods were quite different: groceries could be stored in a chest, or boxed up on shelves, whereas cloth and haberdashery had to be put on show to potential customers. There are echoes here of the shop-show room distinction drawn by Blithe and Lindsey, with different goods, selling techniques and customers being distinguished spatially. Moreover, by arranging different elements of his stock separately, the astute shopkeeper was able to demonstrate not only the wide range of goods at his disposal, but also his specialised knowledge of the trade: careful and thoughtful display symbolised a corresponding orderliness in the retailer and his business. This link between order, knowledge and display was especially true of trades, such as that of apothecary, which were becoming increasingly professionalised.[85] In such cases, but more generally too, the reputation of shopkeepers depended to a significant extent upon the organisation and layout of their premises: in Lefebvre's terms, their representation of the shop space.

Shops were, of course, much more than projected images of the shopkeeper's business acumen. They were real lived spaces, constantly being produced and reproduced through the everyday spatial practices of consumption.[86] This puts emphasis on the behaviour of those who used the shop space (the customers) as well as the intentions of those who conceptualised and represented it (the tradesmen). As we argued earlier, shops were closely associated with new notions of politeness. Just as tradesmen sought to make their shops polite places, so customers wanted to be seen in, and make their purchases from, fashionable shops. As with their London counterparts, provincial shopkeepers attempted to heighten the visual impact and material comfort of their shops, since this helped to attract respectable consumers. Counters formed the point of exchange not simply of goods and money, but also of information and knowledge. Wares were placed there for the customer to inspect and it was over the counter that the shopkeeper was quizzed about use, quality and price. Rails were especially common in the shops of wealthy drapers, allowing cloth to be hung and displayed to best effect. They helped to create the kind of visual impression that encouraged the customer to visit the shop from curiosity and linger from interest.[87] Shop interiors were often further enhanced by providing chairs and other seats, and more occasionally through the use of sconces, looking glasses and pictures to decorate the walls.[88] The four stools in Ambrose Pierpoint's premises, listed in the inventory with his counter, shelves, press, table, coffer, boxes and packets, clearly formed part of the shop fittings, placed for the comfort and convenience of customers. Much the same was probably true of the chairs in William Wright's drapery shop in Coventry, and the two chairs in Robert Rownson's Liverpool shop. Expenditure on such items was often modest, the two chairs and two joint stools in the shop of the Nantwich tailor, Robert Wilkinson, were valued at only 2s 6d, but they contributed to the construction of a congenial environment which encouraged leisurely shopping.[89]

132 *The building*

In this way, we can again see shops as representations of space: the projected messages of orderliness and knowledge discussed earlier, being overlain with those of polite gentility and sociability. Shop space thus comprised an increasingly important part of the polite public sphere for both men and women (see Chapter 6). This links in closely with the idea of shopping as a pleasurable, indeed a leisure, activity: something encouraged by the practice of furnishing shops in an attractive and comfortable manner, and by elaborate arrangement of goods and spaces. The assemblages of tables, chairs and looking glasses in the glassrooms of Coventry offered arenas for more leisurely shopping than the rather utilitarian street-level shops. Similarly, in bringing together suites of furniture, Abner Scholes necessitated a leisurely movement through the display space. It is impossible to be certain, but it seems likely that a visit to his show rooms would be as much to do with leisure and gathering ideas as making purchases. The rural gentry that formed a substantial proportion of his customer base might call at his shop as part of their wider consumption of leisure within Chester. It is probable that these 'rooms' of furniture would be periodically changed (following the sale of items, the manufacture of new ones or the purchase of new sets of pictures or prints), again echoing Wedgwood's constant changing of his London show rooms to 'render the whole a new scene, even to the same Company every time they shall bring their friends to visit us'.[90] The display of goods in eighteenth-century shops thus has significance not only for practices of shopping, but also for wider processes of consumption (both of goods and space) and for the ways in which urban life was structured, represented and perceived.

In sum, the space of the shop and its organisation revolved around creating an appropriate atmosphere for selling, and was designed to present the goods to the customers who came to see and buy. Thus its organisation was centred on the goods that it sold. In other words, the shop was defined by physical space, but also by the spatial practices that were accepted as taking place there, such as buying, sampling, paying bills and acquiring credit.

The politics of space: absence and presence

Much has been made of the easy access to goods in shops: as a result of their spatial organisation and use of display, people could see, touch and talk about the wares on offer.[91] However, access to goods was also controlled. As indicated above, some items were stored elsewhere and most likely brought to the shop when supplies needed replenishing or on special request. This was probably the case with William Cross, a Manchester grocer, who had some sugar candy, bottoms of sugar and a single sugar loaf in his shop, but a further two and a half hundredweight of 'very coarse' sugar in his warehouse.[92] Indeed, as William Stout's memoirs emphasise, bulk grocery goods were often stored out of sight in a cellar or warehouse, with only small ready-packaged parcels offered for sale in the shop. The 1676 inventory of the Bewdley mercer, John Ballard, lists '26 papers yellow & wt Nayles ijd paper', whilst that of the Newcastle-under-Lyme grocer, William Hockenhall, includes 70 lb of tobacco in 10d and 8d parcels.[93] Such practices would have maximised the range of goods that could be kept on display in the shop, thereby helping to project an image of variety and plenty, but also met the purchasing practices of customers who rarely bought in bulk (see Chapter 6). Not all goods were displayed so publicly. Indeed, the division between front-space and back-space, with its implications of 'public' and 'private', was apparent from the location of precious or taboo items. In one sense, this helps to explain the display of valuable glassware in special show rooms, away from the bustle of the street-level shop. It is also apparent in the practices of booksellers who sometimes played an important role in guiding their customers' choice of books, both in the shop and via correspondence.[94] Whilst extensive catalogues were published by many booksellers and the title pages of books were pasted up in shop windows, other tomes were kept more privately.[95] Similarly, certain novel items might be kept aside to be offered to favoured customers. The 'availability' of goods was thus bound up with the space of the shop and the identity of the consumer, certain goods being defined according to the spaces (front or back; public or private) which they occupied. In this way, the shopkeeper was able to control availability of particular items through their presence in or apparent absence from the shop. In Lefebvre's terms, space could assert, negate and deny.[96]

This same duality of presence and absence was apparent in other leisure spaces. Part of the frisson of pleasure gardens was the sexual excitement generated by the press of the crowds and the anonymity which came with them. Mixed with this was the notion of pecuniary gain, both in terms of the leisure facility itself and the ambitions of at least some of the patrons to catch a wealthy marriage partner.[97] These twin features were personified in the figure of the prostitute or gigolo, whose activities clearly mark the ambiguities of display, visibility and consumption.[98] Such characters found cover in the vast crowds who attended the theatre, or the infamous *ridottos* and masquerades of the London pleasure gardens. Their presence both reflected and contributed to the licentiousness of these gatherings, adding to their attraction and their dangers, particularly for women for whom the safeguarding of reputation was of considerable importance. Officially, they were discouraged: at Vauxhall, Tyrer employed so-called 'chaplains' to ensure that the pleasures taken were refined ones. More explicitly, the manager of the theatre in Chester took action against prostitutes who were frequenting the pit 'to the great annoyance of the more respectable members of that part of the house'. He placed advertisements in the local newspaper assuring theatre goers that 'care has been taken to remedy the ill complained of, and the objections are now entirely removed'.[99] Yet, in reality, it was impossible to effectively police such practices, not least because prostitutes played on the role of pleasure gardens or the theatre auditorium as a show-place in which the fashionable could display their personal attributes. In Birmingham's New Street theatre, for example, prostitutes were claimed to have 'infested the box-lobbies' since more moneyed custom was to be found there.[100]

Illicit books and prostitutes, along with smuggled goods and fraudsters, were present within, yet officially absent from, the spaces of polite consumption: their existence was somehow denied or obscured, but was tangible nonetheless. They effectively transgressed the image of refinement and respectability. In this way, they form part of a wider set of activities and behaviour which conflicted with the polite social practices that produced and confirmed the shop, theatre, assembly room or pleasure garden as normative social space. They reflect Lefebvre's depiction of conflict in the consumption of space between the capitalist 'utilizers' and community users of space.[101] The presence of prostitutes, for example, brought conflict over the use and meaning of leisure spaces: they played on and subverted the agendas of sociability and civility, turning these into vehicles of pecuniary gain. Their disreputable behaviour may have been absent from the pages of official town histories and the sanitised accounts of respectable commentators, but their presence in towns throughout provincial England was often recognised in private correspondence, or reported in the newspapers to a public eager for stories of scandal and impropriety.

It might be argued that these individuals and commodities operated within the accepted parameters of behaviour: the intent and meaning of practices and spaces was modified, but not overwhelmed. More injurious, in the longer term, to the ideals of inclusive polite sociability was the fragmentation of public assemblies into smaller parties which created private enclaves in 'public' spaces. One focus for this was the gaming table. Notwithstanding a series of Gaming Acts passed in the years following 1739, gambling remained an important aspect of many leisure activities, from cock-fighting and horse-racing, to the card parties which formed such a central part of assemblies. At one level, this fuelled the critique of the moral credentials of such gatherings, especially at Bath, since gambling was seen as encouraging an underworld of sharps and swindlers.[102] When a gang of shoplifters was arrested in Leominster in 1772, amongst their illicit possessions was listed 'a pack of gambling cards'.[103] In many respects, card-sharps might be viewed in the same way as prostitutes: playing on the social practices of the elite, but twisting them to their own ends. However, gambling was also seen as cutting at the heart of the inclusive sociability of assemblies. The intense concentration induced by gambling, together with its addictive nature, was said to drive its adherents to neglect their social duties. Women gamblers especially were singled out: they engaged in the unfeminine delights of competition and meanwhile ignored eligible suitors.[104]

If gambling brought a threat to polite sociability from within, then the 'mob' threatened to do so from without. We have already seen how the socially heterogeneous crowds at pleasure gardens and particularly race meetings threatened to overwhelm the politeness of such gatherings and spaces. A similar process can also be observed for the theatre. Indeed, the Theatre Act made the problem of popular participation explicit, stating that: 'the excess of theatrical entertainments fills both town and country with idleness and debauchery'.[105] The problem, perhaps more imagined than real, was exacerbated by the practice, noted above, of theatre proprietors admitting people half-price for entry half-way through the show. Whilst proprietors benefited from the additional revenue created, any exclusivity that the ticket price might have afforded was effectively undermined.[106] Many commentators worried that the crowding of the pit brought social disorder:

the behaviour of the lower orders being unseemly for such 'refined' spaces.[107] Indeed, the proprietors of the Birmingham Theatre were sufficiently exercised by the problem that, on one occasion, they advertised a reward for anyone 'who will discover the Ruffians who have thrown ... Bottles, Plates, Apples etc at the Actors and upon the Stage, during and after the Performance'.[108]

The problems of theatre managers ran deep and were redoubled when the theatre became the venue for verbal and physical conflict between local political factions, some of it occurring on stage but much more in the auditorium. Thus, following the election of John Egerton as one of Chester's MPs – breaking the long strangle-hold of the Grosvenors on the city's parliamentary seats – the Theatre Royal experienced a series of vociferous exchanges. These culminated in January 1810 in a riot centred on the theatre. With Grosvenor's supporters, aided by labourers from his estate at Eaton, breaking down the theatre door, inside:

> The first appearance of disturbance was occasioned by a person called Bannister going into the gallery and exclaiming that he saw a member of the Grosvenors there and challenged anyone to fight with him. This conduct was resented and a scuffle ensued. Upon the appearance soon afterwards of Mr Egerton with a party of friends in the boxes, a cry of 'No tyrants' was immediately raised which was resented by the opposite party, and their efforts prevailing over that of Mr Egerton's an officer belonging to Chester Local Militia mounted one of the benches in the pit and exclaimed 'is there a local militia man who will not stretch his arm to support his major?' pointing to Mr Egerton. Several of the gallant officer's friends remonstrated with him on the impropriety of appealing to men in a military capacity to promote a riot. Bannister than came forward on the stage with a jug of ale in his hand, and after having drunk he handed it to a man ... in the pit, who prevailed on his friend Mr Egerton to drink also. Bannister again challenged anyone to fight: then indeed 'confusion raised her crest' and ... the curtain dropped amid shouts of 'Grosvenors for ever'.[109]

Whilst this tells us as much about the culture of elections as it does about the theatre, it is significant how the arrangement of the theatre led to the disturbance spreading to all parts, from the pit to the boxes, and from the gallery to the stage. Moreover, whilst the admittance of the common orders clearly undermined the respectability of the theatre, it is significant that they did so at the behest of MPs and peers of the realm.

Just as problematic were views and uses of the shop which were at odds with its image as a place of visible exchange, polite sociability and respectable consumption. This image was challenged, and the accepted boundaries and uses of the shop transgressed, through acts of theft from or violence against the premises. The problem of shoplifting was inherent to practices of displaying goods and called for close vigilance on the part of the shopkeeper. Its sharp growth – or at least the perception that it was spiralling out of control – around the turn of the eighteenth century is witnessed by the passing of a new Act in 1699. This was directed at the 'Crime of stealing Goods privately out of Shops and Warehouses, commonly called shoplifting', which the wording of the Act suggested was 'of late Years much increased'.[110] It is also apparent from the large volume of pamphlets published at the time, with titles such as 'Hanging Not Punishment Enough: a Case of Traders relating to Shoplifters'; from the burgeoning number of hearings at Quarter Sessions which concerned theft (although it is often unclear whether goods were taken from houses or shops); and from the growing number of 'Associations for the Prosecution of Felons'.[111] To quantify this, the *Worcester Journal* records seven people prosecuted for shoplifting in 1772 alone – many of them women. Moreover, some of these individuals were prolific offenders: Mary Clymer, for instance, admitted to stealing, with her aunt Sarah, from between twenty and thirty shops in and around Worcester over a period of three years. Two other defendants, Mary Turner and Margaret Gatfield, were described as 'old offenders, and very expert in the Art of Shop-Lifting'.[112] The ways in which shoplifters such as Turner and Gatfield operated meshed almost seamlessly with the practices of regular customers (see Chapter 6), and linked closely with the spatial arrangement and display of goods, particularly on the shop counter. As Defoe's Moll Flanders recounted: 'our principal trade was watching shopkeepers' counters, and slipping off any kind of goods we could see carelessly laid anywhere'. This thieving was mixed with regular practices of browsing, designed to allay suspicion. When her partner was apprehended in the act of stealing, Moll herself 'was careful to attempt nothing in the lace chamber, but tumbled the goods pretty much to spend time; then bought a few yards of edging and paid for it'.[113]

If shoplifting was a growing feature of the age, it was not the only threat to the livelihood of the shopkeeper or the image and integrity of the shop. Evidence from the west Midlands suggests that shop-breaking was also a serious problem. The extent and impact of such practices can be illustrated by the activities in and around Coventry of John Rew, William Pickard and their accomplices. In 1750, over the period of a month or so, they broke into and stole from over 25 shops and warehouses. Their plunder included: bowls, dishes and trenchers from a dish turner's shop; a large quantity of hardware from 'Essex Shop'; a piece of linen cloth from Porter's shop; stockings and a worsted cap from Wall's shop; three cheeses from a shop in Bishop street; three bottles of liquors out of Mr Edwardes' shop; sugar from a shop in Bailey Lane; over 5 shillings and a cake of ginger bread from a mercer's shop in Church Lawford; soap and a couple of rabbits from Mr Tuckard's shop, and twisted cloth from the shop below; Lisbon sugar and small cut tobacco from Mr Smith's warehouse in Palmer Lane; 15 yards printed of cotton from Mr Boddington's; a pudding from Admiral Vernon's shop; cloth from a woman in Bailey Lane; three pistols from Warren's shop; two canisters of tea from Mr Ash; and other thefts from butchers and bakers.[114] Whilst these thefts did not, in general, involve high-status shops, they took place across the city's retail space: from the High Street and Cross Cheaping, to the marketplace, Bailey Lane and more peripheral areas such as Gosford Street. Moreover, the extensive list gives an indication of the disorder which would have been created by such acts. Physical damage to property included breaking doors and windows, and forcing locks.[115]

The conventional barriers guarding the integrity of the shop were relatively easily circumvented, and the gang moved freely through the shop and home once inside, as the deposition of Sarah Crow (6 January 1758) makes clear:

> All three went to Maydling's house in Gosford Street [Coventry], and Rew unlocked the entry door, and undid a door in the yard, and got a ladder, and undid the parlour window, and then opened the door out of the Parlour into the yard and then they all went into the parlour of shop and took out three canisters of tea, lump sugar, three pieces of check'd linen, one piece of shirt cloth and several other things.[116]

The ease with which the shop space could be invaded and disturbed is perhaps most telling since it undermined the status of the shop as ordered and formalised space. The integrity of consumer spaces was thus contested, and dominant ideologies pushed aside by the spatial practices of breaking and entering. Significantly, many of the above thefts took place at 'night time'.[117] Whilst, of course, a practical consideration for the thieves, this heightens the impression of transgression as the antithesis of civility: discourses about respectability, sociability and order in the streets were often couched in terms of light and darkness (see Chapter 4). Moreover, the frequency of the thefts from shops, and number of shops involved, must have created an impression of epidemic disorder and highlighted the vulnerability of shop goods and premises.

Similar examples appear in newspaper reports across the west Midlands and north-west England. A sample from the *Worcester Journal* confirms the wide range of goods targeted and the relative ease with which thieves could gain access to shop premises. Through October, November and December 1772, there were break-ins at a baker's shop, from which money was taken; a bookseller's, where paper was stolen; a jeweller's, who lost silver buttons and seals; and a mercer's, where cloth was removed. In addition, thefts were attempted at an apothecary's, a skinner's and several others. One common method of entry was 'to turn the pins in the window-shutters to try if the keys are put in beyond the spring, if not, they easily shake them out, and take down a shutter'. Failing this, more violent means might be adopted, as in the attempted break-in at the shop of Mr Dunn, apothecary, in the High Street, where 'the shop door [was] almost wrenched open'.[118] These examples emphasise the fragility of windows and doors as physical barriers between internal and external space, and underline the importance of social control – and behavioural norms – in the successful operation of polite shopping spaces. Indeed, it is notable that these transgressions of the integrity of the shop were said to have caused 'great terror [in] the inhabitants, many of whom have lately formed themselves into a nightly watch at their own houses'.[119]

The implications of theft from retail shops clearly went above and beyond just the financial loss incurred by shopkeepers. Larceny was a socio-spatial practice that cut into the heart of eighteenth-century principles of retail trade – fair price, good service and visible exchange – and contested the image of the shop that the shopkeepers cultivated. As a consequence, they were a challenge to the wider 'polite' space of the town and more generally consumerism. Assaults on shops, as exemplars of the urban renaissance, could be construed as an attack on the public sphere, a reminder that the eighteenth-century city was a site of struggle behind its polite façade.[120] This conflict was central to the production of urban consumer spaces. Theft disrupted the stock of the shop, causing disorder, took place at night, and often involved breaking into the shop space – broken windows and doors were a visual testament to the contested space of the shop. This challenge struck home at all levels, cutting across the space of sociability, the importance of appearance the shopkeepers upheld, the authority of the shopkeeper over the shop and consequently, the respectability of the shop. In more general terms, these practices subverted the uses and meanings of shop space. They created, at least temporarily, counterspaces in which conflicts over ownership, acquisition and consumption of goods were played out.

Conclusion

The link between an urban renaissance and the emergence of polite culture is well recognised. Yet the spaces which were at the heart of this change, both geographically and metaphorically, were not neutral components of a march towards modernity but part of the ways in which this culture was produced and reproduced. Through access to and social practice within the physical spaces of shops, theatres, assembly rooms and pleasure gardens, both individuals and groups were defined as polite and respectable. At the same time, their presence and activities identified these as polite and respectable places. Thus, the spatiality of the built environment – its inherent social–spatial dialectic – was central to the urban renaissance and rising consumerism. Individual buildings, designed and adapted for the purposes of leisure, were codified spaces which accommodated both the demands of business and the pursuit of pleasure, and the need for a fashionable public front for the leisure and retail sector. This can be seen in the tasteful decoration of assembly rooms and the careful layout of subscription libraries: both calculated to produce space appropriate to their use, yet reflecting the wider agenda of social inclusion and differentiation. At the same time, an innovative agenda was set in response to the new intersection between the availability of novel goods and the privileging of discourses of civility and sociability, giving further impetus to the modernisation of the space of the shop. The shop was newly presented in such a way as to make it the lifeblood of consumer society: one increasingly driven by urbane values and embedded in its spatiality.

The analysis of buildings as public–private space – the product of mutual interaction between proprietors and users – underlines the close relationship between the material structures and spatial practices of polite consumption in the eighteenth century. Display was at the centre of social–spatial interaction, shaping interior layout and public façades, but also the behaviour within these spaces. Thus, even at the level of individual buildings, space was essential in shaping the rituals and material culture which retained and marked social divides: highlighting those with taste and discernment, and distinguishing polite from popular. However, as easily as such images were created, they could be transgressed, displaced and subverted by social practices within these same spaces: the excitement of heterogeneous mixing in pleasure gardens could descend into a threat to social order; the 'public' assembly could become fragmented into private gaming parties; and browsing in shops could become theft. The importance of behaviour in shaping the meaning, character and physical structure of a wide range of spaces of consumption focuses our attention onto the individual and social practices.

6   The individual

Social practices and identity

Introduction

Focusing on the individual consumer returns us to the link between consumption, practice and identity. In terms of material culture, this relationship has been variously styled as one of 'prudent luxury', 'acquisitiveness and self-respect', 'respectability' and 'the domestic environment'.[1] All these readings follow Miller *et al.* in emphasising the importance of the 'symbolic world of consumption' as much as the material world of goods. They also go some way in acknowledging the role in identity formation of the processes whereby goods were acquired which form such an important element of analyses of department stores.[2] As discussed earlier, shopping (and leisure) can be seen as purposeful activities wherein the consumer is an active and knowing agent, often consciously constructing their identity through their shopping practices as much as the goods purchased. In this light, shopping can be linked to sociability and politeness, but also to systems of rational knowledge. Alternatively, it can be seen as intuitive and habitual: identity being created performatively through repeated action. These two positions can, in part, be reconciled through Miller's argument that the identity of consumers is a 'social process that shifts according to social context' and, by extension, spatial setting.[3] But shoppers and pleasure seekers in turn produced these contexts through their co-presence and their social practices of consumption. One way of exploring this spatiality is in terms of the so-called 'cultural contexts' which both framed and promoted the growing demand for consumer goods. These contexts – gentility, luxury, virtue, rational masculinity and feminine domesticity – closely parallel the headings under which Vickery organises her analysis of the social and cultural lives of eighteenth-century genteel women: gentility, love and duty, fortitude and resignation, prudent economy, elegance, civility and vulgarity, and propriety. For Smith, each 'context' was linked to a specific set of goods and spaces, practices and motivations. He binds them together in the wider construct of respectability as an important element of individual and social identity.[4] Smith's analysis can be usefully related to Giddens' notion of structure and agency: cultural contexts form social and spatial structures within and through which operated the agency of individual action.[5] Developing this line of thinking, and linking it to more overtly spatial analysis, leisure and shopping can be viewed as cultural contexts, important in shaping consumption in the eighteenth century. They brought together institutions, sets of 'customary practices or behaviours, particular modes of cognition and discourse, and material objects'.[6] As we have argued in the preceding chapters, they did so in particular spatial contexts which were both the product of social practice and instrumental in structuring behaviour and norms.

So far, we have focused very much on the institutions, built environment and the materiality of leisure and shopping. Smith's framework encourages us to consider spaces of consumption as social constructs. From this perspective, we need to turn our attention from the apparent fixity of the buildings to the spatial and social agency of the consumer. Lefebvre argued that social space incorporates and consists of social action: the everyday or customary practices of individuals and groups. Thus, it was through the activities carried out in the shop, assembly room or promenade – the spatial practices or, as Pred would have it, the daily path of shopping and leisure – that these institutions were experienced, lived and produced as social spaces. However, it would be wrong to see social space as unitary: each set of actions or practices could produce a different social space interpenetrating and/or superimposing itself upon other spaces. In this way, different individuals or groups might perceive, use and produce consumer space in different ways. Equally, as Pred makes clear, it would be mistaken to view social space as atomised: the unique construction and lifeworld of each individual. Space was *socially* produced. It was the product of social interaction between individuals and groups which was itself constrained by the rules and norms of society.[7] As we saw in Chapter 5, these were, in turn, communicated and enforced in and through space: the *active* context for social practice. As Giddens argues, then, the agency of the individual and of social practice operated within and through social and spatial structures.[8] This is not to deny the importance of people in making spaces of consumption. Indeed, the creation of rules and behavioural norms was another way in which people controlled space. The framework of customary practices and behaviour bound up in the 'cultural context' of leisure and shopping may have acted to constrain individual action, but it was central to the social production of space. We therefore need to sharpen the focus on the consumer as a negotiator and producer of the spaces of leisure and shopping if we are to understand more fully the micro-geographies and processes of consumption. In short, we need to repopulate the buildings, streets, towns and regions discussed in earlier chapters, and thus reintegrate the behaviour and spaces of leisure and shopping.

This chapter begins by exploring the patterns and rhythms of leisure and shopping. We emphasise the ways in which both sets of activities involved people coming together in space and time. Shops, theatres and assemblies served as social mixing pots, not least in terms of bringing together town and country through moments of consumption. We then turn more directly to Smith's conceptualisation of the cultural context, and build on Berry's notion of polite consumption to examine the customary behaviour and social practices which characterised shops and leisure facilities. Highlighting that these shared many common characteristics across a range of institutions, we argue that often self-conscious consumer practice was central to the construction of leisure facilities and especially shops as lived spaces. Finally, we consider some of the modes of cognition and discourse associated with leisure and shopping. Here, we draw on Miller's assertion of the pluralism and dynamism of consumer identity, and explore the motivations of consumers, and the identities created and recreated through acts and spaces of consumption.

Material culture and the patterns of leisure and shopping

Both shops and leisure facilities were characterised by patterns of use which varied across space and time. Visits to shops were part of the normal daily routine for many middle-ranking urban residents, particularly women. Fanny Burney's fictional gentlewomen found their mornings 'all spent in gossiping, shopping and dressing', especially when they were in London or at one of the spa resorts. Similarly, Judith Baker's visits to London were marked by wide-ranging shopping trips, and Ann Sneyd, who purchased goods and services throughout the year, spent more time and money on shopping whilst in Bath for the summer season.[9] As Margot Finn reminds us, however, men too could be enthusiastic shoppers when the opportunity arose. Like her better known examples, the rural gentry and urban professionals of north-west England recorded regular purchases in their diaries. Nicholas Blundell travelled to a number of towns, but especially Liverpool to buy goods; the Liverpool attorney, John Plumbe, patronised shops in the town, and made numerous purchases elsewhere, and Henry Prescott's visits to shops in Chester were almost a matter of daily routine.[10]

There were clear temporal patterns to shopping. In Lancaster, Stout noted that most of his shop customers came on market days – a pattern confirmed in our sample of shop account books. The Worcester grocer, Thomas Dickenson, dealt with around 70 per cent more customers on a Saturday, the most important of the town's three market days, when visitors were drawn from a wide hinterland. Similarly, in Newcastle-under-Lyme, the mercers Fletcher and Fenton transacted over one-third of their business on a Monday, the main market day in the town.[11] Overlain on this weekly cycle were seasonal patterns of trade. Dickenson's accounts show peaks in the number of purchases during early March and mid-August, coinciding with Worcester's two assizes, and with the races held in the week following the second court session. Those of Fletcher and Fenton indicate that their busiest times coincided with the town's fairs. Such gatherings provided an enormous fillip for trade: indeed, Coventry's Godiva festival was rejuvenated in 1678 expressly for the purpose of encouraging trade in the town.[12] From the perspective of the consumer, there was the convenience of making purchases when in town on business or pleasure. Thus John Plumbe noted in his diary the purchase of 'gloves for self and wife' whilst at Lancaster assizes in August 1727.[13] Moreover, the influx of extra tradesmen provided an ideal opportunity to make planned purchases. In a letter sent to Sir John Morduant in 1704 concerning the purchase of cloth, Will Clerke states that 'Warwick May Fair is as good a place for ye doing it as any & there will be a great deale of choice'.[14] That said, the dominance of the fixed shop and its growing importance in the shopping routines of the middling sorts increased through the course of the eighteenth century. By 1775, a Chester resident could feel confident in writing to her friend in Flint that 'there is no occasion to be in a violent hurry for there is always great variety of choice in the shops and full as cheap as what the people bring to the fair'.[15] For people such as these, shopping had become in essence, if not literally, an everyday activity.

Patterns of leisure did not take the same form as the patterns of shopping since most leisure activities were available far less frequently. As noted in Chapter 2, some events were held only once every few years: their impact could be enormous, but was temporally limited. The Preston Guild, occurring once every twenty years, was a huge draw for the gentry of the surrounding districts as the Corporation laid on a series of lavish events. More regular were race meetings, which took place annually at major courses such as Chester, Lichfield and Warwick.[16] Meetings in smaller centres were more sporadic, particularly from the mid-eighteenth century when new legislative controls on racing were introduced. From Borsay's survey of seventeen sample years of the *Racing Calendar* between 1730 and 1770, the median number of meetings identified at locations in the five surveyed counties was just two and in many places only a single event is recorded. Such infrequency may, in part, help to explain their enormous attraction both to the rural gentry and a sometimes more plebeian urban audience (see Chapter 5). Musical concerts, assemblies and theatrical performances might occur twice a week during the winter season in larger centres, but were far less frequent in smaller towns (see Chapter 2). Indeed, in places such as Colne and Bromsgrove concerts and assemblies were occasional treats in an otherwise rather barren social calendar.[17] The frequency with which clubs and societies chose to meet also varied considerably, but many were monthly or sometimes weekly events. The famous Lunar Society of Birmingham, for example, met each month on the night of the full moon, so that there would be sufficient light by which to travel home afterwards. Similarly, Bolton's newly established Literary and Philosophical Society met on the second Friday of each month in 1813, whilst the Vale of Evesham Horticultural Society held six exhibitions annually at the town hall from 1827. The more informal Unanimous Society in Liverpool, meanwhile, met every Saturday evening from early September to the end of April.[18]

One effect of the relative infrequency of many events was to heighten their prominence within the social calendar. The Preston Guild was eagerly anticipated, as were the celebrations in towns across the country to mark the coronation of George III in 1761. In Coventry there was a procession through the town followed by fireworks and a grand ball in St Mary's Hall.[19] In smaller towns, where such occasions were rarer, the sense of expectation could be even greater. It was said, for instance, of the Grand Jubilee to celebrate the 1776 opening of the Cloth Hall in Colne, that 'such Doings at such distance from London, but seldom happen and must therefore be the more Marvellous'.[20] More generally the winter and summer season could elicit considerable expectations, particularly in county and resort towns. The *Worcester Journal* commented that the Company at Malvern

Wells was thought likely to be particularly numerous and respectable in 1772. Many 'persons of distinction are daily expected', and 'it is imagined there will be the greatest appearance of genteel Company at the Ball and Public Breakfast at the long Room on Monday next, that has been remembered for several years'.[21] Notwithstanding a bit of 'puffing' by the local rag, it is clear that such periods of excitement added colour to the urban scene, complementing the everyday nature of shops and shopping. Indeed, we can see a layering of activities which together structured patterns of consumption: daily or weekly visits to shops, monthly assemblies or concerts, annual race meetings and periodic major events.

Shops, theatres, assemblies and libraries constituted the coalescence of consumers in space as well as time. Visits to these various institutions involved journeys: for some, merely down the street or across town; for others, from the surrounding countryside or neighbouring towns. As well as selling to fellow townsfolk, Thomas Dickenson – like most shopkeepers – had a large number of rural customers, including squires and the clergy, whilst John Webb counted leading Staffordshire gentry families such as the Chetwynds and Baggotts amongst his best customers.[22] Visits from such customers created a blending of town and country in the space of the shop as well as on the pages of the account books. Much the same was true of leisure facilities, since patrons of the theatres, assembly rooms and concert halls comprised the rural gentry as well as the urban middling sorts. This was especially true of market and county towns, but a significant minority of subscribers to leisure facilities in many industrial centres were from outside the town. Of the 172 people who contributed to the building of new premises for Birmingham's Public Library in 1798, 52 came from outside the town, many from the neighbouring parishes of Aston, Edgbaston and Handsworth. Similarly, the town's music festival drew in people from within 25 miles of the town, including, in 1784, such luminaries as Lady Plymouth, Lord and Lady Ferrers, Sir Robert and Lady Lawley, and Sir Edward Littleton. The more widespread appeal of the festival is, however, clear from the considerable lengths to which the organising committee went, on this occasion, to avoid clashing with similar musical gatherings at Salisbury, Liverpool and Gloucester.[23] Events to mark important occasions also drew the county elite into town. For instance, a grand ball at Liverpool's Infirmary in March 1748 to celebrate peace with France was attended by

> The Countess of Derby and three of the ladies ..., Mr Farrington of Shea Hall and some of Mr Blundell of Ince's family and several officers of St George's Dragoons besides most of the persons of fashion in town, there was all parties there without distinction and the whole conducted with great order, decency and good manners.[24]

Rather than occupying separate spheres, the polite elements of town and country met in the shop, assembly room or theatre. Moreover, as Berry notes, institutions and shops were largely controlled by townspeople which made them instrumental in spreading the values of urban society to a geographically wider constituency. For instance, all those serving on the committee of the Liverpool library between 1769 and 1796 lived in the city, as did those serving on the committee of the library and theatre in Birmingham.[25]

The growing influence exerted by the consumption priorities of polite society made shops and leisure facilities mixing pots in social as well as geographical terms: indeed, this was an important part of the purpose of assemblies, promenades and the like. They formed a context in which the customary practices, modes of discourse and material objects of politeness came together and were spread through society (see Chapters 3 and 5).[26] But this cultural context was, in part, produced by the broader patterns of leisure and shopping. The company assembled and encountered at these events and in these spaces made them what they were. It is therefore important to assess the social composition of 'polite' consumers. To an extent, definitions were place and event specific. At Knutsford in the 1790s, the bar was set high with 'none but gentility' and 'on no account any tradesmen' being admitted to the assemblies. More generally, polite society was defined more broadly. This was particularly true of commercial centres, where much of the elite were in trade, but it was also true of county towns such as Chester, the trading and civic elite of which were increasingly styled as 'urban gentry'. Many shops and leisure facilities drew customers from a surprisingly wide social circle, including the gentry and urban elite, a middling sort of manufacturers, professionals, tradesmen and so on, and often a range of petty tradesmen and artisans. This reflected and indeed stretched the inclusive nature of Addisonian notions of politeness: a set of values and practices open to all who had the time, money and inclination to participate. It served to reinforce the polite nature – or at least pretensions – of both these consumer spaces and their customers. Gentlemen often rubbed shoulders with artisans, labourers and other ruder sorts on the racecourse and in the crowded cockpit. Certainly, diarists and letter writers including the gentlewoman, Ann Sneyd, the attorney, John Plumbe, the flax merchant, Thomas Langton, and Lord Strange, the son of the Earl of Derby regularly mention their attendance at such events.[27] Moreover, polite consumers often took their servants along to assemblies and the theatre, not least as they were needed to reserve seats and to act as a prop for the social display that took place on such occasions.[28] Much the same was true of shops. On a typical day in 1741 the customers of Thomas Dickenson included the apothecary, John Brookes, the cooper, George Lait and the barber, George Saunders, all of Worcester, plus two fellow grocers, Timothy Edwards of Worcester and Frank Webb of Droitwich, and Edmund Taylor, a country squire from Welland, near Malvern.[29]

This social heterogeneity reveals the tensions and contradictions, inherent within the concept of politeness, between inclusivity and exclusivity. The need to keep the 'company' (and the leisure spaces) socially exclusive, at least to some extent, was in the interest of those operating or subscribing to leisure facilities. Without it, the cultural capital attached to participation or membership would be cheapened and the fashionability of the occasion lost. Indeed, as Sweet argues, there was a danger, and indeed a tendency, for the currency of politeness itself to be devalued towards the end of the eighteenth century.[30] Despite this, relatively few institutions or events explicitly debarred access on the grounds of status alone.

Civic ceremonies and entertainments were an exception: at the Preston Guild, the majority of townspeople were debarred from the exclusive junketings of the town's elite and the visiting gentry. Moreover, there was an apparent hierarchy of balls arranged for the meeting in 1762, with two Grand Balls, two Ladies' Assemblies and a Trade Assembly.[31] Outside such gatherings, Shaftesbury's notion of a gentlemanly politeness was rarely expressed in the subscription lists of leisure and cultural facilities, and divisions on the basis of religion and politics were seldom overt. The Liverpool Literary and Philosophical Society was initially dominated by non-conformists, as was the Birmingham library, but both became broader in their membership by the early nineteenth century.[32]

The social status of consumers was policed largely, if rather ineffectively, through price. Subscription rates for theatres and assemblies remained fairly modest throughout the eighteenth century. Jane Healey, owner of the Long Room in Worcester, charged one shilling a night for her card assemblies in 1772, and in Newcastle-under-Lyme the cost of attending the full winter programme of three assemblies in 1789 at the Great Room in the Roe Buck was just 5s, or 10s 6d for an unaccompanied gentleman. Similarly, a Gentleman's Subscription Ticket for the assembly series at Bolton in 1816 could be had for 21 shillings, whilst Ladies paid only 15 shillings.[33] Moreover, from Ann Sneyd's diary it is apparent that, even for someone who regularly participated in a wide range of leisure activities, expenditure on balls, plays and race meetings was fairly modest in comparison to the money spent on consumer goods. Over the period 1766–72 she spent no more than £15 on tickets for social events.[34] This reflected the commercial and social nature of such occasions: their economic viability and success as social events relied on the attraction of a good number of subscribers. In contrast, many libraries were kept exclusive by high initial and annual subscription fees. In Liverpool, the Athenaeum was founded in 1798 on the basis of 350 ten-guinea subscriptions, followed by 150 more at twenty, then thirty guineas. Similarly, the nineteen founding members of the Birmingham Library in 1779 paid the initial sum of a guinea, and then a 6-shilling annual subscription, rising to 10 shillings in 1789.[35] Such rates largely restricted membership of these institutions to wealthy merchants, professionals and the gentry, and signalled the status of both subscribers and institution.

Paralleling this, different shops attracted customers of different social standing. One obvious contrast was between town and country. The village shopkeepers William Wood of Didsbury and John Poyser of Yoxall in Staffordshire sold a wide range of everyday goods to small farmers, artisans and labourers. Few of their customers had honorific titles such as 'Mr', 'Mrs' or gentleman.[36] In contrast, Fletcher and Fenton of Newcastle-under-Lyme, the Stafford mercer John Webb, and the Stafford apothecary Lewis Dickenson each drew 15–20 per cent of their customers from the gentry, clergy and professionals, and over 40 per cent from those entitled Mr or Mrs (see Table 6.1). More particularly, Lewis Dickenson relied heavily on custom from local gentry families who turned to him especially for veterinary medicines for their horses; whilst Fletcher and Fenton earned half of their accounted income in the 1760s from sales to around a dozen high status

Table 6.1 Status of customers at three Staffordshire shops

	Lewis Dickenson (1737–57)			Fletcher and Fenton (1768–9)			John Webb (1738–44)		
	% customers	% accounted income	average spend (£)	% customers	% accounted income	average spend (£)	% customers	% accounted income	average spend (£)
Gentry	11.2	24.9	8.4	10.3	19.9	19.6	13.5	19.5	11.0
Clergy	3.7	0.8	0.8	4.1	4.6	11.3	1.8	3.0	12.6
Profs	7.5	8.3	4.2	1.6	3.6	23.7	4.3	6.2	11.1
Mr/Mrs	54.2	58.6	4.2	43.3	44.6	10.5	59.5	66.1	8.5
Other	23.4	7.4	1.2	40.7	27.3	6.8	20.9	5.2	1.9
	100.0	100.0		100.0	100.0		100.0	100.0	

Source: SRO, D1798 HM 27/4; SRO, D (W) 1788/V/108–11; SRO, D1798 HM28/10.

customers, including a number of country squires.[37] That said, they also served a large proportion of less wealthy customers. Indeed, the proportion of their account customers with no honorific title was double that of the two Stafford tradesmen.

The temporal and spatial patterns of shopping and leisure which emerge from this analysis were closely mapped onto one another, underlining the close relationship between these two activities. The parallel progression of urban improvement and consumption of novel goods tracked by Beckett and Smith should thus be seen as only part of this story: leisure and shopping constituted the twin elements in the production and consumption of urban material culture.[38] As we shall see, they shared common modes of behaviour and discourse, institutions and material objects, and motivations. One basic dimension of this relationship was the overlap between those listed as subscribers and shop customers. Of the 284 subscribers to the Worcester infirmary in 1754, fifty-five also had an account with Thomas Dickenson, amongst them many of the city's aldermen and apothecaries.[39] Some of these men – such as the wealthy clothier Charles Trubshaw Withers, the glover Richard Holdship and the apothecary William Davis – were also generous contributors to Worcester's leisure infrastructure. Withers, for instance, was responsible for laying out gravel paths in the grounds of his house to form Sansome Field Walk, for many years the principal promenade in the city. Holdship and Davis were amongst the founders of the Worcester porcelain factory, itself a notable attraction for visitors.[40]

This same combination of polite shopping and involvement in fashionable leisure activities is chronicled in the domestic accounts of Ann Sneyd. She attended plays on at least fourteen occasions between 1766 and 1772; subscribed to assemblies in Bath, Shrewsbury, Lichfield and Oswestry most years during the 1770s; went annually to the races in Shrewsbury and Lichfield; and was a regular visitor to the Spring Gardens in Bath. She also purchased small fashionable items such as ribbons, handkerchiefs, gloves and fans on an almost weekly basis. In May 1769, for instance, she bought a pair of pearl earrings, tickets for the Spring Gardens, trimming for her red negligee, a hoop, snuff, tickets for 'Mr Plomer's ball', five pairs of white kid gloves, three pairs of gauze worsted stockings, and paid for the hire of a sedan chair. Similarly, John Plumbe bought luxury goods on over thirty occasions during 1727, mostly small items of cloth or haberdashery, but also a teapot, upholstered furniture, French wine, and a dozen knives and forks. He was an enthusiastic sportsman too, attending the races at Preston, Ormskirk and Prescot assiduously, and laying out over £25 for the purchase and repair of a cockpit. The spending patterns of the middle-aged country squire, John Dickenson of Taxal, appear rather modest in comparison (mostly clothing bought for his wife and daughter Sall), whilst his leisure time was primarily spent visiting and dining with friends and family. He was, however, a subscriber to both the Manchester infirmary and the Manchester library in the Old Exchange, and his son Jack attended the music meeting there in 1777 and the races at Mottram in 1779.[41]

Attending the theatre, going to assemblies and concerts, being a member of a subscription library, visiting fashionable shops and subscribing to useful institutions were all elements of a polite lifestyle and all involved the consumption of a specifically urban material culture. Fashionable shops and leisure facilities were polite spaces: a status which both accrued from and reinforced the social standing of their customers and patrons. Critical in this were the ways in which consumers drew on and shaped the spaces of the shop and leisure institution to identify themselves as fashionable and refined.

Socio-spatial practices of leisure and shopping

As a cultural context for consumption, polite leisure and shopping involved a range of spatial practices. Whilst Glennie and Thrift have argued that many of these were intuitive and repetitive, it is clear that they were also structured by a set of behavioural norms, the nature of which varied, as Miller suggests, with social context.[42] The most highly formalised 'rules' governing behaviour in leisure facilities were those drawn up by Beau Nash at Bath. Initially displayed in the Pump Room, they were subsequently published over and again in guides and histories of the town, and thus quickly entered into the collective consciousness of the assembled company and the projected image of the resort.[43] In seeking to guide people's behaviour, Nash effectively framed the social production of Bath's pump rooms and assembly rooms as spaces of polite consumption: a process which was echoed across the country. As we have already seen, rules sometimes shaped the composition of the company at these events. Writing from Derby to his son Robert, for instance, Erasmus Darwin cautioned that 'at Lichfield surgeons are not admitted [to card assemblies] as they are here; but they are to dancing assemblies'. Others informed the organisation of proceedings, the selection of dance partners, and precedence in the dancing that ensued.[44] Significantly, the implementation of these norms generally involved the central figure of a master of ceremonies, as at Liverpool where the assemblies were 'regulated by a lady styled "the Queen", and she rules with very absolute power'. Similarly, Mrs Shaw, who presided over the Otley assemblies in the 1790s, saw that 'everything was conducted with due decorum'. In Leamington Spa, by contrast, the master of ceremonies was less influential, with visitors electing 'presidents' to manage social obligations from amongst their own number.[45] In all these places, though, the assemblies were characterised by norms which encouraged particular social practices and effectively made them polite leisure spaces.

Subscription libraries and learned societies were also regulated and defined by normative codes of behaviour. Those of the Manchester Portico Library were fairly typical. Opening hours of the library were fixed at 1–4pm and 6–9pm, Monday to Saturday, with the later addition of 6–8pm on Sunday, and each member could borrow just one volume at a time. Coffee, tea and soups were allowed only in the newsroom, the library itself being reserved for quiet contemplation and reading.[46] The Liverpool Athenaeum was a little more relaxed regarding drinks, resolving that the 'librarian or housekeeper be allowed to supply the subscribers with tea or coffee either in the Newsroom or Library, but that no wine or other liquors be introduced'. However, it was equally strict on the loan of books, with fines for lost volumes and a prohibition on the removal of reviews, magazines and pamphlets from the newsroom.⁴⁷ In both institutions, a salaried librarian was employed to enforce the rules. The symbolic importance of these regulations was such that, in the case of the Liverpool Athenaeum, it was determined that they would be 'printed at the expense of the Institution; and a copy … delivered to every subscriber on the opening of the Library'.⁴⁸ In addition to this management of space and movement, most libraries, clubs and societies also sought to regulate discussion and debate. The Liverpool Athenaeum, Manchester Portico Library, and the Lunar Society and Subscription Library in Birmingham amongst many others had an avowed non-political foundation. Discussion of politics or religion was strongly discouraged, and proscribed from formal lectures and debates, the focus instead being on trade, natural philosophy or literature.

A parallel set of informal rules framed attendance at the theatre, although behaviour could degenerate into rowdiness and bawdiness. Johanna Schopenhauer noted of the London theatre that:

> etiquette dictates that all ladies attend the theatre in full dress if they wish to sit in the front rows of the boxes … No lady is admitted with a large hat though a small dress one … is allowed. In the pit, however, they can appear in ordinary clothes with large hats which they must remove without objection, if asked to do so. Women of the middle class and gentlemen of any rank frequent the pit. It is quite a respectable place.⁴⁹

Less formal, provincial theatres were still governed by accepted codes of behaviour, suggesting that these norms were embedded in place as well as space. One common pronouncement was that no person was to be 'admitted behind the Scenes' partly, it was argued, 'on account of the machinery', but also as part of a wider agenda of controlling the spatial practices of theatre-goers, and (re)creating the theatre as a respectable and orderly space. The fact that eighteenth-century theatres were often dangerous places, prone to fire or collapse, only reinforced the need for orderly behaviour. And yet it is apparent that rules were often ignored or transgressed, as theatre-goers used subversive tactics to reappropriate the theatre for their own ends. Servants accompanied their masters into boxes, and the gallery in many provincial theatres was often colonised by unruly elements (see Chapter 5). Particularly in moments of crisis or in response to the unexpected, behaviour became spontaneous. In August 1772, for instance, a small fire in the tin pans between the stage and orchestra caused a serious panic at the Theatre Royal in Liverpool:

> many ladies were thrown into fits, and one died of fright. The people in the gallery finding it impossible to get out at the doors, were seized with a temporary frenzy, and many of them dropt from thence into the pit, by which many arms, legs, ribs etc were broken, and the midshipman of a sloop, which lately arrived in the harbour, was trod to death.⁵⁰

On the gravelled walks and public gardens, the imperative of personal display was tempered by polite etiquette. Stepping beyond the boundaries challenged the social construction of these spaces as polite and sociable, and could bring censure or conflict. Ostentatious display was frowned upon, even when it involved the nobility, as is apparent from Mrs Sneyd's caustic account of the public appearances of the Duchess of K- in Bath (see Chapter 4). Equally unacceptable was overt staring, especially at women – the root of the conflict between Henry Bates and a group of Macaronis in London's Vauxhall Gardens.[51] As discussed earlier, pleasure gardens were viewed as places which gave considerable licence to consumers, especially during the popular *ridottos al fresco* and masquerades. As Ogborn argues of the latter, 'their pleasures and dangers lay in the ways in which the masking of identities fragmented notions of the self, levelled hierarchies of class and gender and gave vent – particularly for women – to "frenetic sexual solicitation"'.[52] Whilst they were often laid out in an orderly and tasteful manner, this licentious behaviour made pleasure gardens very particular leisure spaces, and the subject of censure by a moralising press and literati – both Fielding and Smollett wrote critically and satirically of Vauxhall's pretensions at refinement.[53] London pleasure gardens were thus the product of a nexus of spatial planning, commercial imperatives, social practices and moral critique. Provincial gardens and masquerades echoed these same factors, but were less complex and controversial. In particular, behaviour was more restrained. One correspondent wrote in 1736 that Liverpool's 'masquerade or as their printed advertisements called it a Ridotto al Fresco' was attended by 'a good many gentlemen and several young ladies and wives.… There were about a dozen masqu'd and great many unmask'd'.[54] The charade of concealment was equally thin at Pontefract where one female correspondent felt that she would have no trouble in identifying her friends at a masquerade held in 1755. Despite such decorum and transparency, and the 'more socially homogeneous custom' upon which they drew, these events were still subject to critical comment. The masquerades held during the Preston Guild in 1742 were shunned by some of the elite of northern society, whilst John Nicholson noted of the Liverpool masquerade, held in 'Israel's tent on Maiden Green, [that] some good folks call it the devil's dancing house, Spring Gardens and tis by several thought to be a good way from the land of Judea or Promise'.[55] Behaviour was thus circumscribed by wider public opinion, so that pleasure gardens were produced by the social practices of those attending events and by the broader cultural norms of respectability.

Shopping practices were also shaped by widely accepted norms of behaviour, although these varied according to who was shopping and what they were buying. In this context, Berry draws a distinction between 'consumables which are purchased rarely, as a special event, involving pleasure in the exercise of choice, and those repeat-buys which are mundane'.[56] The former, which Berry terms 'polite shopping', was characterised by a 'browse-bargain' framework and could be a lengthy, drawn-out process of looking, choosing and buying, which produced a shop space constructed around notions of display and leisure (see Chapter 5). The latter was more routinised and speedy, sometimes based on the dispatch of servants, but more often for the urban middling sorts, involving the consumer in planned shopping trips based around a preconceived, if purely mental, shopping list. The shop would be a correspondingly simple, if orderly, space. These two different modes of shopping can be seen in the spatial practices of consumers in the west Midlands and north-west England. However, they form the poles on a spectrum of consumer behaviour and retail space.

Shopkeepers' account books suggest that customers visited the shop regularly to purchase a fairly standard 'basket of goods'. Thus, 34 per cent of the entries in Thomas Dickenson's day book between January 1741 and April 1742 are for sugar; a further 15 per cent are for tea, 11 per cent for soap and 10 per cent for spices (see Table 6.2). Within this overall pattern, certain gender differences are apparent, with female account holders far more likely to buy tea and sugar, whilst their male counterparts were over-represented in purchases of rum and tobacco. Such distinctions fit into gender norms of the time, and match Smith's cultural contexts: a female domestic realm of tea-drinking contrasting with a more public coffee-drinking and tobacco-smoking domain frequented by men. However, this picture of uniformity and of gender-related consumption patterns is misleading: few customers were 'typical' either of the customer base as a whole or of their gender. The brazier John Rowell fits the stereotype, as he bought mostly best tobacco from Dickenson, generally in quarter-pound parcels. In contrast, George Woodcock, an innkeeper, usually purchased only a single sugar loaf on his monthly visits, occasionally adding coffee or best bohea tea; whilst the apothecary, John Clements, shopped every other week, buying mainly sugar candy, treacle and brimstone.[57]

These kinds of mundane and routine purchases are precisely those which, Berry argues, could be made by servants or other proxy shoppers. However, Walsh suggests that there were often problems, real or perceived, in trusting servants: they might not inspect goods sufficiently closely or bargain over price, or they might dawdle over the errand.[58] Our evidence for shopping by servants is equivocal. From a total of 853 entries in Thomas Dickenson's account book, 137 refer specifically to the purchaser, as well as the account holder. This suggests that proxy shopping was comparatively rare amongst the customers of a provincial grocer – most of the purchases being made by the account holder (or possibly his wife). Moreover, purchases made in this way were generally of one or two specific items with a total value, on average, of 6 shillings (see Table 6.3). Thus, Mrs Harris sent her maid to Dickenson's shop for 3.5 lb of 'best Bristol soap'; yet she bought 3.5 lb hard soap, 14 oz hops, 1/2 oz green tea, and 1/2 oz bohea tea when she visited the shop herself.[59] This suggests that, at least where groceries were concerned, servants and children were often trusted with running small errands but rarely involved in larger transactions. Nonetheless, basic groceries clearly could be purchased on behalf of others. Carriers feature in Dickenson's account book as third-party shoppers: Sarah Harrison of Droitwich fulfilled this role on a number of occasions, whilst Mrs Foley of Shelsley had two consignments of sugar bought for her and delivered by 'Parkes the carrier'.[60] Such 'mail order' shopping was, in many ways, particularly suited to the purchase of more mundane

Table 6.2 Groceries purchased from Thomas Dickenson of Worcester, grocer: January 1741–April 1742 (percentage of shopping trips)

	No. of purchases	Chocolate	Coffee	Tea	Sugar	Treacle	Spices	Dried fruit	Rum	Tobacco	Soap	Other
Male	720	3.6	4.4	12.4	31.5	4.0	9.4	6.3	10.1	6.4	11.8	29.4
Female	77	3.9	2.6	36.4	54.6	2.6	10.4	7.8	1.3	1.3	7.8	19.5
Total	797	3.6	4.3	14.7	33.8	3.9	9.5	6.4	9.3	5.9	11.4	28.5

Source: SRO, D1798 HM 29/2–4.

Table 6.3 Pattern of proxy purchasing by customers of Thomas Dickenson, 1741–2

Category of purchaser	No. of entries	% of entries noting actual purchaser	Mean no. items purchased
Self	10	7.3	1.1
Wife	2	1.5	1.5
Children	3	2.2	1.0
Individual (forename)	5	3.6	1.0
Other family	2	1.5	2.0
Servant/apprentice	46	33.6	1.6
Individual (surname)	21	15.3	1.6
Carrier	15	10.9	1.6
Others	33	24.1	1.5
Total	137	100.0	1.5

Source: SRO, D1798 HM 29/2–4.

items such as groceries. Prices were generally standardised and close inspection of the goods was not so essential as it was for cloth, furnishings or haberdashery, at least if the purchase was made from a trusted supplier. Indeed, there are myriad examples of gentry customers ordering tea and coffee, as well as wine and other luxury consumables, from London (see Chapter 2).

This portrayal of mundane trips to stock up on a range of necessaries suggests a certain set of consumer practices. There was little need to actively sell the goods: customers had a clear idea of what they wanted before entering the shop, and interaction between shopkeeper and customer was largely structured around assembling the list of goods required. This depiction of routinised, ordered and unimaginatively planned shopping is, of course, a caricature. We have already seen that grocers went to some trouble in arranging and displaying goods in their shops, and some food retailers made considerable effort to woo customers: John Gibbs, for example, made samples of his brandy, rum and gin available for tasting at Mrs Taylor's glass and china warehouse in Coventry.[61] Equally, there is ample evidence that people made unplanned visits to grocers to purchase items seemingly forgotten on an earlier trip. For instance, the apothecary, John Clements went twice to Thomas Dickenson's shop on 30 January 1741, first to buy 1 lb of white sugar candy, then again for 3.5 lb of treacle. A more extreme example comes from the account book of the Didsbury shopkeeper, William Wood, which records the shopping trips of Martha Chase, who bought 1 lb of treacle on 3 January 1787, returning later that day for currants and a clove pepper. On the following day she bought treacle, flour and berm, the next day she had a manchet loaf, and the day after a further loaf, tea and sugar. On 7 January, Martha bought sugar, coffee and bread valued at 8d, and two days later she had treacle and sugar for 7d.[62]

Other consumers spent time and energy finding the best quality or most keenly priced groceries available: they actively shopped for groceries. Writing from London to Sir John Morduant in Warwickshire, W. Collins stated that:

I went to Mr Mason and enquired the price of his best vinegar which is 18d per gallon, the ordinary is 10d, best anchovies are 16d per lb, capers 11d per lb and their best oyle at 3s 6d per qt. I think I have done everything you mentioned in all your letter ....[63]

Here the correspondent is clearly browsing, comparing prices and qualities on behalf of his master. Such behaviour may have been the privilege of the wealthy, with poorer consumers having to take whatever was available and affordable. Yet evidence from shop accounts suggests otherwise. Thomas Dickenson offered a wide variety of groceries, but many of his customers purchased only certain types of goods in his shop. Thus, the Revd Mr Benson, a Worcester clergyman, bought sugar, rum, cocoa, currants, rice and saltpetre. Sugar was purchased about once a month, but other items only once or twice during the study period, and no tea was bought at all: Dickenson cannot have been the only grocer patronised by Benson. Moreover, active shopping for apparently mundane items was not the preserve of the middling sort. Lower status consumers also appear to have bought from more than one shopkeeper. The Worcester joiner, Samuel Richards, made sixteen purchases from Dickenson, but only regularly bought hard soap. Other items, including rum, tea, starch, sugar and lamp black, were purchased on odd occasions and in small quantities, suggesting that Richards was patronising several shops. This could be done quite readily, so long as one's credit was good, but it implies that customers must have been aware of quality and price, and willing to shop around to get the best deal – they were active rather than passive consumers.

All this suggests that the practices involved in buying necessities may not have been so very different from those of shopping for luxuries: differences were in degree, rather than kind. That said, Berry's browse-bargain model clearly fits most readily practices of polite shopping for clothing, furnishings and so on, where choice was more a matter of taste and fashion, and quality had to be carefully judged by visual and manual inspection. Henry Prescott often recorded his shopping in Chester. Although brief, these entries give a clear idea of a man who took some care in making purchases, often inspecting goods in advance. Thus, in June 1711, he carefully reckoned up his expenditure on clothes for the forthcoming Bishop's Visitation: the cloth, trimmings, hat, wig, stockings, gloves and tailor's bill coming to £11 6s 8d. In March the following year, he recorded that he went to 'Randle Minshulls shop [to] look further into Lord Kilmoreys Library, purchasd by him'.[64] A century later, a female diarist from Lutterworth noted frequent trips to the shops with friends. In June 1829, she wrote that 'Sarah [her maid] Miss Duckworth and myself went to Smith to buy a ribbon for my bonnet', and the following month 'After tea Miss S____ and myself went to Miss Middlemist. I bought a handkerchief ... and paid Corrall his bill'.[65] Significantly, both Prescot and this diarist shopped with friends, perhaps, as Berry argues, because, 'company cemented the social pleasures of shopping'.[66]

Direct evidence of browsing or window-shopping remains elusive – these provincial diarists rarely described their activities in such terms – yet they certainly formed part of the shopping practices of provincial customers from an early date. In Fanny Burney's novel *Camilla*, for instance, Mrs Mittin leads the eponymous heroine on an expedition round the shops of Southampton with the intention of inspecting 'all that was smartest, without the expense of buying anything'.[67] In Chester, window-shopping on the Rows was clearly a commonplace well before a mid-nineteenth-century city guide noted their convenience as a 'quiet lounge' for shoppers.[68] This literary evidence is strengthened by the presence of display cabinets, racks and rails and window displays seen in many shops (see Chapter 5), and by the seemingly casual nature of many purchases recorded in shop account books. The ledger of the Stafford draper, John Webb, includes a number of purchases of single items made on the account of William Chetwynd by his daughters.[69] The items bought were mostly hats, ribbon, handkerchiefs or lace – just the sort of trifles that Berry suggests were attractive to the casual browser. In contrast, Chetwynd himself purchased an ensemble of cloth and accessories sufficient to make up a suit of clothing, and further cloth for servant's livery. However, we should be cautious of drawing too easy a distinction: Chetwynd no doubt browsed, carefully inspecting cloths before making his choice. Moreover, men were not averse to making impulse buys. John Byrom wrote to his wife in 1729 that he had 'bought Boetius upon the Consolation of Philosophy at Stafford, to divert me on the road, having forgot to put the Latin one into my pocket'. Similarly, Henry Prescott, walking on the city walls, saw 'a picture, supplying the busienes of a window, in a sordid house, keeping out the weather. Wee enquire after, and I buy it for 1s'.[70]

As we saw in Chapter 5, browsing was encouraged by shopkeepers through the layout of their premises and by their treatment of customers. The social space of the shop was produced by the formal and informal interaction between shopkeeper and customer: the host and his guests.[71] In this light, browsing can be seen as a mechanism for mediating this relationship by placing economic transactions of exchange into a recognised social framework of politeness and sociability. The shop was, in part, the spatial realisation of this relationship. Yet, despite the centrality of this relationship, by no means all purchases of durable luxury goods were made following a period of browsing in one or more shops. Indeed, there is strong evidence that provincial consumers followed a wide variety of shopping practices. Cox differentiates selling through the window from the more service-oriented selling that took place within shops.[72] As with groceries, many consumers appear to have had a preferred supplier for certain items. This was clearly the case for Judith Baker's shopping in London, as she returned year on year to the same suppliers, whilst Henry Prescott could write of 'my tailor' and 'my draper'.[73] There is also evidence of third-party shopping, of the type common amongst those visiting the metropolis. One of John Webb's customers, his brother-in-law John Baxter of Penkridge, appears to have bought goods on behalf of neighbours. Thus his account includes a number of entries noting that the goods purchased are 'for James Wood' or 'for John Ironmonger'.[74] Another shopping strategy used to acquire durable items as well as groceries was ordering by post. Several of the regular customers of John Mountfort, a Worcester bookseller, adopted this approach. Silvester Lamb, ordering on behalf of Bishop Lloyd at Hartlebury, wrote regularly to Mountfort during 1707 requesting specific books.[75] Similarly, a series of letters sent to the Stafford draper Elizabeth Sneyd by Lady Chester of Hams Hall, near Coleshill, contain small squares of cloth clearly used by Sneyd as samples and returned by Lady Chester with her order.[76]

'Remote' shopping for these kinds of goods required detailed instructions and a good degree of trust between customer and shopkeeper. Lamb always gave Mountfort precise details about the book he wished to be purchased. 'An Account of the Earl of Peterborow's Conduct in Spain', for instance, was to be had 'from Jonah Bowyer at the Rose in Ludgate Street'.[77] Lady Chester, too, could be very particular about what she wanted, noting at the end of one letter to Sneyd, that 'to prevent mistakes the green and white stuff must be tammy'. Things could, however, sometimes go wrong: Lady Chester's steward, John Leigh, wrote to Sneyd in February 1742 noting that he was sending back some cloth, which 'is so unlike the pattern it is impossible to make use of it', adding that 'my lady says she does not know whether the master or servants finds the most fault, it being so much a worse cloath than the pattern and the same price'.[78] Similarly, in early nineteenth-century St Helens, the wealthy industrialist Michael Hughes found no end of faults with a carriage from London, despite having placed the order through a friend in the metropolis. He wrote to the makers complaining that it:

> is the most mean paltry thing that ever was sent out of London, & so is deem'd by every Gentleman who has seen it. Whether you look at the Outside or Inside it is equally plain, mean and paltry and this much inferior to any Gentleman's Carriage. From the pompous description of it displayed on your Bill, I should have expected that the Materials at least of which it is made had been of very extraordinary quality. To my great Mortification & Cost they are not so, for the Springs, altho' the Carriage since I had it has not run more than 30 Miles … have already given way and must be replaced.[79]

There was, it seems, no substitute for being able to inspect the quality of goods before purchases were made, and ample opportunity to regret trusting a distant supplier.

Shopping was a serious business requiring the consumer to pay careful attention to the information being provided by the shopkeeper and to inspect goods closely. This businesslike approach framed the relationship between shopkeeper and shopper as they discussed price and quality over the counter. Yet shopping was also a pleasurable activity. The consumer might simply browse, marvelling at or critically assessing the goods on offer. Conversation could encompass novelty and fashion, but might also turn to local news or gossip. In ways that closely parallel Rappaport's reading of nineteenth-century department stores and analyses of modern shopping malls offered by Shields and Goss, the pleasures of shopping shaped the customary practices of shoppers and shopkeepers and linked shopping to wider social and leisure activities. For the shopkeeper, leisurely shopping and sociability encouraged customers to linger and perhaps make additional purchases.

It also deepened his or her relationship with them, helping to tie them into long-term economic relationships with strong social bonds. For these reasons, sociability was something worth investing in, partly in terms of the materiality of the shop and partly through the actions which drew on these material objects and produced the shop as social space. On occasions, this involved laying on specific attractions, as when Mr Keene's Coventry shop hosted the 'surprising Warwickshire young lady ... artist [who] by the help of her toes and feet only, is capable of curious performances; threads needles, picks up money ...'.[80] More often, it meant providing appropriate amenities or quiet 'treating' of valued customers in a back room or local inn. Thus, the inventory of the Wolverhampton bookseller Joshua Cowley states that 'In ye shop there's Books, Coffe, Tea, Glasses, Tables & other furniture'. Clearly, a visit to Cowley's shop involved more than simply inspecting and buying books. The provision of refreshments, and probably chairs, underline his role as a 'skilful host' as well as salesman.[81] Such entertaining was widespread amongst eighteenth-century shopkeepers. In Ashton-in-Makerfield, Roger Lowe noted that 'old Peter Lealand came to me, and sit in shop a good while ... we talked of times and about Mr Woods'. Similarly, Nicholas Blundell records being treated to meals and drinks by a number of shopkeepers in Liverpool; whilst, in a case which came before the Warwick assizes, William Briscoe, a butcher, explained how he and John McNiver, cook for the circuit judges, were invited into the shop of Francis Holmes, a Warwick grocer. There, he 'treated them with a glass or two of his cordials', adding that 'they staid sometime afterwards in the shop'.[82] Such treating was clearly a necessary part of business as well as a social activity which cemented bonds of friendship. When establishing their partnership in the 1780s, Richard Blick and John Fulford set aside £10 'towards accommodating and entertaining customers, goods and carriers'.[83]

In this way, the boundaries between business and pleasure were blurred in the spatial practices of sociability, reinforcing our image of the shop as a space which was at once economic and social. The shop was a centre of sociable activity: a focus for the exchange of gossip as well as goods; a place to linger as well as to buy. Rutherford's account of the fictional town of Cowfold in the 1820s catches this well: 'every customer had something to say beyond his own immediate errand, and the shop was the place where everything touching Cowfold interests was abundantly discussed'.[84] Whilst the material structure of the shop gave physical focus to these processes of exchange, it was the actions of individuals which produced the shop as a vital social and leisure space. Customers came to buy and to talk, to inform and be informed; and the shopkeeper acted as host to these various processes. Both were active agents of social and spatial change.

The shop did not exist in spatial or social isolation: it was a condensation of networks or pathways which intersected in space through the acts of shopping.[85] Shopping practices and spaces were thus enmeshed in wider actions and geographies of sociability. Indeed, many leisure and cultural facilities were 'specifically designed, in their organization and their ethos, to promote sociability'.[86] Whilst they involved a good deal more besides, assemblies were the meeting together of polite society, however that might be (locally) defined. As Macky observed, they were conceived as an opportunity for seeing company and were defined by the gathering together of that company. Defoe clearly recognised this constructed nature, even though he frowned upon their proliferation, when he wrote of the 'new mode of *forming* assemblies, so much, and so fatally now in vogue'.[87] Assemblies, of course, were places of entertainment and display; but above all they provided an opportunity for sociable interaction. The intention was to encourage the free circulation of people and an air of free intercourse between them. The dancing was organised to encourage a circulation of partners and prevent the formation of private cliques. As noted earlier, this was often enshrined in formalised 'rules', but was cemented through the practices of the assembly. Tea was taken communally at large tables, and attempts to create private space or closed groupings within the assembly were strongly discouraged.[88] Such notions and practices of public sociability spread into promenades and public gardens. As Defoe found on the walks at Tunbridge Wells: 'anything that looks like a gentleman, has an address agreeable, and behaves with decency and good manners, may single out whom he pleases'.[89] In this way, the social space of promenades and gardens was produced through the actions of those who walked the gravel paths, socialising with others.

Sociability was also important in structuring the behaviour in less public forms of leisure, including clubs and societies. These provided an opportunity for relaxed social intercourse, sometimes in addition to a more formal rationale for meeting. Thus, the social activities of organisations including guilds and Societies for the Prosecution of Felons, as well as overtly social gatherings such as the Bean Club in Birmingham or the Catch and Glee Club in Liverpool, revolved around food and drink. The genial atmosphere brought together the rural gentry and urban elite socially as well as spatially. For example, Sir Roger Newdigate mingled with the elite of Coventry at the annual Drapers' Feast, and was an active member of the Birmingham Bean Club, joining around 140 other 'gentlemen' at the club's anniversary meeting in 1752.[90] The social space of these clubs was shaped by their meetings and dinners, which often took place in private rooms in the leading inns or coffee houses. The latter constituted informal clubs in their own right. They were lauded as places where men might freely gather and converse, where 'young gentlemen or shopkeepers [might] be sure to meet company, and, by the custom of the house, not such as at other places, stingy and reserved to themselves, but free and communicative'.[91] Indeed, Smith privileges the coffee house as the setting for one of his key cultural contexts: a 'rational masculinity' based on the exchange of news and information within a carefully constructed (semi-) public sphere. Central to this reading of the coffee house was a sociability of conversation, which enjoined 'tolerance of differences of opinion – indeed a desire to hear and participate in debate'.[92] Certainly, the Manchester poet John Byrom found London coffee houses such as Richard's on Fleet Street and George's on Chancery Lane a congenial venue for learning the latest intelligence and engaging in political or religious debate with friends over a bowl of coffee or chocolate. A typical entry in his journal from March 1726 gives a sense of how these spaces were at the heart of his network of sociability: 'went to Slaughter's coffeehouse, Leycester and I played two games at chess, and he beat me the first, I him the second; thence to

Richard's, Mr. Kenn there, sat down and talked with us about the Scotch bill, and Mr Campbell'.[93] What defined the coffee house as a social institution was its role as a meeting place and talking shop, its atmosphere of informed discussion, and its systems of self-regulation. Here again, we see social space being produced through the practices of those who came together in the coffee house.

The customary practices of leisure and shopping discussed here did not operate in isolation from one another. Rather, they were brought together in the minds and actions of consumers, so that spaces of consumption were produced and reproduced through the daily routine of visiting, socialising and consuming. We have seen something of this already, in the way that the diarist in Lutterworth, Henry Prescott and Anne Lister in York combined trips visiting friends with trips to the shops. In effect, shopping was part of the social routine for many consumers, both urban and rural, and they carried with them the same notions of sociability between the shop, the assembly room and the home. On her visits to London, Judith Baker combined shopping with trips to Ranelagh, the theatre and the spa at Saddler's Wells. Similarly in Colne, local gentry gathered at Betty Hartley's general store for tea, 'to be tempted with her fashionable and elegant assortments from London', whilst Nicholas Blundell made purchases at Chester on his way to the Catholic shrine at Holywell.[94] What these examples show is the easy transition from leisure to shopping activities: they were clearly perceived as part of the same social round, driven by similar motivations and involving a parallel set of spatial practices. The social space of consumption might focus on particular sites – shops, assembly rooms, theatres, coffee houses – but, as Borsay argues, it effectively encompassed the whole town. As people passed from one activity to another, their actions not only stitched together urban space so that 'the association of redefined shop spaces and leisure activities was extensive and axiomatic', but also produced the town as a space of polite consumption.[95]

Consumption, space and identity

In this final section, we turn to the modes of cognition and discourse which underpinned shopping and leisure as a cultural context for the consumption of goods, space and time.[96] In doing so, we move beyond the materiality of the built environment and the everyday practices of consumers, to consider the motivations which lay behind, and the identities which were produced and reproduced through, the acts and spaces of consumption. Seeking to understand something of the ethos which drove people to consume – and through which people perceived, presented and understood their participation and their actions – focuses attention on the subjectivity of the consumer.[97] Yet such an undertaking requires a careful reading of the behaviour and writings of eighteenth-century consumers: we must be careful to assess them on their own terms. Whilst metropolitan commentators, journalists, politicians and moralists had much to say about consumption and those who consumed, we must be wary of seeing their discourses as representative of consumers in the provinces and explore local evidence more closely. Borsay identifies two related but contrasting and, in many ways, contradictory forces which shaped England's culture- and consumption-based urban renaissance. The first centred on socio-cultural competition and the pursuit of status; and the second comprised civility, politeness and sociability.[98] We explore each of these in turn.

The pursuit of status, Borsay argues, was predicated on increased levels of disposable income and a gradual relaxation of the definition of gentility. Traditional notions of birthright or the right to coats of arms were increasingly superseded by personal attributes, so that a gentleman was defined by his manners, accomplishments and appearance. As one contemporary commentator put it: anyone with 'either a liberal, or genteel education, that looks gentleman-like … and has wherewithal to live freely and handsomely, is by the courtesy of England usually called a gentleman'.[99] As most of these material and mental trappings of gentility could be openly purchased, this became an important channel through which wealth could be transferred into status. This links to Bourdieu's notion of cultural capital in that social status was being marked through cultural attributes. Of course, eighteenth-century consumers did not think in terms of cultural capital, but they clearly appreciated the benefits or necessity of acquiring the accepted cultural attributes of genteel status. For the middling sort of shopkeepers, professionals, officers and manufacturers, liberalisation of the notion of gentility provided the opportunity to use their wealth to take on the trappings and status of gentlemen. Those who were gentry by birth were caught up in this process since, as Defoe observed: 'virtue, learning, a liberal education, and a degree of natural and acquired knowledge, are necessary to finish the born gentleman … without them the entitled heir will be but the shadow of a gentleman'. Moreover, they sought to use the same devices to improve their own social standing so that 'the poor will be like the rich, and the rich like the great, and the great like the greatest'.[100] The unscrupulous, of course, could short-circuit this social emulation through deliberate fraud. Thus we read of the 'Scots Genius' with 'hair dressed in the macaroni taste' who impersonated a Major on half-pay in order to defraud shopkeepers. According to the *Worcester Journal*, 'he goes to mercers shops, bespeaks fine cloaths, and gives orders to tailors, hatters etc and then takes the opportunity of slipping off without settling his accounts'.[101]

Even without such nefarious activity, this picture of the pursuit of status leading to a spiralling of emulative consumption needs to be treated with some caution (see Chapter 1). The rhetoric of emulation as a harbinger of the dissolution of social distinctions was often repeated, but came largely from metropolitan commentators. In provincial England, urban authorities and tradesmen courted the rural gentry and local aristocracy as benefactors, prime consumers and ornaments for the town, acknowledging the economic and social benefits they could bestow. Moreover, as Smails argues, the urban middling sort 'recognized the social superiority of the gentry and the profound cultural gulf that separated them from the landed elite'. Yet, notwithstanding a collective recognition of their higher status, 'individuals within this group might aspire to become gentlemen'.[102]

The roles of competition and social status in shaping the practices and identities of consumers were manifold. They are explored here through three aspects of consumption; the creation of a fashionable appearance; the acquisition of knowledge and learning, and the production of and association with polite spaces. Personal appearance was central to the pursuit of social status. As Fielding's Mr Wilson noted: 'the character I was ambitious of attaining was that of a fine gentleman, the first requisites to which I apprehended were to be supplied by a tailor, a periwig-maker, and some few more tradesmen, who deal in furnishing out the human body'.[103] The importance of fashionable clothing was especially notable in London and the resorts, from whence letters and descriptions were full of references to the dress and personal appearance of other visitors.[104] Although not always complimentary, these accounts emphasise the importance of how people dressed and looked, with attention focusing on hair and jewellery as well as clothing. They also make clear that public events – such as assemblies, promenading and race meetings – were seen as opportunities for competitive displays of fashion or wealth. For instance, one correspondent from Tunbridge Wells commented that 'the chief diversion of the wells is to stare one at another, and he or she who is best dressed, is the greatest subject of the morning's tittle-tattle'.[105] Accordingly, whilst in Bath Ann Sneyd spent a considerable sum on her personal appearance, including £1 1s to Mr Ruspini 'for cleaning my teeth' and a further 10s for his tincture and tooth powder. On a later occasion she paid Kirby 10s 6d for dressing her hair: adding curls before she attended an important assembly.[106]

Away from the intensity of the admiring or critical gaze in the resorts, attendance to fashion and personal appearance was often more low key and was certainly attuned to local circumstances. Elizabeth Shackleton prided herself in keeping up to date with the latest London fashions, soliciting information from friends in the capital and major resorts. Like her correspondents, however, she derided the absurdities of high fashion, preferring instead clothes that were fashionable but also durable, versatile and appropriate for her age, stature and social standing. Shackleton adopted new styles only when she considered them 'becoming', 'in character' or 'an Easy Fashion'. Nonetheless, fashion and the display of the body was by no means forgotten in the provinces. Sir John Morduant, for instance, observed that 'when the King returns some new fashion may appear'. As a consequence, he decided, '[I] would defer making my clothes as long as I could'.[107] Equally, in rejecting the cloth sent from Elizabeth Sneyd for her servants' livery, Lady Chester was clearly concerned about their appearance to the world and, of course, how this would reflect on her. The cloth was, her steward claimed, so 'sorry' and wanting in both weave and colour that she would be 'ashamed' to be seen in public with her entourage.[108] Very similar concerns troubled Michael Hughes in the early nineteenth century. His complaints about the carriage from London are replete with notions of fashion, taste and the public impression that he might make:

> the Trimmings in the inside do not conform to my ideas of [propriety] … And they are upon the whole much plainer and less showy than I could have wished – My Livery is a light Drab Colour, pretty near the Color [sic] of the Lining with Crimson and Silver. The Inside of the Carriage should have corresponded, & instead of Lace and Trimmings of the same colour, it

should have been a rich Crimson which certainly would have given a much handsomer inside appearance. ... The Carriage in its appearance exhibits the Plainess of a Quaker.[109]

Fashionable adornment and display of the body were of considerable importance to polite consumers, but the pursuit of status did not stop at external decoration. Improvement of the mind through the accretion of appropriate knowledge and learning was critical in demonstrating the taste and discernment that defined genteel status. These cerebral concerns were reflected in a range of leisure and shopping practices, including a widening participation in foreign travel. The Grand Tour had been used as a finishing school for the nobility or wealthy gentry from at least the mid-sixteenth century, and provided an opportunity to learn first-hand about the antiquities, art, architecture and increasingly the landscape of Europe. Travel, and the liberal education which it provided, was thus an important mark of social distinction: an essential marker of gentlemanly education.[110] As such, it became subject to aspirational participation on the part of the expanding middling sorts: a growing number of sons and, to a far lesser extent, daughters of wealthy merchants, professionals and industrialists were sent to the continent. For example, Wedgwood, Boulton and Watt each sent their sons overseas to complete their education, keen for them to become thoroughly European in outlook: James Watt went to Geneva to study geometry, algebra and drawing, and Matthew Boulton to Paris where he studied French science, read widely and immersed himself in the social scene.[111]

Far more important in terms of the numbers participating was the spread of learned societies and subscription libraries to many provincial towns. Few societies were at the cutting edge of scientific progress: the lecture programmes of most were characterised by a wide range of popular topics.[112] However, they did provide important forums for the exchange of knowledge. As Thomas Henry told the Manchester Literary and Philosophical Society in 1785: 'the natural tendency of a cultivation of polite learning is to refine the understanding, humanize the soul, enlarge the field of useful knowledge'.[113] More importantly, perhaps, these institutions were sufficiently exclusive to ensure that membership conferred kudos on the individual. The twinning of learning and exclusivity was explicit in the rationales of many of the grand new subscription libraries which appeared towards the end of the eighteenth century (see Chapter 2). The prospectus for the Athenaeum in Liverpool, published in 1797, stated that:

> It has often been a matter of surprise to many of the inhabitants of this place, and still more so to strangers, that in a town of such commercial and national importance as Liverpool, the conveniences and accommodations for the acquisition of knowledge ... should be so imperfect as they confessedly are ... The present Public Library by no means answers this purpose; it is not sufficiently select in choice of books; the books in it are almost exclusively confined to our own language; and the number of subscribers is now so large ....[114]

The clear desire was for an institution that allowed its members to mark their taste and judgment as well as their wealth – the founding subscription of ten guineas was set deliberately high – and thus to distance themselves from their fellow citizens. Membership quickly became 'a mandatory emblem of status for the Liverpool commercial aristocracy', and shares were soon changing hands for up to forty guineas.[115]

Being *seen* to participate in the correct learned, artistic or philanthropic activities – to be linked to these ideals and the emblematic spaces of their libraries and committee rooms – was, for many, just as important as any improvement it might bring to personal intellect. The published subscription list – for charitable institutions, libraries, town histories and so on – was therefore an important marker of status: it conferred on subscribers 'both the prestige of patronizing some culturally elevating project, and that of being ranked alongside more illustrious contributors'.[116] The possibility of such enhancement of status by association is apparent from the 1754 subscription lists of the Worcester infirmary. Here the names of humble tradesmen such as the baker, Richard Weston and innholder, George Woodcock, are recorded alongside those of aristocrats like Lady Clinton, Lord Sandys and the Earl of Coventry. Subscription was a form of social capital through which one became known to other members of polite society. And being 'known' was crucial in defining status. In this way, subscription was a socially competitive process: one in which men and women alike could engage. Of the 284 subscribers to the Worcester infirmary in 1754, forty were women, amongst them some of the largest contributors: the Countess of Coningsby, for instance, gave £5 5s per year. More numerous and more generous donations increased social and cultural capital, and elevated the status of the subscriber. But by the same token, higher status carried with it the expectation of a larger and more regular contribution. Thus, for example, we see the Earl of Coventry providing £21 per year towards the running costs of the Worcester infirmary, whilst most subscribers paid only £1 1s.[117]

Many of the wealthiest landowners or magnates, of course, spread their subscriptions across a range of different institutions, so that, although individual donations could be relatively modest, their overall expenditure was significant. In addition to laying out Sansome Fields Walk in the grounds of his Worcester residence, Charles Trubshaw Withers gave £2 2s annually to the infirmary in the mid-eighteenth century, and was also a shareholder in the theatre and subscription library.[118] Similarly, in late eighteenth-century Birmingham, Matthew Boulton was a driving force behind the erection of the New Street theatre, and a subscriber to the Birmingham General Hospital and the Birmingham library; whilst the Nicholsons, a prominent Liverpool merchant dynasty, held positions on the committee of the Liverpool infirmary and were also members of the Literary and Philosophical Society, and the Liverpool library.[119] In the early nineteenth century, Michael Hughes gave £100 to the Liverpool infirmary in the year of his presidency and was also a subscriber to the Agricultural Meeting of West Derby Hundred.[120]

Such projects imprinted themselves on the urban landscape as a series of spaces of consumption: concert halls, assembly rooms, libraries and so on. These buildings constituted cultural capital for a status-conscious urban elite, and embodied the taste and discernment – as well as the wealth – which distinguished them from other sections of society (see Chapter 3).[121] Yet these were not the only forms of knowledge that could mark out the individual. In Chester, Mr Durack stressed that his classes were not merely about learning to dance in order to attend balls, but would also teach 'young ladies and gentlemen the art of an easy address'.[122] This emphasis on polite aspirations was made explicit in an advertisement for *The Practical Grammar* which read:

> The necessity of being perfectly well acquainted with our native language is universally acknowledged … The embellishment of being a grammarian is obvious from the ridiculous figure those make who do not understand the construction of the tongue they daily use. He who cannot speak correctly is unfit for conversation; he who cannot write correctly is unfit for business: from correctness springs elegance of expression and composition: an accomplishment more useful and more admired than any in the circle of what is deemed polite and ornamental.[123]

These sentiments link personal accomplishments directly with an Addisonian notion of politeness as a means of oiling the wheels of commercial and social interaction. Correct and elegant modes of expression were portrayed as a necessary prerequisite to any claim to enter polite urban society.

Consumer knowledge was increasingly sought after and actively accreted by fashionable society: it allowed informed choices to be made about which goods would project the correct image of gentility, and where they could be had at the appropriate quality and for the best price. Such knowledge might be mobilised for the benefit of oneself or one's friends: Walsh has written about the practice amongst the London elite of 'proxy shopping' which involved identifying and purchasing fashionable items on behalf of friends.[124] This knowledge was usually acquired through inspecting those who attended the races, crowded the assembly rooms or paraded the walks and gardens – especially when visiting London or one of the fashionable resorts – or more specifically by visiting shops to inspect goods, discover novelties or simply browse. The second of these options was most prevalent in London, where women known as 'Silk-Worms' would 'ramble twice or thrice a Week from Shop to Shop, to turn over all the Goods in Town without buying anything'.[125] Yet it was also a male practice – Pepys, for example, regularly visited shops to inspect goods, and was particularly taken with novel items – and a feature of provincial society: Jane Austen noted that going to Bath to shop was one of the chief attractions of the city.[126] Indeed, the authors of town guides and trade directories from the early nineteenth century often gave great prominence to descriptions of 'numerous and well stocked shops' or 'extensive warehouses and sale rooms', even in one case noting shoppers' preference for the 'showy "establishments" of the larger towns'.[127] Browsing was often encouraged by shopkeepers because window-shoppers were potential customers and would certainly spread intelligence of new goods or fashions to a broader set of consumers. For the consumer, these shopping trips may have been frivolous and pleasure-orientated, but they were also a matter of serious business. The knowledge accreted not only informed their own consumption decisions, but also enhanced their importance as conduits of fashion and as arbiters of taste. Moreover, regular visits to a range of shops added to a person's social capital, making them known to a larger number of shopkeepers. With recognition came trust and favour: perhaps the treats in a back room; more importantly, the extension of credit, which allowed purchases to be made and underlined one's standing in society.[128] At the same time, browsing underlines the importance of the shop as a point of information exchange and as a space that was produced by the everyday actions and motivations of consumers, as well as those of the shopkeeper.[129]

The production of polite consumer space and polite identity went hand-in-hand. Space was rendered fashionable and polite by the social practices of the elite, but, as we argued above and in Chapter 3, it was also important in enhancing the status of those who invested in and occupied that space. In esteemed institutions such as the Portico Library in Manchester or the Birmingham library, mere admission to the facilities could bestow prestige. The exclusivity of other facilities was heightened by the creation of enclaves, such as the grandstands built at many race courses (see Chapter 5) or the provision of separate facilities for those further down the social scale. Thus we see separate assemblies being hosted in the early nineteenth century by at least three of Chester's inns, from the grand balls at the Royal Hotel (formerly the Talbot Inn), to the less prestigious gatherings at the Blossoms Hotel.[130] A similar spatial and social differentiation can be seen in terms of shops, since, in a time before branded goods, kudos came from patronising the best stores. This sometimes meant having goods sent from London shopkeepers, but also involved visiting fashionable shopping streets in provincial towns. In Bath, Milsom Street quickly emerged as the best place to shop and to be seen shopping, and most towns had correspondingly fashionable areas, often compared in local guides with Cheapside or increasingly Regent Street in London (see Chapter 4).

Motivations to consume urban material culture were nothing if not complex, in line with Miller's assertion of the dynamic and plural nature of consumer identity. Running alongside the pursuit of status – which might be seen as individual, exclusive and self-serving – were ideas of civility and polite sociability. These were essentially social, inclusive and, as part of the English Enlightenment, had a nobler ideal of civilising the nation. We have already discussed politeness and sociability at some length, so the focus here is on civility. Despite their polar differences, both status and civilisation were sought through a similar set of activities and were implicated in the production of a common set of consumer spaces. The construction of a new sort of gentility characterised by a civilised nature and polite behaviour certainly opened up the possibility of upward social mobility, but it was also 'intended to reach the very core of a person's identity'.[131] This civilised identity was based on three premises. First, a rational and cultivated mind had to be carefully nurtured. Through the pages of *The Tatler* and *The Spectator*, Steele and Addison argued that the kind of judgment, reason and wisdom, which underpinned civilised humanity, required diligent cultivation. This, of course, made it a rare condition and one to which only the educated might aspire. As one commentator put it: 'taste … is acquired by toil and study, which is the reason so few are possessed of it'.[132] Second, a strong and refined moral code had to be central to an individual's conduct. Morality and truth were central themes of much political writing in the eighteenth century, although then, as now, the definition and exercise of these virtues was always rather fluid. Third, the passions had to be brought in check by reason. Civilised people exercised moderation and avoided both physical and emotional excess. As Steele put it: 'that calm and elegant satisfaction which the vulgar call melancholy, is the true and proper delight of men of knowledge and virtue'.[133]

These three bases of civility were reflected in key social, leisure and consumption activities. The cultivation of taste, judgment and reason was achieved most obviously through those institutions which directly promoted education: clubs, learned societies and subscription libraries. Many of these were consciously exclusive, but they also encouraged both the practice and spirit of rational enquiry and learning. The founders of Birmingham's New Library in 1794, for instance, stated that their aim was to promote 'the diffusion of knowledge and liberality', whilst the first committee of the Literary and Philosophical Society in Bolton argued that their purpose was to further the interests of improvement through 'friendly, literary and philosophical conversation'.[134] Newspapers, journals and books also engendered the spread of knowledge and learning: sometimes, as with *The Tatler* and *The Spectator*, with an overt agenda of promoting politeness and civility. Such publications were held by libraries and newsrooms, or might be read in taverns and coffee houses, but they were also purchased from bookshops and newsmen by individual consumers. Thus, when advertising the opening of his African Coffee-House at the bottom of Lord Street in Liverpool, Leonard Herd took the opportunity to emphasise the polite credentials of the establishment by listing the newspapers and periodicals he took.[135] The thirst for knowledge meant that readers sometimes went to considerable lengths to acquire particular books, whilst circulating and subscription libraries often struggled to meet the demand for popular volumes.[136] The same spirit of enquiry and improvement underpinned the spread of mathematical and scientific instrument makers in provincial towns. In the 1790s they could be found only in Liverpool, Birmingham and Chester, yet by the 1830s over ten towns in the north-west and west Midlands could boast at least one of these skilled craftsmen: Manchester had eight barometer makers, Liverpool twenty-two chronometer makers, and Preston a lecturer in astronomy and philosophy.[137]

Civility and politeness were also promoted through the burgeoning number of charitable foundations and charity events, taken by some commentators to be a sign of 'humanity and public spirit'. In Liverpool, Moss argued for the emergence of an alternative culture based, not on the cultivation of the sciences and fine arts, but on social harmony and humanitarianism.[138] The town boasted a wide range of charities paid for by subscription, private donations or the common council, including an infirmary, dispensary, Seaman's Hospital, School for the Indigent Blind, and Institution for Recovering Persons Apparently Drowned. Alongside such worthy foundations were a host of balls and concerts held to raise money for good causes. In 1828 the proprietor of Ranelagh Gardens in Leamington Spa hosted a Grand Fête in aid of the General Hospital. A year later, over 500 guests attended a fancy-dress ball held at the Royal Hotel, Chester in aid of Spanish and Italian refugees, whilst the Tamworth Music Festival of 1809 raised money for alterations to the parish church and the renovation of its organ.[139]

Such polite gatherings played an important part in the moderation of behaviour and manners – the rejection of crude excess. Boulton made much of the shift in recreational activity which characterised the civilisation of Birmingham. With the decline of 'bull baitings, cock fightings, boxing matches, and abominable drunkenness … the people are more polite and civilized … and we have also made a considerable progress in some of the liberal arts'.[140] As well as specific shifts in fashionable recreation away from the boorish tastes of the rural squire or the lower orders, moderation was effected through general sociability.[141] Many leisure activities were therefore designed to encourage social interaction and spaces were produced to allow polite society to assemble. What such activities both built on and reinforced was the collective identity that constituted polite society. Sociability, and the consumption of urban material culture which underpinned it, were central to politeness: they moderated behaviour and defined membership of this expanding elite. Attendance at sociable gatherings required polite and civilised behaviour: acceptance therein defined one as polite. Whilst the nature of polite leisure activities was important in encouraging sociable interaction, what mattered most was simply being there, interacting with others. An important extension of this was the subscription system: it formed a 'virtual' gathering of polite society and was therefore instrumental in constructing the membership and identity of the urban elite. Overlapping groups of subscribers reflected and defined membership of an elite whose values were reflected in the institutions, organisations and projects to which they subscribed. Subscription was linked to the production of urban spaces of consumption. On a practical level, it drew together the necessary funds to build assembly rooms, concert halls and libraries. At the same time, subscription defined what was polite and fashionable, and, in the list of subscribers, identified those individuals who were similarly favoured.

Conclusions

As Trentmann argues, consumption is ultimately about the attitudes, motivations, behaviour and identity of individuals and the groups in which they express themselves.[142] These shaped the spaces and practices of consumption, and underpinned the creation of a new urban material culture in the eighteenth century. As we have seen, however, motives and actions were themselves informed by the 'cultural context' of polite leisure and shopping. This inter-relationship comprised a number of different dimensions.

First, is the way that the routines or pathways of leisure and shopping brought together diverse individuals and groups in space and time.[143] People congregated in assembly rooms, theatres, race courses, pleasure gardens and, of course, shops at particular times, driven by the daily and weekly routines of shopping and the often seasonal cycles of leisure. Importantly, those crowding the spaces of consumption were drawn from a variety of backgrounds: customers, subscribers and pleasure-seekers came from both town and country, and many different sections of society – from the aristocrat to the artisan. The potential for social mixing should not be overplayed, however: polite leisure was not a jolly free-for-all, just as department stores and malls are far from the being the freely accessible spaces that they might initially appear to be.[144] This underscores the contradiction in eighteenth-century notions of politeness and polite identity between inclusion and exclusion. The spaces of consumption brought together a wide cross-section of society and helped to spread the practices, modes of discourse and material objects of politeness. Yet they also afforded opportunities for display, differentiation and social distanciation. This tension, and the evident (perhaps too evident) inclusivity of many spaces of consumption, goes some way to explain the gradual unravelling of polite sociability as a social structure in the late eighteenth century.

This links to the second point: in giving focus and meaning to the production and consumption of material culture, these events and spaces formed important cultural contexts for consumption. One aspect of this was the way in which customary practices and behaviour acted to produce leisure facilities and shops as lived social spaces. Sometimes, behaviour was framed by formalised sets of rules. At the very least, social etiquette demanded the display of polite and civilised manners in theatres, assembly rooms, libraries and promenades. Behaviour (and with it, to an extent at least, identity) was shaped by customary spatial and social practices. Shopping behaviour was complex, however, and does not easily conform to simplistic interpretations of Berry's nuanced notion of 'polite consumption'. Practices of browsing and choosing seem to have been common to many purchases – of mundane as well as fashionable or luxury items – and underline the liminal nature of shops and shopping. Acquiring goods was both business and pleasure. On the one hand, it involved acquiring detailed knowledge of the availability and suitability of goods; paying careful attention to their price and quality, and building a trusting relationship with the shopkeeper. On the other, it encompassed the excitement of viewing novelty and reviewing fashions, and above all sociability with shopkeepers and fellow shoppers. A second aspect of leisure and shopping as a cultural context is the way in which they built on and reinforced certain modes of cognition and discourse. These drew on spaces of consumption to construct individual and group identities. Paramount in this were the visual, but 'polite' accomplishments which displayed taste and discernment and were also essential to gain admittance to and identity with the social elite. Improvement of the mind came from a wide range of sources, from etiquette books to learned societies, but personal experience was often critical. At one level, this was the guiding rationale for many on the Grand Tour; at another, it provided an extra motivation for window-shopping.

Such a discourse of improvement lay behind the construction of many spaces of consumption – libraries, athenaeums and concert halls, but also fashionable shops. The building and use of these spaces signalled the taste and discernment of the urban elite and the town as a whole (see also Chapter 3). Our third point is to emphasise the way in which the production of polite space and polite identity went hand-in-hand. Space was rendered fashionable and polite by the social practices of the elite, but association with those 'polite' spaces in turn bestowed status on the individual. As Giddens argues, then, the agency of human activity was thus embedded in and acted through socio-spatial structures.[145] In this way, the spatiality of consumption comes to the fore: society and space were mutually constructed. Spaces of consumption were physical structures which focused and shaped behaviour and discourse, but they were also social constructions, produced through the daily lives – the spatial practices – of consumers. They were, in Lefebvre's terms, lived spaces. Yet this spatiality also existed beyond the physical spaces of the shop, theatre, assembly room or race course. Relationships between provider and consumer, process and form, structure and agency, economy and culture were also played out in advertisements in newspapers and on trade cards – the focus of the next chapter.

7 Advertisements

Re-producing spaces of polite consumption

Introduction

Up to this point, we have focused on the physical spaces of consumerism. These were, of course, an essential forum for acting out the spatial practices of consumption, but they formed only part of the eighteenth-century leisure and shopping landscape. In this penultimate chapter, we wish to take the arguments further by re-examining some of the relationships between space, discourse, practice and subjectivity through the virtual spaces constructed in and through advertisements. These spaces existed on the pages of newspapers, trade directories and town guides, and in the minds of both publisher and consumer. They comprised images of goods, people and places, forming a mental landscape of consumption that reflected and shaped the built environment and spatial practices. These images were both a reflection and an important constituent of urban modernity, and their production and consumption were subject to the same pressures of politeness, sociability and competitive differentiation which shaped other spaces of consumption. Use of promotional advertising material in the eighteenth century was widespread and increasingly sophisticated.[1] Many provincial towns sought to assert their identity through the images projected in town guides, trade directories and newspapers, and on coinage and banknotes, all of which acted as signs of urban success and modernity.[2] Advertisements appeared for a wide range of leisure and consumption activities, from theatrical performances to theological discussions, and from horse races to house sales. Central to the construction of a newly urbane provincial culture, however, were the ways in which shops sought to identify themselves with the town as a commercial and cultural entity. Indeed, McKendrick has argued that the modernity and commercialisation of some eighteenth-century advertisements was both characteristic of the age and constitutive of new forms of consumption.[3] Fine and Leopold go further and argue that advertising was also concerned with the ideological reconstruction of use value: giving commodities new and different meanings, and changing the perceptions of consumers.[4] In this way, it shaped consumer tastes and choices, and thus demand especially for novel or fashionable items.[5] Drawing on Hall's encoding/decoding model of communication, we might also interpret advertising as a structured activity in which the individuals and institutions producing messages have the power to define discourses of consumption and materiality. Advertisers set the agenda and provided the cultural categories and frameworks: the 'cultural context' within which leisure and consumption practices took place. Consumers might decode and interpret advertisers' messages in different ways, but the range of their interpretation was constrained and structured by the advertiser.[6]

In this chapter, however, we want to focus on advertising as a spatial practice, with spatial impacts. Advertisements drew on the shop, theatre or library – their physical structure, stock, status and identity – and set these spaces firmly into the context of the street, town and region. In this way, they helped to construct an urbane and commercial culture of consumption in provincial England, and helped to create a virtual consumer landscape in the minds of those reading them. They were, in effect, hybrid material and mental spaces.[7] They drew on the concrete spaces of the town and depended upon the materiality of the printed artefact – the newspaper or the trade card, for instance. Yet they also depended on an audience, itself drawing upon shared social norms and conventions of textual interpretation to decode the message in certain predictable ways. Advertisements show how, in the 'everyday' world, the spaces and practices of consumption were contingent and blurred.

The value of advertisements is manifold. As highly formalised constructions – representations of space – they are suited to a textual reading which not only identifies the evidence they contain about spatial processes, but also how they were grounded in, made reference to and reproduced consumer spaces. This chapter draws on a variety of advertisements to examine the way in which shops and leisure facilities promoted themselves and, more broadly, the consumer spaces of the town and the region. We begin by exploring the ways in which information, images and ideas concerning spaces of consumption were conveyed through advertisements, and how they were used to promote and reproduce those spaces, together with their associated consumption practices. In particular, we emphasise how advertising transcended the different spatial scales of consumer spaces, from the individual to the region. Building on this, we examine how the social and spatial practices of polite shopping and leisure were communicated. Many advertisements assumed knowledge of polite discourse: they were, in a sense, appealing to those already initiated into polite circles. Yet they were also aspirational, offering what might today be called 'lifestyle choices' and guidance as to how to enter the world of polite consumption. Finally, we look at advertisements as projections of polite and modern images of the individual, shop and town, and as a virtual representation of the town and its manifold spaces of consumption, made real on the page of the newspaper. Thus, this chapter brings together themes of the spatiality of consumer processes and the production of consumer space; the inter-locking of material culture and the town, and of provincial and metropolitan identity.

Advertising (and) consumer spaces

At a fundamental level, trade cards and newspaper advertisements were designed to encourage more business for the advertiser, in terms of goods sold, seats taken at the theatre, dancing lessons paid for, and so on. It is unsurprising, then, that much emphasis was placed on the goods, events or services being offered to the consumer. Indeed, at first glance, many newspaper advertisements for shops can appear to be rather pedestrian listings of commodities (see Figure 7.1). Yet such readings underplay their importance and impact as a virtual display. In their text and imagery, they highlighted the cornucopia on offer and contributed to growing consumer knowledge. Listing goods brought to the attention of the pubic not simply what was available in a particular shop, but also the broader range of consumption possibilities. Importantly, the construction of these virtual displays was not restricted to durable goods. The Wigan nursery and seedsman, William Pinkerton, advertised a 'valuable stock of young Nursery trees' – including ash, beech, birch, horse and Spanish chestnut, English and Dutch elm, hornbeam, larch, lime, oak, Weymouth pine, poplar, sycamore, walnut and willow – plus 'all other kinds of forest and fruit trees, evergreen and flowering shrubs, bass mats, garden seeds, transplanted thorn quicksets &c.'. For the bewildered, he also advised that, 'on application, Gentlemen may be accommodated with experienced gardeners',

---

To be sold

By William Cart, Hatter and Haberdasher, from Leicester

At Mr. Fulford's Shop, next door to Mr. Remington's near the

Cross in Coventry during the fair

An entire new Assortment of the following Articles:____Six-fourths, Ell-wide, and Yard-wide. Muslins of al sorts, flower'd, strip'd and plain gauze, flower'd, strip'd and plain lawns, silks and satins, all colours, Barcelona and Sarcenet Handkerchiefs, Catgut and Paris nett, Linen Handkerchiefs, Sufeer ditto, Silk and cotton hats of the newest fashion, great variety of drest caps, in the newest taste; new Ranelagh Cloaks, figur'd and plain ribbons of the choicest patterns, Minionet and trolley laces, Edgeing and footings, all sorts of Women's Leather Gloves and Mitts...Boys silk and sattin Hats and Caps, with feather for ditto, Garnet and Pearl necklaces and earings, French and English ditto, Garnet and Paskes Hair pins and crosses, Italian flowers and Egret with every other Article in the Haberdashery and millinery way.

Articles in the hatting branch.

Men's Carline Hats...n.b Ladies and Gentlemen who please to favour me with their custom in either of the above branches. May depend on being served with as neat Goods, and as cheap as they can be bought in any warehouse in London.

Figure 7.1 Advertisement of William Cart, Coventry, 1767

Source: *Jopson's Coventry Mercury*, 15 June 1767.

hinting at the ways in which shopkeepers more generally operated as arbiters of taste: introducing new goods and ideas, and advising on consumption choices.[8]

The emphasis on plenty, variety and choice was presented visually on trade cards which, especially in the 1720s and 1730s, often illustrated a montage of different objects and sometimes a whole world of goods.[9] At a basic level, this allowed shopkeepers to communicate something of the range of goods which they had available, reminding or informing consumers where they might be viewed and purchased. The trade card of the bookseller and stationer John Sibbald, for example, pictured books, quadrants, mathematical instruments and reading glasses. These illustrations reinforced messages of variety and choice carried in the list of goods appearing beneath.[10] In this way, Sibbald signalled his Liverpool shop as a place where these goods were available, but also hinted at its suitability as a meeting place for the cognoscenti of the town – a suggestion supported by the fact that he also operated a circulating library.[11] In essence, Sibbald's card and the ways in which it promotes his shop are quite straightforward. More complex images aimed at communicating something of the quality as well as the quantity and range of goods available. For instance, the billhead of James Shardlow, a Leicester tinplate worker, shows the products of his industry including kettles, urns and lanterns, but also the tradesman himself at work. The careful craftsmanship depicted in the illustration projected into the homes of his customers the quality of the items purchased. In a similar manner, though far more ornately, the trade card of Benjamin Pearkes of Worcester includes vignettes depicting the manufacture of tobacco and snuff, from the picking and drying of leaves, to the milling process.[12] Here, the excellence of the goods being offered for sale is represented through the quality of the visual imagery of the card: the fine detail of the vignettes being set within a fashionable rococo frame.

When leisure institutions or activities were advertised, it was the service or event being 'sold' that formed the focus of the advertisement. Playbills were not lavishly illustrated, but instead provided a wealth of textual information about the performance, with greatest emphasis placed on the title of the play and the names of the leading actors. Thus, what stands out on a Chester playbill from the 1780s, are the plays – 'King Henry the Second', 'GALLANT SAILORS', 'VILLAGE GHOST' – and the key performers – 'Mr. GARLAND and Signior TOLVARE From the Opera House in *Paris* and lately from the Theatre Royal in *Dublin*'.[13] Similarly, newspaper advertisements for concerts and assemblies focused attention on the event itself: the largest type-face was invariably reserved for the words 'Musick', 'Assembly', 'Oratorio' or 'Lecture'. Somewhat less prominence was given to the venue, the performer and the date of the performance. Information about the price and availability of tickets, when present, appeared in smaller text, relegated to the bottom of the advertisement. The emphasis was very much on the event, in part because these advertisements were appealing to a knowledgeable audience, familiar with the theatre and assemblies. They required information about the play and the performers, the dates and times, rather than the nature of the event *per se*.

Goods, services and events might form the focus of advertisements, but they were often linked to the shopkeeper, professional, impresario or proprietor, whose name often dominated the advertisement. In doing so, they played on the reputation of the individual as an incentive to patronise particular shops or leisure activities. Indeed, reputation was vital for success in eighteenth-century business. Many transactions depended on the easy flow of credit, and credit relationships were mediated by trust, which was itself central to the construction of long-term customer relationships. This was especially true of those trades where the authenticity of goods was difficult for customers to assess (for example, goldsmiths) or which relied most heavily on the skill and knowledge of the service provider (most notably, apothecaries).[14] The importance and selling power of a tradesman's good name is clear from the way in which visiting retailers, such as William Cart, traded on the name of established local men. Cart's advertisement refers to both Fulford, in whose shop he has rented space, and his neighbour Remington. This underscores the extent to which provincial shopkeepers operated within the lived spaces of the local community: they expected to be known to their customers personally or, at least, through association. Moreover, by heading advertisements with their name, shopkeepers effectively projected themselves into the public sphere and broadcast their good name. Much the same was true of notices for polite leisure events where the reputation of the performer, composer or playwright was important in assuring the public of the quality of the production. Thus, a 1751 newspaper advertisement boasted that a concert at the Guildhall in Worcester would be given by 'the Celebrated Miss Cassandra Frederica', with whose performances 'Mr HANDEL himself (*that Great* MASTER *of harmony*) had often thought proper to express the utmost Satisfaction'.[15] Here, both composer and performer give extra kudos to the event, the former used to endorse the credentials of the latter. The importance of the performer's renown becomes particularly apparent in a series of advertisements which was placed in the Liverpool newspaper, *Gore's Advertiser*, in October 1770. In the first, the largest lettering is given to the nature of the event: 'The FIRST OF A COURSE OF SIX LECTURES on the *Art* of *Speaking* in *Public*'. Towards the bottom of the notice, in smaller print, we are told the name of the speaker: the Rev. J. Herries of London. As the lecture programme proceeded, Herries was given ever greater prominence in the advertisements, so that by the final lecture his name was printed in typeface as large as that of the event itself. Apparently, the speaker was becoming a big part of the attraction: his reputation – like those of shopkeepers – communicated notions of reliability, quality or discernment.[16]

Whilst they emphasised the individual, advertisements also locked them into urban space. At one level, the advertisement can be seen as a representation of the shop, theatre or concert room: the virtual counterpart to the façade. As such, advertisements can be read as sign-boards for the spaces and practices for which they formed the public front. Walsh argues that, first and foremost, trade cards served to maintain the customer's awareness of the shop, stamping its image into their consciousness and memory.[17] In an age before brand names were widely used beyond patent medicines, cards were an effective means of reminding the customer where and from whom goods had been bought. Whether as billheads preserved in the ledgers of household accounts or as labels, sometimes – as with trunks and hats, for example[18] – quite literally pasted onto the products, they established and maintained a link between the product and its place of purchase. This carried the shop into the home, the illustration on the card being a potent representation of the shopkeeper and his business.

Through their adoption of fashionable tropes, trade cards carried symbolic capital; by representing goods, shopping practices and sometimes manufacturing processes, they produced an image of the 'private' spaces of the interior. In both their imagery and their use, they formed the boundary and bridge between public and private realms. Moreover, as *aides-mémoire*, trade cards provided a recollection of the shop as a space and shopping as a practice of consumption.[19] In this manner, we can see them as important links between the act of purchasing and the subsequent ownership, associations and meanings of the item. They allowed consumers to relive the shopping experience and to imagine future visits and additional purchases. It is significant, then, that trade cards often carried an image of the shop itself, and thus linked virtual to physical space. The card of Turnbull's Cheltenham Exchange portrays a showroom with an orderly display of writing desks, travelling cases, work boxes, umbrellas and so on, whilst chairs are ranged around the room for the comfort of customers. The scene is one of plenty, order and comfort. Mary Rollason of Birmingham goes a stage further, depicting an elaborate, albeit clearly idealised, showroom. Chandeliers and lamps hang from the ceiling, held in place by cherubs, figurines occupy niches on the far walls, and classical columns frame the whole.[20] The image is one of carefully orchestrated and tasteful refinement: a representation of the shop as an emporium of goods, but also a place of fashion, taste and respectability. Other shopkeepers illustrated the exterior of the premises. Hill and Turley of Worcester, for instance, used an image of their mercer's and draper's shop: a grand three-storey edifice with a pedimented colonnade above the ground floor (see Figure 7.2). The architectural image is a conscious representation of the retail space, sending a clear message about the quality of the shop and, by implication, the goods within. Moreover, its location within a town guide carried this representation beyond the physical bounds of the city.

Advertisements for particular shops and cultural events also made reference to the wider urban environment – its polite credentials and geographies of consumption – and thus served to project an image of the street and town into the homes of individual consumers. Merridew, the Warwick bookseller and stationer, for example, illustrated his trade card with an image of the castle and the town, aligning himself with the local aristocracy and with Warwick as an archetype of polite provincial society.[21] More typically, both newspaper advertisements and trade cards were integral to mental maps of the town's polite topography. A clear statement of location was paramount, both pragmatically and symbolically. This practice was widespread amongst shopkeepers (see Chapter 5), but was also apparent amongst those providing leisure services. Mrs A. Whytell advertised that she painted portraits for ladies and gentlemen, and also sold fancy pieces and prints, noting that 'she is to be spoke with' at her premises in Duke Street, Liverpool, 'where the pictures are to be seen'. Similarly, the dancing master, Mr Winder, was careful to specify that his classes would take place in the Dun-horse

Figure 7.2 Trade card of Hill and Turley of Worcester
Source: *Guide to Worcester*, 1837.

assembly room in Blackburn.[22] In this way, he unmistakably situated himself not only in urban space, but also the consumer landscape of the town – his classes took place in precisely the venue where their benefit would be felt. His advertisement, like those of Rollason, Turnbull and others, constructed and broadcast a virtual reality of that landscape.

Advertisements played an important role in producing an integrated region and projecting this construction through the printed page. At one level, shopkeepers and professionals boasted of their links with other centres – as when the Sheffield dentist, Mr Oliver, advertised that he had previously worked in Liverpool and Manchester.[23] At another, some advertisements sketched out links between networks of towns. The Chester newspaper, *Adams Weekly Courant*, carried notices for assemblies in a number of surrounding towns, including Wrexham, Holywell and Whitchurch, as well as those in the city itself. Similarly, the *Blackburn Mail* advertised the races in Preston, Newton-le-Willows, Leeds and Hexham.[24] In both cases, a regional matrix of events was created through the pages of the newspaper. Whilst it is unlikely that many citizens of Chester would travel to assemblies in other towns, the act of reading these notices set them in a broader framework of polite leisure activities. On a more practical level, Mr Durack, the Chester dancing master, carefully listed the times and places where his classes would be held: 'at Wrexham, on Monday the 21st May Inst. at Chester, on Wednesday the 31st Inst. and at Ellesmere, on Monday the 5th June'.[25] These towns were linked together on the page of the newspaper, by the service provided by Durack, and by the collective desire to gain some of the basic trappings of politeness. Virtual space, the built environment and social discourse were thus united in constructing a regional consumer landscape.

The spaces of consumption drawn on and reproduced through advertisements transcended the town and region. They linked consumers to national and international circuits of exchange and cultures of consumption through the pages of newspapers and town guides, and in the images on trade cards. Nationally, the usual point of reference was London.[26] In a sample of newspaper advertisements taken from the *Worcester Journal* (1742–52), *Gore's Advertiser* (1770) and the *Blackburn Mail* (1793–4), nearly one-fifth made specific reference to London, often as the provenance of goods. Mrs Coppell of Liverpool was typical of many, announcing that she had 'returned from London, where she has purchased a very genteel assortment of goods in the millinery way'. Similarly, J. Wraith advertised that he had 'just received from London, a large quantity of raisin and cowslip wines of excellent qualities'.[27] References to London locked the shopkeeper into a network of ideas, knowledge and supply, a point made clear by the Liverpool mercer, P. Prichard, who announced that:

> he has just come down from London as great a variety of the different new patterns calculated for the spring, as the earliness of the season would admit of, and will make a point of furnishing himself, by all the weekly conveyances, with such others, and those of the most elegant fancy, that are now making for the approaching months.[28]

Prichard's point was threefold: first, fashions were changing rapidly; second, London was the supply centre for these fashions; and third, he was well-placed to supply consumers with both knowledge of the latest trends and the goods themselves. The metropolis could thus recommend the shopkeeper or professional as well as the goods. Time served in London could be used to communicate, *inter alia*, awareness of fashion, skilled craftsmanship and knowledge of particular production techniques. J. Meller, the Knutsford upholsterer, thus advertised that:

> As he has had the Advantage of being for some Time in some of the most capital Shops in London, he makes no Doubt but he has acquired sufficient Share of Knowledge in the various Parts of his Business as to render him capable of executing any Part of it with Skill and Exactness. Those who please to favour him with their Commands, may depend upon having them executed in the neatest manner.[29]

Similar motivations appear to have been in the mind of James Smith, a Worcester gunsmith, who emphasised 'the assistance of a hand from *London*'.[30] Equally, a Liverpool playbill from July 1767 noted that a forthcoming performance of 'Romeo and Juliet' would be given by 'Comedians from the Theatre-Royal in London', and Mr Winder, the Blackburn dancing master, advertised that he was 'late a pupil of Mr Holiway, London'.[31] The metropolis was not the only point of reference, however: other provincial towns formed a cultural matrix which linked local consumer landscapes to a broader context. Winder linked himself to Richmond as well as London, and his local rival, Mr Corbyn, added Windsor to the list of reference points. In Chester, Mr Durack was 'late of Sheffield, and some time since one of the principal dancers in the opera-house, London'.[32] In this way, a general awareness and experience of the wider world of goods and cultural references effectively complemented explicit and functional cosmopolitan links. And both offered a counterpoint to the shopkeeper's or professional's embeddedness in what we might now call the local cultural-economy.

Overall, it is clear that the images on trade cards and newspaper advertisements helped to create a culture of consumption in eighteenth-century provincial England. This culture was based on products, services and events, but also encompassed the varied spaces of consumption. Moreover, advertisements helped to project shops, theatres and so on into virtual and mental space, linking the materiality of the urban environment to the imaginations of consumers. Unlike the buildings themselves, they were transportable and thus carried their representations into the domestic sphere and individuals' mental maps of the consumer landscape of the town. Yet advertisements drew on, broadcast and reproduced not just the spaces of consumption, but also spatial practices of polite shopping and leisure. In the following section, we examine advertisements in this light, emphasising in particular the ways in which they were embedded in a rhetoric of politeness and social aspiration.

Promoting politeness: the social practices of consumption

As we have seen, advertisements were, quite literally, representations of space. They were conceived abstractions produced by the shopkeeper or entrepreneur to project key messages about their business. They drew on and reproduced in virtual form a range of consumption spaces. At the same time, they re-presented and communicated many of the new practices of consumption discussed earlier. Sometimes, they stressed retail innovations such as fixed prices and the 'Advantages of ready money',[33] but more often emphasis was placed on shopping as a pleasurable experience – akin to Berry's notion of 'polite consumption' (see Chapter 6). This practice is most evident in the trade cards of London tradesmen. Dorothy Mercier's card, for example, shows wealthy patrons leisurely shopping in her print and stationery shop on Windmill Street, whilst that of Masefield has the proprietor showing some of his stock of wallpaper to three well-dressed customers in his elegant shop on the Strand.[34] Much the same attempt to link visual imagery and consumer practice is evident in provincial advertisements, such as that of Hill and Turley of Worcester. This shows not just their shop, but also a number of well dressed customers inspecting window displays and entering the premises, and a carriage with four horses and two footmen waiting outside (see Figure 7.2). Similarly, through the open door of Lillington's 'Hosiery, Glove and London Hat Warehouse' in Worcester, we can see fashionably-dressed customers being served by one of the shop assistants.[35]

In representing these practices, such advertisements helped to abstract polite consumption from the physical space of the shop and the street. Politeness was thus communicated through the printed media of advertisements as well as through social practice learned through daily repetition or the study of etiquette manuals. Furthermore, the advertisements themselves became part of polite discourse, drawing on established tropes and appropriate linguistic and artistic constructions. Newspaper advertisements were styled as legitimate 'notices' – a useful device for imparting information about the availability of goods or services at specific locations, whilst remaining within the bounds of politeness and avoiding the impression of vulgar self-promotion. Wedgwood was clearly exceptional in his distaste for advertising in newspapers or via trade cards: his preference for elaborate sales catalogues was a reflection of his reading of the elite market at which he aimed his wares. Yet it is equally clear that provincial shopkeepers and professionals were careful to avoid accusations of tasteless puffing by keeping their advertising within generally accepted boundaries of good taste.[36] The language and conventions adopted by advertisers consciously extended courtesy beyond the boundary of the shop, assembly room or theatre. To illustrate, the Coventry brush-maker, J. Lee, advertised his new shop in the High Street, writing that: 'he most ardently solicits their encouragement, as every endeavour shall be entered to give satisfaction to all that please to confer the least favour upon him, which will, with the greatest Gratitude, be acknowledged'.[37] The courteous language employed and sense of flattery towards the client appears to have furthered the illusion of the genteel customer. Words were carefully chosen and the tone was very much in keeping with the refined culture of shopping engendered in many county towns – at least in the better shops.[38] Phrases such as 'humble servant', 'begs leave to acquaint', and 'most sincere thanks' were used as a matter of course by both shopkeepers and others providing leisure services.

Perhaps more importantly, advertisers, and particularly shopkeepers, also played on their intimacy with established customers by addressing their advertisements to 'friends' and 'the public': differentiating a set of privileged (and self-identifying) customers from the general reader.[39] Friends were valued customers with whom personal bonds were strong: the sort of person who might receive one of the ornate billheads or be invited into the backspace of the shop (see Chapter 5). In focusing on these people in their advertisements, shopkeepers looked to cultivate an atmosphere of sociability which was increasingly associated with the cultures of shopping and leisure. It is significant, then, that this form of advertisement seems to have become increasingly the norm as the century progressed. Entirely absent from the pages of the *Worcester Journal* in the 1740s and 1750s, notices to 'friends' were almost standard practice a generation later. Moreover, they were often styled as personal notes. Thus, John King, a Coventry grocer and haberdasher, wrote in 1778 that he 'embraces the opportunity to return his thanks to his friends for his past favours, and at the same time assures them they may depend upon being supplied with the best goods'. Similarly, John Bridge of Liverpool advertised that he was taking

> this opportunity to return his most grateful thanks to the Ladies and Gentlemen, for the great encouragement they have been pleased to show him, and that he intends opening The Card Assembly on Tuesday the 3rd of May next, and he humbly hopes for a continuance of their favours.[40]

These notices strike a quasi-intimate tone, hinting at the different grades of personal connections which existed between shopkeepers and consumers, and serving as a reminder that customers were not all of equal status.[41] Advertisements, of course, aimed to drum up new business as well as cementing established relationships. The public was thus addressed, and was linked to as well as differentiated from friends: they were kept informed of the goods available and given the implicit invitation to (re)define their relationship with the shopkeeper or service-provider, establishing, through their regular custom, their status as friends.

These various ideas are brought together in the carefully crafted language of John Grimes' advertisement for his Coventry shop (see Figure 7.3). He first gives his reason for advertising – the importuning of his friends – thus distinguishing them from the public to whom the notice is addressed. He then goes on to itemise in a careful manner the various goods and services on offer. Above all, though, Grimes' advertisement draws on and projects ideas of respectability, reflecting the importance of representing the shop as genteel and an integral part of the polite consumer spaces of the town. The privileging of civility became a form of

---

Coventry, Oct. 19 1767

JOHN GRIMES, Cabinet and Chair-maker, Upholster, and Sworn Appraiser, being advised by several of his Friends, has thought proper to acquaint the Public, that he buys and sells all Sorts of Household Furniture, &c: Whosoever pleases to favour him with their Commands, may depend upon being served with the utmost Expedition, by

Their humble Servant,

John Grimes.

Variety of Chairs and Cabinet-Work at his Warehouse at the bottom of Cross Cheaping; Barometers made and carefully repaired; Looking-Glasses silver'd.

Figure 7.3 Advertisement of John Grimes, Coventry, 1767

Source: *Jopson's Coventry Mercury*, 19 October 1767.

urbane etiquette, and a formative part of shopkeepers' practice. Thus shopping was subject to the wider agendas of politeness and respectability so central to the urban renaissance. By presenting a picture of the obliging shopkeeper and genteel customer, for instance, a relationship was constructed which imbued the consumers with certain social status and hinted at the way in which shopping began to play with identity. These relationships were constructed through personal contact and through advertisements. Both in person and in print, they drew on and enhanced the reputation and standing of the tradesman within the urban and business community.

Advertisements established and broadcast the identity and status of the shop, service or event, and that of their providers and their customers, carrying ideals of politeness into a virtual space of newspapers, trade cards and playbills. They also played on the competitive aspect of politeness, appealing to the aspirations of consumers and offering what we might term 'lifestyle choices' and guidance as to how to enter the world of polite consumption. Embedded within the polite language and imagery was the rhetoric of persuasion which aimed to tempt customers to the shop, subscribers to the assembly room or clients to the dancing master. Advertisements conveyed direct and powerful references to the rise of fashion, the emergence of new goods, emulation, the cultural cachet of London, and importantly, pleasure-seeking. From our sample of shop advertisements, just under one-quarter made reference to the genteel or fashionable nature of the goods on offer, often linking the arrival of fresh stock with the new season. Fashion, of course, was most important – and changed most rapidly – in the field of clothing so it is unsurprising that mercers and milliners were prominent in their emphasis of the newness and fashionability of their wares. Thus, in 1770, we see Mr Pickersgill of Liverpool announcing that he has just acquired a 'very large and fresh supply of every article both of the millinery and haberdashery goods calculated for the spring trade'; whilst Sebastian Finglass, also of Liverpool, noted that he made 'all sorts of stays after the newest and neatest fashion'.[42] Indeed, such notions of fashion appear to have penetrated all forms of material culture: L. Hall, a Blackburn saddler, cap, whip and harness-maker, informed 'his friends and the public in general' that 'those who please to favour him with their orders, may depend upon being served with the newest and most fashionable articles'. They also influenced leisure practices, especially those linked to sociability and display. Mr Corbyn, the Blackburn dancing master, was fairly typical, announcing his intention to teach 'some of the newest and most fashionable dances'.[43]

This emphasis of newness and fashionability underscored the importance of taste in constructing an identity as polite and discerning. Choosing the right goods, shops and leisure events enhanced the cultural capital of the consumer.[44] Advertisements reflected this, playing on notions of quality and authenticity to promote goods and performances. Thus, William Cart emphasised the quality of his goods. There were garnet and pearl necklaces and earrings, Ranelagh cloaks, printed cloths, and the promise of the newest taste. Moreover, these were 'genuine' and 'exotic' articles: Barcelona handkerchiefs, French necklaces, Paris net and Italian flowers.[45] Similarly, a display of 'Four Hundred fine Figures in Sculpture', exhibited at the King's Head in Worcester was likened to the statuary of ancient Rome, and described as being found among the treasure taken from a French ship – a selling point which was still being pursued when the display turned up in Lancaster (now for sale) in 1770. In a somewhat different vein, but still emphasising the authentic nature of the event, were the 'feats of activity on the slack and streit rope and the wire' to be undertaken by a 'Company of Italians' visiting Liverpool in 1770.[46] The use of visual metaphors allowed shopkeepers to communicate far more complex messages through their trade cards. The stock figure of the Chinese man with tea chests and ginger jars appears on the cards of many grocers and tea dealers. That of Samuel Daniell of Stourbridge is fairly typical (see Figure 7.4).[47] The central figure, together with the pagodas, coolies and junks in the background, affirms the provenance and authenticity of the produce, whilst adding an aspect of the exotic to what were, by the late eighteenth century, widespread and increasingly mundane commodities. This notion of authenticity is carried a stage further in the trade card of Joseph Ward of Coventry,[48] the single figure being replaced by a group of Chinese people taking tea, whilst alongside them the figure of a black 'native' smokes a long earthenware pipe. The message is clear: the products are exotic imports, and their consumption is part of a set of 'authentic' practices. In drawing on these stock figures, shopkeepers such as Daniell and Ward were able to present their shops as exotic spaces, linked to a broad network of supply, and themselves not only as purveyors of desirable imported goods, but also gatekeepers of a range of pleasurable and exotic experiences.

Advertisements also drew on the discernment and knowledge of consumers in making allusions both to artistic conventions and familiar genres of commercial imagery. Thus, in an interesting twist on the Chinese tea motif, the trade card of Henry Waterfall's 'Provision Warehouse' places a classical female figure in the

Figure 7.4 Trade card of Samuel Daniell of Stourbridge

Source: Bodleian Library, University of Oxford, John Johnson Collection, Trade Cards 11 (98).

184 *Advertisements*

midst of a pastoral rural scene (see Figure 7.5).[49] The image cleverly draws on the growing fashion for pastoral scenes – the type of engraving or painting that would adorn the walls of polite customers to whom Waterfall's card was directed – but the specific point of reference is clear. A windmill appears in place of the pagoda, whilst sacks of grain, barrels of butter and hams replace the tea chests and ginger jars. The allusion is clear and deliberate, yet its success relies upon the consumer being aware of both idioms. This is sophisticated advertising. The illustration operates at a number of levels: an advertisement for the goods, a visual pun and as a fashionable image which drew on and reinforced notions of taste and polite discernment.

The advertising system of provincial shopkeepers and leisure services of the eighteenth century was complex and highly nuanced. Advertisers were careful to conform to expectations of what was socially acceptable, whilst promoting new discourses of shopping and buying. Their notices and trade cards were polite, informative and innovative, giving information about stock and services, as well as location. But the messages they conveyed were more powerful than this. Shopkeepers encouraged people to buy and infused their goods and their premises with an aura of status and respectability. The language in which advertisements were constructed was a code to politeness and a respectable way of life in the provincial town. In this way the advert was designed and styled on the same principles as the shop. Moreover, through the emphasis on fashionability, politeness and the shopkeepers' reputation, they portrayed the shop as a front space, and like the shop, presented a selective and partial image. The virtual representation of the shop in advertisement or trade card drew on many of the same discourses as the shop space itself – both used by the shopkeeper as vehicles to promote new polite consumer 'lifestyles'. In doing this, advertisements projected images of the individual, shop, social event and town as polite and modern. They were, in effect, virtual representations of the town and its manifold spaces of consumption, made

Figure 7.5 Trade card of Henry Waterfall of Coventry

Source: Bodleian Library, University of Oxford, John Johnson Collection, Trade Cards 11 (76).

real on the printed page. It is to the characteristics of these virtual consumer spaces, and their relationship with real spaces in the town and on the page, that we turn in the final section.

Advertising, space and the printed page

Advertisements formed an important channel of communication between those supplying goods and services – or organising social and cultural events – and a set of literate, urbane and respectable consumers. They provided information about what was available in particular places and at particular times, but also informed the public about wider notions of novelty, fashionability and taste: what we might term polite cultures of consumption. Moreover, in the subtext of their persuasive rhetoric, they generated important ideas about the provincial town as a place for shopping and leisure, and a site of consumption. In essence, they defined and communicated the spatialisation of modernity in the urban arena through their portrayal of consumer spaces.[50] The shop was represented through the medium of the advert and its physical presence in either a newspaper or trade card. It was also re-presented in the context of the fashionable urban arena, with new and plentiful goods, organised and sold in the latest mode. Through using advertising space to promote the shop, its wares and the reputation of the shopkeeper, the space of the shop was transformed. This re-presentation added to its impact as a space of consumption.

But the significance of using this medium was greater still. Advertisements not only represented these spaces, they also produced and re-produced them, creating new forms of consumer spaces. This virtual or abstract space lay at the intersection between perceived and conceived space. The printed advertisement was the medium through which notions of abstract space were transmitted; it was one step removed from the world that it represented, it was commodified, and it was the product of capitalist exchange.[51] This liminal space contributed to the production of consumer landscapes at different spatial scales, outside the realm of the concrete space of the shop, theatre or assembly room. And it helped to knit together the different spatial scales of consumption as they were lived and experienced on the ground. This was achieved in a number of related ways.

First, in listing, describing and illustrating goods, shops, plays, theatres, and so on, advertisements linguistically and pictorially constructed both a culture of consumption, and the shop, theatre and assembly room as consumer space. For example, in the 1787 advertisement of the shoemaker J. Brown, the reader seems to be taken around the shop. We start with Ladies' shoes, including those of silk and stuff, Italian glazed heels, sandals and different types of clogs. Then we move on to Gentlemen's boots and dress shoes, and finally come to an assortment of lasts.[52] This virtual tour is reinforced by the subtle and polite rhetoric contained in the advertisement which was, as we discussed earlier, designed to encourage people to consume and more specifically to patronise Brown's shop. Yet it also constructs the shop as a space of polite consumption, reinforcing the codes and mores of such consumer spaces. A similar feel of being in the space described by the advertisement comes with Joseph Sillen and Chesrea Chikertou's notice of their firework display in New Square, Liverpool. Within the confined space of the square, the viewer is to be treated to the spectacle of:

> Stars, snakes, and serpents, globes, and wheels of fire, a flower-pot full of flowers all on fire, the Italian mill all on fire, the sun, moon, and seven stars, a palm-tree full of roses, a pigeon flying on the cord sets fire to the grand piece, a fountain all on fire.[53]

Such textual representations within media space not only created a picture of the new consumer landscapes; it was also part of their production. It created and transmitted particular ideas about the shop, public space and the town.

Second, as printed artefacts, the advertisements were themselves mobile. Newspapers were carried by networks of newsmen across the county and beyond, those from Chester, for example, reaching far into north Wales. As a consequence, the advertisements that they contained moved from Chester to Llangollen, Bangor and Caernarfon, and from tradesman or entrepreneur, to printer, to newsrooms, coffee houses and private houses. Similarly, trade cards and billheads were transferred into account ledgers, taking the shop into the domestic sphere, whilst playbills were pasted onto walls, projecting an image of the theatre onto the street.[54] This meant that the consumer did not have to go to the shop for a taste of the new fashions or knowledge of new goods. They could acquire these vicariously via the printed advertisement. In this way, advertisements served to draw together the consumer landscape of the region: linking town to country and integrating a network of centres of consumption. Moreover, purchasing and reading provincial newspapers, perusing trade cards and billheads, and studying playbills all encouraged new patterns of consumption and constituted a form of consumption in themselves. Newspapers especially, as disposable commodities, were indicative of the privileging of novelty over antiquity. Through this consumption of the printed media, access was gained to the spaces of consumerism that it embodied. And, of course, these spaces were instrumental in promoting consumer knowledge and desires, since the advertisements in the newspaper were both produced (physically and conceptually) and productive (they evoked a response).[55]

Third, advertisements as a virtual representation of the town and its manifold spaces of consumption were made real on the page of the newspaper. Here advertisements for different products, services, businesses and institutions jostled for attention and offered the reader a kaleidoscope of images, ideas, and representations, all of which had to be decoded in subtly different ways. Notices from shopkeepers or for leisure activities were therefore subject to a very particular type of contextualisation, sitting alongside other advertisements for the stagecoaches to and goods from London, public lectures and drawing lessons, music concerts, and commodious new-built brick houses. The matrix of advertisements fed off each other, providing a virtual guide to politeness and consumerism, and a montage of the street, the town and the region as spaces of consumption (see Figure 7.6). In a sense, the visual and perceptual collage of the newspaper page mirrored the shop

Tarvin Fair	Shop: leather seller (Chester)	Auction: tenement (Shotton)
To Let: estate (Plumley)	For Sale: farm (Salop)	
Wreck to be raised	Dancing assembly (Wrexham)	Auction: house (Warrington)
For Sale: fire engine (Denbigh)	Dancing Assembly (Whitchurch)	
Auction: coffee house (Chester)	Assembly (Holywell)	Auction: house (Great Neston)
	For Sale: house (Wrexham)	
Auction: house (Alpraham)	Subscription for lighthouse	Stationers' Hall: almanacs
	Shop: gardener (Chester)	
Stolen: horse	Notice to creditors (Whitchurch)	
Auction: cheese farm, etc.	Notice to creditors (Warrington)	Shop: bookshop (Chester)
	Auction: farm (Sevenoaks)	

Figure 7.6 Media space: a matrix of advertisements

Source: *Adams Weekly Courant*, 5 December 1775.

fronts and street signs, with their juxtapositioning of competing imagery – a visual assault described so vividly by Benjamin.[56] Indeed, it is possible to see the mixture of advertisements as representing the mixing of premises along the street. At the same time, the range and variety of shops, institutions and events being advertised mirrored the listing of shopkeepers and institutions in trade directories. As such, they reflected the cornucopia of shopping and leisure opportunities offered in the town or region. Shops and leisure facilities in different towns competed for custom in real space, and continued this competition within the pages of the newspaper, each advert trying to outdo the next in its appeal to the discerning and respectable consumer. The page of advertisements helped bind the region together, as did the real consumer decisions and choices which they were designed to influence.

This montage of ideas and images, which together represented urbane culture, had a provincial twist that was the result of closely maintained relationships with the country. Scattered amongst advertisements for urban shops and theatres were notices concerned with issues such as poaching, damage to woodland, lost animals, and advertisements for farms or stud horses. Links between town and country were close and mutual, but provincial advertisers, be it through trade cards or newspapers, embraced the opportunity to exemplify the town as the site for modern living. At the same time, a strong sense of community crept into many advertisements. The use of names of shopkeepers and sometimes their friends and neighbours (as discussed earlier) suggests at least a familiarity with their general audience. The provincial town was clearly not a place of anomie and anonymity.

Conclusion

By the late eighteenth century, provincial shopkeepers and leisure providers were using a range of means to advertise their shops, goods and services, and themselves. The concrete space of the premises themselves, combined with newspaper advertisements and trade cards, represented the provincial town as a matrix of spaces of consumption. They helped to produce and project 'modern' shopping and leisure practices which lay at the heart of urban consumption, and thus cemented the axiomatic link between consumerism and the town. In this way, advertisements underscored processes which were enacted in the physical space of the shop, library, theatre and street. However, advertising through the printed media had greater implications, since advertisements located the consumer landscape beyond the spatial boundary of, for example, the shop and the street, thereby producing an abstract space of consumption. This, in turn, extended the influence of the shop and the wider realm of consumerism. The advert not only re-created but also re-presented the shop, assembly room and theatre.

The representation of the shop has two interrelated aspects. In practical terms, it gave access to the shop without the consumer needing to go there and was instrumental in promoting consumer knowledge and desires. Through advertisements, consumer space was no longer just concrete or absolute, but was embedded in the collective psyche. In the words of Lefebvre, each system 'maps out its own territory, takes it out and signposts it'.[57] Advertisements were indeed a map and signpost to the world of goods found in the town. They were critical, not only in engineering a desire to buy, but also in elevating a consciousness of consumerism beyond its spatial location. In conceptual terms, the advertisement was a hybrid derived from the concrete space of the shop and the materiality of the goods, and the mental space of the consumer's perceptions of the consumption landscape. Together, the material and the mental produced the image of consumer spaces presented in advertisements. The physicality of the image made it mobile yet fixed, so that it could be embedded in the physical space of the street, the pages of the newspaper and the lifeworld of the consumer. Through their references to new goods and practices, they constructed the shop and leisure space as modern. Through their portrayal of consumer spaces, they communicated and transmitted the spatialisation of modernity. They re-presented the shop, theatre and so on in the context of the fashionable urban arena, thereby contributing to the production of new spaces of consumption. These spaces were re-produced in the mind of the reader, and this was important as it was this abstract space which symbolised the invasion of consumerism into new spaces. The newspaper advertisements depended on the perception of the reader and potential customer: consumer spaces were not just concrete, but also perceived, lived and imagined.

8   Conclusions

Consumption lay at the geographical and ideological heart of the provincial town. In presenting an integrated analysis of leisure and shopping in eighteenth-century England, we have argued that they drew on related social and cultural imperatives, were intermeshed in the daily lives of consumers, and were set within and drew upon overlapping spaces of consumption. Central to our argument is an understanding that the practices of leisure and shopping produced and reproduced consumer space, whilst they were themselves moulded by those spaces. The playing out of this socio-spatial dialectic has been a continual theme; but we have also sought to reconsider this simple dichotomy, drawing on Lefebvre's trialectic of spatiality – (everyday) spaces, (preconceived) representations of space, and (perceived or felt) spaces of representation – to uncover the complex spatialities of consumption in eighteenth-century towns.[1] In doing so, the objective was not to present a critique of spatial theory. Rather, we sought to draw on these ideas to further our understanding of the character and development of consumption during this critical period, often characterised as being the birth of a consumer society. To this end, we consciously linked this spatialisation of urban history to contemporary discourses – of politeness, modernity and sociability – and to the subjectivity and identity of consumers – through notions of performance, representation and display.[2] Exploring the spatiality of consumption at various scales both embeds practices in a layering of space and highlights the ways in which different imperatives surfaced at each scale.

Examining leisure and retail provision at the regional scale establishes (conceptually and practically) the existence of consumer space above the level of the built environment of the town. At one level, this regional space of consumption comprised an urban system in and through which goods and services were distributed. The spread of leisure activities and a range of shops in many towns across the west Midlands and north-west England – even those at the margins of urban status – reflected growing demand from the rural gentry and a burgeoning urban middling sort. In this way, the regional space of consumption was produced by the social practices of consumers. Yet, as Soja argues, society was also shaped by space: the hierarchical and spatial structuring of retailing and leisure facilities focused consumer activity into certain favoured locations. Provision was not restricted to larger towns, but they tended to have earlier, more and better quality goods and services. As improvements in transport and communications in the late eighteenth and early nineteenth century made travel easier and the spread of consumer knowledge more rapid, these larger towns grew in dominance, even as they arguably declined in national significance as centres of consumption.[3] The local availability of goods and services, via a hierarchically structured urban system, meant that consumers could make choices where to shop and take their leisure. As is apparent from the activities of Nicholas Blundell, John Plumbe, Ann Sneyd and many others, these choices were determined in part by the relative attractions of different towns: what we have styled here the consumption hierarchy. But they were also shaped by individuals' readings of the consumer landscape and their personal preference systems. The regional space of consumption thus comprised the geographical and hierarchical space of the urban system, overlain with and integrated through the mental maps and behaviour patterns of individual consumers. Thus, by exercising choice, consumers contributed to the production of the regional consumer.

Towns were the effective building blocks of this regional space. They were differentiated not just by the level of provision afforded to (polite) consumers, but also in terms of their credentials as polite places. In part, this politeness was constructed through, and judged in terms of, the assemblage of appropriate infrastructure and fashionable shops – a representation of space, conceived and codified by the urban and sometimes the rural elite. On the ground, this often led to the construction of particular geographies of polite space: concentrations of functions and infrastructure which became self-reinforcing as the lived spaces of polite leisure and shopping. In more abstract terms, many centres attempted to re-imagine and project themselves as polite places.[4] This was frequently undertaken through the pages of town histories and guides which can be seen as representations of space and place: blueprints of urban ambition and identity as much as records of past events and contemporary achievements and characteristics. At the same time, they broadcast this polite image to a literate polite audience, carrying the materiality of the town into a world of text and images which, as Sweet argues, were carefully chosen to encourage, guide, celebrate or berate urban achievement.[5] Yet these histories also highlighted the existence of different interpretations of what comprised politeness, for the individual and for the town. For much of the eighteenth century, many town histories, corporations and citizens viewed politeness as Shaftesbury had conceived it: a model of behaviour (or urban/civic accomplishment) which distinguished and justified the position of the gentlemanly elite and the established urban hierarchy. Yet the meanings of politeness were always slippery, commercial and Enlightenment ideals being overlain on the concept as it took on distinctively urban associations. Towards the end of the eighteenth century, Barker notes the growing strength of another provincial and commercial perspective which portrayed politeness increasingly in terms of civility, individual and urban improvement, and civic pride – a bourgeois recipe which increasingly defined the identity of towns in the nineteenth century.[6]

These re-conceptions of the town were firmly grounded in improvement of the urban environment and urban society. The improved street, in particular, was a key element of the wider idealisation of the town as polite and civilised, and underpins our understanding of the changing built environment of the eighteenth-century town.[7] Streets were moulded by environmental upgrading and architectural makeovers into public spaces designed for particular activities and informed by discourses of politeness and improvement. Ogborn offers a reading of the street in political terms – as part of a (male) public sphere. Yet it was also a public space in much broader terms: a thoroughfare, a venue for leisure and shopping, and a site of contestation and conflict – one which was populated by both men and women.[8] This layering of functions and meanings made its position as a key space of representation within the town – produced by urban elites through Improvement Acts and the implementation of the principles of classical architecture – all the more telling. Streets were conceived and engineered to be orderly and rational: a reflection of the ideals of urban civility. They were also the stage-sets for conscious and sub-conscious performances which moulded and projected individual identities.[9] Performances on eighteenth-century streets, as in nineteenth-century department stores and twentieth-century malls, were often guided by ritual, etiquette and itineraries. We should be wary, however, of giving too much weight to the polemic of courtesy writers: performances were also iterative and relational, shaped by their context and the actions and reactions of others. As Glennie and Thrift, Miller *et al.*, and others have argued, consumer behaviour drew on the active context of the built environment, whilst in turn shaping the street and its meanings as well as the identity of individuals and groups of actors.[10] Moreover, these carefully constructed environments, performances and meanings could be disrupted by everyday activities with, for example, a commercial, plebeian or criminal imperative. The image, spaces and practices of politeness were all fragile: open to alternative interpretations and to penetration by different ideologies and activities.[11]

The street was suffused with other spaces of consumption, most notably the buildings with which it was lined. These buildings were themselves representations of space. Their public façades were imbued with symbolic capital which projected key messages about the 'private' spaces that lay behind and formed the boundary between Goffman's front and back regions.[12] This demarcation allowed the production and definition of specialist spaces as shops, libraries, assembly rooms and so on. These were then spatially sorted as they vied for the best locations. However, the spatiality of consumption was not just the geography of where individual shops and leisure facilities were located; it also encompassed embedded references to other polite spaces and the privileging of some spaces over others. All this was a crucial part of the production of new consumer landscapes, as a consumer ethos penetrated the morphology of the town. At the same time, internal sub-divisions of shops and leisure facilities created a hierarchy of privacy, affording differential access and conferring status accordingly. This complicates any simple dichotomy between public and private, and further challenges established readings of the gendered nature of space.[13] What comprised public and private space within a shop, for example, when it was segregated physically, but also conceptually differentiated? As Walsh argues, shopkeepers actively used space to organise their business, convey different meanings and differentiate customers, serving some through the window and allowing others access to more private show rooms.[14] The division of space thus created a spatiality that embodied the culture of consumerism; both in the way these spaces were consumed and how they facilitated the consumption of other aspects of urban material culture. Moreover, the layering of space also accommodated different modes of display: to promote wares, facilitate certain leisure activities, enhance social status or encourage particular modes of living. It thus brought together representations of space with the lived spaces of everyday action. These actions, as de Certeau suggests, might transgress and subvert these careful conceptions of consumer space, creating, through theft for example, counterspaces which contested identities and meanings.[15]

As Trentmann argues, consumption is ultimately about the motivations, attitudes and behaviour of individuals.[16] These shaped the spaces and practices of consumption as lived spaces, and underpinned the creation of a new material culture in eighteenth-century provincial England. Yet these motives and actions were in turn informed by a variety of 'cultural contexts' – the socio-spatial structures within and through which operated the agency of individual action. In focusing on polite shopping and leisure as one such context, we have argued that imperatives of sociability and status competition – motivations which Borsay sees as lying at the heart of an urban renaissance – were reflected in the polite practices and social mixing which characterised many leisure and shopping environments.[17] Relatively few spaces of consumption were overtly exclusive, and many accommodated men and women from a range of social and geographical backgrounds. As Berry argues, the rural gentry shared space, even if they were reluctant to rub shoulders with urban tradesmen, and even artisans. Moreover, perhaps in contrast to Estabrook's assertions, this suggests a certain commonality in terms of the values of rural and urban consumers.[18] Sometimes, behaviour was governed by formal rules (as at assembly rooms); more often, it was shaped by a set of behavioural norms which conformed with ideals of politeness, civility and commercial practice. But the production of polite space and polite identity were mutually constitutive: linked through social practices. As research on contemporary shopping highlights, the agency of the consumer is central to the construction and meaning of a range of socio-spatial structures: the mall, high street, car-boot sale and so on.[19] In the eighteenth century, these structures included shops, theatres and assemblies, and also advertisements which transcended the physicality of the urban environment and created an abstract spatial context for individual action.

Through the course of the eighteenth century, advertisements for shops, assemblies, concerts, plays, auctions and so on, appeared in ever greater numbers in the provincial press, and on trade cards, play bills, and later in trade directories. Through these media spaces, 'modern' shopping and leisure practices were produced and projected, and the town was re-presented as a complex matrix of spaces of consumption. In this way, advertisements cemented the link between consumerism and the town – a relationship which was mediated through the emphasis on politeness which pervaded both the language and imagery of the advertisements and the events, spaces and services which they promoted. In doing this, advertisements drew on and reproduced physical spaces of consumption. But they also transcended the different spatial scales of consumer spaces, taking the norms and practices of polite consumption, as well as knowledge about goods and services, into an abstract consumer landscape. Moreover, advertisements helped to embed these ideas and values into the collective psyche. They were, therefore, a hybrid derived from the materiality of the shop and goods, and the mental space of the consumer's perceptions. At the same time, their physical presence on the printed page produced a montage of images of consumption which reflected the intense visual impact of the street and the shop that so struck Benjamin in nineteenth-century Paris.[20] This underlines the variegated nature of consumer spaces – incorporating physical, perceived, lived and imagined dimensions – and the ways in which these different aspects were woven together through the personal experience of individual consumers.

Our analysis has highlighted the importance of leisure and shopping in shaping the built environment, and the social and cultural dynamics of the eighteenth-century provincial town. We have placed particular emphasis on the role of politeness in structuring urban society and space, but have consciously sought to problematise both its conception and its impact. That it was a mutable ideal is a commonplace. Yet, in its varied interpretations as an ideal and a set of normative practices, politeness was closely linked with the consumption of goods, time and space. In turn, these processes were shaped by a consumer landscape which comprised the lived spaces of the urban environment; the conceptions of town histories, architects' plans and shopkeepers' displays, and the perceptions of individual consumers. It was on this ground, then, that eighteenth-century discourse met with twentieth-century spatial theory. And it is in the creative dialogue that ensued that we sought to create fresh insights into notions of politeness, processes of consumption and the dynamics of urban change. From this, four broad observations can be made about the production of consumer space in the eighteenth-century town which link us back to Lefebvre's spatial trialectic.

The first, and most obvious, is that this production of space did indeed take place at a variety of different geographical scales, from the self-aware individual, through the shop, street and town, to the region, and beyond to the abstract space of advertisements. At all these levels, space was produced by, engaged with and influenced the social and spatial practices of consumers. Further, these spaces did not exist in isolation from one another: actions which took place on one scale (for example, visiting a particular shop) contributed to the production of space at a larger scale (the creation of specialist areas within the town and the construction of hierarchies of consumption across the region and beyond). This both indicates the interdependency, even fluidity, of different spaces, and is critical to an understanding of consumer behaviour and spaces as being mutually constituted.

The second is that consumer spaces were conceived spaces: they were planned, regulated and shaped as fashionable, polite and modern. In this way, they were *representations of space* which were codified and had imbedded within them ideologies of improvement and progress which lay at the heart of Enlightenment ideals. Notwithstanding the involvement of rural elites, especially in the early eighteenth century, these representations were urban in their manifestation and in their conception. The association between civilisation, politeness, modernity and consumerism was embodied in the town as the quintessential enlightened environment.[21] The emphasis was placed on order, regularity and the visual, with the façade becoming an increasingly important feature of the urban landscape. Behind this, however, were internal spaces which were also carefully planned to structure behaviour, to send important messages about status and probity, and to assist in the display of goods and the self.

Third, and cutting across the geographical and concrete hierarchy of space, is a different understanding of spatiality which emphasises the importance of processes or spatial practices. These were the *lived spaces* of consumers, as they experienced, negotiated, and in turn shaped their immediate environment. They were constituted through the meanings invested in places through actions which were sometimes conscious, but often the repeated routines of daily life.[22] Shopping and leisure spaces in the eighteenth-century town were dependent upon consumers for their making, most obviously through the acts of shopping and taking leisure, but also in the social meanings invested in these activities and therefore in the spaces in which and through which they took place. Consumers therefore emerge as active agents who experienced their environment as lived space, at once social and practical, and attached significance to the knowledge-making process that came about through, for example, shopping. Conversely, consumer spaces evoked particular forms of behaviour, informed by politeness and sociability as well as the practicalities and hedonism of acquiring goods and services, thereby asserting the mutually reinforcing relationship between space and practice.

Fourth, whilst the production of consumer spaces is largely portrayed as modern, polite and improving, contradictions and contestation existed on many levels. Traditional places and times of shopping and leisure – fairs, markets and festivals – remained important and sat alongside the more 'modern' spaces of the shop, assembly room and library. The two were spatially and socially contingent, shops doing much of their business on market days and often being clustered around the marketplace; yet the former were often portrayed as the antithesis of modernity and politeness. In addition, consumer spaces were subject to transgression and disorder, and were thus re-made as *spaces of representation* by counter-cultures with very different sets of values and norms. Most dangerous to the prevailing order were the socio-spatial practices which overtly contested polite and commercial discourses, including blood sports and shop-breaking. The last of these challenged the codes of conduct associated with shopping and its spaces, and serves as a reminder that socially constructed spaces were dependent upon social consensus as to how they should be used.

These conclusions reveal consumer spaces of eighteenth-century towns as spatially and socially produced and negotiated. They were constructed geographically and ideologically, and permeated the lifeworld of individuals at different scales, from the lived environment of the shop, street and town, to the abstract spaces of media representation. Consumerism lay at the heart of the eighteenth-century town, and space lay at the heart of consumerism: it was produced through, and in turn served to shape, spatial practices and social relationships. Only by understanding the critical spatiality of the historic processes of consumerism can we begin to fathom their evolution.

Notes

1 Leisure, consumption and shopping

1 Miller, D. et al., *Shopping, Place and Identity*, London: Routledge, 1998, p. 1; Berg, M., *Luxury and Pleasure in Eighteenth-Century Britain*, Oxford: Oxford University Press, 2005, p. 27. For a critique of the overweening importance of consumption, see White, J., 'A world of goods? The "Consumption Turn" and eighteenth-century British history', *Cultural and Social History*, 3:1, 2006, pp. 93–104.
2 Trentmann, F., 'Beyond consumerism: new historical perspectives on consumption', *Journal of Contemporary History*, 39, 2004, p. 373. See also Sombart, W., *Luxury and Capitalism*, 1922, Ann Arbor, MI: University of Michigan Press, 1967; Veblen, T., *The Theory of the Leisure Class: An Economic Study of Institutions*, Basingstoke: Macmillan, 1912; Baudrillard, J., *Selected Writings*, Oxford: Blackwell, 1988.
3 Miller *et al.*, *Shopping, Place and Identity*, pp. 2–7; Trentmann, 'Beyond consumerism'. See also Stearns, P., *Consumerism in World History: The Global Transformation of Desire*, London: Routledge, 2001; Cohen, L., *A Consumer's Republic: The Politics of Mass Consumption in Post-War America*, New York: Knopf, 2003; the various contributions to Daunton, M.J. and Hilton, M. (eds), *Politics of Consumption: Material Culture and Citizenship in Europe and America*, London: Berg, 2001.
4 Trentmann, F., 'Knowing consumers – histories, identities and practices', in F. Trentmann (ed.) *The Making of the Consumer: Knowledge, Power and Identity in the Modern World*, London: Berg, 2006, pp. 1–27; Shields, R., 'Spaces for the subject of consumption', in R. Shields (ed.), *Lifestyle Shopping: The Subject of Consumption*, London: Routledge, 1992, pp. 1–20; Gregson, N. and Crewe, L., *Second-Hand Cultures*, London: Berg, 2003; Rappaport, E., *Shopping for Pleasure. Women in the Making of London's West End*, Princeton, NJ: Princeton University Press, 2000.
5 Compare, for example, the discussion of leisure in Borsay, P., *The English Urban Renaissance: Culture and Society in the Provincial Town, 1660–1770*, Oxford: Oxford University Press, 1989, pp. 115–96, to that of consumption in Smith, W.C., *Consumption and the Making of Respectability, 1600–1800*, London: Routledge, 2002. An implicit link is made in Vickery, A., *The Gentleman's Daughter: Women's Lives in Georgian England*, New Haven, CT: Yale University Press, 1998. Stobart, J., 'Shopping streets as social space: consumerism, improvement and leisure in an eighteenth century county town', *Urban History*, 25, 1998, pp. 3–21, and Beckett, J. and Smith, C., 'Urban Renaissance and consumer revolution in Nottingham 1688–1750', *Urban History*, 27, 2000, pp. 31–50, do so more explicitly, but in relation to a single town.
6 For rare exceptions, see Berry, H., 'Polite consumption: shopping in eighteenth-century England', *Transactions of the Royal Historical Society*, 12, 2002, pp. 375–94; Walsh, C., 'Social meaning and social space in the shopping galleries of early-modern London', in J. Benson and L. Ugolini (eds), *A Nation of Shopkeepers: Five Centuries of British Retailing*, London: Tauris, 2003, pp. 52–79; Peck, P., *Consuming Splendor: Society and Culture in*

Seventeenth-Century England, Cambridge: Cambridge University Press, 2005, pp. 25–72.
7 See Weatherill, L., *Consumer Behaviour and Material Culture*, second edition, London: Routledge, 1996, pp. 137–90; Vickery, *Gentleman's Daughter*; Smith, *Consumption and Respectability*; Finn, M., 'Men's things: masculine possession in the consumer revolution', *Social History*, 25, 2000, pp. 133–55; Berg, *Luxury and Pleasure*, pp. 199–246; Berry, H., 'Prudent luxury: the Metropolitan tastes of Judith Baker, Durham gentlewoman', in P. Lane and R. Sweet (eds), *Out of Town: Women and Urban Life in Eighteenth-Century Britain*, Aldershot: Ashgate, pp. 130–54; Peck, *Consuming Splendor*, pp. 21–2, 61–71, 135–9.
8 Soja, E., *Postmodern Geographies: The Reassertion of Space in Critical Social Theory*, London: Verso, 1989, pp. 10–24.
9 See Arnade, P., Howell, M. and Simons, W., 'Fertile spaces: the productivity of urban space in Northern Europe', *Journal of Interdisciplinary History*, 32, 2002, pp. 515–48.
10 De Vries, J., *European Urbanization, 1500–1800*, London: Methuen, 1984.
11 Berg, *Luxury and Pleasure*, p. 216.
12 Braudel, F., *Capitalism and Material Life, 1400–1800*, London: Fontana, 1974, p. 389.
13 See Borsay, *Urban Renaissance*, p. 223; Glennie, P. and Thrift, N.J., 'Modernity, urbanism and modern consumption', *Environment and Planning A: Society and Space*, 10, 1992, pp. 423–43.
14 Estabrook, C., *Urbane and Rustic England: Cultural Ties and Social Spheres in the Provinces, 1660–1780*, Manchester: Manchester University Press, 1998, p. 7.
15 Borsay, P., 'The culture of improvement', in P. Langford (ed.), *The Eighteenth Century*, Oxford: Oxford University Press, 2002, pp. 183–212.
16 Ogborn, M., *Spaces of Modernity: London's Geographies 1680–1780*, New York: Guildford Press, 1998, p. 3.
17 See Habermas, J., *The Structural Transformation of the Public Sphere*, Cambridge, MA: MIT Press, 1989.
18 Ogborn, *Spaces of Modernity*, pp. 1–38; Breen, T.H., 'The meanings of things', in J. Brewer and R. Porter (eds), *Consumption and the World of Goods*, London: Routledge, 1993, p. 257.
19 Elliot, P., 'Towards a geography of English scientific culture: provincial town identity and literary and philosophical culture in the English county town, 1750–1850', *Urban History*, 32, 2005, p. 391; Borsay, *Urban Renaissance*, p. 317.
20 Borsay, P., 'Bath an Enlightenment City?', in P. Borsay, G. Hirschfelder and R.-E. Mohrmann (eds), *New Directions in Urban History*, Münster: Waxmann, 2000, p. 3.
21 These ideas are discussed in more detail in the following section and in Chapter 3.
22 Stobart, J. 'County, town and country: three histories of urban development in eighteenth-century Chester', in P. Borsay and L. Proudfoot (eds), *Provincial Towns in Early Modern England and Ireland*, Oxford: Oxford University Press, 2002, pp. 178–86; Ellis, J., 'Industrial and urban growth in Nottingham, 1680–1840', in J. Stobart and N. Raven (eds), *Towns, Regions and Industries*, Manchester: Manchester University Press, 2005, pp. 147–60.
23 Weatherill, *Consumer Behaviour*, pp. 70–90; Overton, M. et al., *Production and Consumption in English Households, 1600–1750*, London: Routledge, 2004, pp. 153–65; Estabrook, *Urbane and Rustic England*.
24 Sweet, R., 'Topographies of politeness', *Transactions of the RHS*, 12, 2002, p. 355.
25 Hutton, W., *An History of Birmingham to the End of the Year 1780*, Birmingham: Pearson and Rollason, 1781, p. 259. Copper, A.A., Third Earl of Shaftesbury, *Characteristics of Men, Manners, Opinions, Times*, ed. Lawrence Klein, Cambridge: Cambridge University Press, 1999, p. 31; Carter, P., *Men and the Emergence of Polite Society, Britain 1660–1800*, Harlow: Longman, 2002, Chapter 2.

26 Bourdieu, P., *Distinction: A Social Critique of the Judgement of Taste*, London: Routledge, 1986. See also Berg, *Luxury and Pleasure*, pp. 6, 41, 234; Smith, *Consumption and Respectability*, pp. 41–3.
27 Vickery, *Gentleman's Daughter*, p. 202; Klein, L., 'Politeness for plebes. Consumption and social identity in early eighteenth-century England', in J. Brewer and A. Bermingham (eds), *The Culture of Consumption: Image, Object, Text*, London: Routledge, 1995, pp. 367–71; Carter, *Men and Polite Society*, Chapter 2; Berg, *Luxury and Pleasure*, pp. 219–46.
28 Berg, *Luxury and Pleasure*, p. 233.
29 Borsay, *Urban Renaissance*, pp. 267–83.
30 Peck, *Consuming Splendor*, pp. 188–229; Borsay, *Urban Renaissance*, pp. 49–59, 289–91.
31 Ogborn, *Spaces of Modernity*, p. 75.
32 Falkus, M., 'Lighting in the dark ages of English economic history: town streets before the industrial revolution', in D.C. Coleman and A.H. John (eds), *Trade and Economy in Pre-Industrial England*, London: Weidenfeld and Nicolson, 1976, pp. 248–73; Sweet, R., *The English Town, 1680–1840*, Harlow: Longman, 1999, pp. 81–4.
33 Plumb, J., 'The commercialization of leisure in eighteenth-century England', in N. McKendrick, J. Brewer and R. Porter (eds), *The Birth of a Consumer Society*, London: Hutchinson, 1982, pp. 266–88.
34 Sweet, 'Topographies of politeness'; Girouard, M., *The English Town*, New Haven, CT: Yale University Press, 1990, pp. 45–56; Borsay, *Urban Renaissance*, pp. 101–13.
35 Borsay, *Urban Renaissance*, pp. 283, 243–8, 267–82; Hayton, D., 'Contested kingdoms, 1688–1756', in P. Langford (ed.), *The Eighteenth Century*, Oxford: Oxford University Press, 2002, pp. 46–55.
36 Griffin, E., *England's Revelry: A History of Popular Sports and Pastimes 1660–1830*, Oxford: Oxford University Press, 2005, *passim*. For a more general discussion of the interaction between so-called high and popular cultures, see the various contributions to Harris, T. (ed.), *Popular Culture in England, c.1500–1850*, Basingstoke: Macmillan Press, 1995.
37 Reid, D., 'Beasts and brutes: popular blood sports *c.*1780–1860', in R. Holt (ed.), *Sport and the Working Class in Modern Britain*, Manchester: Manchester University Press, 1990, pp. 18–19; McCormack, M., *The Independent Man*, Manchester: Manchester University Press, 2005, pp. 57, 65–7.
38 Sweet, 'Topographies of politeness', pp. 358, 373. See also Klein, L., 'The polite town: shifting possibilities of urbanness, 1660–1714', in T. Hitchcock and H. Shore (eds), *The Streets of London: From the Great Fire to the Great Stink*, London: Rivers Oram Press, 2003, pp. 27–39.
39 Smith, *Consumption and Respectability*, pp. 189–201; Sweet, 'Topographies of politeness', p. 358.
40 Ellis, J., 'Regional and county centres, 1700–1840', in P. Clark (ed.), *The Cambridge Urban History of Britain, Volume II, 1540–1840*, Cambridge: Cambridge University Press, 2000, pp. 697–702.
41 See Sweet, 'Topographies of politeness', pp. 355, 360–2; McInnes, A., 'The emergence of a leisure town: Shrewsbury, 1660–1760', *Past and Present*, 120, 1988, pp. 53–87.
42 Defoe, D., *A Tour through the Whole Island of Great Britain*, 1724–6, Harmondsworth: Penguin, 1971, pp. 411, 144, 405; Fiennes, C., *The Journeys of Celia Fiennes*, ed. C. Morris, London: Cresset Press, 1947, pp. 114–15.
43 Defoe, *Tour through Britain*, p. 374.
44 Defoe, *Tour through Britain*, p. 218.
45 Stobart, J., 'Culture versus commerce: societies and spaces for elites in eighteenth-century Liverpool', *Journal of Historical Geography*, 28, 2002, pp. 471–85.
46 Sweet, 'Topographies of politeness', p. 365.
47 Trentmann, 'Beyond consumerism', p. 374. See also Brewer, J., 'The error of our ways: historians and the birth of consumer society', Cultures of Consumption Programme, Working Paper 12, 2003.

48 Peck, *Consuming Splendor*; McCracken, G., *Culture and Consumption: New Approaches to the Symbolic Character of Consumer Goods and Activities*, Bloomington, IN: Indiana University Press, 1988, pp. 11–15; Welch, E., *Shopping in the Renaissance: Consumer Cultures in Italy, 1400–1600*, New Haven, CT: Yale University Press, 2005; Musgrave, P., *Early Modern European Economy*, Basingstoke: Macmillan, 1999, pp. 59–83; Trentmann, 'Beyond consumerism', p. 378.
49 Brewer, 'Error of our ways'; Stearns, P., 'Stages of consumerism: recent work on the issues of periodization', *Journal of Modern History*, 69, 1997, pp. 102–17.
50 Weatherill, *Consumer Behaviour*, pp. 70–90; Overton *et al.*, *Production and Consumption*, pp. 153–65; Estabrook, *Urbane and Rustic England*, pp. 128–63.
51 Berg, *Luxury and Pleasure*, pp. 85–110, 199–246; Cox, N., *The Complete Tradesman: A Study of Retailing, 1550–1820*, Aldershot: Ashgate, 2000, pp. 110–11.
52 Nenadic, S., 'Middle-rank consumers and domestic culture in Edinburgh and Glasgow 1720–1840', *Past and Present*, 145, 1994, pp. 122–56; Berg, *Luxury and Pleasure*, pp. 206–34; Weatherill, *Consumer Behaviour*, pp. 79–87.
53 Veblen, *Leisure Class*; Simmel, G., *On Individuality and Social Forms*, Chicago, IL: University of Chicago Press, 1971, esp. pp. 294–323. For a useful summary of Veblen's ideas, see Corrigan, P., *The Sociology of Consumption*, London: Sage, 1997, pp. 21–6.
54 Veblen, *Leisure Class*, p. 75.
55 McKendrick, N., 'The consumer revolution of eighteenth-century England', in N. McKendrick, J. Brewer and J.H. Plumb (eds), *The Birth of a Consumer Society*, London: Hutchinson, 1982, p. 11.
56 See, *inter alia*, de Vries, J., 'Between purchasing power and the world of goods', in J. Brewer and R. Porter (eds), *Consumption and the World of Goods*, London: Routledge, 1993, pp. 85–132; Campbell, C., 'Understanding traditional and modern patterns of consumption in eighteenth-century England: a character-action approach', in J. Brewer and R. Porter (eds), *Consumption and the World of Goods*, London: Routledge, 1993, pp. 40–57; Thrift, N. and Glennie, P., 'Historical geographies of urban life and modern consumption', in G. Kearns and C. Philo (eds), *Selling Places: The City as Cultural Capital, Past and Present*, Oxford: Pergamon, 1993, pp. 33–48.
57 See Weatherill, *Consumer Behaviour*; Overton *et al.*, *Production and Consumption*; Shammas, C., *The Pre-industrial Consumer in England and America*, Oxford: Oxford University Press, 1990; Berg, *Luxury and Pleasure*, pp. 291–4, 306–14.
58 De Vries, 'Purchasing power'; Borsay, *Urban Renaissance*; Berg, *Luxury and Pleasure*, pp. 113–92, 206–19; Thrift and Glennie, 'Historical geographies', p. 36.
59 Berg, M., 'New commodities, luxuries and their consumers in eighteenth-century England', in M. Berg and H. Clifford (eds), *Consumers and Luxury: Consumer Culture in Europe, 1650–1850*, Manchester: Manchester University Press, 1999, p. 69. See also Weatherill, *Consumer Behaviour*, pp. 145–57; Overton *et al.*, *Production and Consumption*, pp. 98–108.
60 Thrift and Glennie, 'Historical geographies', p. 37.
61 Corrigan, *Sociology of Consumption*, p. 20.
62 Miller, D., *Material Culture and Mass Consumption*, Oxford: Blackwell, 1987, p. 149.
63 Smith, *Consumption and Respectability*, pp. 5–24, 139–61. For discussion of the growing independence of the consumer, see Giddens, A., 'Structuralism, post-structuralism and the production of culture', in A. Giddens and J. Turner (eds), *Social Theory Today*, Cambridge: Polity Press, 1987, pp. 195–223.
64 Weatherill, *Consumer Behaviour*; Nenadic, 'Middle rank consumers'.
65 Overton *et al.*, *Production and Consumption*; Blondé, B., 'Cities in decline and the dawn of a consumer society: Antwerp in the 17th–18th centuries', in B. Blondé, E. Briot, N. Coquery and L. Van Aert (eds), *Retailers and Consumer Changes in Early Modern Europe*, Tours: University of Tours, 2005, pp. 37–52.
66 Berg, 'New commodities', p. 69. See also Berg, *Luxury and Pleasure*, pp. 219–34.

67 Dolan, B., *Josiah Wedgwood: Entrepreneur to the Enlightenment*, London: HarperCollins, 2004, *passim*; Berg, *Luxury and Pleasure*, p. 253; Bianchi, M., 'In the name of the tulip. Why speculation?', in M. Berg and H. Clifford (eds), *Consumers and Luxury: Consumer Culture in Europe, 1650–1850*, Manchester: Manchester University Press, 1999, pp. 85–102.
68 See Berg, *Luxury and Pleasure*, p. 250.
69 Estabrook, *Urbane and Rustic England*, p. 7; Finn, 'Men's things'; Campbell, C., *The Romantic Ethic and the Spirit of Modern Consumerism*, Oxford: Oxford University Press, 1987, p. 288.
70 Smith, *Consumption and Respectability*, pp. 171–87. See also Weatherill, *Consumer Behaviour*, pp. 137–42; Lemire, B., *Fashion's Favourite: The Cotton Trade and the Consumer in Britain, 1660–1800*, Oxford: Oxford University Press, 1991, pp. 55–61; Berg, M., 'Women's consumption and the industrial classes of eighteenth-century England', *Journal of Social History*, 30, 1996, pp. 415–34; Vickery, A., 'Women and the world of goods', in J. Brewer and R. Porter (eds), *Consumption and the World of Goods*, London: Routledge, 1993, pp. 274–301.
71 For discussion of this idea, see Vickery, A., 'Golden age to separate spheres', *Historical Journal*, 36, 1993, pp. 383–414; Tosh, J., *A Man's Place: Masculinity and the Middle-Class Home in Victorian England*, New Haven, CT: Yale University Press, 1999.
72 Berg, 'Women's consumption', p. 421; Vickery, *Gentleman's Daughter*, pp. 13–37, 64–7.
73 Finn, 'Men's things'; Nenadic, S., 'Print collecting and popular culture in eighteen-century Scotland', *History*, 82, 1997, pp. 203–22; Uglow, J., 'Vase mania', in M. Berg and E. Eger (eds), *Luxury in the Eighteenth-Century: Debates, Desires and Delectable Goods*, Basingstoke: Palgrave, 2003, pp. 151–64.
74 Nenadic, 'Middle-rank consumers', p. 127.
75 Berg, 'New commodities', p. 67.
76 See Borsay, *Urban Renaissance*, pp. 201–30.
77 Copeland, E., *Women Writing About Money: Women's Fiction in England 1790–1820*, Cambridge: Cambridge University Press, 1995, p. 90.
78 Sweet, 'Topographies of politeness', p. 357. See also Klein, L., 'Politeness and interpretation of the British eighteenth century', *Historical Journal*, 43, 2002, pp. 869–98; Smith, *Consumption and Respectability*.
79 Vickery, *Gentleman's Daughter*; Cohen, *Consumer's Republic*.
80 Shields, 'Spaces for consumption', pp. 11–17.
81 Pennell, S., 'Consumption and consumerism in early modern England', *The Historical Journal*, 42, 1999, pp. 549–64. See also Brewer, 'Error of our ways'.
82 Trentmann, 'Beyond consumerism', pp. 377, 380.
83 Gregson and Crewe, *Second-Hand Cultures*; Shields, 'Spaces for consumption', pp. 1–6; Miller, D., 'Consumption as the vanguard of history, a polemic by way of introduction', in D. Miller (ed.), *Acknowledging Consumption: A Review of New Studies*, London: Routledge, 1995, pp. 1–57, 17.
84 Fine, B. and Leopold, E., *The World of Consumption*, London: Routledge, 1993; Styles, J., 'Clothing the North: the supply of non-elite clothing in the eighteenth-century north of England', *Textile History*, 25, 1994, pp. 139–66; Berg, *Luxury and Pleasure*.
85 Jefferys, J.B., *Retailing in Britain 1850–1950*, Cambridge: Cambridge University Press, 1954; Mathias, P., *Retailing Revolution: A History of Multiple Retailing in the Food Trades*, London: Longmans, 1967; Blondé, B. *et al.*, 'Retail circuits and practices', in B. Blondé, P. Stabel, J. Stobart and I. Van Damme (eds), *Buyers and Sellers*, Antwerp: Brepols, 2006, p. 2; Trentmann, 'Beyond consumerism', p. 385.
86 It fits better with a European historiography of retail development which has long focused on guilds as systems of retail organisation and governance. But, even here, research is moving to recognise the flexibility and dynamism of early-modern retailing. See Blondé *et al.*, 'Retail circuits', pp. 4–5.

87 Willan, T., *The Inland Trade: Studies in English Internal Trade in the Sixteenth and Seventeenth Centuries*, Manchester: Manchester University Press, 1976; Mui, H.-C. and Mui, L., *Shops and Shopkeeping in Eighteenth-Century England*, London: Routledge, 1989; Shammas, *Pre-industrial Consumer*; Glennie, P. and Thrift, N.J., 'Consumers, identities and consumption spaces in early-modern England', *Environment and Planning A*, 28, 1996, pp. 25–45.
88 Walsh, C., 'Shop design and the display of goods in eighteenth-century London', *Journal of Design History*, 8, 1995, pp. 157–76; Cox, *Complete Tradesman*; Berry, 'Polite consumption'; Stobart, J. and Hann, A., 'Retailing revolution in the eighteenth century: evidence from north-west England', *Business History*, 46, 2004, pp. 171–94; Peck, *Consuming Splendor*.
89 Mui and Mui, *Shops and Shopkeeping*, p. 29.
90 De Vries, 'Purchasing power'.
91 Reed, M., 'The cultural role of small towns in England 1600–1800', in Clark, P. (ed.), *Small towns in Early Modern Europe*, Cambridge: Cambridge University Press, 1995, pp. 121–47.
92 Berg, *Luxury and Pleasure*, p. 258.
93 Postlethwayt, 'Fairs', *Universal Dictionary*, 1774, quoted in Berg, *Luxury and Pleasure*, p. 258.
94 Everitt, A., 'The marketing of agricultural produce', in J. Thirsk (ed.), *The Agrarian History of England and Wales, Volume IV: 1500–1640*, Cambridge: Cambridge University Press, 1967, p. 537.
95 Mui and Mui, *Shops and Shopkeeping*, Chapter 4.
96 Cox, *Complete Tradesman*, pp. 85, 125; Fowler, C., 'Changes in provincial retail practice during the eighteenth-century, with particular reference to central-southern England', *Business History*, 40, 1998, pp. 37–54.
97 Welch, E., 'The fairs of early modern Italy', in B. Blondé, P. Stabel, J. Stobart and I. Van Damme (eds), *Buyers and Sellers*, Antwerp: Brepols, 2006, pp. 31–50; Blondé *et al.*, 'Retail circuits', p. 17.
98 Walsh, C., 'The advertising and marketing of consumer goods in eighteenth-century London', in C. Wischermann and E. Shore (eds), *Advertising and the European City: Historical Perspectives*, Aldershot: Ashgate, 2000, pp. 79–95.
99 Cox, *Complete Tradesman*, pp. 79–81.
100 Walsh, 'Advertising', pp. 79–95.
101 Cox, *Complete Tradesman*, pp. 96–8; Walsh, C., 'The newness of the department store: a view from the eighteenth century', in G. Crossick and S. Jaumain (eds), *Cathedrals of Consumption*, Aldershot: Ashgate, 1999, pp. 46–71; Walsh, 'Advertising', pp. 79–85.
102 Hann, A. and Stobart, J., Sites of consumption: the display of goods in provincial shops in eighteenth century England', *Cultural and Social History*, 2, 2005, pp. 181–6.
103 Davis, D., *A History of Shopping*, London: Routledge and Kegan Paul, 1966, pp. 185–8.
104 Cox, *Complete Tradesman*, pp. 127–39.
105 Stobart, 'Shopping streets'.
106 Beckett and Smith, 'Urban Renaissance'.
107 Miller, D., *A Theory of Shopping*, Cambridge: Polity Press, 1998, pp. 5–9. On the subject of shopping for others, see Walsh, C., 'Social relations of shopping', in B. Blondé, P. Stabel, J. Stobart and I. Van Damme (eds), *Buyers and Sellers*, Antwerp: Brepols, 2006, pp. 331–51.
108 Miller *et al.*, *Shopping, Place and Identity*, pp. 10, 17–18.
109 Borsay, P., 'Sounding the Town', *Urban History*, 29, 2002, pp. 92–102; Fiennes, *Journeys*, p. 133; Shields, 'Spaces for consumption', p. 7.
110 Shields, 'Spaces for consumption', p. 1; Smith, *Consumption and Respectability*, pp. 13–15; Berry, 'Polite consumption'.
111 Glennie and Thrift, 'Consumption spaces', p. 39.

202 Notes

112 Peck, *Consuming Splendor*, p. 27; Miller *et al.*, *Shopping, Place and Identity*, p. 15.
113 Berry, 'Polite consumption', p. 377; Stobart, 'Shopping streets'.
114 Letter written to Robert Cecil, Earl of Salisbury, by Francis Carter, the surveyor of the New Exchange, quoted by Peck, *Consuming Splendor*, p. 56; Walsh, 'Social meaning', pp. 62–72; Glennie and Thrift, 'Consumption spaces', pp. 28–31.
115 Schopenhauer, J., *A Lady Travels: Journeys in England and Scotland from the Diaries of Johanna Schopenhauer*, London: Routledge, 1988, pp. 150–2.
116 Miller *et al.*, *Shopping, Place and Identity*, pp. 10, 20–1; Shields, 'Spaces for consumption', pp. 11–17; Goss, J., 'The "magic of the mall": an analysis of form, function and meaning in the contemporary retail built environment', *Annals of the Association of American Geographers*, 83, 1993, pp. 18–47; Jackson, P., 'Domesticating the street: the contested spaces of the high street and the mall', in N.R. Fyfe (ed.), *Images of the Street: Planning, Identity and Control in Public Space*, London: Routledge, 1998, pp. 176–91.
117 On gender and consumption in the early-modern period, see, for example: Vickery, *Gentleman's Daughter*; Berg, *Luxury and Pleasure*, pp. 234–46; Peck, *Consuming Splendor*, pp. 61–71.
118 Glennie and Thrift, 'Consumption spaces', p. 41.
119 Berry, 'Polite consumption', pp. 376–7; Ogborn, *Spaces of Modernity*, p. 21.
120 Crewe, L., 'Progress report: geographies of retailing and consumption', *Progress in Human Geography*, 24, 2000, pp. 276–80.
121 Miller *et al.*, *Shopping, Place and Identity*; Arnade *et al.*, 'Fertile spaces', p. 518.
122 Stobart, 'Shopping streets'; Glennie and Thrift, 'Consumption spaces', pp. 31–6.
123 Goffman, E., *The Presentation of Self in Everyday Life*, New York: Doubleday, 1956; Shields, 'Spaces for consumption'; Glennie and Thrift, 'Consumption spaces; Miller *et al.*, *Shopping, Place and Identity*.
124 See Soja, E., 'The socio-spatial dialectic', *Annals of the Association of American Geographers*, 70, 1980, pp. 207–25; Soja, *Postmodern Geographies*, pp. 76–93.
125 These are expressed most clearly in the work of the Berkeley School and in Wirth, L., 'Urbanism as a way of life', *American Journal of Sociology*, 44, 1938, pp. 1–44.
126 Gregory, D., *Geographical Imaginations*, Oxford: Blackwell, 1994, p. 234; Wolin, R., *Walter Benjamin: An Aesthetic of Redemption*, New York: Columbia University Press, 1982, p. 100. This approach, of course, makes his writing difficult to summarise and to interpret – see Benjamin, W., *The Arcades Project*, Cambridge, MA: Harvard University Press, 1999.
127 Valentine, G., *Social Geographies: Space and Society*, Harlow: Longman, 2001, p. 109.
128 Harvey, D., *The Condition of Postmodernity*, Oxford: Blackwell, 1989, pp. 66–98.
129 Soja, *Postmodern Geographies*, pp. 79–88, 190–221; Gregory, *Geographical Imaginations*, pp. 209–56.
130 Crang, M. and Thrift, N. (eds), *Thinking Space*, London: Routledge, 2000, p. 2.
131 Soja, E., 'Reassertions: towards a spatialised ontology', in J. Agnew, D. Livingstone and A. Rogers (eds), *Human Geography: An Essential Anthology*, Oxford: Blackwell, 1996, p. 625.
132 See Frisby, D., *Fragments of Modernity*, Cambridge, MA: MIT Press, 1986, p. 71; Castells, M., *The City and the Grassroots*, London: Edward Arnold, 1983.
133 Hägerstrand, T., 'What about people in Regional Science?', *Papers and Proceedings of the Regional Science Association*, 24, 1970, pp. 7–21; Pred, A., 'The choreography of existence: comments on Hägerstrand's Time-Geography and its usefulness', in J. Agnew, D. Livingstone and A. Rogers (eds), *Human Geography: An Essential Anthology*, Oxford: Blackwell, 1996, pp. 636–49.
134 Pred, A., *Lost Words and Lost Worlds: Modernity and the Language of Everyday Life in Late Nineteenth-Century Stockholm*, Cambridge: Cambridge University Press, 1990. See also Gregory, *Geographical Imaginations*, pp. 248–52.
135 De Certeau, M., *The Practice of Everyday Life*, reprinted in G. Bridge and S. Watson (eds), *The City Reader*, Oxford: Blackwell, 2002, p. 386.

136 See Gregory, *Geographical Imaginations*, p. 112.
137 Wirth-Nesher, H., *City Codes: Reading the Modern Urban Novel*, Cambridge: Cambridge University Press, 1996, p. 1.
138 Soja, 'Reassertions', p. 626.
139 This montage of projections and images is carried in both the content and the structure of *The Arcades Project*. For more specific discussion of the notion of phantasmagoria, see Cohen, M., 'Walter Benjamin's phantasmagoria', *New German Critique*, 48, 1989, pp. 87–107.
140 Rendell, J., 'West-End rambling: gender and architectural space in London 1800–1830', *Leisure Studies*, 17, 1998, pp. 108–22; Walsh, 'Social meaning'; Chambers, R.W., 'Images, acts and consequences: a critical review of historical knowing', in A.R.H. Baker and M. Billinge (eds), *Period and Place*, Cambridge: Cambridge University Press, 1992, p. 200.
141 Lefebvre, H., *The Production of Space*, Oxford: Blackwell, 1991. For brief reviews of the influence of Lefebvre's work, see Arnade *et al.*, 'Fertile spaces'; Elden, S., 'Politics, philosophy, geography: Henri Lefebvre in recent Anglo-American scholarship', *Antipode*, 33, 2001, pp. 809–25.
142 Dear, M., 'The production of space', *Urban Geography*, 14, 1993, p. 493.
143 See Soja, E., *Thirdspace*, Oxford: Blackwell, 1996.
144 Kerr, D., 'The production of space', *Urban Studies*, 29 1992, p. 1020.
145 Often translated as *representational space*. Stewart notes that this term can be confusing and *spaces of representation* is closer to the French and 'more suggestive'. See Stewart, L., 'Bodies, visions and spatial practices', *Environment and Planning A: Society and Space*, 13, 1995, p. 616.
146 De Certeau, *Practice of Everyday Life*, pp. 110–12; Merrifield, A., 'Henri Lefebvre: a socialist in space', in M. Crang and N. Thrift (eds), *Thinking Space*, London: Routledge, 2000, p. 174. See also Gregory, *Geographical Imaginations*, p. 404.
147 For a rare exception, see the special issue of *Journal of Interdisciplinary History*, 32:4. Studies more loosely informed by these ideas include: Ogborn, *Spaces of Modernity*; Nead, L., 'Mapping the self: gender, space and modernity in mid-Victorian London', *Environment and Planning A*, 29, 1997, pp. 659–72; Melville, J.D., 'The use and organisation of domestic space in late seventeenth-century London', unpublished PhD thesis, Cambridge University, 1999; Walsh, 'Social meaning'.
148 The middling sort have been variously defined as those with an income of £40–50 per year and liability for payment of the poor rates; or as a broad grouping of occupations, including professionals, (retired) military personnel, and substantial artisans and tradesmen. See Berg, *Luxury and Pleasure*, pp. 208, 212.
149 See Stobart, J., *The First Industrial Region: North-West England 1700–1760*, Manchester: Manchester University Press, 2004, and the various contributions to Stobart, J. and Raven, N. (eds), *Towns, Regions and Industries*, Manchester: Manchester University Press, 2005.

2 The region

1 Arnade *et al.*, 'Fertile spaces', p. 518; Hudson, P., 'Regional and local history: globalisation, postmodernism and the future', *Journal of Regional and Local Studies*, 20, 1999, pp. 5–24.
2 Soja, *Postmodern Geographies*, pp. 10–24.
3 Christaller, W., *Central Places in Southern Germany*, Englewood Cliffs, NJ: Prentice Hall, 1966.
4 Elliott, 'English scientific culture', p. 393.
5 Information on the range and scale of retail provision is derived from occupation data in probate records (for the early eighteenth century) and from trade directories (the *Universal British Directory* (*UBD*) for the 1790s and Pigot & Co.'s *National Commercial*

Directory for *c*.1830). A comprehensive survey of the former provides us with a reasonably good picture of the type of retailer present in each town, but absolute numbers are difficult to accurately gauge in the absence of indexes which include occupational titles (see Stobart, *First Industrial Region*, pp. 229–33; Stobart, J., 'Leisure and shopping in the small towns of Georgian England', *Journal of Urban History*, 31:4, 2005, pp. 487–9). Directories are more helpful here, despite the less than complete coverage of early examples, and are used to calculate both the number and variety of retailers. Data on the first appearance and range of key leisure facilities are drawn from a wide variety of primary and secondary sources, including directories, town histories, newspapers and diaries. Here, there are problems with achieving systematic coverage: some towns (usually the larger ones) are inevitably better served by the documentary evidence than are others. Moreover, whereas the recorded presence of a facility shows that it was there, absence might simply reflect a lack of evidence.

6 See Ogborn, *Space of Modernity*, pp. 116–57; Carter, *Men and Polite Society*, Chapter 2; Borsay, *Urban Renaissance*, pp. 67–83.
7 Sweet, *English Town*, p. 254.
8 In such places, inns were especially important in providing a focal point for economic, social, cultural and political life. See Sweet, *English Town*, p. 231; Clark, P., *The English Alehouse: A Social History*, London: Longmans, 1983.
9 *Berrow's Worcester Journal*, 8 September 1748.
10 Borsay, *Urban Renaissance*, pp. 183–5.
11 Warwick County Record Office (WaRO), Newdigate MSS. In 1778 racing at Stratford seems to have ceased altogether. *Berrow's Worcester Journal*, 6 August 1772; Bearman, R., 'Captain James Saunders of Stratford upon Avon: a local antiquary', *Dugdale Society Occasional Papers*, 33, 1990, p. 36.
12 Kennett, A. (ed.), *Georgian Chester*, Chester: Chester City Record Office, 1987, p. 36; Abram, W., *Memorials of the Preston Guilds*, Preston: G. Toulmin, 1882, *passim*; Hembry, P., *British Spas from 1815 to the Present: A Social History*, London: Athlone Press, 1997, pp. 8–9, 23; Barfoot, P. and Wilkes, J., *Universal British Directory*, Vol. 3, London: Barfoot and Wilkes, 1798, p. 592.
13 Many theatres and concert halls in commercial towns were built by subscription, reflecting the willingness of merchants and industrialists to ornament their towns with such cultural facilities (see Chapter 3).
14 Astle, W., *History of Stockport*, Stockport: Swain, 1922, p. 124; Beattie, D., *Blackburn: The Development of a Lancashire Cotton Town*, Halifax: Ryburn, 1992, p. 115; Smith, W., *A New and Compendious History of the County of Warwick*, Birmingham, 1830, p. 251; Lunn, J., *A History of Leigh*, Runcorn: Riley, 1993, p. 64; Elbourne, R., *Music and Tradition in Early Industrial Lancashire*, Woodbridge: Brewer, for the Folklore Society, 1980, pp. 64–5.
15 Corry, J., *The History of Macclesfield*, London: Ferguson, 1817, p. 98. See also Allan, D., 'Eighteenth-century private subscription libraries and provincial urban culture: the Amicable Society of Lancaster, 1769–*c*.1820', *Library History*, 17, 2001, pp. 57–76; Brewer, J., *The Pleasures of the Imagination*, Chicago, IL: University of Chicago Press, 1997, pp. 176–80.
16 For a full listing of book clubs, subscription and circulating libraries, see the 'Library History Database' at www.r-alston.co.uk.
17 Price, J., *The Worcester Guide*, Worcester: W. Smart, 1799, p. 54; Roberts, H., *The Chester Guide*, Chester, 1851, p. 64; Pigot & Co., *National Commercial Directory*, London: Pigot & Co., 1835, p. 601; Pye, C., *A Description of Modern Birmingham*, Birmingham, 1818, p. 10.
18 *UBD*, Vol. 2, p. 672.
19 Broster, P., *The Chester Guide*, Chester: P. Broster, 1782, p. 24; Picton, J., *City of Liverpool: Municipal Archives and Records, 1700–1835*, Liverpool: Walmsley, 1886, p. 137; Wallace, J., *A General and Descriptive History of the Ancient and Present State of the Town of Liverpool*,

Liverpool: R. Phillips, 1795, p. 85; Stobart, J., 'In search of a leisure hierarchy: English spa towns in the urban system', in P. Borsay, G. Hirschfelder and R. Mohrmann (eds), *New Directions in Urban History*, Münster: Waxmann, 2000, p. 27.
20 Whitehead, D., 'Urban renewal and suburban growth: the shaping of Georgian Worcester', *Worcestershire Historical Society, Occasional Publications*, 5 1989, pp. 36–40; Stobart, J., 'Rus et Urbe? The hinterland and landscape of Georgian Chester', in M. Palmer and P. Barnwell (eds), *Post-Medieval Landscapes in Britain: Landscape History after Hoskins*, Vol. 3, Macclesfield: Windgather Press, forthcoming, 2007.
21 Broster, *Chester Guide*, p. 69; *Schofield's Middlewich Journal*, 1 February 1757; Vickery, *Gentleman's Daughter*, p. 264; Harrison, D., *The History of Colne*, Barrowford: Pendle Heritage Centre, 1988, p. 153.
22 Barton, B., *History of the Borough of Bury and Neighbourhood*, Bury, 1874, pp. 18–23.
23 Lancashire Record Office (LRO), DDX 211/21, Playbill (1789).
24 Ward, T., *History of the Athenaeum, 1824–1925*, London, 1926, pp. 4–27.
25 Hamlyn, H., 'Eighteenth-century circulating libraries in England', *Library*, 5th series, I, 1947, pp. 197–218.
26 Picton, *Liverpool Archives*, pp. 255–6; Picton, J., *Memorials of Liverpool*, London: Longmans Green, 1873, Vol. 2, pp. 206–7, 268–9; Muir, R., *A History of Liverpool*, Liverpool: University Press of Liverpool, 1907, p. 282; Smith, J., *The Story of Music in Birmingham*, Birmingham: Cornish Brothers Ltd, 1945, pp. 10–11; Orton, G., *Maps of Wolverhampton*, Wolverhampton: Wolverhampton Public Libraries, 1976.
27 Picton, *Memorials of Liverpool*, Vol. 2, p. 281; Upton, C., *A History of Birmingham*, Chichester: Phillimore, 1993, pp. 35–6; Hunt, 'A tale of two squares'.
28 Borsay, *Urban Renaissance*, pp. 156–7; Vickery, *Gentleman's Daughter*, p. 241.
29 Kennett, *Georgian Chester*, p. 37.
30 Alston, 'Library History Database'.
31 Stobart, 'Culture versus commerce', p. 475; Smith, *History of Warwick*, pp. 352–3; Clark, P., *British Clubs and Societies, 1580–1800*, Oxford: Oxford University Press, 2000, pp. 133–7.
32 Aikin, J., *A Description of the Country from Thirty to Forty Miles round Manchester*, London: J. Stockdale, 1795, p. 200; Kidd, A., *Manchester*, Keele: Keele University Press, 1993.
33 See, for example, Lane, J., 'Worcester infirmary in the eighteenth century', *Worcester Historical Society Occasional Publications*, 6, 1992, pp. 1–2.
34 Shammas, *Pre-industrial Consumer*, pp. 157–93; Smith, *Consumption, passim*; Berg, *Luxury and Pleasure*, pp. 199–246; Vickery, *Gentleman's Daughter*, pp. 161–94; Brewer, *Pleasures of the Imagination*, pp. 201–51.
35 *UBD*, Vol. 4, pp. 14–16.
36 Mui and Mui, *Shops and Shopkeeping*, pp. 45, 297; Shammas, *Pre-industrial Consumer*, pp. 225–65.
37 Cox, *Complete Tradesman*, pp. 58–65; Stobart, 'Leisure and shopping'.
38 Blome, R., *Britannia or a Geographical Description of the Kingdoms of England, Scotland, and Ireland*, London: T. Rycroft, 1673, p. 205.
39 Cheshire and Chester Archives (CCA), WS 1709 William Jordan.
40 CCA, WS 1732 Edward Twambrooks; WS 1711 John England.
41 Stobart, J. and Trinder, B., 'New towns of the industrial coalfields: Burslem and West Bromwich', in J. Stobart and N. Raven (eds), *Towns, Regions and Industries*, Manchester: Manchester University Press, 2005, pp. 125–7.
42 Barker, H., '"Smoke cities": northern industrial towns in late Georgian England', *Urban History*, 31, 2004, p. 183.
43 Lewis, C.P. and Thacker, A.T. (eds), *Victoria County History of Chester*, Vol. 5, Part 1, London: Boydell and Brewer, 2003, pp. 175–7.
44 Berg, 'New commodities'; Weatherill, *Consumer Behaviour*, pp. 25–69; Vickery, *Gentleman's Daughter*, pp. 251–2.
45 Trusler, J., *The Way to be Rich and Respectable*, London, 1766, p. 5.

46 Sweet, *English Town*, pp. 251–5; Barker, 'Smoke cities', pp. 176–7.
47 Stobart, 'Culture versus commerce', pp. 473–81; Elliott, 'English scientific culture', pp. 391–7; Morris, R.J., 'Structure, culture and society in British towns', in M. Daunton (ed.), *The Cambridge Urban History of Britain, Volume III: 1840–1950*, Cambridge: Cambridge University Press, 2000, p. 402.
48 See Stobart, 'Culture versus commerce'.
49 Coventry was some way below Worcester and Birmingham, sharing the effective status as county town with Warwick, and failing to attract large numbers of or investment from the rural gentry; yet it possessed an impressive array of leisure and retail facilities. See Morgan, V., 'Producing consumer space in eighteenth-century England: shops, shopping and the provincial town', unpublished PhD thesis, Coventry University, 2003.
50 Stobart, 'County, town and country'.
51 Defoe, *Tour through Britain*, pp. 548, 405, 549.
52 Stobart, 'Leisure and shopping', pp. 487–93.
53 The National Archives (TNA), E 182 Shop Tax.
54 Blome, *Britannia*, p. 204; Schwarz, L., 'On the margins of industrialisation: Lichfield', in J. Stobart and N. Raven (eds), *Towns, Regions and Industries*, Manchester: Manchester University Press, 2005.
55 Sellers, I., *Early Modern Warrington 1520–1847*, Lampeter: Edwin Mellen Press, 1998, pp. 119–24.
56 Defoe, *Tour through Britain*, pp. 547–8.
57 Letter from Alice Ainsworth of Bolton, 1816, quoted in Vickery, *Gentleman's Daughter*, p. 277.
58 For detailed biographies of the members of the Lunar Society, see Uglow, J., *The Lunar Men*, London: Faber and Faber, 2002.
59 Sweet, R., *The Writing of Urban Histories in Eighteenth-Century England*, Oxford: Oxford University Press, 1997, pp. 125–41.
60 Borsay, *Urban Renaissance*, pp. 139–44.
61 Olleson, P., 'The Tamworth Music Festival of 1809', *Staffordshire Studies*, 5, 1993, pp. 81–106.
62 M. Richardson, Brierley, to M. Warde, Hooton Pagnell, quoted in Vickery, *Gentleman's Daughter*, p. 261.
63 *Berrow's Worcester Journal*, 1772. A similar season characterised Chester – see Broster, *Chester Guide*, p. 69.
64 LRO, DP 282/15, Programme of the Bolton Assemblies 1816–17; *Blackburn Mail*, 25 September 1793; 20 November 1793; 1 January 1794.
65 Hembry, *British Spas*, pp. 17–18.
66 *Berrow's Worcester Journal*, 20 August 1772.
67 *Gore's Liverpool Advertiser*, 1770.
68 *Schofield's Middlewich Journal*, 11–18 January 1757; Broster, *Chester Guide*, p. 69.
69 LRO, DDX/274/13–17, Diary of John Dickenson II (1776–82).
70 Vickery, *Gentleman's Daughter*, pp. 168–72.
71 Chambers, J., *A General History of Worcester*, Worcester, 1819, p. 360.
72 Mui and Mui, *Shops and Shopkeeping*, pp. 211–16.
73 Stobart and Hann, 'Retailing revolution', pp. 181–4.
74 Elliott, 'English scientific culture', p. 392.
75 The rates payable and the charging scales changed on several occasions between the introduction of the tax in 1696 and its eventual demise in 1851. Dowell, S., *A History of Taxation and Taxes in England*, London, 1888, Vol. III, pp. 168–77.
76 Stobart and Hann, 'Retailing revolution', pp. 181–4.
77 Stobart and Trinder, 'New towns', pp. 125–6; Hann, A., 'Industrialisation and the service economy', in J. Stobart and N. Raven (eds), *Towns, Regions and Industries*, Manchester: Manchester University Press, 2005, pp. 53–8.

78 Corry, *Macclesfield*, p. 223. See also Aikin, *Manchester*, p. 423; Pigot's *Directory*, p. 11. The gentry, of course, also sourced goods from London: see the following section.
79 Bentley, J., *History, Gazetteer, Directory and Statistics of Worcestershire*, Worcester: Bull and Turner, 1841, Vol. III, p. 15.
80 Lepetit, B., *The Pre-Industrial Urban System: France, 1740–1840*, Cambridge: Cambridge University Press, 1994, p. 97.
81 Borsay, P., 'The landed elite and provincial towns in Britain 1660–1800', *The Georgian Group Journal*, XIII, 2003, pp. 281–94; Clark, P., 'Elite networking and the formation of an industrial small town: Loughborough, 1700–1840', in J. Stobart and N. Raven (eds), *Towns, Regions and Industries*, Manchester: Manchester University Press, 2005, pp. 163–4.
82 Everitt, A., 'Country, county and town: patterns of regional evolution in England', *Transactions, Royal Historical Society*, 5th series, 29, 1979, p. 94.
83 Liverpool Record Office (LivRO), 614 INF/5/1, Annual Report and Subscription Book for the Liverpool Infirmary 1748–1780; Worcestershire Record Office (WRO), 899:93 BA 1558/19, Account of the Worcester Infirmary, 1754; Lane, 'Worcester Infirmary', pp. 10–26.
84 Hutton, *History of Birmingham*, p. 127; White, F., *History, Gazetteer and Directory of Staffordshire*, Sheffield: White, F., 1834, p. 132.
85 CCA, WS 1711 John England of Knutsford; LRO, WCW 1732 Edward Twambrooks of Warrington.
86 Mitchell, S.I., 'The development of urban retailing 1700–1815', in P. Clark (ed.), *The Transformation of English Provincial Towns 1600–1800*, London: Hutchinson, 1984, pp. 261–3.
87 CCA, WS 1756 Abner Scholes of Chester.
88 Elliott, 'English scientific culture', p. 394.
89 Raven, N. and Stobart, J., 'Networks and hinterlands: transport in the Midlands', in J. Stobart and N. Raven (eds), *Towns, Regions and Industries*, Manchester: Manchester University Press, 2005, pp. 81–6; Stobart, *First Industrial Region*, pp. 185–92.
90 Lepetit, *Urban System*, p. 347.
91 Staffordshire Record Office (SRO), D1798 HM27/5, Account Book of Thomas Dickenson (1740–50).
92 Parish, C., *History of the Birmingham Library*, London: Library Association, 1966, pp. 105–31
93 LivRO, 614 INF/5/1.
94 Anderson, B.L., 'The attorney and the early capital market in Lancashire', in J.R. Harris (ed.), *Liverpool and Merseyside*, London: Frank Cass, 1969, pp. 59–69.
95 Morgan, 'Producing consumer space', p. 105; *Keating's Stratford and Warwick Mercury*, 9 March 1752; Lowe, R., *The Diary of Roger Lowe of Ashton in Makerfield*, ed. W. Sasche, London: Longmans, Green & Co., 1938, pp. 5–6.
96 WaRO, CR1596/Box 90/7/7, Briefs for the Warwick Assizes.
97 SRO, D (W) 1788/V/108–111, Sales Ledgers of Fletcher and Fenton (1768–83). See also WaRO, CR439 Thomas Burbidge's Shop Book.
98 Morgan, 'Producing consumer space', pp. 106–11.
99 For a general overview of Blundell's shopping habits, see Cox, *Complete Tradesman*, pp. 122, 136, 208, 228.
100 Tyrer, F., 'The great diurnal of Nicholas Blundell of Little Crosby, Lancashire', *Record Society of Lancashire and Cheshire*, 3 volumes (1968–72), 16 May 1718; 15 October 1710.
101 Coventry City Record Office (CRO), PA208/13, Lutterworth Woman's Diary (1829–30).
102 Shakespeare Birthplace Trust Record Office (SARO), DR 18/5, Leigh Estate Vouchers; Morgan, Producing consumer space', pp. 108–11, 219–23.
103 Mitchell, 'Urban retailing', pp. 262–3.

104 Vickery, *Gentleman's Daughter*, pp. 168–72; Barker, T.C. and Harris, J.R., *A Merseyside Town in the Industrial Revolution: St Helens 1750–1900*, Liverpool: Liverpool University Press, 1954, pp. 152–4.
105 Hanley Reference Library (HRL), D4842/14/4/7, bundle of John Wood's bills and receipts.
106 LivRO, 920 PLU PT9, Account book of John Plumbe (1697–1757); LRO, DDX/274/13–17.
107 SRO, D1798 HM 24/3, Domestic Accounts of Ann Sneyd.
108 These are discussed, respectively, in Chapters 6 and 3, but see also Vickery, *Gentleman's Daughter*, Berry, 'Polite consumption', Estabrook, *Urbane and Rustic England*.
109 Vickery, *Gentleman's Daughter*, p. 13.
110 See Stobart, 'Leisure hierarchy'.

3 The town

1 Ogborn, *Spaces of Modernity*, pp. 75–91; Borsay, *Urban Renaissance*, p. 80; Sweet, 'Topographies of politeness'; Ellis, J., '"For the honour of the town": comparison, competition and civic identity in eighteenth-century England', *Urban History*, 30, 2003, pp. 325–37.
2 Borsay, *Urban Renaissance*, p. 85.
3 Lefebvre, *Production of Space*, pp. 38, 84–6, 232–3, 413–14.
4 Sweet, 'Topographies of politeness', pp. 355–7.
5 Klein, L., 'Coffeehouse civility, 1660–1714: an aspect of post-courtly culture in England', *Huntington Library Quarterly*, 59, 1997, pp. 30–51; Borsay, *Urban Renaissance*, pp. 263–83.
6 Hume, D., *Essays and Treatises on Several Subjects*, London: A. Millar, 1758, p. 38; Ogborn, *Spaces of Modernity*, p. 88.
7 Habermas, *Public Sphere*; Ogborn, *Spaces of Modernity*, pp. 75–9.
8 Smith, *Consumption and Respectability*, p. 147; Vickery, *Gentleman's Daughter*, pp. 288, 290.
9 Sweet, 'Topographies of politeness', p. 356.
10 Ellis, 'For the honour of the town', pp. 329–32.
11 Sweet, 'Topographies of politeness', p. 357.
12 See, for example, Stobart, 'Shopping streets'; Smith, *Consumption and Respectability*, pp. 139–70; Borsay, P., 'All the town's a stage: urban ritual and ceremony, 1660–1800', in P. Clark (ed.), *The Transformation of English Provincial Towns, 1600–1800*, London: Hutchinson, 1984, pp. 228–58; Corfield, P.J., 'Walking the city streets: the urban odyssey in eighteenth-century England', *Journal of Urban History*, 16, 1990, pp. 132–74.
13 Gutkind, E.A., *Urban Development in Western Europe: The Netherlands and Great Britain*, New York: The Free Press, 1971, pp. 223, 251–5.
14 Peck, *Consuming Splendor*, pp. 188–229; Gutkind, *Urban Development*, pp. 264–77; Rosen, A., 'Winchester in transition, 1580–1700', in P. Clark (ed.), *Country Towns in Pre-Industrial England*, Leicester: Leicester University Press, 1981, pp. 180–1.
15 Enfield, W., *An Essay towards the History of Leverpool*, London: Johnson, 1773, p. 20.
16 Borsay, *Urban Renaissance*, pp. 96–7.
17 Whellan & Co., *A New Alphabetical and Classified Directory of Manchester and Salford*, Manchester: Whellan & Co., 1853, p. 685.
18 WaRO, CR 1563/299, Building Land in the New Town at Leamington Priors, 1822; Cave, L., *Royal Leamington Spa: Its History and Development*, Chichester: Phillimore, 1988, pp. 33–4.
19 Cave, *Royal Leamington Spa*, pp. 53–5; Hembry, *British Spas*, pp. 20–1.
20 WaRO, CR 351/220, The Upper Part of the New Town, Leamington Spa, c.1826.

21 *Warwick Advertiser*, 19 August 1826. See also Chaplin, R., 'The rise of Royal Leamington Spa', *Warwickshire History*, 2, 1972, pp. 13–29.
22 *Warwick Advertiser*, 19 August 1826.
23 For detailed discussion, see Borsay, P., 'A county town in transition: the Great Fire of Warwick, 1694', in Borsay, P. and Proudfoot, L. (eds), *Provincial Towns in Early Modern England and Ireland*, Oxford: Oxford University Press, 2002, pp. 151–70.
24 Borsay, *Urban Renaissance*, p. 95.
25 Defoe, *Tour through Britain*, p. 543; Chalklin, C., *The Provincial Towns of Georgian England: a Study of the Building Process, 1740–1820*, London: Arnold, 1974, pp. 98–102; Enfield, *History of Liverpool*, pp. 20–1.
26 Wilson, A., 'Cultural identity of Liverpool, 1790–1850', *Transactions, Historic Society of Lancashire and Cheshire*, 147, 1997, p. 62; Stobart, 'Culture versus commerce', p. 481.
27 Dalziel, N. 'Trade and transition, 1690–1815', in A. White (ed.), *A History of Lancaster*, Edinburgh: Edinburgh University Press, 2001, pp. 117–27, 135–44.
28 Dalziel, 'Trade and transition', pp. 146–7.
29 Hemingway, J., *History of the City of Chester*, Chester: J. Fletcher, 1831, Vol. 1, p. 417.
30 Defoe, *Tour Through Britain*, p. 392; Stobart, 'Shopping streets', pp. 17–18.
31 Falkus, 'Lighting'.
32 Smart, J., *Directory of Wolverhampton*, Wolverhampton, 1827, p. xxxvi.
33 Ellis, J., *The Georgian Town*, Basingstoke: Palgrave, 2001, p. 92; Griffin, *England's Revelry*, pp. 122–40.
34 LRO, PMC/1/2, Preston White Book, 11 November 1726.
35 *Birmingham Journal*, 10 March 1851, quoted in Reid, 'Beasts and brutes', pp. 16–17.
36 CRO, shelved, Coventry Statutes, 1558–1830.
37 30 Geo III cap. 77 [1790], 'An Act for paving, lighting and cleansing the City of Coventry and its suburbs …'.
38 Smith, W.A., *The Town Commissioners in Wolverhampton, 1777–1848*, p. xxxv.
39 Ogborn, *Spaces of Modernity*, pp. 14–17, 87–91; Hume, *Essays*, p. 111.
40 Borsay, 'County town', pp. 163–8.
41 Cave, *Leamington Spa*, p. 61.
42 Langford, P., *Polite and Commercial People. England 1727–1783*, Oxford: Oxford University Press, 1989, pp. 424–32.
43 Scola, R., *Feeding the Victorian City: The Food Supply of Manchester 1770–1870*, Manchester: Manchester University Press, 1992, pp. 23–7, 150–6; Smith, *Town Commissioners*, p. viii.
44 Sweet, *English Town*, p. 196; Stobart, 'Rus et Urbe'; Borsay, 'Landed elite'; Herson, J., 'Victorian Chester: a city of change and ambiguity', in R. Swift (ed.), *Victorian Chester*, Liverpool: Liverpool University Press, 1996, pp. 22–3.
45 Hemingway, *History of Chester*, Vol. II, p. 333.
46 Green, V., *Survey of the City of Worcester*, Worcester, 1764, p. 235.
47 Smart, *Worcester Guide*, p. 35.
48 Aikin, *Manchester*, p. 192; Smith, *History of Warwick*, p. 311; Baines, E., *History, Directory and Gazetteer of the County Palatine of Lancaster*, 2 volumes, 1824–5, Newton Abbot: David and Charles, 1968, p. 203.
49 Corry, *Macclesfield*, p. 97; Smith, *History of Warwick*, p. 172; White, *Directory of Staffordshire*, p. 380; Bentley, *History of Worcestershire*, Vol. IV, p. 62.
50 Moss, W., *The Liverpool Guide*, Liverpool, 1796, pp. 118–19; Dalziel, 'Trade and transition', p. 154; Hemingway, *History of Chester*, Vol. 2, p. 230; Troughton, T., *The History of Liverpool*, Liverpool: W. Robinson, 1810, pp. 92–4; Smith, W., *Picture of Birmingham*, Birmingham: J. Drake, 1831, p. 83; Hutton, *History of Birmingham*, p. 134.
51 Barker, 'Smoke cities', p. 189.
52 Ellis, 'For the honour of the town'; Sweet, 'Topographies of politeness'.
53 Wallace, *History of Liverpool*, p. 2.

54 Sweet, *Writing of Urban Histories*, pp. 100–41.
55 Ellis, 'For the honour of the town', pp. 329–32; Sweet, *Writing of Urban Histories*, pp. 238–41, 252–5.
56 Sweet, *Writing of Urban Histories*, pp. 130, 149–50.
57 Wallace, *History of Liverpool*, p. 268; Brooke, R., *Liverpool As It Was: 1775 to 1800*, Liverpool, 1853, pp. 37, 118–21.
58 Enfield, *History of Leverpool*, p. 20.
59 Aikin, *Manchester*, p. 192.
60 Defoe, *Tour Through Britain*, p. 482; Stevens, W. (ed.), *Victoria County History of Warwickshire*, Vol. 8, Oxford: Oxford University Press, 1969, p. 222.
61 Butterworth, J., *An Historical and Descriptive Account of the Town and Parochial Chapelry of Oldham in the County of Lancaster*, Oldham, 1817, pp. 14–15.
62 Fraser, N., 'Rethinking the public sphere: a contribution to the critique of actually existing democracy', in C. Calhoun (ed.), *Habermas and the Public Sphere*, Cambridge, MA: MIT Press, 1992, pp. 109–42; Wallace, *History of Liverpool*; Moss, *Liverpool Guide*; Sweet, *Writing Urban Histories*, pp. 130–1.
63 Hanshall, J., *The History of the County Palatine of Chester*, Chester, 1817, p. 267; Ormerod, G., *The History of the County Palatine and City of Chester*, London, 1819, p. 286; Green, *City of Worcester*, pp. 228–30.
64 Brooke, *Liverpool*, pp. 71–4; Baines, *History of Lancaster*, pp. 193–4.
65 Corry, *Macclesfield*, pp. 228, 230; Ingamells, J., *Directory of Newcastle-under-Lyme*, Newcastle-under-Lyme: D. Dilworth, 1871, pp. 31–2.
66 *VCH, Chester*, Vol. 5, Part 1, p. 144.
67 Quoted in Hewitson, A., *History of Preston in the County of Lancaster*, Preston: Chronicle Office, 1883, p. 320; Borsay, *Urban Renaissance*, pp. 162–3; Dalziel, 'Trade and transition', p. 138.
68 Brailsford, D., *A Taste for Diversions: Sport in Georgian England*, Cambridge: Cambridge University Press, 1999, p. 25; Dalziel, 'Trade and transition', p. 140.
69 *Berrow's Worcester Journal*, 7 May 1772; Race Card from 1776 reproduced in Dalziel, 'Trade and transition', p. 141; LRO, DDPr 34/1, Race bills, Lancaster (1811–27); Willmore, F., *A History of Walsall and its Neighbourhood*, Walsall: Robinson, 1887, p. 396.
70 *Worcester Journal*, 8 September 1748.
71 See Stobart, J., 'Building an urban identity. Cultural space and civic boosterism in a "new" industrial town: Burslem, 1761–1911', *Social History*, 29, 2004, pp. 486–9; Hill, K., '"Thoroughly imbued with the spirit of ancient Greece": symbolism and space in Victorian civic culture', in A. Kidd and D. Nicholls (eds), *Gender, Civic Culture and Consumerism: Middle Class Identity in Britain 1800–1940*, Manchester: Manchester University Press, 1999, pp. 99–102; Gunn, S., *The Public Culture of the Victorian Middle Class*, Manchester: Manchester University Press, 2000, pp. 24–30.
72 Massey, D. and Pile, S. (eds), *City Worlds*, London: Routledge, 1999, p. 149. See also Jacobs, J., *Edge of Empire: Postcolonialism and the City*, London: Routledge, 1996.
73 Sweet, *Writing Urban Histories*, pp. 236–75; Stobart, 'Building an urban identity', pp. 489–91.
74 Barker, 'Smoke cities', p. 180; Ellis, 'For the honour of the town', p. 332.
75 Borsay, 'The landed elite'; Stobart, 'Rus et Urbe'; Sweet, *English Town*, p. 60.
76 Aikin, *Manchester*, p. 294; *VCH, Chester*, Vol. 5, Part 1, pp. 157–8.
77 White, *Directory of Staffordshire*, p. 310; Duggan, M., *Ormskirk: The Making of a Modern Town*, Stroud: Sutton, 1998, pp. 58–60; Baines, *History of Lancaster*, p. 600.
78 White, F., *History, Gazetteer and Directory of Cheshire*, Sheffield: White, F., 1860, pp. 272–3.
79 Borsay, 'Warwick', pp. 159–68, quotation from p. 167.
80 Cave, *Leamington Spa*, pp. 44–65.
81 Wilson, K., *The Sense of the People. Politics, Culture and Imperialism in England, 1715–85*, Cambridge: Cambridge University Press, 1998, pp. 76–7; Chalklin, C., 'Capital

expenditure on building for cultural purposes in provincial England, 1730–1830', *Business History*, 22, 1980, pp. 51–70.
82 White, *Directory of Staffordshire*, pp. 539–43; Schmiechen, J. and Carls, K., *The British Market Hall: A Social and Architectural History*, New Haven, CT: Yale University Press, 1999, p. 269; Alston, 'Library History Database'.
83 Stobart, 'Shopping streets', p. 7.
84 Berry, H., 'Creating polite space: the organisation and social functions of the Newcastle assembly rooms', in H. Berry and J. Gregory (eds), *Creating and Consuming Culture in North-East England, 1660–1830*, Aldershot: Ashgate, 2004, p. 125.
85 Kennett, *Georgian Chester*, pp. 36–7; Borsay, *Urban Renaissance*, p. 192; *Cumberland Pacquet*, 25 June 1782; Corry, *Macclesfield*, p. 229.
86 Stobart, 'Building an urban identity', p. 490; Chalklin, 'Capital expenditure', p. 63; Birmingham City Archives (BCA), Minute book of the Theatre Royal, Birmingham (1773–1937), MS 3375 Lee Crowder 387.
87 Letter from Matthew Boulton to the Earl of Dartmouth, 1777, quoted in Pemberton, T.E., *The Theatre Royal Birmingham 1774 to 1901*, Birmingham, 1901, pp. 6–7.
88 Berry, 'Creating polite space', p. 126.
89 BCA, MS 3375.
90 LivRO, 027 LYC 1/1/1, Minute Books of the General Committee, Liverpool Library (1769–96).
91 Lane, 'Worcester Infirmary', pp. 258–9; Aikin, *Manchester*, pp. 199, 395; Hutton, *History of Birmingham*, pp. 258–9.
92 LivRO, 614 INF/5/1.
93 *The Chester Chronicle*, 15 October 1815.
94 Dalziel, 'Trade and transition', p. 139; Pearce, T., *The History and Directory of Walsall*, Birmingham, 1813, p. 132; Smart, *Worcester Guide*, p. 42.
95 Dalziel, 'Trade and transition', p. 138; Hembry, *British Spas*, p. 16.
96 Hall, J., *A History of the Town and Parish of Nantwich*, Nantwich: printed for the author, 1883, p. 218; Bentley, *History of Worcestershire*, Vol. II, p. 50; Crossley, F.H., *Cheshire*, London: Robert Hale, 1949, pp. 75–6; Barton, *History of Bury*; Harrison, *History of Colne*, p. 169; Smith, *History of Warwick*, p. 352; Pearce, *History of Walsall*, pp. 131–2.
97 Stobart, 'Shopping streets', p. 10; Poole, B., *Coventry: Its History and Antiquities*, London, 1870, p. 405.
98 Smith, *Music in Birmingham*, pp. 10–11; Gwilliam, B., *Old Worcester: People and Places*, Bromsgrove: Halfshire Books, 1993.
99 LivRO, 920 NIC 3/3/4, Letter to Samuel Nicholson, 1736.
100 Ogborn, *Spaces of Modernity*, pp. 122–8; LivRO, 920 NIC 3/3/4, Letter to Samuel Nicholson, 1736.
101 Brooke, *Liverpool*, p. 87; SRO, D1798 HM 24/3.
102 Pemberton, *Theatre Royal, Birmingham*, pp. 5–6. For more general discussion of the opposition to theatres, see: Baker, J., 'Theatre, law and society in the provinces: the case of Sarah Baker', *Cultural and Social History*, 1, 2004, pp. 159–78.
103 Borsay, *Urban Renaissance*, pp. 284–96.
104 See Ogborn, *Spaces of Modernity*; Lefebvre, *Production of Space*, passim.
105 Pigott, J.M.R., *History of the City of Chester*, Chester, 1815, p. 157.
106 Chambers, *History of Worcester*, pp. 303–4; Poole, *Coventry*, p. 130.
107 Hutton, *History of Birmingham*; Brooks, A. and Haworth, B., *Boomtown Manchester: 1800–1850. The Portico Connection*, Manchester: The Portico Library, 1993, pp. 10–11.
108 Stobart, 'Culture versus commerce', pp. 473–6; Brooke, *Liverpool*, pp. 80–8, 429; Muir, *History of Liverpool*, p. 293.
109 Orton, *Maps of Wolverhampton*; Smart, *Directory of Wolverhampton*, pp. xxxvii–xxxviii; White, *Directory of Staffordshire*, pp. 184–7.

110 Platt, J., *The History and Antiquities of Nantwich*, London: Longman *et al.*, 1818, pp. 76–7.
111 Hembry, *British Spas*, p. 11.
112 *Manchester Mercury*, 6 July 1790; *Aris's Birmingham Gazette*, 19 June 1780.
113 Hann and Stobart, 'Sites of consumption', p. 6.
114 These concentrations parallel those noted for Manchester food retailers: see Scola, *Feeding the Victorian City*, pp. 237–42.
115 Lawton, R., 'The age of great cities', *Town Planning Review*, 43, 1972, p. 206.
116 See Pearce, *History of Walsall*.
117 Mui and Mui, *Shops and Shopkeeping*, pp. 124–7.
118 Morgan, 'Producing consumer space', pp. 119–28; Lancaster, J.C., 'Coventry', in M.D. Lobel (ed.), *The Atlas of Historic Towns*, Vol. 2, London: Scolar Press, 1975, pp. 12–13.
119 *Worcester Directory*, Worcester: John Grundy, 1788.
120 Green, *City of Worcester*, p. 235.
121 Mitchell, 'Urban retailing'; Dyke, E. (ed.), 'Chester's Earliest Directories', *Journal of the Chester Archaeological Society*, XXXVII, 1949.
122 Hughes, T., *Ancient Chester: A Series of Illustrations of the Streets of this Old City*, London, 1880.
123 Roberts, *Chester Guide*, p. 65.
124 Hemingway, *History of Chester*, Vol. 1, p. 387.
125 CCA, CR 63/2/133/17, P. Broster, *Sketch Plan of Eastgate Street* (c.1754).
126 Mui and Mui, *Shops and Shopkeeping*, pp. 124–8; Whitehead, 'Urban renewal', pp. 10–12.
127 Upton, *History of Birmingham*, pp. 35–8.
128 Picton, *Memorials of Liverpool*, p. 281.
129 Borsay, 'Warwick', 161; Morgan, 'Producing consumer space', pp. 115–19.
130 TNA, PROB3 32/108, Inventory of John Fairfax, mercer of Warwick 1733.
131 Cowdroy, W., *The directory and guide for the City and County of Chester*, Chester, 1784. This parallels developments taking place in Macclesfield and Stockport – see Mitchell, 'Urban retailing'.
132 *Autobiography of Francis Place*, Vol. II, p. 56, quoted in Cox, *Complete Tradesman*, p. 70.
133 Berg, *Luxury and Pleasure*, p. 268. See also Berry, 'Polite consumption', pp. 375–94; Walsh, 'Social meaning'; Walsh, 'Social relations'.
134 Meteyard, *The Life of Josiah Wedgwood, 1866*, pp. 31–2, quoted in Berry, 'Polite consumption', p. 383.
135 Chambers, *History of Worcester*, p. 360.
136 Poole, *Coventry*, pp. 336, 406; Reader, W., *The History and Antiquities of the City of Coventry*, Coventry, 1810, pp. 96, 103, 181–99.
137 Sweet, 'Topographies of politeness', pp. 358–62.
138 Smart, *Worcester Guide*, pp. 36–7; Brooke, *Liverpool*, p. 118.
139 Sweet, 'Topographies of politeness', pp. 363–74; Barker, 'Smoke cities', pp. 189–90.
140 Hutton, W., *The History of Derby*, London: J. Nichols, 1791, p. 186.

4 The street

1 Corfield, 'Walking', pp. 148–9.
2 Benjamin, *Arcades Project*. Much the same has been suggested for twentieth-century malls, shopping streets and even car boot sales, see Shields, 'Spaces for consumption'; Jackson, 'Domesticating the street'; Goss, 'Magic of the mall'; Miller, *Theory of Shopping*; Gregson and Crewe, *Second-Hand Cultures*.
3 Benjamin, *Arcades Project*, p. 394; Shoemaker, R.B., 'The London "mob" in the early eighteenth century', *Journal of British Studies*, 26, 1987, pp. 273–304; Borsay, 'All

the town's a stage', pp. 246–9; Kilmartin, J., 'Popular rejoicing and public ritual', unpublished PhD thesis, Warwick University, 1987, pp. 343–50.
4   Goffman, *Presentation of Self*. See also Glennie and Thrift, 'Consumption, shopping and gender', p. 226; Borsay, 'All the town's a stage'.
5   Shields, 'Spaces for consumption'; Glennie and Thrift, 'Consumption spaces'; Miller *et al.*, *Shopping, Place and Identity*.
6   Gregson, N. and Rose, G., 'Taking Butler elsewhere: performativities, spatialities and subjectivities', *Environment and Planning D: Society and Space*, 18, 2000, p. 434; Gregory, *Geographical Imaginations*, p. 404.
7   These intersections form a major element of Pred's analysis of spatiality in nineteenth-century Stockholm: Pred, *Lost Words*, pp. 229–35.
8   See Ogborn, *Spaces of Modernity*, pp. 79–84, 87–91.
9   Sennett, R., *The Fall of Public Man*, Cambridge: Cambridge University Press, 1977, p. 17.
10 Ogborn, *Spaces of Modernity*, p. 75.
11 CCA, A/B/1/111v; A/B/2/156v; A/B/2/169v; A/B/3/10v; A/B/3/163v; A/B/3/264v. See Sweet, *English Town*, p. 79; Corfield, 'Walking the streets', p. 150.
12 Wallace, *History of Liverpool*, pp. 275–6; Touzeau, *Liverpool*, Vol. I, p. 429.
13 Wallace, *History of Liverpool*, p. 273; Berg, *Luxury and Pleasure*, p. 262; Aikin, *Manchester*.
14 Smith, *History of Warwick*, p. 33.
15 Falkus, 'Lighting', pp. 251–60.
16 Stobart, 'Shopping streets', pp. 15–16; *VCH Warwickshire*, Vol. 8, pp. 263–75.
17 Falkus, 'Lighting', p. 259.
18 Webb, S. and Webb, B., *English Local Government: Statutory Authorities for Special Purposes*, London: Longmans, Green and Co., 1922, pp. 254–5; Borsay, *Urban Renaissance*, pp. 72–4.
19 Hutton, W., *A Journey from Birmingham to London*, Birmingham, 1785, pp. 22–3.
20 Johannes Neiner, *Vienna Curiosa & Gratiosa* (1720), quoted in Koslofsky, C., 'Court culture and street lighting in seventeenth-century Europe', *Journal of Urban History*, 28, 2002, p. 751; Sweet, *The English Town*, p. 81.
21 Fox, L., 'Coventry constables presentments 1629–1742', *Dugdale Society Publications*, XXXV, 1986, pp. 35–81.
22 *Piercy's Coventry Gazette*, 17 December 1778.
23 *Blackburn Mail*, 10 July 1793; *Gore's Liverpool Advertiser*, 2 November 1770.
24 TNA 17, Geo III cap. 25 [1777], 'An Act for widening the several Streets, lanes, Alleyways and other public passages within the town of Wolverhampton'; Smith, *Town Commissioners in Wolverhampton*, pp. xviii, xxxv.
25 Chandler, G. and Hannah, I.C., *Dudley as it was and is Today*, London: Batsford, 1949, pp. 151–4.
26 Moore, E., *Liverpool in King Charles the Second's Time*, Liverpool: Henry Young and Sons, 1899, p. 150; Borsay, *Urban Renaissance*, p. 64.
27 Farr, M. (ed.), 'The Great Fire of Warwick 1694', *Dugdale Society Publications*, XXXVI, 1992, pp. 123–4.
28 Borsay, *Urban Renaissance*, p. 65.
29 Picton, *Liverpool Archives*, pp. 264–72.
30 Brooke, *Liverpool*, pp. 118–19. See also Stobart, 'Culture versus commerce'.
31 *The Coventry Guide*, Coventry: Merridew and Son, 1824.
32 Mitchell, 'Urban retailing'.
33 Hemingway, *History of Chester*, Vol. 1, pp. 413, 419 and Vol. 2, p. 12; Chester City Library (CCL), MF 1/12, Plan of Chester: I. Stockdale, 1796.
34 CCA, A/B/5/185; A/B/5/207; Seacombe, J., *The Chester Guide*, Chester, 1836, p. 139.

35 *Scarborough Gazette*, 11 August 1853, cited in Schmiechen and Carls, *British Market Hall*, pp. 17–18. See also Hemingway, *History of Chester*, Vol. 2, p. 24.
36 CCA, A/B/4/148v; CR 63/2/133/17; Cowdroy, *Directory of Chester*.
37 Poole, *Coventry*, p. 330.
38 See Girouard, *English Town*, pp. 155–88; Borsay, *Urban Renaissance*, pp. 39–113; Gutkind, *Urban Development*, pp. 255–62.
39 Borsay, 'Warwick', p. 166; Borsay, P., 'The London connection: cultural diffusion and the eighteenth-century provincial town', *London Journal*, 19, 1994, pp. 21–2.
40 Borsay, 'Warwick', 166–7; Wallsgrove, S.G., 'Town planning in Warwick after the Fire: the making of a new square', *Warwickshire History*, 9, 1995, pp. 183–9.
41 Wood, J., *A Description of Bath*, 1742–4, London: W. Bathoe and T. Lownds, 1969, p. 345.
42 Brooke, *Liverpool*, p. 146.
43 Touzeau, *Liverpool*, Vol. II, pp. 480–5.
44 Quoted in Hill, J. and Dent, R., *Memorials of the Old Square*, Birmingham, 1897, p. 17; Borsay, *Urban Renaissance*, p. 209.
45 *VCH, Chester*, Vol. 5, Part 1, p. 225; Pigot, *Commercial Directory*, pp. 98–107; Schwarz, 'Lichfield', p. 178.
46 Hutton, *History of Birmingham*, p. 249; Smith, *History of Warwick*, p. 319.
47 Wallace, *History of Liverpool*, p. 82; Picton, *Memorials of Liverpool*, Vol. 2, p. 281; Hunt, *Tale of Two Squares*; Stobart, 'Culture versus commerce'.
48 See Herson, 'Victorian Chester', pp. 21–2.
49 Borsay, *Urban Renaissance*, pp. 75, 77; Girouard, *English Town*, pp. 157–65.
50 Girouard, *English Town*, pp. 155–6.
51 Borsay, *Urban Renaissance*, pp. 61–2.
52 CCA, A/B/4/217–8, A/B/4/243, A/B/4/243v, A/B/267; Hemingway, *History of Chester*, Vol. 2, p. 12.
53 Broster, *Directory*; Toldervy, W., *England and Wales Described in a Series of Letters*, London, 1762, p. 349.
54 Nash, T.R., *Collections for the History of Worcestershire*, London: Payne, 1781–2, Vol. II, pp. cxv–cxvi; Brooke, *Liverpool*, pp. 386–7; Picton, *Liverpool Archives*, pp. 258, 264–72; Styles, P., *Studies in Seventeenth Century West Midlands History*, Kineton: Roundwood Press, 1978, p. 210.
55 Hutton, *History of Birmingham*, p. 132.
56 See Lefebvre, *Production of Space*, pp. 220–6.
57 *Berrow's Worcester Journal*, 16 April 1772; *Gore's Liverpool Advertiser*, 20 April 1770; *Gore's Liverpool Advertiser*, 16 March 1770.
58 See, for example, West, W., *The History, Topography and Directory of Warwickshire*, R. Wrightson, 1830, pp. 175–290.
59 Borsay, *Urban Renaissance*, p. 66.
60 Borsay, 'London connection', p. 30; Girouard, *English Town*, pp. 52–6, 125–6, 155–70; Gutkind, *Urban Development*, pp. 302–451.
61 *VCH Chester*, Vol. 5, Part 2, pp. 225–8; Brown, *Rows of Chester*, p. 167.
62 WRO, B. WAR at C.711 Tar (p). 'Fire damage and urban renewal in the late seventeenth and eighteenth centuries', paper by M. Turner.
63 Quoted in Farr, 'Great Fire', pp. 87–8; TNA, 6 William III cap. 1 [1694], 'An Act for Rebuilding the Town of Warwick …'; Borsay, 'Warwick', pp. 155–9.
64 Moore, *Liverpool*, p. 127.
65 Fiennes, *Journeys*, p. 184; Defoe, *Tour through Britain*, p. 543.
66 *Gore's Liverpool Advertiser*, 15 June 1770.
67 Hann and Stobart, 'Sites of consumption', pp. 176–7.
68 Green, *City of Worcester*, p. 235.
69 *VCH Chester*, Vol. 5, Part 2, p. 224; Brown, *Rows of Chester*, pp. 168–9, 177–9, 180–1, 183–5.

70 CCA, A/B/4/298; A/B/4/25.
71 Hanshall, *Stranger in Chester*, p. 34; CCA 658/60; 'Watergate Street Row, Chester', etching published by T. Catherall (Chester, 1852); CCA, Views of Chester Streets: 'Eastgate Row, Chester', Evans and Ducker (Chester, no date).
72 Hemingway, *History of Chester*, Vol. 1, p. 410.
73 West, *History of Warwickshire*, p. 182.
74 See Savage, M., 'Walter Benjamin's urban thought', in M. Crang and N. Thrift (eds), *Thinking Space*, London: Routledge, 2000, pp. 33–53.
75 Panelli, R., *Social Geographies. From Difference to Action*, London: Sage, 2004, p. 248.
76 Glennie and Thrift, 'Consumption spaces', p. 37; Weiss, M.R., *The Leen Valley at Work, 1785–1985*, Barnsley: Wharncliffe, 1996, p. 3.
77 See Gregson and Rose, 'Performativities'; Jackson, 'Domesticating the street', pp. 176–91.
78 Goffman, *Presentation of Self*, p. 252. See also McCormack, *Independent Man*, pp. 35–44.
79 Rappaport, *Shopping for Pleasure*, esp. pp. 74–107; Gregson and Rose, 'Performativities', p. 434; Butler, J., *Gender Trouble: Feminism and the Subversion of Identity*, London: Routledge, 2000, p. 25; Glennie and Thrift, 'Consumption spaces', pp. 39–40.
80 Borsay, 'All the town's a stage'; Postles, D., 'The market place as space in early modern England', *Social History*, 29, 2004, pp. 41–58.
81 Hardwick, C., *History of the Borough of Preston and its Environs in the County of Lancaster*, Preston: Worthington, 1857, pp. 291–4.
82 Kuerden, *Preston*, quoted in Hardwick, *History of Preston*, p. 293.
83 Borsay, 'All the town's a stage', pp. 239–43.
84 See Glennie and Thrift, 'Consumption, shopping and gender', p. 226; Goheen, P., 'Parades and processions', in R.L. Gentilcore (ed.), *Historical Atlas of Canada, Volume II: The Land Transformed, 1800–1891*, Toronto: University of Toronto, 1993, pp. 150–1.
85 See Goffman, *Presentation of Self*.
86 Crossley, *Cheshire*, p. 65; Borsay, 'All the town's a stage', p. 247; Cawte, E.C., *Ritual Animal Disguise: A Historical and Geographical Study of Animal Disguise in the British Isles*, Cambridge: Brewer, 1978, p. 29.
87 Hardwick, *History of Preston*, p. 295.
88 Petrie, A., *The Rules of Good Deportment*, 1720, in *The Works of Adam Petrie*, Edinburgh: Scottish Literary Club, 1877, pp. 6–7; Towle, M., *The Young Gentleman and Lady's Private Tutor*, Oxford, 1771, pp. 148–9. See also Corfield, 'Walking the city streets', p. 154.
89 Montagu, M. (ed.), *The Letters of Elizabeth Montagu*, London, 1810, Vol. II, p. 81.
90 Borsay, *Urban Renaissance*, p. 172.
91 Smith, *History of Warwick*, p. 311; Smart, *Worcester Guide*, pp. 53–4; White, F., *History, Gazetteer and Directory of Warwickshire*, Sheffield: White, F., 1874, p. 713; Roberts, *Chester Guide*, p. 64.
92 Bath Central Library (BaCL), Letters of Mrs M. Sneyd, 20 May 1771.
93 Carter, *Men and Polite Society*, pp. 126–8.
94 Corfield, 'Walking the city streets', p. 136.
95 See Carter, *Men and Polite Society*, pp. 149–50.
96 West, *History of Warwickshire*, p. 184.
97 West, *History of Warwickshire*, pp. 182, 210.
98 Bentley, J., *Bentley's History and Guide to Dudley, Dudley Castle, and the Castle Hill*, Birmingham, 1841, pp. 14–37.
99 De Certeau, *Practice of Everyday Life*, reproduced in Bridge and Watson, *City Reader*, pp. 386–7.
100 Soja, *Thirdspace*, pp. 73–82.
101 Butler, *Gender Trouble*; Gregson and Rose, 'Performativities'.
102 Berry, 'Polite consumption', pp. 384–91; Cox, *Complete Tradesman*, pp. 116–45; Berg, *Luxury and Pleasure*, pp. 257–70.

103 Cited in Vickery, *The Gentleman's Daughter*, pp. 250–1.
104 Whitbread, H. (ed.), *I Know My Own Heart: The Diaries of Anne Lister, 1791–1840*, London: Virago, 1988, pp. 249–50.
105 Addy, J. (ed.), 'The diary of Henry Prescott, Vol. I', *Records Society of Lancashire and Cheshire*, 127, 1987, 24 April 1705.
106 Fawcett, T., *Voices of Eighteenth-Century Bath: An Anthology*, Bath: RUTON, 1995, p. 85; BaCL, *Diary of a Tour by Three Students from Cambridge*, 1725, p. 118.
107 E. Shackleton to R. Parker, quoted in Vickery, *Gentleman's Daughter*, p. 252.
108 Jane Austen, *Northanger Abbey*, 1818, quoted in Towner, *Recreation and Tourism*, p. 83.
109 Addy, J. and McNiven, P. (eds), 'The diary of Henry Prescott, Vol. II', *Records Society of Lancashire and Cheshire*, 132, 1994, *passim*; Whitbread, *Diaries of Anne Lister*, 12 May 1823.
110 Cited in Vickery, *The Gentleman's Daughter*, p. 250.
111 Schopenhauer, *A Lady's Travels*, pp. 35–6; Hughes, *Ancient Chester*; West, *History of Warwickshire*, pp. 175–290.
112 Postles, 'Market place', pp. 41–2; Griffin, *England's Revelry*.
113 Hutton, *History of Birmingham*, p. 153; Kennett, A., *Chester and the River Dee: An Illustrated History of Chester and its Port*, Chester: Chester City Council, 1982; White, *Directory of Staffordshire*, pp. 167–8.
114 Ormerod, *History of Chester*, Vol. I, p. 302; Hewitson, *History of Preston*, pp. 300–1; Griffin, *England's Revelry*, p. 68; Arrowsmith, P., *Stockport: A History*, Stockport: Stockport Metropolitan Borough Council, 1997; Troughton, *History of Liverpool*, pp. 93–4.
115 Griffin, *England's Revelry*; Borsay, 'All the town's a stage', pp. 239–43.
116 Hutton, *History of Birmingham*, p. 134.
117 Addy and McNiven, 'Diary of Henry Prescott', 25 March 1718.
118 Kennett, *Chester*, p. 38.
119 Chambers, *History of Worcester*, p. 355.
120 'Memorial Received from Shopkeepers in the Old Market Place', quoted in Schmiechen and Carls, *British Market Hall*, p. 18.
121 *Berrow's Worcester Journal*, 28 May 1772.
122 Whitbread, *Diaries of Anne Lister*, 1 April 1824.
123 Hutton, *History of Birmingham*, p. 134.
124 Reader, *History of Coventry*, p. 80; White, *Directory of Staffordshire*, p. 168.
125 It is not the intention here to provide a full account of street trading. For more detailed studies, see Spufford, M., *The Great Reclothing of Rural England: Petty Chapmen and their Wares in the Seventeenth Century*, London: Hambledon Press, 1984; Lemire, B., *The English Clothing Trade before the Factory, 1660–1800*, Basingstoke: Macmillan, 1997, pp. 97–104.
126 *Precott's Manchester Journal*, 13 March 1779.
127 Lemire, *English Clothing Trade*, p. 100.
128 'Proceedings of the Society – Food Committee', *Journal of the Society of Arts*, 10 January 1868, p. 124.
129 Schmiechen and Carls, *British Market Halls*, p. 27.
130 Lefebvre, *Production of Space*, pp. 33–4, 86.
131 Giddens, *Central Problems*, pp. 49–95.
132 Blome, *Brittania*.
133 De Certeau, *Practice of Everyday Life*, pp. 110–12.

5 The building

1 Borsay, *Urban Renaissance*, pp. 62–8, 101–13.
2 Glennie and Thrift, 'Consumption spaces', pp. 31–6.
3 Rutherford, M., *Catherine Furze*, London: Unwin, p. 28.

4 Peck, *Consuming Splendor*, pp. 188–229; Borsay, *Urban Renaissance*, pp. 41–60, 101–13; Hill, 'Symbolism and space'; Stobart, 'Building an urban identity'.
5 Arnade *et al.*, 'Fertile spaces', p. 518.
6 See de Certeau, *Practice of Everyday Life*; Fraser, 'Rethinking the public sphere'.
7 Borsay, *Urban Renaissance*, pp. 257–308; Langford, *Polite and Commercial People*, pp. 99–121.
8 Vickery, *Gentleman's Daughter*, p. 290.
9 Carter, *Men and Polite Society*, Chapter 2; Ogborn, *Spaces of Modernity*, pp. 79–91, 110–11, 133–42; Klein, 'Politeness for plebes', pp. 369–71.
10 Lefebvre, *Production of Space*, p. 33. For further elucidation see Merrifield, A., 'Place and space: a Lefebvrian reconciliation', *Transactions of the Institute of British Geographers*, 18, 1993, p. 523.
11 Morris, R.J., 'The industrial town', in P. Waller (ed.), *The English Urban Landscape*, Oxford: Oxford University Press, 2000, p. 198.
12 Chambers, *History of Worcester*, pp. 298–9; Green, *City of Worcester*, pp. 227–8; Girouard, *English Town*, pp. 52–3.
13 *VCH Chester*, Vol. 5, Part 1, p. 225.
14 Dent, R.K., *Old and New Birmingham: A History of the Town and Its People*, Birmingham: Houghton and Hammond, 1880, pp. 144, 191, 203.
15 West, *History of Warwickshire*, p. 188.
16 Lefebvre, *Production of Space*, p. 363.
17 Rutherford, M., *Revolution in Tanner's Lane*, 1887; Oxford: Oxford University Press, 1936, p. 48.
18 Cox, *Complete Tradesman*, pp. 95–7.
19 For a broader survey, see Hann and Stobart, 'Sites of consumption'.
20 WRO, Henry Bolt, 1702; LRO, WCW Robert Rownson, 1709; Lichfield Joint Record Office (LRRO), Isaac Stretch, 1716. The use of lattices highlights the tension in shops between, on the one hand, the desire for display and access, and, on the other, the need to safeguard stock from theft.
21 CCA, A/B/4/259v.
22 Brooks and Haworth, *Boomtown Manchester*, pp. 18–24; Shaw, G.T., *History of the Athenaeum, Liverpool, 1798–1898*, Liverpool: Committee of the Athenaeum, 1898, pp. 4–27; Parish, *Birmingham Library*, pp. 38–46.
23 See Jackson, 'Domesticating the street'; Shields, 'Spaces for consumption'; Goss, 'Magic of the mall'.
24 WRO, Joseph Bourn, 1737; WRO, Nicholas Paris, 1716.
25 LRO, WCW Robert Rownson, 1709; LJRO, B/C/11, John Finney, 1740.
26 LRO, WCW Edward Clifton, 1715; LJRO, P/C/11, Simon Ames, 1711.
27 Cox, *Complete Tradesman*, pp. 135–9.
28 Tyrer, 'Diurnal of Nicholas Blundell', 16 May 1718; 15 October 1710.
29 WRO, 2612/W213, Hatton Atkins, 1683; LJRO, B/C/11, Jonathon Daniel, 1703.
30 LRJO, B/C/11, Nicholas Blithe, 1710.
31 Aston, J., *The Manchester Guide*, Manchester: J. Aston, 1804, pp. 236–9; Troughton, *History of Liverpool*, p. 289.
32 Girouard, *English Towns*, pp. 138–9; Berry, 'Creating polite space', p. 124.
33 Aston, *Manchester Guide*, p. 236.
34 Willshaw, E.M., 'The inns of Chester, 1775–1832', unpublished MA thesis, University of Leicester, 1979, p. 13.
35 Clark, *Clubs and Societies*, pp. 248–50.
36 Shaw, *Athenaeum*, p. 68. The original plan to incorporate shops on the ground floor and thus defray some of the costs of construction was quickly abandoned.
37 Shaw, *Athenaeum*, pp. 12, 7.
38 Wyke, T. and Rudyard, N., *Manchester Theatres*, Manchester: Manchester Central Library, 1994, p. 55; Baker, 'Theatre, law and society', pp. 174–5.

39 Vickery, *Gentleman's Daughter*, p. 234; Schopenhauer, *A Lady Travels*, p. 171; Brooke, *Liverpool*, pp. 275–6. There is little evidence that this was a regional characteristic – in Chester and Manchester, boxes were favoured.
40 Brooke, *Liverpool*, pp. 275–6.
41 *Birmingham Gazette*, 15 June 1795; Derrick, S., *Letters Written from Liverpool, Chester … Bath*, London, 1767, Vol. I, p. 21.
42 See Ogborn, *Spaces of Modernity*, pp. 122–8.
43 Smollett, T., *The Expedition of Humphry Clinker*, 1771, Oxford: Oxford University Press, 1966, pp. 143, 149.
44 Van Muyden, *Letters of De Saussure*, p. 48, quoted in Vickery, *Gentleman's Daughter*, p. 250.
45 LivRO, 920 NIC 3/3/4.
46 Vickery, *Gentleman's Daughter*, p. 244.
47 Historical Manuscripts Commission, *Hastings MSS*, iii, 18.
48 Addy, 'Diary of Henry Prescott', 23 April 1705.
49 Tyrer, 'Diurnal of Nicholas Blundell', Vol. III, p. 161.
50 Aston, *Manchester Guide*, p. 244; Upton, C., *A History of Birmingham*, Chichester: Phillimore, 1993, p. 113; Bruton, F., *A Short History of Manchester and Salford*, Manchester: Sherratt and Hughes, 1924, p. 199.
51 White, *Directory of Staffordshire*, p. 167; Pearce, *History of Walsall*, pp. 130–1.
52 SRO, D1798 HM 24/3; Vickery, *Gentleman's Daughter*, p. 267.
53 Otter, C., 'Making liberalism durable: vision and civility in the late Victorian city', *Social History*, 27, 2002, p. 4.
54 Hewitson, *History of Preston*, p. 320; Covins, F., *The Arboretum Story*, Worcester: Arboretum Residents' Association, 1989, pp. 7–8.
55 Borsay, *Urban Renaissance*, pp. 162–72, 350–4.
56 Addy and McGiven, 'Diary of Henry Prescott', 7 August 1717. See also Fiennes, *Journeys*, p. 227.
57 Quoted in Vickery, *Gentleman's Daughter*, p. 241.
58 This underlines the importance of assemblies and other leisure activities as marriage markets – see Vickery, *Gentleman's Daughter*, pp. 267–9; Borsay, *Urban Renaissance*, pp. 185–96, 243–8.
59 Green, *City of Worcester*, p. 228; Pearce, *History of Walsall*, pp. 131–2.
60 Berry, 'Creating polite space', pp. 131–2.
61 Green, *City of Worcester*, pp. 228–30; Aston, *Manchester Guide*, p. 236.
62 Troughton, *History of Liverpool*, p. 177.
63 Borsay, *Urban Renaissance*, p. 160; Goldsmith, O., 'The life of Richard Nash', in A. Friedman (ed.), *Collected Works of Oliver Goldsmith*, 5 volumes, Oxford: Oxford University Press, 1966, Vol. 2, p. 33.
64 Laird, F.C., *The Beauties of England and Wales*, London: J. Harris, Longman and Co., 1813, xii, Part 1, p. 149.
65 Vickery, *Gentleman's Daughter*, p. 234.
66 *Birmingham Gazette*, 15 June 1795.
67 For more detailed analysis of these activities, see Hann and Stobart, 'Sites of consumption'.
68 Walsh, 'Shop design'.
69 LJRO, B/C/11, Simon Ames, 1711; WRO, 2612/W251, John Chamberlain, 1688; LRO, WCW Thomas Taylor, 1720.
70 *Worcester Journal*, 23–30 March 1744.
71 LJRO, B/C/11, Thomas Clarke, 1717.
72 Berry, 'Polite consumption', pp. 386–7. Rails and racks are absent from even the Kentish probate inventories before 1680, suggesting that they were a novel item in eighteenth-century provincial shops.
73 CCA, WS Ralph Edge, 1683; LRO, WCW Ambrose Pierpoint, 1723.

74 See Walsh, 'Newness', pp. 60–2.
75 LJRO, B/C/11, Nicholas Blithe, 1710; B/C/11, Richard Lindsey, 1710.
76 McKendrick, N., 'Josiah Wedgwood and the commercialization of the Potteries', in N. McKendrick, J. Brewer and J.H. Plumb (eds), *The Birth of a Consumer Society*, London: 1982.
77 CCA, WS Abner Scholes, 1736.
78 Bianchi, 'In the name of the tulip'; Saumarez-Smith, C., *Eighteenth-century Decoration and Design in Domestic Interiors in England*, London: Weidenfeld and Nicolson, 1993, pp. 11–13, 132–3.
79 For more detailed discussion of these points, see Hann and Stobart, 'Sites of consumption' and, for a London comparison, Walsh, 'Shop design and the display of goods'.
80 West, *History of Warwickshire*, p. 187.
81 Benjamin, *Arcades Project*, pp. 31–61; Lefebvre, *Production of Space*, pp. 40–6.
82 Walsh, 'Shop design', p. 163.
83 Defoe, D., *The Complete English Tradesman*, 1726, Stroud: Sutton, 1987, pp. 182–3.
84 TNA, PROB 4 4125 Julius Billers, PROB 3 35/26 Samuel Gibbard.
85 Wallis, P., 'Consumption, retailing and medicine in early modern London', *Economic History Review*, forthcoming.
86 See Lefebvre, *Production of Space*, pp. 16–18.
87 Walsh, 'Shop design', pp. 370–1; Hann and Stobart, 'Sites of consumption', pp. 181–6. See also Chapter 7.
88 Cox, *Complete Tradesman*, pp. 90–5.
89 LRO, WCW Ambrose Pierpoint, 1723; LJRO, B/C/11, William Wright, 1709; LRO, WCW Robert Rownson, 1709; CCA, WS Robert Wilkinson, 1721.
90 Quoted in McKendrick, 'Josiah Wedgwood', p. 119.
91 See the extract from the *Spectator* discussed in Kowleski-Wallace, E., *Consuming Subjects: Women, Shopping and Business in the Eighteenth Century*, New York: Columbia University Press, 1997, pp. 82–6.
92 LRO, WCW William Cross, 1734.
93 Stout, W., *Autobiography of William Stout of Lancaster, 1665–1752*, Manchester: Manchester University Press, 1967; Cox, *Complete Tradesman*, pp. 83–4; LJRO, B/C/11, William Hockenhull, 1733.
94 Jacobs, E.H., 'Buying into classes: the practice of book selection in eighteenth-century Britain', *Eighteenth-Century Studies*, 33, 1999, pp. 43–64.
95 For fuller discussion of these ideas, see Johns, A., *The Nature of the Book*, Chicago, IL: University of Chicago Press, 1998.
96 Lefebvre, *Production of Space*, p. 99.
97 Ogborn, *Spaces of Modernity*, pp. 122–33. The London pleasure gardens in particular were criticised and parodied for the high cost of food and drink provided.
98 On this subject, see Nead, L., 'From alleys to courts: obscenity and the mapping of mid-Victorian London', *New Formations*, 32, 1999, pp. 32–45.
99 Ogborn, *Spaces of Modernity*, p. 128; *The Chester Chronicle*, 11 October 1815.
100 Vickery, *Gentleman's Daughter*, p. 338; Cunningham, J., *Theatre Royal: The History of the Theatre Royal in Birmingham*, Oxford: Oxford University Press, 1950, p. 44.
101 Lefebvre, *Production of Space*, p. 360.
102 Borsay, P., *The Image of Bath. Towns, Heritage and History*, Oxford: Oxford University Press, 2000, pp. 32–3.
103 *Berrow's Worcester Journal*, 9 April 1772.
104 Borsay, *Urban Renaissance*, pp. 248–50.
105 Quoted in Borsay, *Urban Renaissance*, p. 304.
106 Baker, 'Theatre, law and society', pp. 173–5.
107 Vickery, *Gentleman's Daughter*, pp. 332–3.
108 Quoted in Cunningham, *Theatre Royal*, p. 42.

109 *The Chester Chronicle*, 12 January 1810. For a full account of these riots, see Edwards, J., 'Events at the Theatre Royal Chester, 1807–1810', *Cheshire History*, 38, 1998–9, pp. 55–70.
110 TNA 10 and 11, William III cap. 23 [1699], 'Act … for the better apprehending of Felons that commit Burglary, Housebreaking or Robbery from Shops …'. See also Cox, *Complete Tradesman*, p. 101; Berry, 'Polite consumption', p. 384; Segrave, K., *Shoplifting: A Social History*, London: Mcfarland & Co., 2001.
111 Beattie, J.M., *Policing and Punishment in London 1660–1750: Urban Crime and the Limits of Terror*, Oxford: Oxford University Press, 2001, pp. 328–30; 'Proceedings in Quarter Sessions 1690–1696', *Warwick County Records*, Vol. IX, 1964, which list thefts of clothing, linen, muslin, silk tippets, sheets, a silver thimble and wool, as well as items such as coals and a harness; Clark, *Clubs and Societies*, pp. 102–3.
112 *Berrow's Worcester Journal*, 26 November 1772; 16 January 1772.
113 Defoe, D., *Moll Flanders*, 1722, London: Oxford University Press, 1971, pp. 209, 211.
114 CRO, BA/E/B/7/3, 'Theft examinations and inventory of stolen goods, 1750'. It is significant that the shopkeepers had their stock sufficiently well ordered that they could specify exactly those goods which had gone missing.
115 CRO, BA/E/B/7/2.
116 CRO, 347–96, James Hewitt's Journal, 98.
117 CRO, BA/E/B/7/2.
118 *Worcester Journal*, 1 October 1772; 17 December 1772.
119 *Worcester Journal*, 17 December 1772.
120 Lefebvre, *Production of Space*, p. 386.

6 The individual

1 Berry, 'Prudent luxury'; Berg, *Luxury and Pleasure*, pp. 199–246; Smith, *Consumption and Respectability*; Weatherill, *Consumer Behaviour*, pp. 137–65.
2 Miller *et al.*, *Shopping, Place and Identity*, p. 23. See, for example, Rappaport, *Shopping for Pleasure*, and the various contributions to Crossick, G. and Jaumain, S. (eds), *Cathedrals of Consumption*, Aldershot: Ashgate, 1999.
3 Miller *et al.*, *Shopping, Place and Identity*, p. 20. See Berry, 'Polite consumption'; Vickery, *Gentleman's Daughter*, pp. 250–2; Berg, *Luxury and Pleasure*, pp. 247–78; Glennie and Thrift, 'Consumption spaces', pp. 39–40.
4 Smith, *Consumption and Respectability*, pp. 189–221.
5 See Giddens, A., *The Constitution of Society*, Cambridge: Polity Press, 1984. For useful critiques of these ideas, see Gregory, *Geographical Imaginations*, pp. 109–24; Thrift, N., *Spatial Formations*, London: Sage, 1996, pp. 53–61.
6 Smith, *Consumption and Respectability*, p. 13.
7 Lefebvre, *Production of Space*, pp. 33–4, 86; Pred, *Lost Words*, pp. 200–35.
8 See Gregory, *Geographical Imaginations*, p. 112; Giddens, *Constitution of Society*, and, for historical analyses, the various contributions to French, H. and Barry, J. (eds), *Identity and Agency in England, 1500–1800*, Basingstoke: Macmillan, 2004.
9 Berry, 'Polite consumption', p. 380; Berry, 'Prudent luxury', pp. 144–8; SRO, D1798 HM 24/3.
10 Finn, 'Men's things'; Tyrer, 'Diurnal of Nicholas Blundell'; LivRO, 920 PLU PT 9; Addy and McGiven, 'Diary of Henry Prescott'.
11 Stout, *Autobiography*, p. 79; SRO, D1798 HM 29/2–4; SRO, D (W) 1788/V/108–11, Sales ledgers of Fletcher and Fenton of Newcastle-under-Lyme, 1768–83.
12 Kilmartin, 'Popular rejoicing', p. 350.
13 LRO, 920 PLU PT9.
14 WaRO, CR1368, Vol. 4/41, Morduant Family Letters.
15 Quoted in Stobart, 'County, town and country', p. 178.

16 *The Guild Merchant of Preston, with an Extract of the Original Charter*, Manchester: T. Anderton, 1762, pp. 16 and 17; Vickery, *Gentleman's Daughter*, pp. 242–4; Borsay, *Urban Renaissance*, pp. 143, 155–6, 355–67.
17 Aston, *Manchester*, pp. 240–1; Stobart, 'Leisure hierarchy', pp. 25–8; *Schofield's Middlewich Journal*, 1 February 1757; Vickery, *Gentleman's Daughter*, p. 264; *Berrow's Worcester Journal*, 9 January 1772.
18 Uglow, *Lunar Men*, p. xiii; Brooke, *Liverpool*, p. 290; LRO, DP 282/14, Address and Code of Laws from a Committee of the Literary and Philosophical Society of Bolton, 18 October 1813; Bentley, *History of Worcestershire*, Vol. III, p. 20.
19 Reader, *History of Coventry*, p. 98.
20 Letter from W. Ramsden to E. Shackleton, quoted in Vickery, *Gentleman's Daughter*, p. 264.
21 *Berrow's Worcester Journal*, 13 August 1772.
22 SRO, D1798 HM29/2–5; SRO D1798 HM28/10, Customer's Account Book of John Webb of Stafford, mercer.
23 Parish, *Birmingham Library*, pp. 105–31; Dent, *Birmingham*, pp. 176–81.
24 LivRO, 920 NIC 3/4/9.
25 Berry, 'Creating polite space', p. 126; LivRO, 027 LYC 1/1/1; Parish, *Birmingham Library*; BCA, MS 3375.
26 Borsay, *Urban Renaissance*, pp. 257–83; Smith, *Consumption and Respectability*, pp. 13–19.
27 SRO, D1798 HM 24/3; LivRO, 920 PLU PT 9; Wilkinson, J. (ed.), 'The Letters of Thomas Langton, Flax Merchant of Kirkham, 1771–1788', *Chetham Society*, 3rd series, 38, 1994; LRO, DDX 334/10–18, Letters from James, Lord Strange to Sir William Horton of Chadderton, esquire (1752–9).
28 See SRO, D1798 HM 24/3; *Gore's Liverpool Advertiser*, 7 September 1770; LRO, DDPr 28/1, Playbill for Blackburn New Theatre, 4 May 1787.
29 SRO, D1798 HM 29/2–4.
30 Sweet, 'Polite topographies'.
31 Borsay, *Urban Renaissance*, p. 155.
32 See Stobart, 'Culture versus commerce', pp. 478–81; Parish, *Birmingham Library*, pp. 9–70.
33 *Berrow's Worcester Journal*, 24 September 1772; *Aris's Birmingham Gazette*, 2 February 1789; LRO, DP/282/15.
34 SRO, D1798 HM 24/3.
35 Shaw, *History of the Athenaeum*, pp. 4–27; Parish, *Birmingham Library*, pp. 11–23.
36 Mui and Mui, *Shops and Shopkeeping*, pp. 211–16; Shammas, *Pre-industrial Consumer*, pp. 243–8.
37 SRO, D1798 HM 27/4, Account book of Lewis Dickenson of Stafford, apothecary (1737–57); SRO, D (W) 1788/V/108–11.
38 Beckett and Smith, 'Urban renaissance'. See also Berry, 'Creating polite space', p. 126.
39 WRO, 899:93 BA1558/19, Account of Worcester Infirmary and List of Annual Subscribers (1753–4); SRO, D1798 HM27/5.
40 Covins, *Arboretum Story*, pp. 5–8; *Gentleman's Magazine*, August 1752; Green, *City of Worcester*, pp. 231–3.
41 SRO, D1798 HM 24/3; LivRO, 920 PLU PT9; LRO, DDX/274/13–17.
42 Glennie and Thrift, 'Consumption spaces', pp. 39–40; Miller *et al.*, *Shopping, Place and Identity*, p. 20.
43 Borsay, *English Urban Renaissance*, pp. 275–6.
44 Letter from Erasmus Darwin to his son Robert, 17 December 1790, in Krause, E., *Erasmus Darwin*, London: Murray, 1879, p. 40; Berry, 'Creating polite space', p. 135.
45 Derrick, *Letters*, p. 20; Vickery, *Gentleman's Daughter*, p. 241; Hembry, *British Spas*, pp. 10–11.
46 Brooks and Haworth, *Boomtown Manchester*, pp. 10, 27.

47 Shaw, *Athenaeum*, pp. 14, 69.
48 Shaw, *Athenaeum*, p. 70.
49 Schopenhauer, *A Lady Travels*, p. 171.
50 *Berrow's Worcester Journal*, 3 September 1772.
51 Ogborn, *Spaces of Modernity*, pp. 116–18.
52 Ogborn, *Spaces of Modernity*, p. 129.
53 Smollett, *Humphrey Clinker*, pp. 88–90. See also Fielding, H., *The Masquerade*, London, 1728.
54 LivRO, 920 NIC 3/3/4.
55 Vickery, *Gentleman's Daughter*, pp. 248, 244; LCA, 920 NIC 3/3/4.
56 Berry, 'Polite shopping', p. 379.
57 SRO, D1798 HM 29/2–4.
58 Walsh, C., 'Why it was better to shop yourself – shopping for the household in early-modern England and the problem of servants', CHORD workshop, University of Wolverhampton, April 2004.
59 SRO, D1798 HM 29/2–4.
60 SRO, D1798 HM 29/2–4. For discussion of correspondence and 'proxy' shopping, see Walsh, 'Social relations', and below.
61 *Piercy's Coventry Gazette*, 28 February 1778.
62 SRO, D1798 HM 29/2; Mui and Mui, *Shops and Shopkeeping*, pp. 212–13.
63 WaRO, CR 1368, Vol. 4/57 Morduant Family Letters.
64 Addy and McGiven, 'Diary of Henry Prescott', 8 June 1711; 26 March 1712.
65 CRO, PA208/13, 15 June 1829; 29 July 1829.
66 Berry, 'Polite shopping', p. 380.
67 Burney, F., *Camilla, or a Picture of Youth*, 1796, New York: Oxford University Press, 1983, p. 607.
68 Roberts, *Chester Guide*, p. 64.
69 SRO, D1798 HM 28/10.
70 Parkinson, R. (ed.), 'The private journal and literary remains of John Byrom', Vol. I, *Chetham Society*, 32 and 35, 1854–55, Vol. I, Part II, p. 324; Addy and McGiven, 'Diary of Henry Prescott', 17 September 1717.
71 See Johns, *Nature of the Book*, pp. 120–1.
72 Cox, *Complete Tradesman*, pp. 77–83, 90–102.
73 Berry, 'Prudent luxury', pp. 144–6; Addy and McGiven, 'Diary of Henry Prescott', *passim*.
74 SRO, D1798 HM28/10.
75 Cooper M., 'The Worcester book trade in the eighteenth century', *Worcester Historical Society Occasional Publications*, 8, 1997, pp. 30–1.
76 SRO, D1798 HM 37/36, Papers of Mrs Elizabeth Sneyd of Stafford (1713–52).
77 WRO, 705:781 B.A. 7537/1, Mountfort Collection.
78 SRO, D1798 HM 37/36.
79 Letter to Messrs Chamberlayne & Co., 23 October 1809, quoted in Barker, T.C. and Harris, J.R., *A Merseyside Town in the Industrial Revolution: St Helens 1750–1900*, Liverpool: Liverpool University Press, 1954, p. 155.
80 *Piercy's Coventry Gazette*, 27 June 1788.
81 LJRO B/C/11 1734 Joshua Cowley; Johns, *Nature of the Book*, p. 120.
82 Lowe, *Diary*, 7 April 1664; Tyrer, 'Diurnal of Nicholas Blundell', 16 May 1718; 15 October 1710; WaRO, CR1596, Box 84, no.16.
83 WaRO, CR1596, Box 90/7/7.
84 Rutherford, *Revolution in Tanner's Lane*, p. 161.
85 See Pred, *Lost Words*, pp. 229–35.
86 Borsay, *Urban Renaissance*, p. 268.
87 Macky, J., *A Journey through England and Scotland*, London: J. Pemberton, 1722–3, Vol. ii, p. 41; Defoe, *Tour of Britain*, p. 115 (emphasis added).

88 Borsay, *Urban Renaissance*, pp. 273–4.
89 Defoe, *Tour of Britain*, p. 126.
90 WaRO, CR136, Newdigate MSS, 31 December 1753; 17 July 1752.
91 'Coffee-Houses Vindicated', 435, quoted in Borsay, *Urban Renaissance*, p. 269.
92 Smith, *Consumption and Respectability*, p. 154.
93 Parkinson, 'John Byrom', Vol. I, Part I, p. 227.
94 Berry, 'Prudent luxury', p. 148; Elizabeth Shackleton to Robert Parker, quoted in Vickery, *Gentleman's Daughter*, pp. 251–2; Tyrer, 'Diurnal of Nicholas Blundell', 24 June 1707.
95 Glennie and Thrift, 'Consumption spaces', p. 33; Berry, 'Polite consumption', pp. 377–82.
96 Smith, *Consumption and Respectability*, pp. 16–17.
97 Trentmann, 'Knowing consumers', pp. 2–6.
98 Borsay, *Urban Renaissance*, pp. 225–83.
99 Miège, *The New State of England*, 3rd edition, London, 1699, p. 149.
100 Defoe, D., *The Compleat English Gentleman*, 1728–9, London: D. Nutt, 1890, p. 5; Defoe, *Complete English Tradesman*, pp. 73–4.
101 *Berrow's Worcester Journal*, 8 October 1772.
102 Quoted in Vickery, *Gentleman's Daughter*, p. 14. See also Ellis, 'For the honour of the town'.
103 Fielding, H., *Joseph Andrews*, 1742, London: Methuen, 1987, p. 155.
104 Borsay, *Urban Renaissance*, pp. 238–40; Williams, J., 'The geographies of genteel women and the production of space in Bath, 1702–1761', unpublished MSc thesis, University of Oxford, 2003, pp. 175–85.
105 'Letter from Tunbridge Wells', in *Tunbridge and Bath Miscellany*, London, 1714.
106 SRO, D1798 HM 24/3.
107 Vickery, *Gentleman's Daughter*, pp. 172–7; WaRO CR 1368, Vol. 1/4.
108 SRO, D1798 HM 37/36.
109 Letter to Chamberlayne & Co., 5 August 1809, quoted in Barker and Harris, *St Helens*, p. 154.
110 Towner, J., *An Historical Geography of Recreation and Tourism in the Western World, 1540–1940*, Chichester: Wiley, 1996, pp. 96–106.
111 Uglow, *Lunar Men*, pp. 405–6.
112 The Lunar Society in Birmingham, with its close contacts to the Royal Societies in London and Paris, was an exception, as was the Manchester Literary and Philosophical Society. Uglow, *Lunar Men, passim*; Wilson, 'Cultural identity of Liverpool', p. 65. See also Borsay, 'Bath', p. 6; Clark, *Clubs and Societies, passim*.
113 Quoted in Porter, R., 'Science, provincial culture and public opinion in Enlightenment England', in P. Borsay (ed.), *The Eighteenth-Century Town: A Reader in English Urban History 1688–1820*, Harlow: Longman, 1990, p. 256.
114 Shaw, *Athenaeum*, pp. 5–6.
115 Wilson, 'Cultural identity of Liverpool', p. 64; Chalklin, 'Capital expenditure', 64.
116 Borsay, *English Urban Renaissance*, p. 251.
117 WRO, 899:93 BA 1558/19.
118 Cavins, *Arboretum Story*, pp. 5–7; WRO, 899:93 BA 1558/19.
119 BCA, MS 3375; Parish, *Birmingham Library*, p. 89; LRO, 614 INF/5/1; LRO, 027 LYC 1/1/1.
120 Barker and Harris, *St Helens*, pp. 155, 165.
121 Stobart, 'Building an urban identity'; Borsay, *Urban Renaissance*, pp. 250–6.
122 *Adams Weekly Courant*, 23 May 1775.
123 *Adams Weekly Courant*, 23 May 1775.
124 Walsh, 'Social relations'; Vickery, *Gentleman's Daughter*, pp. 168, 183. See also Peck, *Consuming Splendor*, pp. 37–8.
125 *The Spectator*, 11 August 1712, quoted in Berry, 'Polite shopping', p. 387.

126 See, Glennie and Thrift, 'Consumer spaces', pp. 28–31; Towner, *Recreation and Tourism*, p. 83.
127 White, *Directory of Staffordshire*, p. 62; Baines, *History of Lancaster*, p. 534; Palmer, C.F., *The History of the Town and Castle of Tamworth*, Tamworth: J. Thompson, 1845, p. 208.
128 Muldrew, C., *The Economy of Obligation: The Culture of Credit and Social Relations in Early-Modern England*, Basingstoke: Macmillan, 1998, pp. 148–72.
129 See Lefebvre, *Production of Space*, pp. 360, 362.
130 Kennett, *Georgian Chester*, pp. 36–7; Wilshaw, 'Inns of Chester', p. 13. This echoes the hierarchy of events offered at the Preston Guild of 1762 – see Chapter 4.
131 Borsay, *Urban Renaissance*, p. 263.
132 *Weekly Register*, 6 February 1731; *The Tatler*, No. 89, 1–3 November 1709, quoted in Ross, A. (ed.), *Selections from The Tatler and The Spectator*, Harmondsworth: Penguin, 1982, pp. 123, 210.
133 Ross, *Tatler and The Spectator*, p. 128.
134 Parish, *Birmingham Library*, p. 60; LRO, DP/282/14.
135 *Gore's Liverpool Advertiser*, 27 July 1770. For details of the reading interests of the middling sorts, see, for example, Fergus, J., 'Eighteenth-century readers in provincial England: the customers of Samuel Clay's circulating library and workshop at Warwick, 1770–72', *Papers of the Bibliographical Society of America*, 78, 1984, pp. 155–213.
136 Cooper, 'Worcester book trade', pp. 30–1. Many of the most frequently borrowed books were, of course, popular novels, rather than weighty tomes.
137 Barfoot and Wolkes, *UBD*, Vols II–V; Pigot, *National Directory*.
138 Enfield, *History of Leverpool*, p. 48; Moss, *Liverpool Guide*, pp. 117–18.
139 *Leamington Spa Courier*, 1828; Kennett, *Georgian Chester*, p. 37; Olleson, 'Tamworth Music Festival', p. 84.
140 Historical Manuscript Commission, *Dartmouth MSS*, iii, p. 235.
141 Hutton, *History of Birmingham*, p. 259.
142 Trentmann, 'Knowing consumers', pp. 2–6.
143 See Pred, *Lost Words*, p. 200.
144 See Rappaport, *Shopping for Pleasure*; Shields, 'Spaces for consumption'; Goss, 'Magic of the mall'.
145 See Giddens, *Central Problems*, pp. 49–95.

7 Advertisements

1 For a useful overview, see Wischermann, C., 'Placing advertising in the modern cultural history of the city', in C. Wischermann and E. Shore (eds), *Advertising and the European City: Historical Perspectives*, Aldershot: Ashgate, 2000, pp. 1–12.
2 Morgan, V., 'Beyond the boundary of the shop: retail advertising spaces in 18th-century provincial England', in J. Benson and L. Ugolini (eds), *Cultures of Selling: Perspectives on Consumption and Society since 1700*, Aldershot: Ashgate, 2006.
3 McKendrick, N., 'George Packwood and the commercialisation of shaving: the art of eighteenth century advertising', in N. McKendrick, J. Brewer and J.H. Plumb (eds), *The Birth of a Consumer Society*, London: Hutchinson, 1982, pp. 146–96. See also Mui, and Mui, *Shops and Shopkeeping*, Chapter 12; Cox, *Complete Tradesman*, pp. 102–10.
4 Fine and Leopold, *World of Consumption*, pp. 194–218.
5 Berg, M. and Clifford, H., 'Commerce and the commodity: graphic display and selling new consumer goods in eighteenth-century England', in M. North and D. Ormrod (eds), *Art Markets in Europe, 1400–1800*, Aldershot: Ashgate, 1998, p. 191–2.
6 Hall, S., 'Encoding and decoding in the TV discourse', in S. Hall, D. Hobson, A. Lowe and P. Willis (eds), *Culture, Media and Language*, London: Routledge, 1992, pp. 128–38.
7 It is this unity between mental and material space that Lefebvre seeks to highlight. Lefebvre, *Production of Space*, pp. 6, 12, 413.

8 *Blackburn Mail*, 20 November 1793.
9 Berg, and Clifford, 'Commerce', p. 196.
10 Bodleian Library, University of Oxford, John Johnson Collection (JJC), Book-trade: Lancashire.
11 Lambert, J., *A Nation of Shopkeepers: Trade Ephemera from 1654 to the 1860s in the John Johnson Collection*, Oxford: Bodleian Library, 2001, p. 116.
12 JJC, Bill Headings 31 (16); JJC, Trade Cards 28 (26).
13 Reproduced in Edmonds, 'Theatre royal', p. 75.
14 Muldrew, *Economy of Obligation*, pp. 148–72; Wallis, 'Consumption, retailing and medicine'.
15 *Worcester Journal*, 2 January 1751.
16 *Gore's Advertiser*, 5 October 1770; 12 October 1770; 19 October 1770.
17 Walsh, 'Advertising'.
18 Hat sellers often produced circular trade cards or labels to paste onto the inside of the hat. See, for example, the trade card of Cooke & Co. of Leamington, Northampton and Rugby: JJC, Trade Cards 13 (68).
19 Berg and Clifford, 'Commerce', p. 193.
20 JJC, Trades and Professions 6 (48); JJC, Trade Cards 6 (39).
21 British Museum (BM), Banks Collection 17.69, (MY17 – MRR).
22 *Gore's Advertiser*, 21 September 1770; *Blackburn Mail*, 2 October 1793.
23 Barker, 'Smoke cities', pp. 184–5.
24 *Adams Weekly Courant*, 5 December 1775; *Blackburn Mail*, 19 June 1793, 10 July 1793.
25 *Adams Weekly Courant*, 28 November 1775
26 See Borsay, 'The London connection', pp. 24, 31.
27 *Gore's Advertiser*, 25 May 1770; *Blackburn Mail*, 19 June 1793.
28 *Gore's Advertiser*, 23 February 1770.
29 *Adams Weekly Courant*, 23 May 1775.
30 *Worcester Journal*, 23 July 1752 – original emphasis.
31 Brooke, *Liverpool*, p. 84; *Blackburn Mail*, 2 October 1793.
32 *Blackburn Mail*, 2 October 1793; *Adams Weekly Courant*, 23 May 1775.
33 *Jopson's Coventry Mercury*, 15 June 1767.
34 These trade cards are reproduced in, respectively: Cox, *Complete Tradesman*, p. 91 and Walsh, 'Shop design', 163.
35 *Guide and Directory to the City and Suburbs of Worcester, for 1837*, Worcester: T. Stratford, 1837; JJC, Trade Cards 13 (47).
36 See Walsh, 'Advertising', pp. 83–4; Morgan, 'Beyond the boundary'.
37 *Piercy's Coventry Gazette*, 18 July 1778.
38 This polite tone is shared with the London advertisements: Walsh, 'Advertising', p. 83. For a more general discussion of the language of politeness, see Klein, 'Coffeehouse civility'.
39 See, for example, the advertisements of Thomas Ewbank (Chemist and Druggist) and J. Ratheram (clock and watchmaker) in the *Coventry Mercury*, 31 December 1787.
40 *Piercy's Coventry Gazette*, 3 December 1778, Vol. XII, no. 516; *Gore's Advertiser*, 13 April 1770.
41 See Cox, *Complete Tradesman*, pp. 127–39.
42 *Gore's Advertiser*, 20 April 1770, 27 April 1770.
43 *Blackburn Mail*, 11 September 1793, 2 October 1793.
44 See Andersson, G., 'A mirror of oneself: possessions and the manifestation of status among a local Swedish elite, 1650–1770', *Cultural and Social History*, 3, 2006, pp. 21–44 and, more generally, Bourdieu, *Distinction*.
45 *Jopson's Coventry Mercury*, 15 June 1767.
46 *Worcester Journal*, 14 July 1748; *Gore's Advertiser*, 15 June 1770, 14 December 1770.
47 JJC, Trade Cards 11 (98). See also the commentary on a similar image in Lambert, *A Nation of Shopkeepers*, p. 140.

48 BM, Banks Collection 68.143 (MY17 - WRDJ).
49 JJC, Trade Cards 11 (76).
50 Soja, *Postmodern Geographies*, notes that urbanisation is a summative metaphor for the spatialisation of modernity.
51 This depiction of Lefebvre's 'abstract' space is seen in Gregory, *Geographical Imaginations*, p. 401.
52 *Jopson's Coventry Mercury*, 31 December 1787. This mirrors the way goods are described in the probate inventory – see Chapter 5.
53 *Gore's Advertiser*, 26 January 1770.
54 Morgan, 'Producing consumer space', pp. 188–9; Stobart, 'County, town and country', pp. 185–6.
55 Lefebvre describes abstract space as result and container, as a representation of space and also a representational space, unlimited, an ensemble of signs, images and symbols and 'full of juxtapositions': Lefebvre, *Production of Space*, p. 288.
56 See Benjamin, *Arcades Project, passim*.
57 Quoted in Gregory, *Geographical Imaginations*, p. 401.

8 Conclusions

1 Lefebvre, *Production of Space*; Soja, *Thirdspace*; Soja, 'Towards a spatialised ontology'; Arnade *et al.*, 'Fertile spaces'; Glennie and Thrift, 'Consumption spaces'.
2 See Miller *et al.*, *Shopping, Place and Identity*; Trentmann, 'Beyond consumerism'; Shields, 'Spaces for consumption'; Goss, 'Magic of the mall'; Glennie and Thrift, 'Consumption spaces'.
3 Ellis, 'Regional and county centres', pp. 697–702.
4 Sweet, 'Topographies of politeness'; Stobart, Shopping streets'.
5 Sweet, *Writing Urban Histories*.
6 Barker, 'Smoke cities', pp. 189–90. See also, Stobart, 'Building an identity'; Gunn, *Public Culture*.
7 Borsay, *Urban Renaissance*, pp. 39–113.
8 Ogborn, *Spaces of Modernity*, pp. 75–104. See also Vickery, *Gentleman's Daughter*, pp. 6–7, 288–90.
9 Goffman, *Presentation of Self*; Glennie and Thrift, 'Consumption, shopping and gender'; Borsay, 'All the town's a stage'.
10 Glennie and Thrift, 'Consumption spaces', pp. 39–41; Miller *et al.*, *Shopping, Place and Identity*, pp. 14–17; Gregson and Rose, 'Performativities'.
11 See Ogborn, *Spaces of Modernity*, pp. 111–14; Rappaport, *Shopping for Pleasure*, pp. 48–73; Miller *et al.*, *Shopping, Place and Identity*, pp. 24–8; Lefebvre, *Production of Space*, pp. 33–4.
12 Goffman, *Presentation of Self*. See also Glennie and Thrift, 'Consumption spaces'; Shields, 'Spaces for consumption'.
13 Vickery, *Gentleman's Daughter*, pp. 6–7, 288–90; Klein, 'Coffeehouse civility'; Smith, *Consumption and Respectability*, pp. 139–87.
14 Walsh, 'Shop design'. See also Hann and Stobart, 'Sites of consumption'.
15 De Certeau, *Practice of Everyday Life*; Fraser, 'Rethinking the public sphere'.
16 Trentmann, 'Knowing consumers', pp. 2–6. See also Giddens, *Central Problems*, pp. 49–95.
17 Smith, *Consumption and Respectability*, pp. 13–24; Borsay, *Urban Renaissance*, pp. 225–308.
18 Berry, 'Creating polite space', pp. 125, 136; Estabrook, *Urbane and Rustic England*.
19 See Shields, 'Spaces for consumption'; Miller *et al.*, *Shopping, Place and Identity*; Gregson and Crewe, *Second-Hand Cultures*; and the various contributions to Trentmann, F. (ed.), *The Making of the Consumer: Knowledge, Power and Identity in the Modern World*, London: Berg, 2006.

20 Benjamin, *Arcades Project*.
21 Ogborn, *Spaces of Modernity*, pp. 22–8, 91–104; Borsay, 'Landed elite'; Borsay, 'Bath', p. 3.
22 See Crewe, 'Geographies of retailing'; Pred, *Lost Words*; Glennie and Thrift, 'Consumption spaces'.

Select bibliography

Manuscript sources

Bath Central Library

Letters of Mrs M. Sneyd.
Diary of a Tour by Three Students from Cambridge, 1725.

Birmingham Central Library, City Archives

MS 3375 Lee Crowder 387, Minute book of the Theatre Royal, Birmingham, 1773–1937.
MS 1342, A collection of miscellaneous bills, circulars and receipts, 1782–1923.

Bodleian Library, University of Oxford

John Johnson Collection: Trade Cards.

British Museum

Banks Collection of trade cards.

Cheshire and Chester Archives

Views of Chester Streets: Eastgate Row, Chester by Evans and Ducker, Chester, no date.
658/60, 'Watergate Street Row, Chester' etching published by T. Catherall, Chester, 1852.
A/B/1–5, Chester Assembly Books.
CR 63/2/133/17, Peter Broster's *Sketch Plan of Eastgate Street*, c.1754.
Probate records for Cheshire.

Chester City Library

MF 1/12, Plan of Chester: I. Stockdale, 1796.

Coventry City Record Office

BA/E/B/7/1–4, Theft examinations and inventory of stolen goods, 1750.
347-96, James Hewitt's Journal.
PA208/13, Lutterworth Woman's Diary, 1829–30.

House of Lords Record Office

6 William III cap. 1 [1694], 'An Act for Rebuilding the Town of Warwick…'.
10 and 11 William III cap. 23 [1699], 'Act … for the better apprehending of Felons that commit Burglary, Housebreaking or Robbery from Shops …'.
17 Geo III cap. 25 [1777], 'An Act for widening the several Streets, lanes, Alleyways and other public passages within the town of Wolverhampton'.
30 Geo III cap. 77 [1790], 'An Act for paving, Lighting and Cleansing the City of Coventry and its suburbs…'.

Lancashire Record Office

DDCs 26/40, John Jackson's Account for the Erection of the Market House at Prescot, 1808.
DDPr 28/1, Playbill for Blackburn New Theatre, 4 May 1787.
DDPr 34/1, Race bills, Lancaster, 1811–27.
DDX 211/21, Playbill, 1789.
DDX 274/13–17, Diary of John Dickenson II, 1776–82.
DDX 334/10–18, Letters from James, Lord Strange to Sir William Horton of Chadderton, esquire (1752–9).
DP 282/6A, Trade Card of R. Constantine of Bolton, early nineteenth century.
DP 282/14, Address and Code of Laws from a Committee of the Literary and Philosophical Society of Bolton, 18 October 1813.
DP 282/15, Programme of the Bolton Assemblies, 1816–17.
PMC/1/2, Preston White Book.
Probate records for Lancashire

Lichfield Joint Record Office

Probate records for the diocese of Lichfield.

Liverpool Record Office

027 LYC 1/1/1, Minute Book of the General Committee of the Liverpool Library, 1769–96.
614 INF/5/1, Annual Report and Subscription Books of the Liverpool Infirmary, 1748–80.
920 NIC 3/4/9, Letter to Samuel Nicholson from his brother, James Nicholson, 19 March 1748.
920 PLU PT 9, Diary and Account Books of John Plumbe of Wavertree Hall, 1697–1757.

The National Archives

E 182, Exchequer Tax Accounts, Land and Assessed Taxes: Shop Tax.
TNA PROB3 32/108, Inventory of John Fairfax, mercer of Warwick, 1733.

Shakespeare Birthplace Trust Record Office

DR 18/5, Leigh Estate Vouchers and Receipts Ledger.

Staffordshire Record Office

D1798 HM 24/3, Domestic Accounts of Ann Sneyd, 1765–82.
D1798 HM 27/4, Account Book of Lewis Dickenson of Stafford, apothecary, 1737–57.
D1798 HM 28/10, Customers Account Book of John Webb of Stafford, mercer.
D1798 HM 29/2–5, Day Books and Account Books of Thomas Dickenson of Worcester, grocer, 1740–52.
D1798 HM 37/36, Papers of Mrs Elizabeth Sneyd of Stafford, 1713–52.
D (W) 1788/V/108–11, Sales Ledgers of Fletcher and Fenton of Newcastle-under-Lyme, 1768–83.

Stoke-on-Trent City Archives

D4842/14/4/7, bundle of John Wood's bills and receipts.

Warwickshire County Record Office

B. WAR at C.711 Tar (p). 'Fire damage and urban renewal in the late seventeenth and eighteenth centuries', paper by M. Turner.
CR136, Newdigate MSS.
CR 351/220, The Upper Part of the New Town, Leamington Spa, c.1826.
CR439, Thomas Burbidge's Shop Book.
CR1368, Morduant Family Letters.
CR 1563/299, Building Land in the New Town at Leamington Priors, 1822.
CR1596, Box 84/16 and Box 90/7/7, Briefs regarding cases for the Warwick Assizes.
CR1596, Box 9/8/9 and Box 9/8/10, Partnership deeds for shopkeepers.
Probate records for the town of Warwick.

Worcestershire Record Office

899:93 BA 1558/19, An Account of the Worcester Infirmary and List of Annual Subscribers, 1753–54.
705:781 B.A. 7537/1, Mountfort Collection.
Probate records for the diocese of Worcester.

Printed primary sources

Adams Weekly Courant.
Addy, J. (ed.), 'The diary of Henry Prescott, Vol. I', *Records Society of Lancashire and Cheshire*, 127, 1987.
Addy, J. and McNiven, P. (eds), 'The diary of Henry Prescott, Vol. II', *Records Society of Lancashire and Cheshire*, 132, 1994.
Aikin, J., *A Description of the Country from Thirty to Forty Miles round Manchester*, London: J. Stockdale, 1795.
Aris's Birmingham Gazette.
Aston, J., *The Manchester Guide*, Manchester: J. Aston, 1804.
Baines, E., *History, Directory and Gazetteer of the County Palatine of Lancaster*, 2 volumes, 1824–5, Newton Abbot: David and Charles, 1968.
Barfoot, P. and Wilkes, J., *Universal British Directory*, 5 volumes, London: Barfoot and Wilkes, 1793–8.
Bentley, J., *History, Gazetteer, Directory and Statistics of Worcestershire*, Worcester: Bull and Turner, 1841.
—— *Bentley's History and Guide to Dudley, Dudley Castle, and the Castle Hill*, Birmingham, 1841.
Blackburn Mail.
Blome, R., *Britannia or a Geographical Description of the Kingdoms of England, Scotland, and Ireland*, London: T. Rycroft, 1673.
Broster, P., *The Chester Guide*, Chester: P. Broster, 1782.
Burney, F., *Camilla, or a Picture of Youth*, 1796; New York: Oxford University Press, 1983.
Butterworth, J., *An Historical and Descriptive Account of the Town and Parochial Chapelry of Oldham in the County of Lancaster*, Oldham, 1817.
Chambers, J., *A General History of Worcester*, Worcester, 1819.
Chester Courant.
Copper, A.A., Third Earl of Shaftesbury, *Characteristics of Men, Manners, Opinions, Times*, ed. Lawrence Klein, Cambridge: Cambridge University Press, 1999.
Corry, J., *The History of Macclesfield*, London: Ferguson, 1817.
The Coventry Guide, Coventry: Merridew and Son, 1824.
Cowdroy, W., *The Directory and Guide for the City and County of Chester*, Chester, 1784.
Defoe, D., *The Compleat English Gentleman*, 1728–9; London: D. Nutt, 1890.
—— *Moll Flanders*, 1722, London: Oxford University Press, 1971.
—— *A Tour through the Whole Island of Great Britain*, 1724–26, Harmondsworth: Penguin, 1971.
—— *The Complete English Tradesman*, 1726, Stroud: Sutton, 1987.
Derrick, S., *Letters Written from Leverpoole, Chester … Bath*, 2 volumes, London, 1767.
Dyke, E. (ed.), 'Chester's earliest directories', *Journal of the Chester Archaeological Society*, XXXVII, 1949.
Enfield, W., *An Essay towards the History of Leverpool*, London: Johnson, 1773.
Fielding, H., *The History of the Adventures of Joseph Andrews and his Friend Mr Abraham Adams*, 1742, London: Methuen, 1987.
Fiennes, C., *The Journeys of Celia Fiennes*, ed. C. Morris, London: Cresset Press, 1947.
Fox, L., 'Coventry Constables Presentments 1629–1742', *Dugdale Society Publications*, XXXV, 1986.
Gay, J., *Trivia: Or the Art of Walking the Street of London*, London: B. Lintott, 1716.
Gentleman's Magazine.
Gore's Liverpool Advertiser.

232 *Select bibliography*

Green, V., *Survey of the City of Worcester*, Worcester, 1764.
The Guild Merchant of Preston, with an Extract of the Original Charter, Manchester: T. Anderton, 1762.
Hanshall, J., *The Stranger in Chester*, Chester: J. Fletcher, 1816.
—— *The History of the County Palatine of Chester*, Chester, 1817.
Hemingway, J., *History of the City of Chester*, 2 volumes, Chester, 1831.
Historical Manuscripts Commission, *Dartmouth MSS*, iii.
—— *Hastings MSS*, iii.
Hughes, T., *Ancient Chester: A Series of Illustrations of the Streets of this Old City*, London, 1880.
Hume, D., *Essays and Treatises on Several Subjects*, London: A. Millar 1758.
Hutton, W., *An History of Birmingham to the End of the Year 1780*, Birmingham: Pearson and Rollason, 1781.
—— *A Journey from Birmingham to London*, Birmingham, 1785.
—— *The History of Derby*, London: J. Nichols, 1791.
Ingamells, J., *Directory of Newcastle-under-Lyme*, Newcastle-under-Lyme: D. Dilworth, 1871.
Keating's Stratford and Warwick Mercury.
Kuerdon, R., *A Brief Description of the Burrough and Town of Preston*, Preston, 1818.
Lowe, R., *The Diary of Roger Lowe of Ashton in Makerfield*, ed. W. Sasche, London: Longmans, Green & Co., 1938.
Macky, J., *A Journey through England and Scotland*, 3 volumes, London: J. Pemberton, 1722–3.
Manchester Mercury.
Mannex & Co., *History, Topography and Directory of Mid-Lancashire*, Preston, 1854.
Miège, *The New State of England*, 3rd edition, London, 1699.
Montagu, M. (ed.), *The Letters of Elizabeth Montagu*, London, 1810.
Moss, W., *The Liverpool Guide*, Liverpool, 1796.
Nash, T.R., *Collections for the History of Worcestershire*, London: Payne, 1781–2.
Ormerod, G., *The History of the County Palatine and City of Chester*, London, 1819.
Palmer, C.F., *The History of the Town and Castle of Tamworth*, Tamworth: J. Thompson, 1845.
Parkinson, R. (ed.), 'The private journal and literary remains of John Byrom', Vol. I, *Chetham Society*, 32 and 35, 1854, 1855.
Pearce, T., *The History and Directory of Walsall*, Birmingham: Thomson and Wrightson, 1813.
Petrie, A., *The Rules of Good Deportment* (1720), in *The Works of Adam Petrie*, Edinburgh: Scottish Literary Club, 1877.
Picton, J., *Memorials of Liverpool*, 2 volumes, London: Longmans Green, 1873.
—— *City of Liverpool: Municipal Archives and Records, 1700–1835*, Liverpool: Walmsley, 1886.
Piercy's Coventry Gazette.
Pigot & Co., *National Commercial Directory, Comprising a Classification of … in the Counties of Derby, Hereford, Leicester…*, London: Pigot & Co., 1835.
Pigott, I.M.B., *History of the City of Chester*, Chester, 1815.
Platt, J., *The History and Antiquities of Nantwich*, London: Longman *et al.*, 1818.
Prescott's Manchester Journal.
Price, J., *The Worcester Guide*, Worcester: W. Smart, 1799.
'Proceedings in Quarter Sessions 1690–1696', *Warwick County Records*, Vol. IX, 1964.
Pye, C., *A Description of Modern Birmingham*, Birmingham, 1818.
Reader, W., *The History and Antiquities of the City of Coventry*, Coventry, 1810.
Roberts, H., *The Chester Guide*, Chester, 1851.
Ross, A. (ed.), *Selections from The Tatler and The Spectator*, Harmondsworth: Penguin, 1982.
Rutherford, M., *Catherine Furze*, London: Unwin, no date.

—— *Revolution in Tanner's Lane*, 1887, Oxford: Oxford University Press, 1936.
Schofield's Middlewich Journal.
Schopenhauer, J., *A Lady Travels: Journeys in England and Scotland from the Diaries of Johanna Schopenhauer*, London: Routledge, 1988.
Seacombe, J., *The Chester Guide*, Chester, 1836.
Smart, J., *Directory of Wolverhampton*, Wolverhampton, 1827.
Smith, W., *A New and Compendious History of the County of Warwick*, Birmingham, 1830.
—— *Picture of Birmingham*, Birmingham: J. Drake, 1831.
Smollett, T., *The Expedition of Humphry Clinker*, 1771, Oxford: Oxford University Press, 1966.
Stout, W., *Autobiography of William Stout of Lancaster, 1665–1752*, Manchester: Manchester University Press, 1967.
Swinney's Birmingham and Stafford Chronicle.
Toldervy, W., *England and Wales Described in a Series of Letters*, London, 1762.
Towle, M., *The Young Gentleman and Lady's Private Tutor*, Oxford, 1771.
Troughton, T., *The History of Liverpool*, Liverpool: W. Robinson, 1810.
Trusler, J., *The Way to be Rich and Respectable*, London, 1766.
Tunbridge and Bath Miscellany, London, 1714.
Tyrer, F., 'The great diurnal of Nicholas Blundell of Little Crosby, Lancashire', *Record Society of Lancashire and Cheshire*, 3 volumes, 1968–72.
Wallace, J., *A General and Descriptive History of the Ancient and Present State of the Town of Liverpool*, Liverpool: R. Phillips, 1795.
Warwick Advertiser.
Weekly Register.
West, W., *The History, Topography and Directory of Warwickshire*, Birmingham: R. Wrightson, 1830.
Whellan & Co., *A New Alphabetical and Classified Directory of Manchester and Salford*, Manchester: Whellan & Co., 1853.
Whitbread, H. (ed.), *I Know My Own Heart: The Diaries of Anne Lister, 1791–1840*, London: Virago, 1988.
White, F., *History, Gazetteer and Directory of Staffordshire*, Sheffield: White, F., 1834.
—— *History, Gazetteer and Directory of Cheshire*, Sheffield: White, F., 1860.
—— *History, Gazetteer and Directory of Warwickshire*, Sheffield: White, F., 1874.
Wilkinson, J. (ed.), 'The letters of Thomas Langton, flax merchant of Kirkham, 1771–1788', *Chetham Society*, 3rd series, 38, 1994.
Wood, J., A *Description of Bath*, 2nd edition, London: W. Bathoe and T. Lownds, 1765.
The Worcester Directory, Worcester: John Grundy, 1788.
Worcester Journal, later *Berrow's Worcester Journal*.

Secondary sources

Allan, D., 'Eighteenth-century private subscription libraries and provincial urban culture: the Amicable Society of Lancaster, 1769–*c*.1820', *Library History*, 17, 2001, pp. 57–76.
Alston, R., 'Library History Database', www.r-alston.co.uk (accessed 28/05/04).
Arnade, P., Howell, M. and Simons, W., 'Fertile spaces: the productivity of urban space in Northern Europe', *Journal of Interdisciplinary History*, 32, 2002, pp. 515–48.
Baker, J., 'Theatre, law and society in the provinces: the case of Sarah Baker', *Cultural and Social History*, 1, 2004, pp. 159–78.

Barker, H., '"Smoke cities": northern industrial towns in late Georgian England', *Urban History*, 31, 2004, pp. 175–90.
Barker, T.C. and Harris, J.R., *A Merseyside Town in the Industrial Revolution: St Helens 1750–1900*, Liverpool: Liverpool University Press, 1954.
Barton, B., *History of the Borough of Bury and Neighbourhood*, Bury, 1874.
Baudrillard, J., *Selected Writings*, Oxford: Blackwell, 1988.
Bearman, R., 'Captain James Saunders of Stratford upon Avon: a local antiquary', *Dugdale Society Occasional Papers*, 33, 1990.
Beckett, J. and Smith, C., 'Urban Renaissance and consumer revolution in Nottingham 1688–1750', *Urban History*, 27, 2000, pp. 31–50.
Benjamin, W., *The Arcades Project*, Cambridge, MA: Harvard University Press, 1999.
Berg, M., 'Women's consumption and the industrial classes of eighteenth-century England', *Journal of Social History*, 30 1996, pp. 415–34.
—— 'New commodities, luxuries and their consumers in eighteenth-century England', in M. Berg and H. Clifford (eds), *Consumers and Luxury: Consumer Culture in Europe, 1650–1850*, Manchester: Manchester University Press, 1999, pp. 63–87.
—— *Luxury and Pleasure in Eighteenth-Century Britain*, Oxford: Oxford University Press, 2005.
Berg, M. and Clifford, H., 'Commerce and the commodity: graphic display and selling new consumer goods in eighteenth-century England', in M. North and D. Ormrod (eds), *Art Markets in Europe, 1400–1800*, Aldershot: Ashgate, 1998, pp.187–200.
Berry, H., 'Polite consumption: shopping in eighteenth-century England', *Transactions of the Royal Historical Society*, 12, 2002, pp. 375–94.
—— 'Creating polite space: the organisation and social functions of the Newcastle assembly rooms', in H. Berry and J. Gregory (eds), *Creating and Consuming Culture in North-East England, 1660–1830*, Aldershot: Ashgate, 2004, pp. 120–40.
—— 'Prudent luxury: the Metropolitan tastes of Judith Baker, Durham gentlewoman', in P. Lane and R. Sweet (eds), *Out of Town: Women and Urban Life in Eighteenth-Century Britain*, Aldershot: Ashgate, 2005, pp. 130–54.
Bianchi, M., 'In the name of the tulip. Why speculation?', in M. Berg and H. Clifford (eds), *Consumers and Luxury: Consumer Culture in Europe, 1650–1850*, Manchester: Manchester University Press, 1999, pp. 85–102.
Blondé, B., Stabel, P., Stobart, J. and Van Damme, I., 'Retail circuits and practices', in B. Blondé, P. Stabel, J. Stobart and I. Van Damme (eds), *Buyers and Sellers*, Antwerp: Brepols, 2006, pp. 1–29.
Borsay, P., 'All the town's a stage: urban ritual and ceremony, 1660–1800', in P. Clark (ed.), *The Transformation of English Provincial Towns, 1600–1800*, London: Hutchinson, 1984, pp. 228–58.
—— *The English Urban Renaissance: Culture and Society in the Provincial Town, 1660–1770*, Oxford: Oxford University Press, 1989.
—— 'The London connection: cultural diffusion and the eighteenth-century provincial town', *London Journal*, 19, 1994, pp. 21–35.
—— 'Bath an Enlightenment City?', in P. Borsay, G. Hirschfelder and R.-E. Mohrmann (eds), *New Directions in Urban History*, Münster: Waxmann, 2000, pp. 3–17.
—— 'A county town in transition: the Great Fire of Warwick, 1694', in P. Borsay and L. Proudfoot (eds), *Provincial Towns in Early Modern England and Ireland*, Oxford: Oxford University Press, 2002, pp. 151–70.
—— 'The landed elite and provincial towns in Britain 1660–1800', *The Georgian Group Journal*, XIII, 2003, pp. 281–94.

Bourdieu, P., *Distinction: A Social Critique of the Judgement of Taste*, London: Routledge, 1986.
Braudel, F., *Capitalism and Material Life, 1400–1800*, London: Fontana, 1974.
Brewer, J., *The Pleasures of the Imagination*, Chicago, IL: University of Chicago Press, 1997.
—— 'The error of our ways: historians and the birth of consumer society', Cultures of Consumption programme, Working Paper 12, 2003.
Brooke, R., *Liverpool As It Was: 1775 to 1800*, Liverpool, 1853.
Brooks, A., and Haworth, B., *Boomtown Manchester: 1800–1850. The Portico Connection*, Manchester: The Portico Library, 1993.
Brown, A., *The Rows of Chester*, London: English Heritage, 1999.
Butler, J., *Gender Trouble. Feminism and the Subversion of Identity*, London: Routledge, 2000.
Campbell, C., *The Romantic Ethic and the Spirit of Modern Consumerism*, Oxford: Oxford University Press, 1987.
—— 'Understanding traditional and modern patterns of consumption in eighteenth-century England: a character-action approach', in J. Brewer and R. Porter (eds), *Consumption and the World of Goods*, London: Routledge, 1993, pp. 40–57.
Carter, P., *Men and the Emergence of Polite Society, Britain 1660–1800*, Harlow: Longman, 2002.
Cave, L., *Royal Leamington Spa: Its History and Development*, Chichester: Phillimore, 1988.
Chalklin, C., 'Capital expenditure on building for cultural purposes in provincial England, 1730–1830', *Business History*, 22, 1980, pp. 51–70.
Chandler, G. and Hannah, I.C., *Dudley as it was and is Today*, London: Batsford, 1949.
Christaller, W., *Central Places in Southern Germany*, Englewood Cliffs, NJ: Prentice Hall, 1966.
Clark, P., *British Clubs and Societies, 1580–1800*, Oxford: Oxford University Press, 2000.
Cooper M., 'The Worcester book trade in the eighteenth century', *Worcester Historical Society Occasional Publications*, 8, 1997, pp. 1–48.
—— *'A More Beautiful City': Robert Hooke and the Rebuilding of London after the Great Fire*, Stroud: Sutton, 2003.
Corfield, P.J., 'Walking the city streets: the urban odyssey in eighteenth-century England', *Journal of Urban History*, 16, 1990, pp. 132–74.
Corrigan, P., *The Sociology of Consumption*, London: Sage, 1997.
Covins, F., *The Arboretum Story*, Worcester: Arboretum Residents' Association, 1989.
Cox, N., *The Complete Tradesman: A Study of Retailing, 1550–1820*, Aldershot: Ashgate, 2000.
Crang, M. and Thrift, N. (eds), *Thinking Space*, London: Routledge, 2000.
Crewe, L., 'Progress report: geographies of retailing and consumption', *Progress in Human Geography*, 24, 2000, pp. 275–90.
Cunningham, J., *Theatre Royal: The History of the Theatre Royal in Birmingham*, Oxford: Oxford University Press, 1950.
Dalziel, N., 'Trade and transition, 1690–1815', in A. White (ed.), *A History of Lancaster*, Edinburgh: Edinburgh University Press, 2001, pp. 117–73.
Davis, D., *A History of Shopping*, London: Routledge and Kegan Paul, 1966.
De Certeau, M., *The Practice of Everyday Life*, reprinted in G. Bridge and S. Watson (eds), *The City Reader*, Oxford: Blackwell, 2002, pp. 383–92.
De Vries, J., 'Between purchasing power and the world of goods', in J. Brewer and R. Porter (eds), *Consumption and the World of Goods*, London: Routledge, 1993, pp.85–132.
Dear, M., 'The production of space', *Urban Geography*, 14, 1993, pp. 489–94.
Dent, R.K., *Old and New Birmingham: A History of the Town and Its People*, Birmingham: Houghton and Hammond, 1880.
Dolan, B., *Josiah Wedgwood: Entrepreneur to the Enlightenment*, London: HarperCollins, 2004.

Edmonds, J., 'Events at the Theatre Royal Chester, 1807–1810', *Cheshire History*, 38, 1998–9, pp. 55–70.
Elbourne, R., *Music and Tradition in Early Industrial Lancashire*, Woodbridge: Brewer, 1980.
Elliot, P., 'Towards a geography of English scientific culture: provincial town identity and literary and philosophical culture in the English county town, 1750–1850', *Urban History*, 32, 2005, pp. 391–412.
Ellis, J., 'Regional and county centres, 1700–1840', in P. Clark (ed.), *The Cambridge Urban History of Britain, Volume II, 1540–1840*, Cambridge: Cambridge University Press, 2000, pp. 673–704.
—— *The Georgian Town*, Basingstoke: Palgrave, 2001.
—— '"For the honour of the town": comparison, competition and civic identity in eighteenth-century England', *Urban History*, 30, 2003, pp. 325–37.
Estabrook, C., *Urbane and Rustic England: Cultural Ties and Social Spheres in the Provinces, 1660–1780*, Manchester: Manchester University Press, 1998.
Everitt, A., 'Country, county and town: patterns of regional evolution in England', *Transactions, Royal Historical Society*, 5th series, 29, 1979, pp. 79–108.
Falkus, M., 'Lighting in the dark ages of English economic history: town streets before the industrial revolution', in D.C. Coleman and A.H. John (eds), *Trade and Economy in Pre-Industrial England*, London: Weidenfeld and Nicolson, 1976, pp. 248–73.
Farr, M. (ed.), 'The Great Fire of Warwick 1694', *Dugdale Society Publications*, XXXVI, 1992.
Fergus, J., 'Eighteenth-century readers in provincial England: the customers of Samuel Clay's circulating library and workshop at Warwick, 1770–72', *Papers of the Bibliographical Society of America*, 78, 1984, pp. 155–213.
Fine, B. and Leopold, E., *The World of Consumption*, London: Routledge, 1993.
Finn, M., 'Men's things: masculine possession in the consumer revolution', *Social History*, 25, 2000, pp. 133–55.
Fraser, N., 'Rethinking the public sphere: a contribution to the critique of actually existing democracy', in C. Calhoun (ed.), *Habermas and the Public Sphere*, Cambridge, MA: MIT Press, 1992, pp. 109–42.
Giddens, A., *Central Problems in Social Theory: Action, Structure and Contradiction in Social Analysis*, London: Macmillan, 1979.
—— *The Constitution of Society*, Cambridge: Polity Press, 1984.
—— 'Structuralism, post-structuralism and the production of culture', in A. Giddens and J. Turner (eds), *Social Theory Today*, Cambridge: Polity Press, 1987, pp. 195–223.
Girouard, M., *The English Town*, New Haven, CT: Yale University Press, 1990.
Glennie, P. and Thrift, N.J., 'Consumers, identities and consumption spaces in early-modern England', *Environment and Planning A*, 28, 1996, pp. 25–45.
—— 'Consumption, shopping and gender', in N. Wrigley and M. Lowe (eds), *Retailing, Consumption and Capital: Towards the New Retail Geography*, Harlow: Longman, 1996, pp. 221–37.
Goffman, E., *The Presentation of Self in Everyday Life*, New York: Doubleday, 1956.
Goss, J., 'The "magic of the mall": an analysis of form, function and meaning in the contemporary retail built environment', *Annals of the Association of American Geographers*, 83, 1993, pp. 18–47.
Greenslade, M.W. (ed.), *Victoria County History of Staffordshire*, Vol. 7, London: Oxford University Press, 1996.
Gregory, D., *Geographical Imaginations*, Oxford: Blackwell, 1994.
Gregson, N. and Crewe, L., *Second-Hand Cultures*, London: Berg, 2003.

Gregson, N. and Rose, G., 'Taking Butler elsewhere: performativities, spatialities and subjectivities', *Environment and Planning D: Society and Space*, 18, 2000, pp. 433–52.
Griffin, E., *England's Revelry. A History of Popular Sports and Pastimes 1660–1830*, Oxford: Oxford University Press, 2005.
Gunn, S., *The Public Culture of the Victorian Middle Class*, Manchester: Manchester University Press, 2000.
Gutkind, E.A., *Urban Development in Western Europe: The Netherlands and Great Britain*, New York: The Free Press, 1971.
Gwilliam, B., *Old Worcester: People and Places*, Bromsgrove: Halfshire Books, 1993.
Habermas, J., *The Structural Transformation of the Public Sphere*, Cambridge, MA: MIT Press, 1989.
Hägerstrand, T., 'What about people in Regional Science?', *Papers and Proceedings of the Regional Science Association*, 24, 1970, pp. 7–21.
Hall, J., *A History of the Town and Parish of Nantwich*, Nantwich: printed for the author, 1883.
Hann, A., 'Industrialisation and the service economy', in J. Stobart and N. Raven (eds), *Towns, Regions and Industries*, Manchester: Manchester University Press, 2005, pp. 42–61.
Hann, A. and Stobart, J., 'Sites of consumption: the display of goods in provincial shops in eighteenth century England', *Cultural and Social History*, 2, 2005, pp. 165–87.
Hardwick, C., *History of the Borough of Preston and its Environs in the County of Lancaster*, Preston: Worthington, 1857.
Harrison, D., *The History of Colne*, Barrowford: Pendle Heritage Centre, 1988.
Hembry, P., *British Spas from 1815 to the Present: A Social History*, London: Athlone Press, 1997.
Herson, J., 'Victorian Chester: a city of change and ambiguity', in R. Swift (ed.), *Victorian Chester*, Liverpool: Liverpool University Press, 1996, pp. 13–52.
Hewitson, A., *History of Preston in the County of Lancaster*, Preston: Chronicle Office, 1883.
Hill, J. and Dent, R., *Memorials of the Old Square*, Birmingham, 1897.
Hill, K., '"Thoroughly imbued with the spirit of ancient Greece": symbolism and space in Victorian civic culture', in A. Kidd and D. Nicholls (eds), *Gender, Civic Culture and Consumerism: Middle Class Identity in Britain 1800–1940*, Manchester: Manchester University Press, 1999, pp. 99–111.
Hodgkinson, J.L. and Pogson, R., *The Early Manchester Theatre*, London: A. Blond, 1960.
Hunt, M., *A Tale of Two Squares: St. John's and St. James's*, on http://www.localhistory.scit.wlv.ac.uk/interesting/squares/whhs_twosquares.htm (accessed 30/07/04).
Jackson, P., 'Domesticating the street: the contested spaces of the high street and the mall', in N.R. Fyfe (ed.), *Images of the Street: Planning, Identity and Control in Public Space*, London: Routledge, 1998, pp. 176–91.
Jefferys, J.B., *Retailing in Britain 1850–1950*, Cambridge: Cambridge University Press, 1954.
Johns, A., *The Nature of the Book*, Chicago, IL: University of Chicago Press, 1998.
Kennett, A. (ed.), *Chester and the River Dee: An Illustrated History of Chester and its Port*, Chester: Chester City Council, 1982.
—— *Georgian Chester*, Chester: Chester City Record Office, 1987.
Kerr, D., 'The production of space', *Urban Studies*, 29, 1992, pp. 1020–3.
Kilmartin, J., 'Popular rejoicing and public ritual', unpublished PhD thesis, Warwick University, 1987.

238 Select bibliography

Klein, L., 'Politeness for plebes: consumption and social identity in early eighteenth-century England', in J. Brewer and A. Bermingham (eds), *The Culture of Consumption: Image, Object, Text*, London: Routledge, 1995, pp. 362–82.

—— 'Coffeehouse civility, 1660–1714: an aspect of post-courtly culture in England', *Huntington Library Quarterly*, 59, 1997, pp. 30–51.

—— 'The polite town: shifting possibilities of urbanness, 1660–1714', in T. Hitchcock and H. Shore (eds), *The Streets of London: From the Great Fire to the Great Stink*, London: Rivers Oram Press, 2003, pp. 27–39.

Kowleski-Wallace, E., *Consuming Subjects: Women, Shopping and Business in the Eighteenth Century*, New York: Columbia University Press, 1997.

Lancaster, J.C., 'Coventry', in M.D. Lobel (ed.), *The Atlas of Historic Towns*, London: Scolar Press, 1975.

Lane, J., 'Worcester infirmary in the eighteenth century', *Worcester Historical Society Occasional Publications*, 6, 1992, pp. 10–26.

Langford, P., *Polite and Commercial People: England 1727–1783*, Oxford: Oxford University Press, 1989.

Lefebvre, H., *The Production of Space*, Oxford: Blackwell, 1991.

Lemire, B., *Fashion's Favourite: The Cotton Trade and the Consumer in Britain, 1660–1800*, Oxford: Oxford University Press, 1991.

Lepetit, B., *The Pre-industrial Urban System: France, 1740–1840*, Cambridge: Cambridge University Press, 1994.

Lewis, C.P. and Thacker, A.T. (eds), *Victoria County History of Chester*, Vol. 5, Part 1, London: Boydell and Brewer, 2003.

McCormack, M., *The Independent Man*, Manchester: Manchester University Press, 2005.

McCracken, G., *Culture and Consumption: New Approaches to the Symbolic Character of Consumer Goods and Activities*, Bloomington, IN: Indiana University Press, 1988.

McInnes, A., 'The emergence of a leisure town: Shrewsbury, 1660–1760', *Past and Present*, 120, 1988, pp. 53–87.

McKendrick, N., 'The consumer revolution of eighteenth-century England', in N. McKendrick, J. Brewer and J.H. Plumb (eds), *The Birth of a Consumer Society*, London: Hutchinson, 1982, pp. 9–33.

—— 'Josiah Wedgwood and the commercialisation of the Potteries', in N. McKendrick, J. Brewer and J.H. Plumb (eds), *The Birth of a Consumer Society*, London: Hutchinson, 1982, pp. 100–45.

—— 'George Packwood and the commercialisation of shaving: the art of eighteenth century advertising', in N. McKendrick, J. Brewer and J.H. Plumb (eds), *The Birth of a Consumer Society*, London: Hutchinson, 1982, pp. 146–96.

Melville, J.D., 'The use and organisation of domestic space in late seventeenth century London', unpublished PhD thesis, Cambridge University, 1999.

Merrifield, A., 'Henri Lefebvre: a socialist in space', in M. Crang and N. Thrift (eds), *Thinking Space*, London: Routledge, 2000, pp. 167–82.

Miller, D., *Material Culture and Mass Consumption*, Oxford: Blackwell, 1987.

—— 'Consumption as the vanguard of history, a polemic by way of introduction', in D. Miller (ed.), *Acknowledging Consumption: A Review of New Studies*, London: Routledge, 1995, pp. 1–57.

—— *A Theory of Shopping*, Cambridge: Polity Press, 1998.

Miller, D., Jackson, P., Thrift, N., Holbrook, B. and Rowlands, M., *Shopping, Place and Identity*, London: Routledge, 1998.

Mitchell, S.I., 'The development of urban retailing 1700–1815', in P. Clark (ed.), *The Transformation of English Provincial Towns 1600–1800*, London: Hutchinson, 1984, pp. 259–83.

Moore, E., *Liverpool in King Charles the Second's Time*, Liverpool: Henry Young and Sons, 1899.

Morgan, V., 'Producing consumer space in eighteenth-century England: shops, shopping and the provincial town', unpublished PhD thesis, Coventry University, 2003.

Mui, H.-C. and Mui, L., *Shops and Shopkeeping in Eighteenth-Century England*, London: Routledge, 1989.

Muir, R., *A History of Liverpool*, Liverpool: University Press of Liverpool, 1907.

Muldrew, C., *The Economy of Obligation: The Culture of Credit and Social Relations in Early-Modern England*, Basingstoke: Macmillan, 1998.

Nead, L., 'Mapping the self: gender, space and modernity in mid-Victorian London', *Environment and Planning A*, 29, 1997, pp. 659–72.

Nenadic, S., 'Middle-rank consumers and domestic culture in Edinburgh and Glasgow 1720–1840', *Past and Present*, 145, 1994, pp. 122–56.

—— 'Print collecting and popular culture in eighteen-century Scotland', *History*, 82, 1997, pp. 203–22.

Ogborn, M., *Spaces of Modernity: London's Geographies 1680–1780*, New York: Guildford Press, 1998.

Olleson, P., 'The Tamworth Music Festival of 1809', *Staffordshire Studies*, 5, 1993, pp. 81–106.

Orton, G., *Maps of Wolverhampton*, Wolverhampton: Wolverhampton Public Libraries, 1976.

Overton, M., Whittle, J., Dean, D. and Hann, A., *Production and Consumption in English Households, 1600–1750*, London: Routledge, 2004.

Parish, C., *History of the Birmingham Library*, London: Library Association, 1966.

Peck, P., *Consuming Splendor: Society and Culture in Seventeenth-Century England*, Cambridge: Cambridge University Press, 2005.

Pemberton, T.E., *The Theatre Royal Birmingham 1774 to 1901*, Birmingham, 1901.

Pennell, S., 'Consumption and consumerism in early modern England', *The Historical Journal*, 42, 1999, pp. 549–64.

Plumb, J., 'The commercialization of leisure in eighteenth-century England', in N. McKendrick, J. Brewer and R. Porter (eds), *The Birth of a Consumer Society*, London: Hutchinson, 1982, pp. 266–88.

Poole, B., *Coventry: Its History and Antiquities*, London, 1870.

Postles, D., 'The market place as space in early modern England', *Social History*, 29, 2004, pp. 41–58.

Pred, A., *Lost Words and Lost Worlds: Modernity and the Language of Everyday Life in Late Nineteenth-Century Stockholm*, Cambridge: Cambridge University Press, 1990.

—— 'The choreography of existence: comments on Hägerstrand's Time-Geography and its usefulness', in J. Agnew, D. Livingstone and A. Rogers (eds), *Human Geography: An Essential Anthology*, Oxford: Blackwell, 1996, pp. 636–49.

Rappaport, E., *Shopping for Pleasure: Women in the Making of London's West End*, Princeton, NJ: Princeton University Press, 2000.

Raven, N. and Stobart, J., 'Networks and hinterlands: transport in the Midlands', in J. Stobart and N. Raven (eds), *Towns, Regions and Industries*, Manchester: Manchester University Press, 2005, pp. 80–101.

Reed, M., 'The cultural role of small towns in England 1600–1800', in P. Clark (ed), *Small Towns in Early Modern Europe*, Cambridge: Cambridge University Press, 1995, pp. 121–47.

Reid, D., 'Beasts and brutes: popular blood sports c.1780–1860', in R. Holt (ed.), *Sport and the Working Class in Modern Britain*, Manchester: Manchester University Press, 1990, pp. 12–28.

Rendell, J., 'West-End rambling: gender and architectural space in London 1800–1830', *Leisure Studies*, 17, 1998, pp. 108–22.

Savage, M., 'Walter Benjamin's urban thought', in M. Crang and N. Thrift (eds), *Thinking Space*, London: Routledge, 2000, pp. 33–53.

Schmiechen, J. and Carls, K., *The British Market Hall: A Social and Architectural History*, New Haven, CT: Yale University Press, 1999.

Schwarz, L., 'On the margins of industrialisation: Lichfield', in J. Stobart and N. Raven (eds), *Towns, Regions and Industries*, Manchester: Manchester University Press, 2005, pp. 176–88.

Scola, R., *Feeding the Victorian City: The Food Supply of Manchester 1770–1870*, Manchester: Manchester University Press, 1992.

Segrave, K., *Shoplifting: A Social History*, London: Mcfarland & Co., 2001.

Shammas, C., *The Pre-industrial Consumer in England and America*, Oxford: Oxford University Press, 1990.

Shaw, G.T., *History of the Athenaeum, Liverpool, 1798–1898*, Liverpool: Committee of the Athenaeum, 1898.

Shields, R., 'Spaces for the subject of consumption', in R. Shields (ed.), *Lifestyle Shopping: The Subject of Consumption*, London: Routledge, 1992, pp. 1–20.

Simmel, G., *On Individuality and Social Forms*, Chicago, IL: University of Chicago Press, 1971.

Smith, J., *The Story of Music in Birmingham*, Birmingham: Cornish Brothers Ltd, 1945.

Smith, W.A., *The Town Commissioners in Wolverhampton, 1777–1848*, unpublished manuscript.

Smith, W.C., *Consumption and the Making of Respectability, 1600–1800*, London: Routledge, 2002.

Soja, E., *Postmodern Geographies: The Reassertion of Space in Critical Social Theory*, London: Verso, 1989.

—— 'Reassertions: Towards a Spatialised Ontology', J. Agnew, D. Livingstone and A. Rogers (eds), *Human Geography: An Essential Anthology*, Oxford: Blackwell, 1996.

—— *Thirdspace*, Oxford, Blackwell, 1996.

Sombart, W., *Luxury and Capitalism*, 1922, Michigan: University of Michigan Press, 1967.

Stevens, W. (ed.), *Victoria County History of Warwickshire*, Vol. 8, Oxford: Oxford University Press, 1969.

Stobart, J., 'Shopping streets as social space: consumerism, improvement and leisure in an eighteenth century county town', *Urban History*, 25, 1998, pp. 3–21.

—— 'In search of a leisure hierarchy: English spa towns in the urban system', in P. Borsay, G. Hirschfelder and R. Mohrmann (eds), *New Directions in Urban History*, Münster: Waxmann, 2000, pp. 19–40.

—— 'County, town and country: three histories of urban development in eighteenth-century Chester', in P. Borsay and L. Proudfoot (eds), *Provincial towns in Early Modern England and Ireland*, Oxford: Oxford University Press, 2002, pp. 178–86.

—— 'Culture versus commerce: societies and spaces for elites in eighteenth-century Liverpool', *Journal of Historical Geography*, 28, 2002, pp. 471–85.

—— 'Building an urban identity: cultural space and civic boosterism in a 'new' industrial town: Burslem, 1761–1911', *Social History*, 29, 2004, pp. 485–98.
—— *The First Industrial Region: North-West England 1700–1760*, Manchester: Manchester University Press, 2004.
—— 'Leisure and shopping in the small towns of Georgian England', *Journal of Urban History*, 31:4, 2005, pp. 479–503.
—— 'Rus et Urbe? The hinterland and landscape of Georgian Chester', in M. Palmer and P. Barnwell (eds), *Post-Medieval Landscapes in Britain: Landscape History after Hoskins*, Vol. 3, Macclesfield: Windgather Press, forthcoming, 2007.
Stobart, J. and Hann, A., 'Retailing revolution in the eighteenth century: evidence from north-west England', *Business History*, 46, 2004, pp. 171–94.
Stobart, J. and Trinder, B., 'New towns of the industrial coalfields: Burslem and West Bromwich', in J. Stobart and N. Raven (eds), *Towns, Regions and Industries*, Manchester: Manchester University Press, 2005, pp. 121–33.
Sweet, R., *The Writing of Urban Histories in Eighteenth-Century England*, Oxford: Oxford University Press, 1997.
—— *The English Town, 1680–1840*, Harlow: Longman, 1999.
—— 'Topographies of politeness', *Transactions of the RHS*, 12, 2002, pp. 355–74.
Thrift, N., *Spatial Formations*, London: Sage, 1996.
Thrift, N. and Glennie, P., 'Historical geographies of urban life and modern consumption', in G. Kearns and C. Philo (eds), *Selling Places: The City as Cultural Capital, Past and Present*, Oxford: Pergamon, 1993, pp. 33–48.
Touzeau, J., *The Rise and Progress of Liverpool*, Liverpool: The Liverpool Booksellers Co. Ltd, 1910.
Towner, J., *An Historical Geography of Recreation and Tourism in the Western World, 1540–1940*, Chichester: Wiley, 1996.
Trentmann, F., 'Beyond consumerism: new historical perspectives on consumption', *Journal of Contemporary History*, 39, 2004, pp. 373–401.
—— 'Knowing consumers – histories, identities and practices', in F. Trentmann (ed.), *The Making of the Consumer. Knowledge, Power and Identity in the Modern World*, London: Berg, 2006, pp. 1–27.
Uglow, J., *The Lunar Men*, London: Faber and Faber, 2002.
—— 'Vase mania', in M. Berg and E. Eger (eds), *Luxury in the Eighteenth-Century: Debates, Desires and Delectable Goods*, Basingstoke: Palgrave, 2003, pp. 151–64.
Upton, C., *A History of Birmingham*, Chichester: Phillimore, 1993.
Veblen, T., *The Theory of the Leisure Class: An Economic Study of Institutions*, Basingstoke: Macmillan, 1912.
Vickery, A., 'Golden age to separate spheres', *Historical Journal*, 36, 1993, pp. 383–414.
—— *The Gentleman's Daughter: Women's Lives in Georgian England*, New Haven, CT: Yale University Press, 1998.
Wallis, P., 'Consumption, retailing and medicine in early modern London', *Economic History Review*, forthcoming.
Walsh, C., 'Shop design and the display of goods in eighteenth-century London', *Journal of Design History*, 8, 1995, pp. 157–76.
—— 'The newness of the department store: a view from the eighteenth century', in G. Crossick and S. Jaumain (eds), *Cathedrals of Consumption*, Aldershot: Ashgate, 1999, pp. 46–71.

—— 'The advertising and marketing of consumer goods in eighteenth-century London', in C. Wischermann and E. Shore (eds), *Advertising and the European City: Historical Perspectives*, Aldershot: Ashgate, 2000, pp. 79–95.

—— 'Social meaning and social space in the shopping galleries of early-modern London', in J. Benson and L. Ugolini (eds), *A Nation of Shopkeepers. Five Centuries of British Retailing*, London: Tauris, 2003, pp 52–79.

—— 'Social relations of shopping', in B. Blondé, P. Stabel, J. Stobart and I. Van Damme (eds), *Buyers and Sellers*, Antwerp: Brepols, 2006, pp.331–51.

Ward, T., *History of the Athenaeum, 1824–1925*, London, 1926.

Weatherill, L., *Consumer Behaviour and Material Culture*, 2nd edition, London: Routledge, 1996.

White, J., 'A world of goods? The 'Consumption Turn' and eighteenth-century British history', *Cultural and Social History*, 3, 2006, pp. 93–104.

Whitehead, D., 'Urban renewal and suburban growth: the shaping of Georgian Worcester', *Worcestershire Historical Society, Occasional Publications*, 5, 1989, pp. 36–40.

Wilson, A., 'Cultural identity of Liverpool, 1790–1850', *Transactions, Historic Society of Lancashire and Cheshire*, 147, 1997, pp. 55–80.

Wischermann, C., 'Placing advertising in the modern cultural history of the city', in C. Wischermann and E. Shore (eds), *Advertising and the European City: Historical Perspectives*, Aldershot: Ashgate, 2000, pp. 1–31.

Wyke, T. and Rudyard, N., *Manchester Theatres*, Manchester: Manchester Central Library, 1994.

Index

advertisements 2, 25, 170, 192–3; and architectural images 176; and consumer spaces 172–9; as counterpart to façade 175; and creation of culture of consumption 179, 185–6; and customer awareness 175–6; and emphasis on plenty, variety, choice 174; and identity/status of shop 182, 184–5; implications of 188; and the individual 175, 178–9; interpretation of 171–2; and knowledge of consumers 183–4; leisure institutions/activities 174; link to shopkeeper, professional, proprietor 174–5; and links between towns/regions 177–8; and listing of goods/services 173; and location 176–8; mobility of 186; as mode of communication 185–7; as montage of ideas/images 186–7; and newness/fashionability 182–3; and the printed page 185–7; and promoting politeness 179–85; and representation of shops 173–4, 176, 179–80, 185–6, 188; and reputation 175; and shaping of consumer choice 171; and shopkeeper/customer relationship 179–82; trade cards 172–6, 187; use/value of 171, 172; variety of 188; as virtual representations of towns 186–7; wide range of 171

assemblies 7, 18, 27, 28–9, 31, 32, 112, 113; access to/social practice within 138, 139, 146; and advertisements 177, 185; arrangement, decoration, use of space 124–5; attendance at 148; building of 95; cultural context 145; flexibility of space 118–19; funding for 76; group distinctions 125; location of 78; occurrence of 143; and personal display 124–5; as places for sociable interaction 159; provision of 70–1, 73; quality/fashionability of company in 124; social etiquette in 169; and social status 165, 166; spatial patterns of 144

booksellers 31, 35, 36, 44, 81, 82, 105, 106, 133, 137, 156, 158, 174, 176

buildings 2, 5, 6; architectural styles 113–15; arrangement of 95–6; classical style 96; cultural/symbolic capital of 112; and display 112–13, 123–32; and division/re-division of space 112, 116, 117–23; front/back regions 191; front/back space 111; in harmony with streets 97–8; importance of façades 111, 112, 114–16; inter-/intra-building distinction 111; ornamentation of 96–7, 112, 114–15; planning of 60; and politics of space 113, 132–8; public buildings 95; public/private distinction 111, 112, 113–16, 117–23; reconstruction of 97; residential squares 92–4; role of 114; and status-conscious urban elite 165; uniformity of appearance 94–7

bull-baiting 7, 65, 91, 107

charities 28, 29, 60, 103, 164, 167, 168

clubs 31, 79, 80, 116, 119, 120, 149–50, 159, 163

coffee/coffee houses 6, 11, 17, 19, 33, 45, 53, 58, 84, 106, 119, 121, 149, 152, 154, 159–60, 167, 186

consumers 1–2; and advertisements 172, 174, 176, 178–9, 181–3, 185; agency of 1; attracting/courting 130, 131, 161; and choice 23, 54, 55, 190; cognitive/mental space 121; concentration of 3; daily lives/social practices of 2; and display 123; and entertainment 17; expectations of 44; as fashionable/refined 149; and gender 105; and identity 140, 161, 189; as innovative/acquisitive 9; and link with commodities 13; and lived space 194; motivations 17, 23, 142, 166; normative actions of 98; numbers of 29, 47; polite 106, 110, 130, 145, 163; and preferred suppliers 156; and status 146, 161; tactics/practices of 22, 24, 27, 53, 54, 59, 92, 152, 154, 160, 166, 170, 171, 189, 193; urban/rural 48–9, 54, 72, 77, 156, 192

consumption, centrality of 189; cultural context 140–1; development of 8–9; and the exotic/novel 11; flexibility of concept/practice 1; and gender 2, 11–12, 152; hierarchies of 38–49; and identity 11–13, 17, 160–8; integration of 49–55; motivations 9–11, 166–7, 192; as ostentatious 10–11; polite 5, 98–9; and provision of goods and services 33–6; rise of 1–2; and rituals 11–13; and social differentiation 10–11; social-geographical variations 9; spatiality of 18–22; themes/analysis 22–5

corporations 65–6, 70–2, 87–8, 90; and assembly rooms 70–1; and horse racing 71; motivations for investment 71–2; and promenades 71; and provision of leisure 70–2

cultural capital 5, 10, 11, 12, 69, 72, 74, 145, 161, 164, 165, 182

cultural context 140–1; and leisure/shopping interaction 168–70; and patterns of shopping/leisure 142–9; and shopping 17–18, 140–1; and social status 146–8; socio-spatial practices 149–60

display 138–9; and assembly rooms 124–5; aural/visual 124; centrality/impact of 123–32; and etiquette 151; ostentatious 151; and public walks/gardens 123–4; and shops 126–32; and theatres 125–6

Enlightenment 3–4, 57–8, 190, 194

fairs 15, 91, 107–8
Firstspace *see* lived space

gardens and parks 6, 7, 30, 31–2, 55, 77, 79, 116, 122, 123–4, 133, 148, 151, 159, 165, 168

gender 2, 11–12, 58, 152
gentry 4–8, 22, 28, 32, 42, 45–6, 48, 53, 62, 71–3, 80, 82, 100, 105, 107, 122–3, 132, 143–4, 145–6, 159–60, 161, 163

hierarchies of consumption 23–4, 27; changes in 42, 44–5; and choice of venue 54–5; and individual decision-making 53–5; and internal divisions of space 117–23; positioning 38; quantitative distinctions 40; retail provision 40–2; secondary towns 40; social cycles 45–6; socio-economic character 48–9; spatial ordering 46–8; structure of 53; trends 44–5; upper tier 38–40

hierarchies of space 23–5; assembly rooms 118–19; and blurring of public–private 117–23; clubs, newsrooms, libraries 119, 120; outdoor leisure 122–3; shop–home distinctions 117–18; theatres 119, 121

horse races 27, 28, 31, 32, 47, 71, 122–3, 143

identity 11, 24–5; and acquisition of knowledge/learning 163–6, 167; and consumption 160–8; creation of 140; and fashionable appearance 162–3; and politeness 12–13; and production of/association with polite spaces 166–8; and social status 161–8

Improvement Commissions/Acts 7, 65, 66–7, 89–91, 191

infirmaries 28, 33, 49, 73, 75, 78, 164

leisure 23; access to 116, 145–6; centrality of corporations to 70–2; commercialization of 6, 33, 73–7, 113; cultural context 140–1; and hierarchies of space 121–2; and industrial growth 56; institutions 28; link with polite shopping 148–9; location/distribution of 78–9; and population size 47; presence/importance of 33; process/practice of 19; provision of 189–90; range/distribution of 28–33; rules for behaviour 149; and shopping 17; and sociability/civility 27–8, 158–60; socio-spatial practices 149–51, 149–60, 189; spatial patterns of 144–5; temporal patterns of 143–4; traditional 7
libraries 18, 28, 30, 31, 32, 113; access to 116, 146; codes of behaviour 149;

funding for 73, 74, 75; location of 79, 95; membership of/attendance at 144, 145, 148; public-private spaces 118–19, 120; social etiquette in 169; and social status 163–5, 166; spatial patterns of 144
lighting 88–9
literary societies 30, 32–3, 143, 146, 163, 164, 167
lived space 22, 113, 131; firstspace 22, 104; secondspace 22, *see also* spaces of consumption; spaces of representation

markets 15, 48, 49, 50, 65, 73; criticisms of 91; location of 79–80, 82, 91, 91–2; as sites of performance 106–7
middling sorts 3, 5, 6, 9, 10, 11, 12, 37, 53, 55, 62, 74, 77, 79, 84, 91, 94, 107, 108, 143, 144, 152, 163
music 29–30, 31, 32, 77, 78, 83, 143, 144, 148

newspapers 30, 36, 50–1, 171, 177, 186, 187, 188

performance 24, 191; as central to politeness 98; and cock-fighting/bull-baiting 107; definition of 98; and fairs 107–8; guides to walking 95, 102–4; and itinerant tradesmen/hawkers of goods 108–9; and marketplaces 106–7; and orchestrated processions 99–101; as polite 99–106; and promenading 101–2; and shopping 101–2, 105–6; and street as lived space 104–5; tensions in 98–9, 106–9; traditional arenas 106–9
philosophical societies 28, 30, 32–3, 143, 146, 163, 164, 167
planning, changes in 63–5; classical/ Renaissance influence on 62–3, 65; developments/extensions 62–5; lack of coherent tradition in 59; and modernising/improving space/society 65–9; and new towns 60; and ordering of space 62–7; and rebuilding 59, 60–2; restrictions/difficulties 59–60; scope/ importance of 60
pleasure gardens 7, 113; access to/social practice within 138, 139; behaviour in 151; criticisms of 151; and lack of spatial/social boundaries 122; location of 79, 80; as private ventures 77; prostitutes in 133; *ridottos*/masquerades in 133, 151; and social status 112; and use of façades 116
politeness 24, 141, 190; and appearance at events 168; changes in concept/ principle 7; and civility 167–8; and commerce 8, 84, 85; construction of 84; and consumption 113, 169; and corporations 70–2; courtesy writers views on 4; as cultural capital 5; devaluation of 145–6; and development of fashionable resorts 60; and gender 5; and the gentry 72–3; geographies/ spatial practices of 78–84; and identity 12–13; importance of visibility 87; influence of consumption on 145; and keeping up standards 69–70; link with consumption 5; lived spaces of 59; meeting places for 144–6; and moderation of behaviour/manners 168; and new urban elite 67; and ordering/regulating of space 65–7; and performance 98, 99–106; and private entrepreneurs 76–7; as product of social practices 84–5; production of 70–8, 192; promotion through advertisements 179–85; and public order 65–6; role of 193; shopping-leisure link 148–9; and sociability/ civility 27–8; and spatial arrangements of shops 126, 128–30, 131; and status/ character of towns 67–9; and street as public space 87; and subscription system 73–6, 168; tensions/ contradictions in 6, 145–6; and town planning 59–70; and traditional values, customs, activities 7; transgressions 134–8; as urban concept 4, 5; and urban equality 7–8; venue for 4, 57–8
politics of space, and gambling 134; and identity of customers 133; and illicit/ taboo items 133; and the 'mob' 134–5; and presence/absence of goods/people 132–8; and prostitutes/gigolos 133–4; and storage of goods 132–3; and theft of goods 135–8
population, growth 2–3, 30; relationship with retail/leisure provision 47
promenades 71, 79, 83; cultural context 145; and personal display 124; sociability of 159; social etiquette in 169; and social mixing 122
prostitutes 133–4
public–private space 7, 19, 28, 191–2; as anathema to polite society 113; and

blurring of distinctions 117–23; broad concept of 113; conflicting use of 134–5, 139; development of 3–4; disruptions in 133–8; duplicitous nature of 116; as gendered 58, 113; and hierarchies of privacy 117; and internal divisions 117–23; and location of precious/taboo goods 133; and presence/absence of goods/people 132–8

regional space 2, 189–90; and business connections 52–3; central place theory 26–7; and hierarchies of consumption 38–49; influences on 55–6; and integration of consumption 49–55; and leisure consumption/industrial growth link 56; north–south differences 37; and similarity of experiences 56; and spatial interaction 26; transport services 51–2; and urban renaissance 36–8

representations of space 22, 24, 53, 193–4; and advertisements 179; and planning proposals 63–5; shops as 128, 132

Secondspace *see* representations of space

servants 77, 121, 145, 150, 152, 154, 157

shopbreaking 136–7

shopkeepers 16, 18, 97, 169, 191–2; and advertisements 174–5, 179–82; image/professionalism of 126, 129–30, 131; and mixing of public–private spheres 117–18; and use of shop space 111–12; and window-dressing 111, 116

shoplifting 135–6

shopping 23; businesslike approach to 157–8, 169; cultural context 17–18, 140–1; development of 15, 16–18; and gender 142, 152, 156; as leisure activity 83; link with fashionable leisure activities 148–9; and mundane/routine purchases 2, 142, 152–4; and norms of behaviour 151–2; as part of social round 17–18; as performance 101–2, 105–6; as pleasurable activity 2, 132, 157–8; postal 156–7; process/practice of 19; as social routine 160; and social status 165–6; socio-spatial practices 149–50, 151–60, 189; spatial patterns of 2, 144; and street improvements 90; temporal patterns of 142–3; third-party/remote 156–7, 165

shops 98, 113; and access to goods 126, 127–9, 131–3; access to/social practice within 138; and advertisements 173–4, 176, 179–80, 185–6, 188; architectural styles 115; and attractiveness of goods 16; browsing in 151, 154, 155–6, 165, 166, 169; as centres of sociable activity 158; and creation of spectacle 129; and cultivation of image 128–30; development of 13–15; and display of goods/people 126–32; fixtures/fittings 15–16, 126–30, 131; front-space/back-space 117–19, 133; guides to 165–6; hierarchical distribution of 34–6; layout 128–30; and link with the domestic 117–18; as lived spaces 131, 141–2, 169; location/concentration of 79–84; organisation of space 130–1, 132; patterns of use 142; as polite spaces 126, 128–30, 131; and price of goods 16; ratio of population to 33; as representations of space 128, 132; role of 15; service-oriented selling 118; and the showroom 16; and social status 112; specialist 80–2; and status of customers 146–8; and storing of goods 132–3; and theft/violence 135–8; and use of preferred suppliers 156; and use of space 111–12; variety/distribution of 33–6; visual impact of 82, 126–30; and window presentations 111, 116

sociability, and assemblies 159; and blurring of business/pleasure 158–9; and clubs 159; and coffee houses 159–60; and leisure/politeness 27–8; and promenades/gardens 159; and shopping 157–9; and spaces of consumption 166–8, 169, 170; streets as sites of 98–109, 110; and structuring of leisure 159–60

social practices 140–1; active context 141; and consumption/identity 160–8; framework for 141; inclusivity/exclusivity of 145–6; and individual agency 141; and patterns of leisure/shopping 142–9; polite shopping/fashionable leisure link 148–9; spatial range 149–60

social status, and cultural attributes 161; and emulative consumption 161; and fashion/personal appearance 162–3; and identity 161–6; and membership of libraries/societies 163–5, 166, 167; nefarious routes to 161; pursuit of 161–6; and shopping 165–6; traditional notions 161

spaces of consumption, access to 169; and advertisements 172–9, 188; and civility, politeness, sociability 166–8, 169, 170; and competition 161–6; contradictions/contestations 194; and discourse of improvement 170; and focus/meaning of 169; as lived spaces of consumers 194; as physical structures 170; as planned, regulated, shaped 193–4; and politeness 169; production of 193, 194–5; and pursuit of status 161–6; and routines of leisure/shopping 169; tensions in 169; writings on 160–1
spaces of representation 22, 53, 70, 109, 194, *see also* spaces of consumption
spatial theory 189; built form 19–20, 21; central place theory 21, 26–7; and consumption 18–22; and production of space 21–2; and representations of space 22; socio-cultural processes 18–19; and spaces of representation 22; as way of life 19, 20
squares 6, 30, 60, 92–4
streets 5–6, 190–1; architectural features 92–8; arrangement/appearance of buildings on 95–8; in harmony with buildings 97–8; and Improvement Commissions 89–91; investment in 88–9; lighting of 88–9; as lived spaces 86; markets in 91–2; naming of 63, 66; as ordered public sphere 113; orderliness of 87; paving of 87–8, 92; planning of 65; and polite society 87, 90, 91; as principal spatial unit 109–10; as public space 87–92; re-modelling/rebuilding of 90, 110; reconceptualisation of 91; refuse in 87–8, 89; regulation/improvements in 6, 87–92, 97; as sites of performance/sociability 98–109, 110; social mixing in 86; as space of representation 109; as spaces of commerce 86; and squares 92–4; and terraces 94–5; tours/tourists of 95, 102–4; as visual space 97; widening of 60–1
subscriptions 168; and commercialization of leisure 73–6; contributors to 73–4; and motivations of subscribers 74–5; networks of subscribers 75–6; philanthropic 75; and private enterprise 76–7; success of 76, *see also* libraries

tea/tea-drinking 7, 10, 11, 33, 36, 54, 105, 118, 119, 121, 136, 149, 152, 154, 155, 159, 160, 183
terraces 94–5
theatres 27, 29, 31, 32, 49–50, 113; access to/social practice within 138; admission to 77; and advertisements 185; architectural styles 115; attendance at 148; funding for 74, 76; and hierarchy of internal space 119, 121; illumination of 125–6; location of 79, 80; and location within auditorium 126; occurrence of performances 143; and personal display 125–6; prostitutes in 133; rules of behaviour 150; socal disorder in 134–5; social etiquette in 169; spatial patterns of 144; and use of façades 116
Thirdspace *see* spaces of representation
town halls, 39, 72–3, 80, 90, 95, 119, 143
towns 190–1; built form 19–20, 21; as central to consumption 3; character of 68; as civilised/polite space 2, 57–9; conception/perception of 57–9; county/industrial distinction 31–2; critiques of 69–70; and the Enlightenment 4; and environment 4–8; formal/informal facilities 30–1; growth of 2–3; hierarchy of space in 61–2; impact of differing groups on 70–8; improvements to 65–8; and inclusivity 67; and leisure 5–8; leisure facilities 78–9; lighting in 65; and link with countryside/hinterlands 4, 5, 28, 47, 48–9, 50; literature/histories on 69–70; maps of 57; market areas 48, 49, 50; navigating through 66; planning of 59–65; and politeness 4–8, 57–8; and population growth 30; and provision of leisure/retail facilities 58–9; and regularising/civilising space in 62, 65–7; remodelling of 30, 57; retail space in 79–84; rivalry between 72; socio-economic character of 48–9; sociocultural aspects 3–4; specialist 4; status of 67–8; topographical setting 4; travel to 46–7; and urban renaissance 36–8; as way of life 19, 20; and wealth of inhabitants 48
transport 51–2

urban renaissance 28, 36–8, 58, 111, 138

walks 30, 79, 83, 95, 102–4, 116, 123–4, 159, 165

eBooks – at www.eBookstore.tandf.co.uk

A library at your fingertips!

eBooks are electronic versions of printed books. You can store them on your PC/laptop or browse them online.

They have advantages for anyone needing rapid access to a wide variety of published, copyright information.

eBooks can help your research by enabling you to bookmark chapters, annotate text and use instant searches to find specific words or phrases. Several eBook files would fit on even a small laptop or PDA.

NEW: Save money by eSubscribing: cheap, online access to any eBook for as long as you need it.

Annual subscription packages

We now offer special low-cost bulk subscriptions to packages of eBooks in certain subject areas. These are available to libraries or to individuals.

For more information please contact webmaster.ebooks@tandf.co.uk

We're continually developing the eBook concept, so keep up to date by visiting the website.

www.eBookstore.tandf.co.uk